FOR THE FRIENDS OF MY YOUTH; BOBBY BLACKWELL, BOBBY UHER, CY COLE, LANCE DORMAN, KATIE B., RUSS WOOTEN AND JESSE DEGRAFFE

California Newt, 5-7¾"

Iron West

By Doug TenNapel

Joe Potter - Cover
Snocone Studios - Lettering
Tom Krajewski - Proofreader

Image Comics, Inc.

Erik Larsen - Publisher
Todd McFarlane - President
Marc Silvestri - CEO
Jim Valentino - Vice-President

Eric Stephenson - Executive Director
Jim Demonakos - PR & Marketing Coordinator
Mia MacHatton - Accounts Manager
Traci Hui - Administrative Assistant
Joe Keatinge - Traffic Manager
Allen Hui - F   action Manager
Jonathan Chan - Production Artist
Drew Gill - Production Artist

www.imagecomics.com
www.tennapel.com

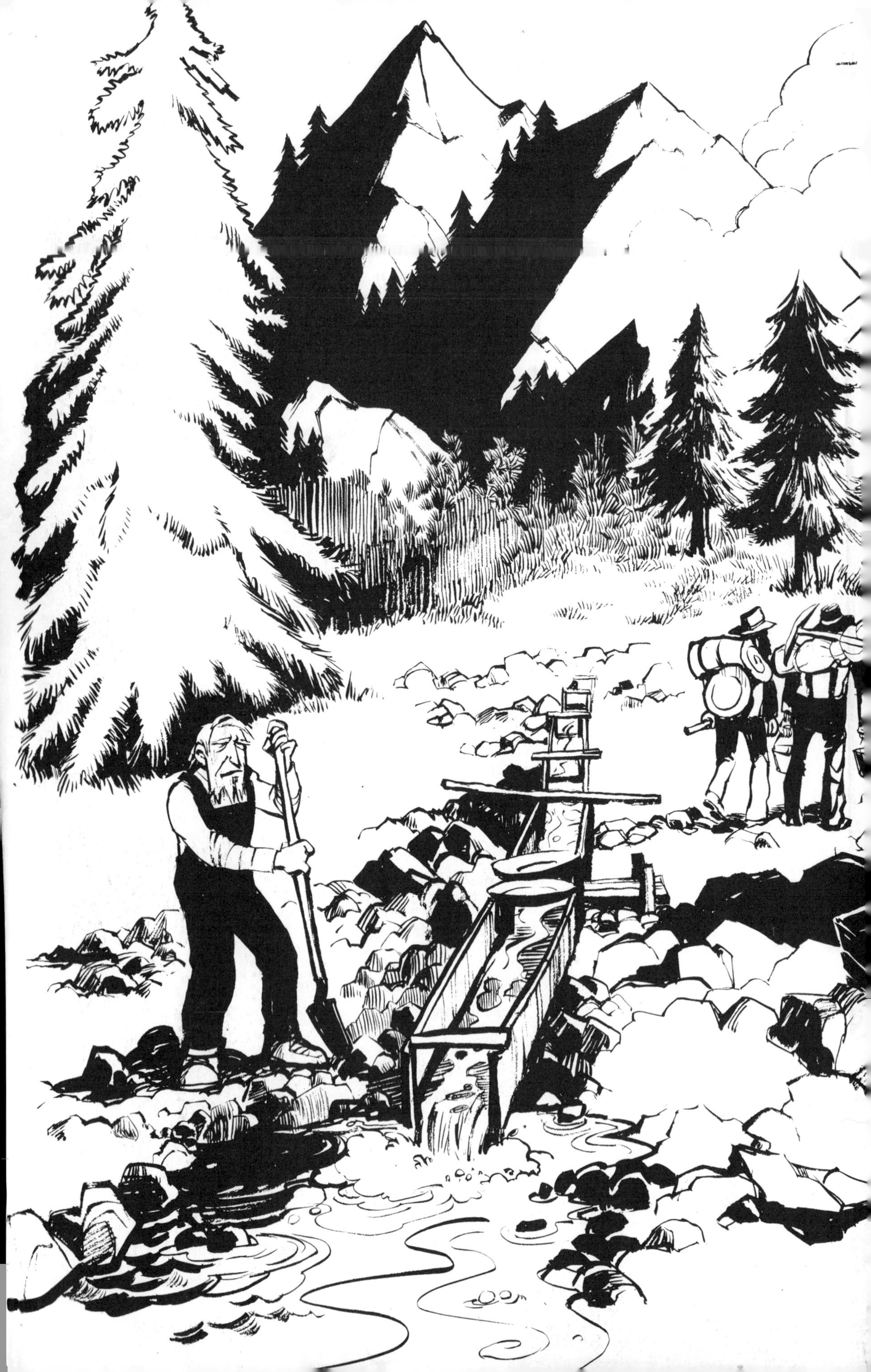

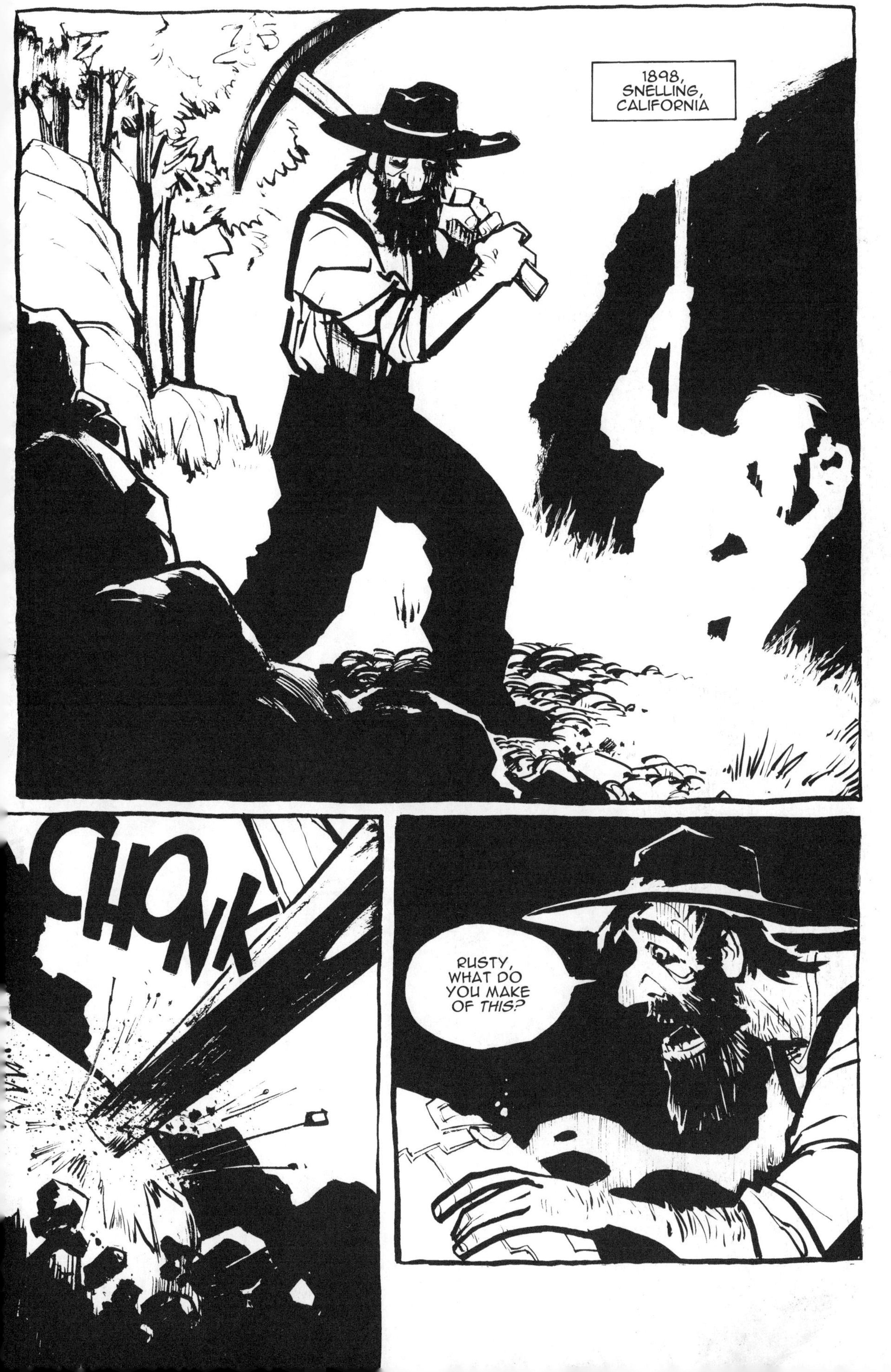
1898,
SNELLING,
CALIFORNIA
CHONK
RUSTY,
WHAT DO
YOU MAKE
OF THIS?

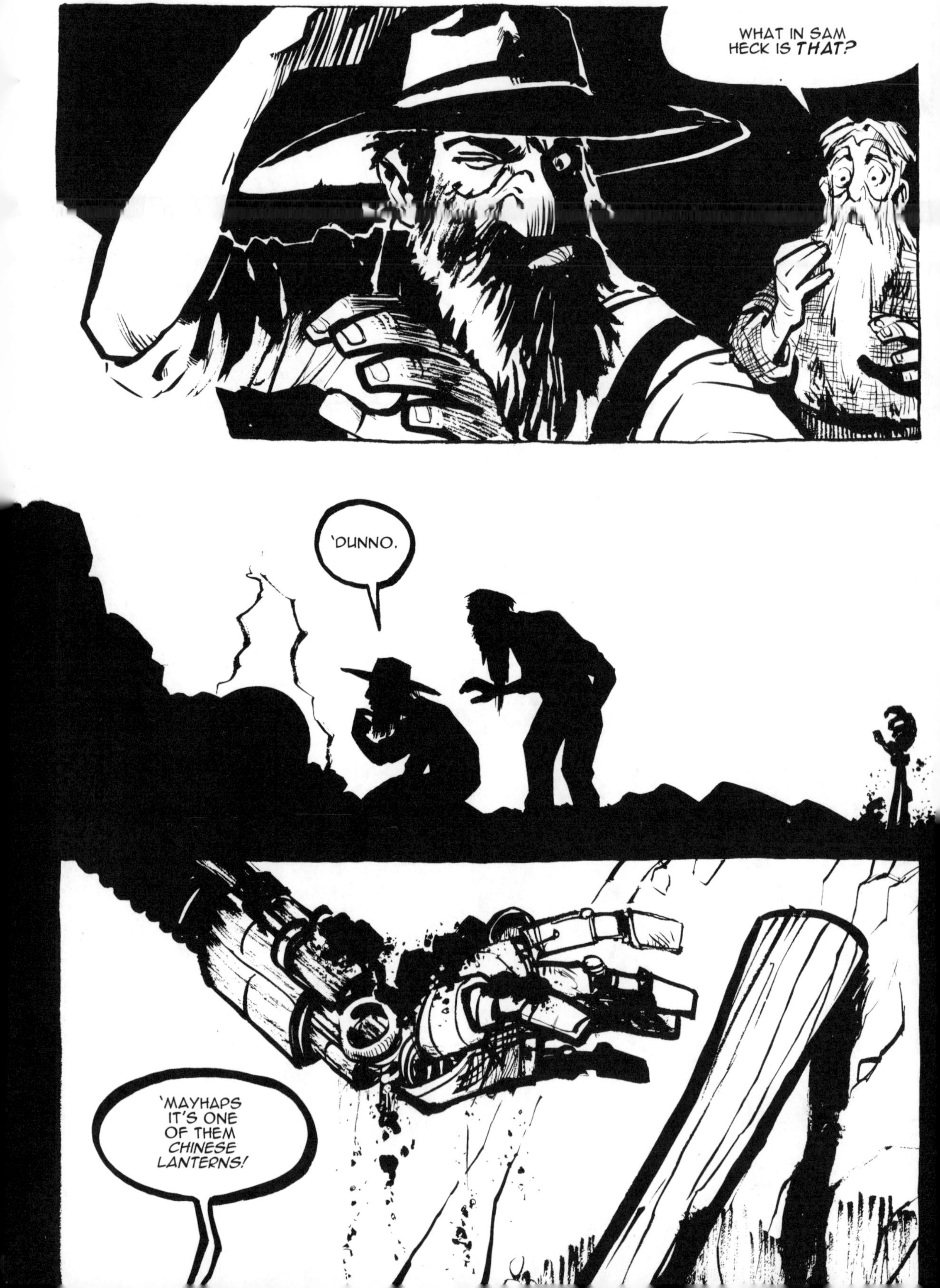
WHAT IN SAM HECK IS THAT?
'DUNNO.
'MAYHAPS IT'S ONE OF THEM CHINESE LANTERNS!

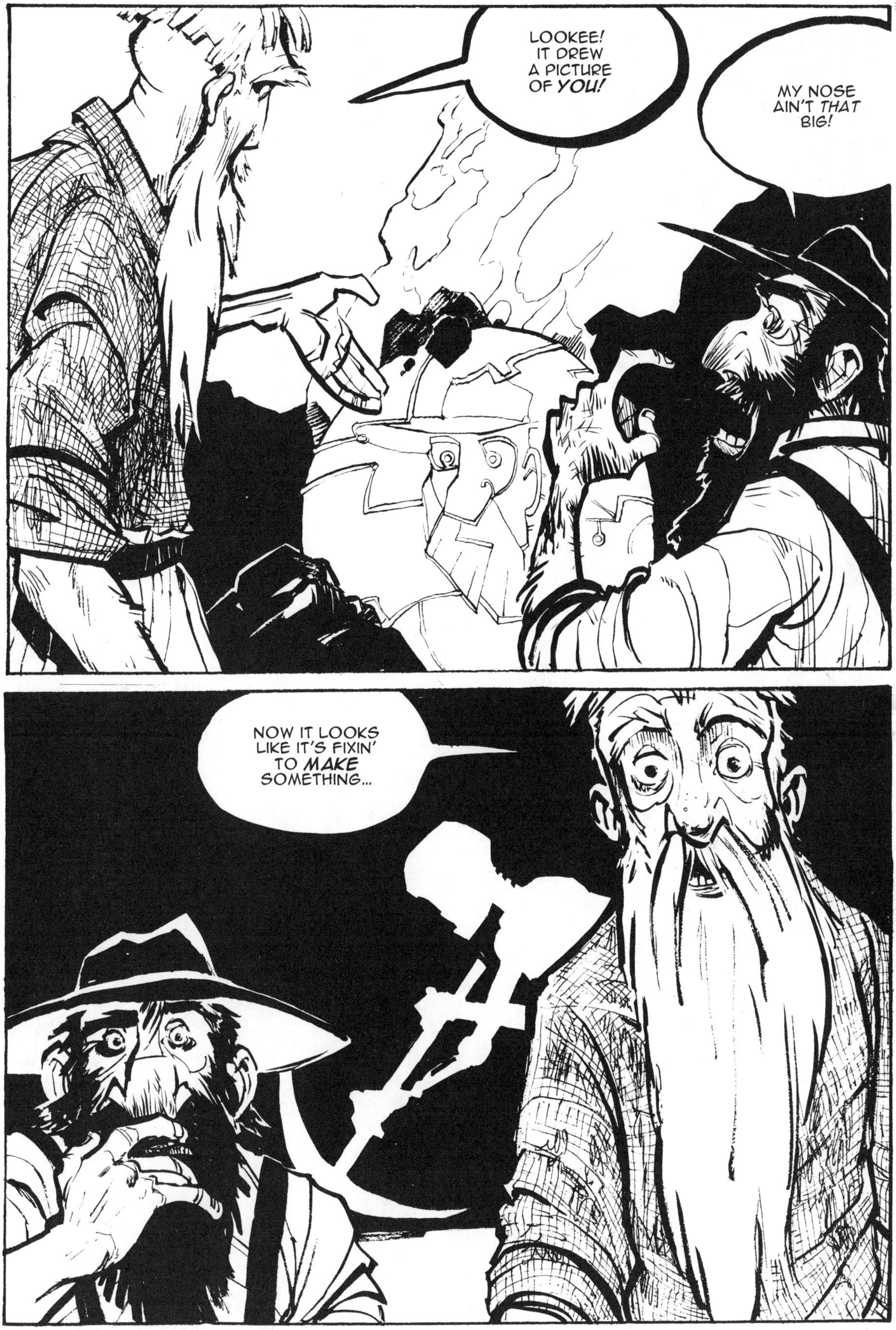
LOOKEE! IT DREW A PICTURE OF *YOU!*
MY NOSE AIN'T *THAT* BIG!
NOW IT LOOKS LIKE IT'S FIXIN' TO *MAKE* SOMETHING...

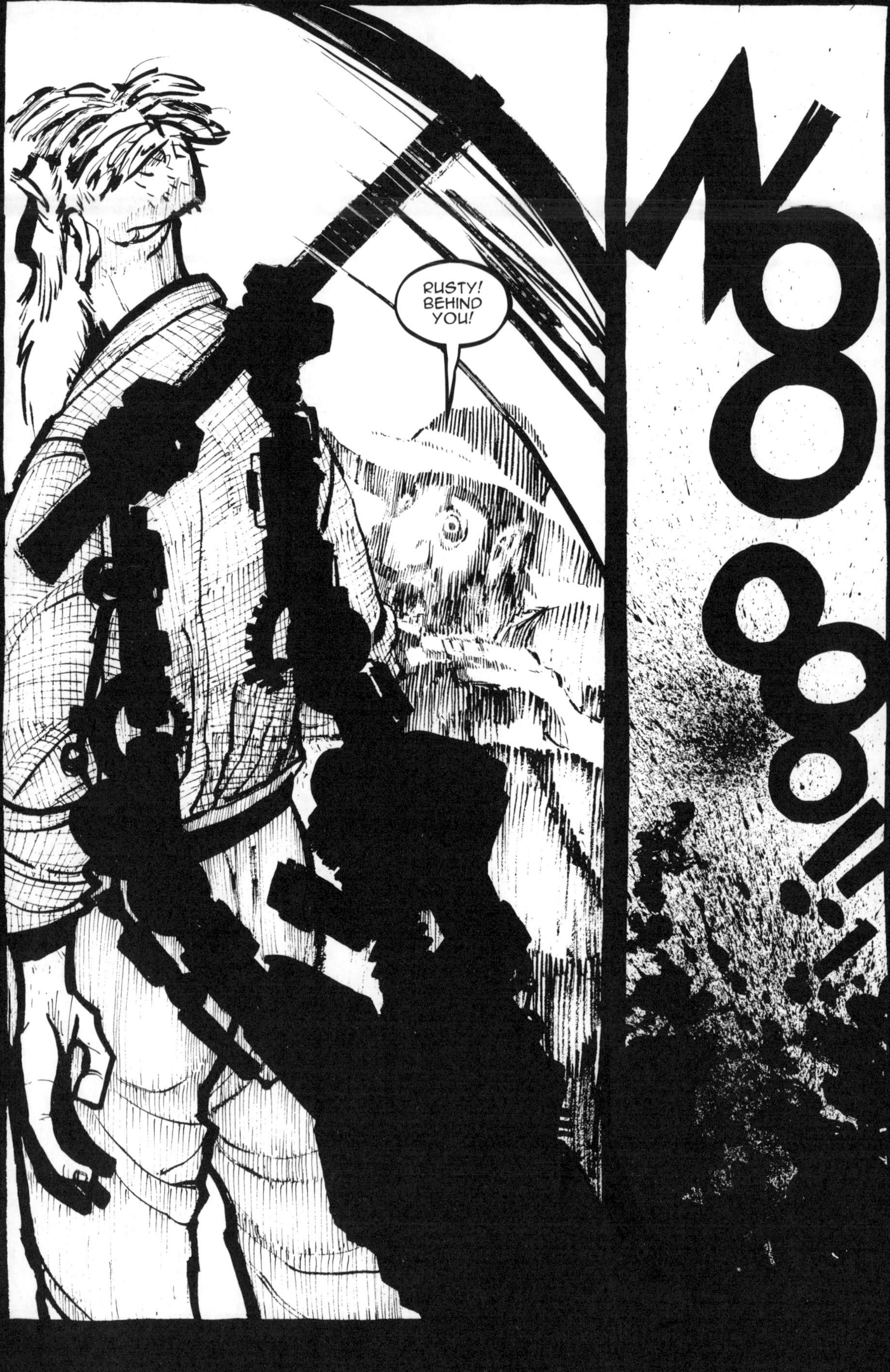
RUSTY! BEHIND YOU!

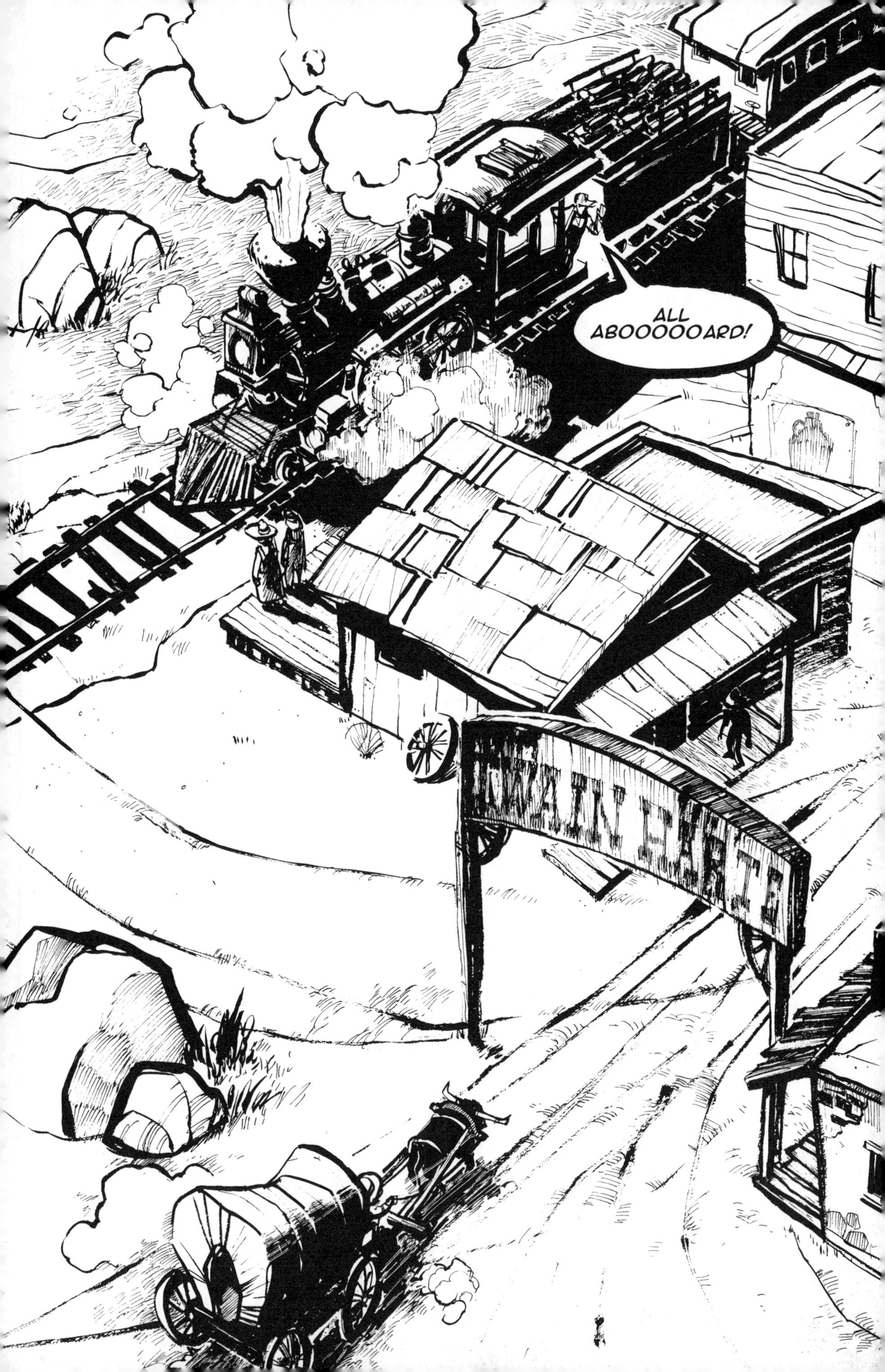
ALL ABOOOOOARD!

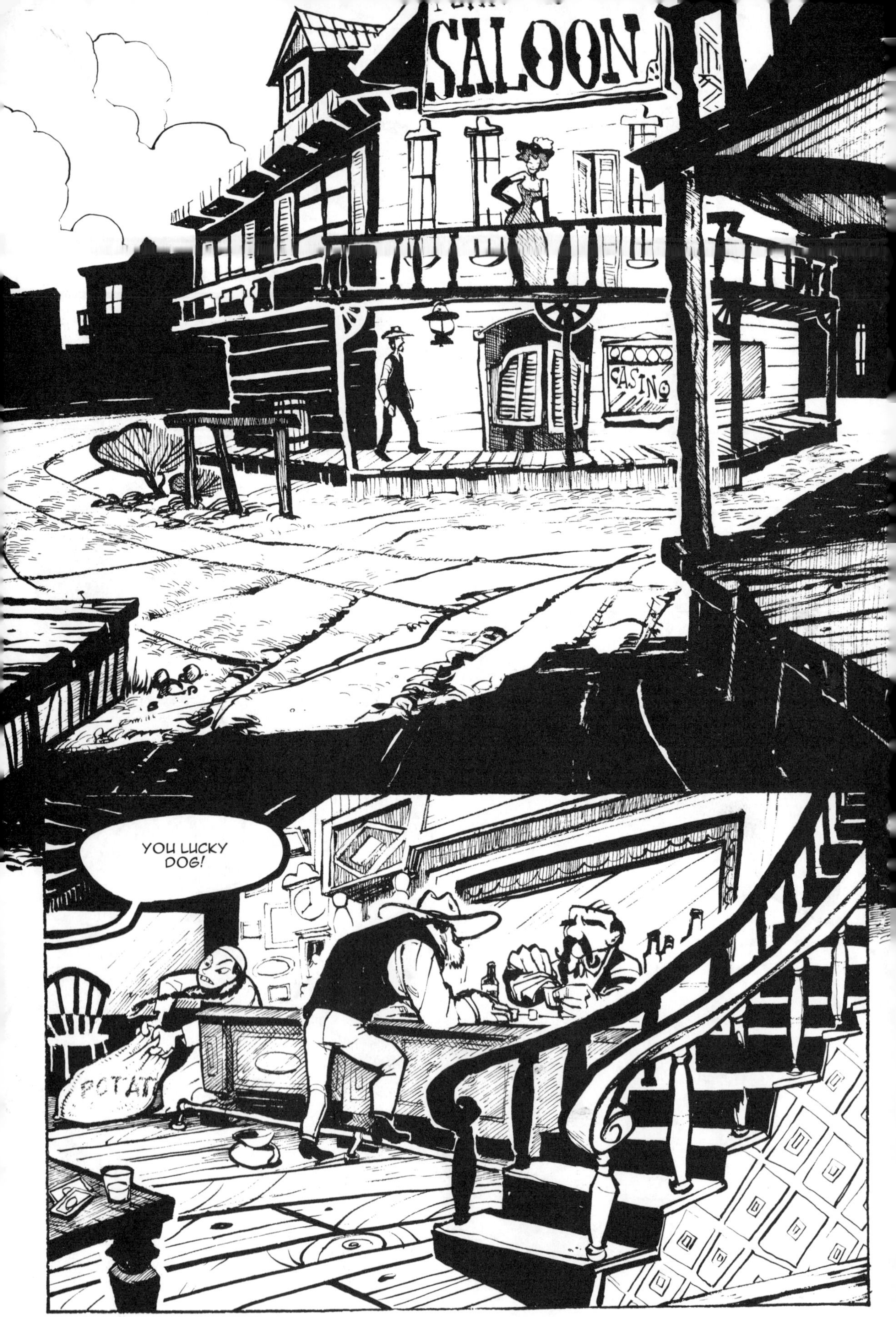
SALOON
CASINO
YOU LUCKY DOG!
POTAT

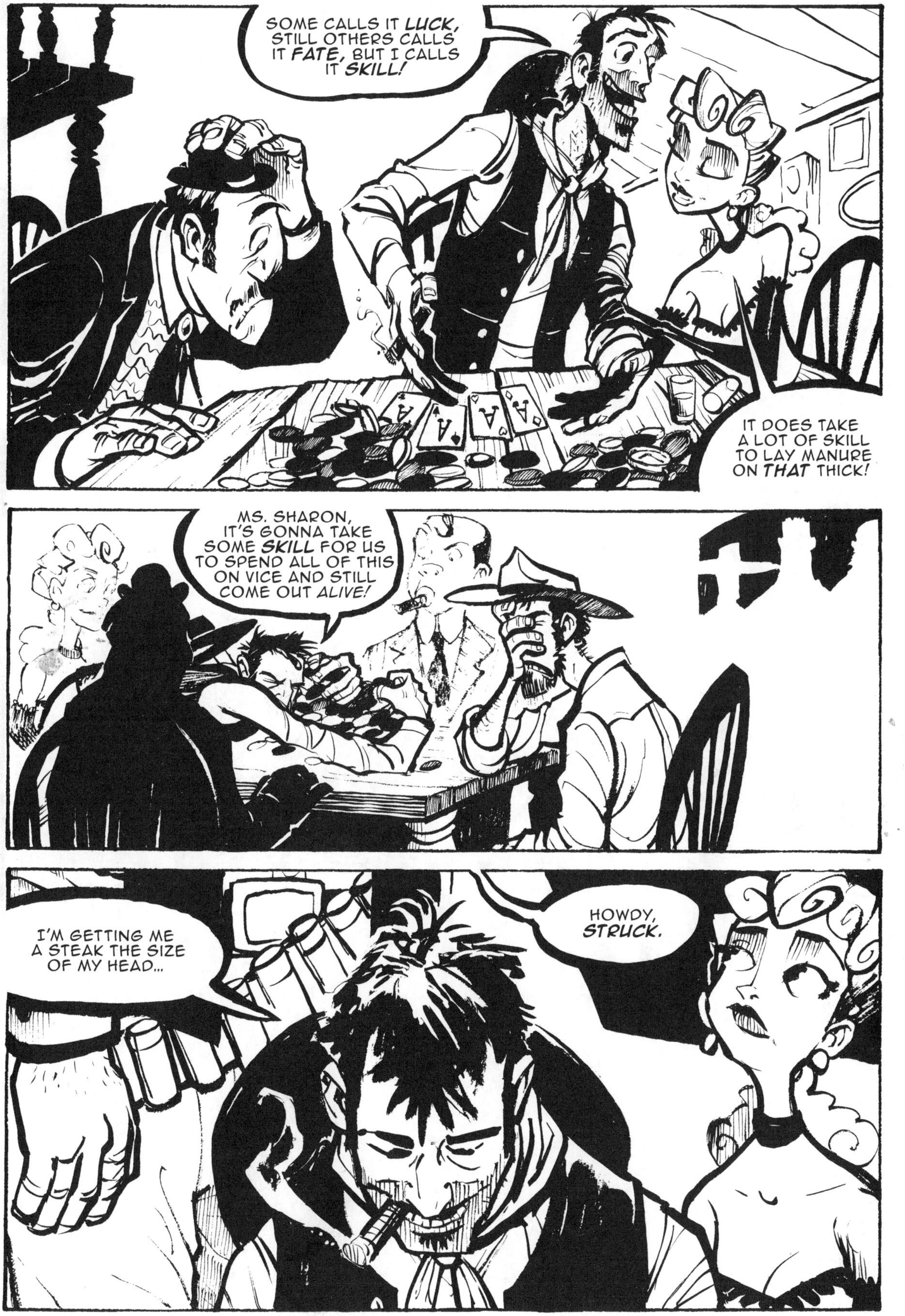
SOME CALLS IT LUCK, STILL OTHERS CALLS IT FATE, BUT I CALLS IT SKILL!
IT DOES TAKE A LOT OF SKILL TO LAY MANURE ON THAT THICK!
MS. SHARON, IT'S GONNA TAKE SOME SKILL FOR US TO SPEND ALL OF THIS ON VICE AND STILL COME OUT ALIVE!
I'M GETTING ME A STEAK THE SIZE OF MY HEAD...
HOWDY, STRUCK.

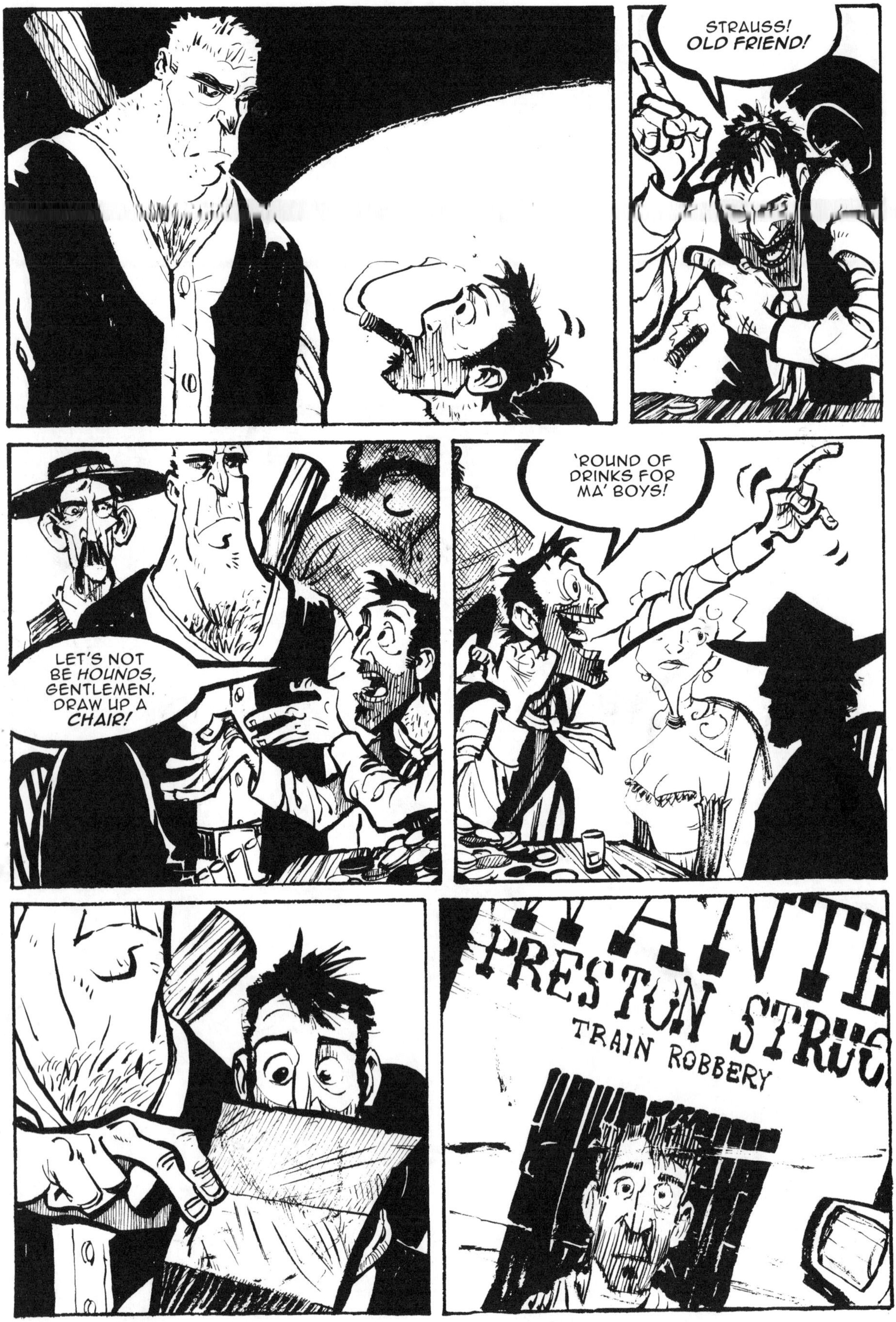
STRAUSS! OLD FRIEND!
LET'S NOT BE HOUNDS, GENTLEMEN. DRAW UP A CHAIR!
'ROUND OF DRINKS FOR MA' BOYS!
PRESTON STRUC
TRAIN ROBBERY

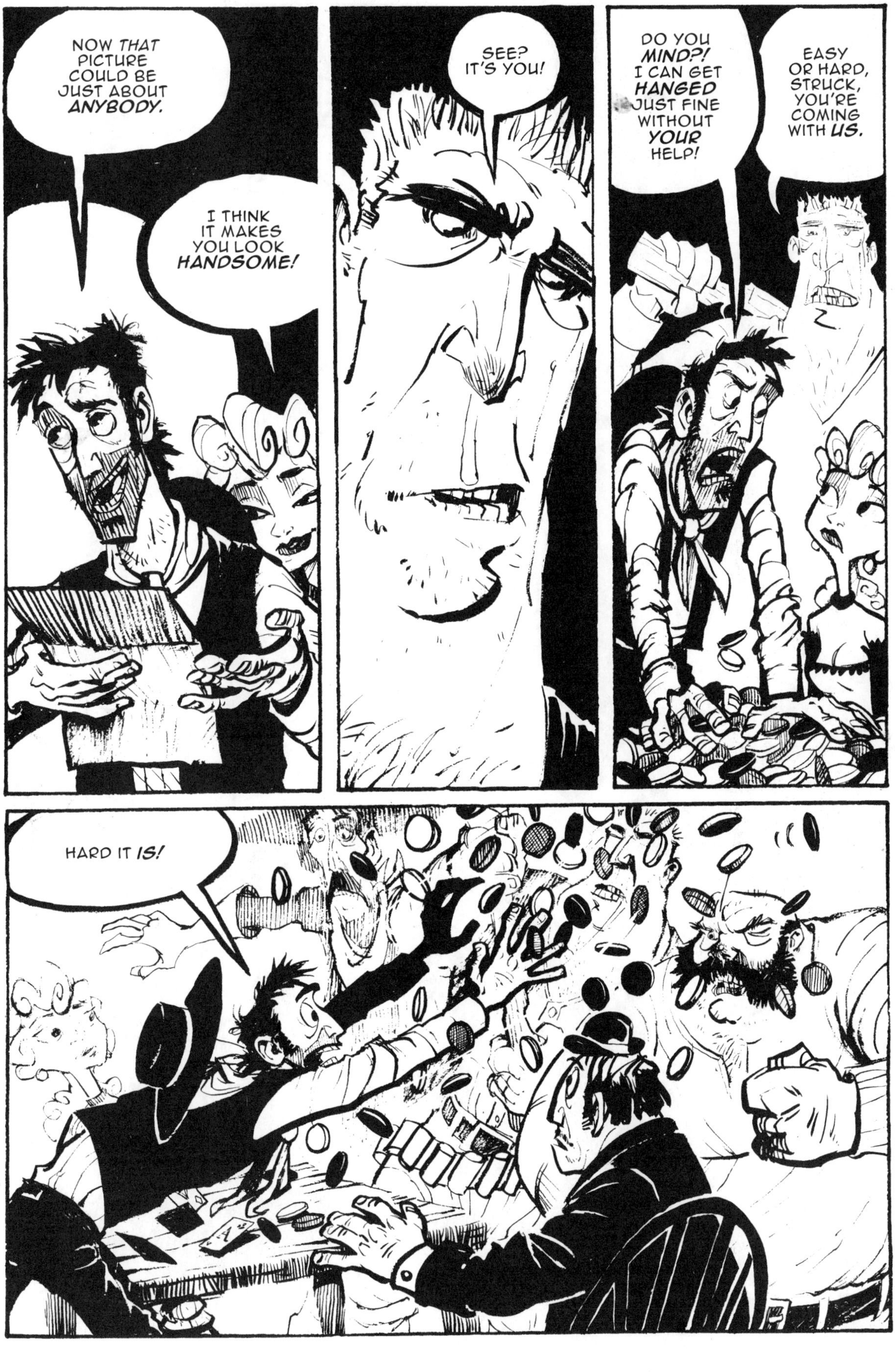
NOW THAT PICTURE COULD BE JUST ABOUT ANYBODY.
I THINK IT MAKES YOU LOOK HANDSOME!
SEE? IT'S YOU!
DO YOU MIND?! I CAN GET HANGED JUST FINE WITHOUT YOUR HELP!
EASY OR HARD, STRUCK, YOU'RE COMING WITH US.
HARD IT IS!

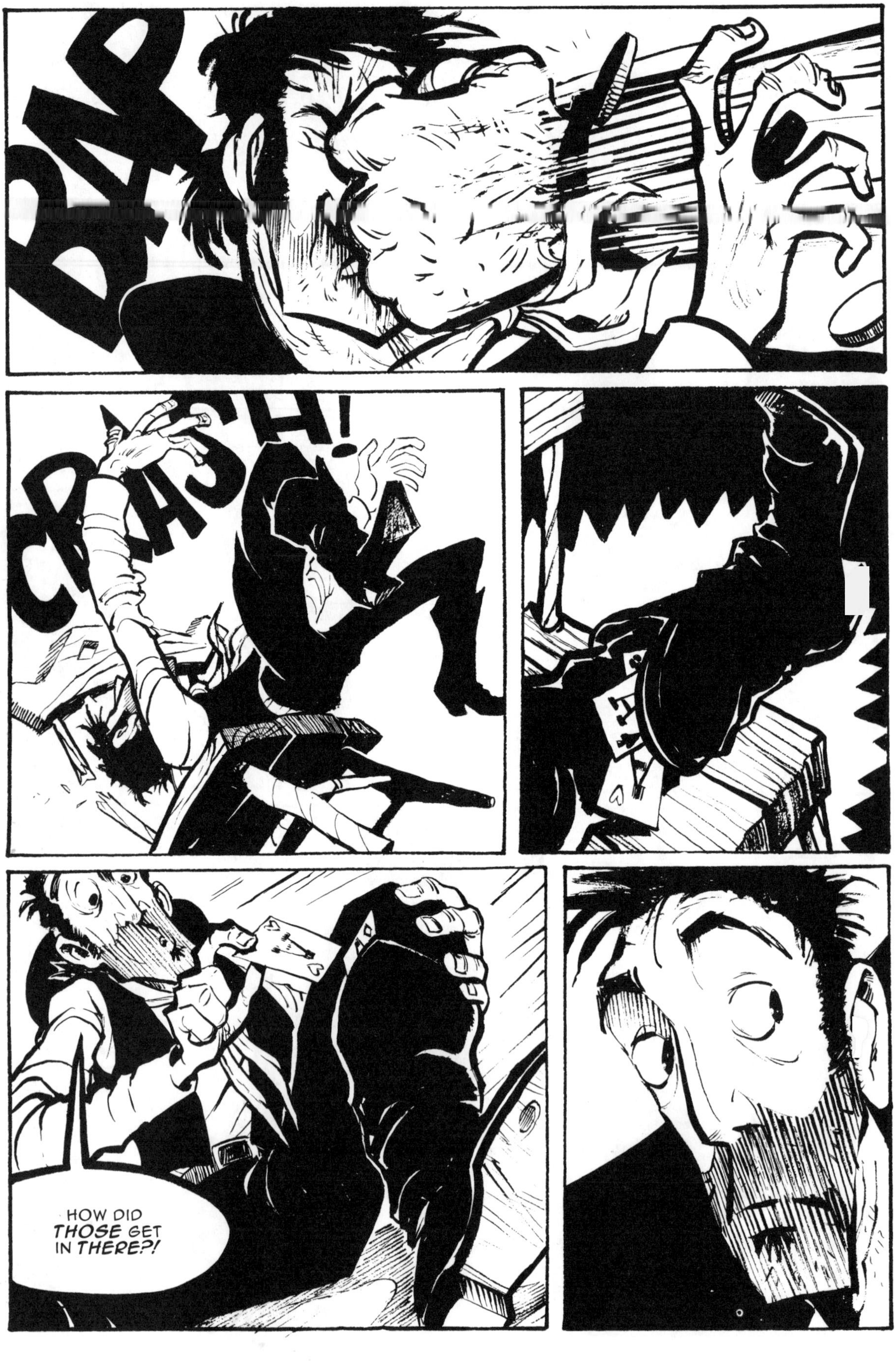
BAP
CRASH!
HOW DID THOSE GET IN THERE?!

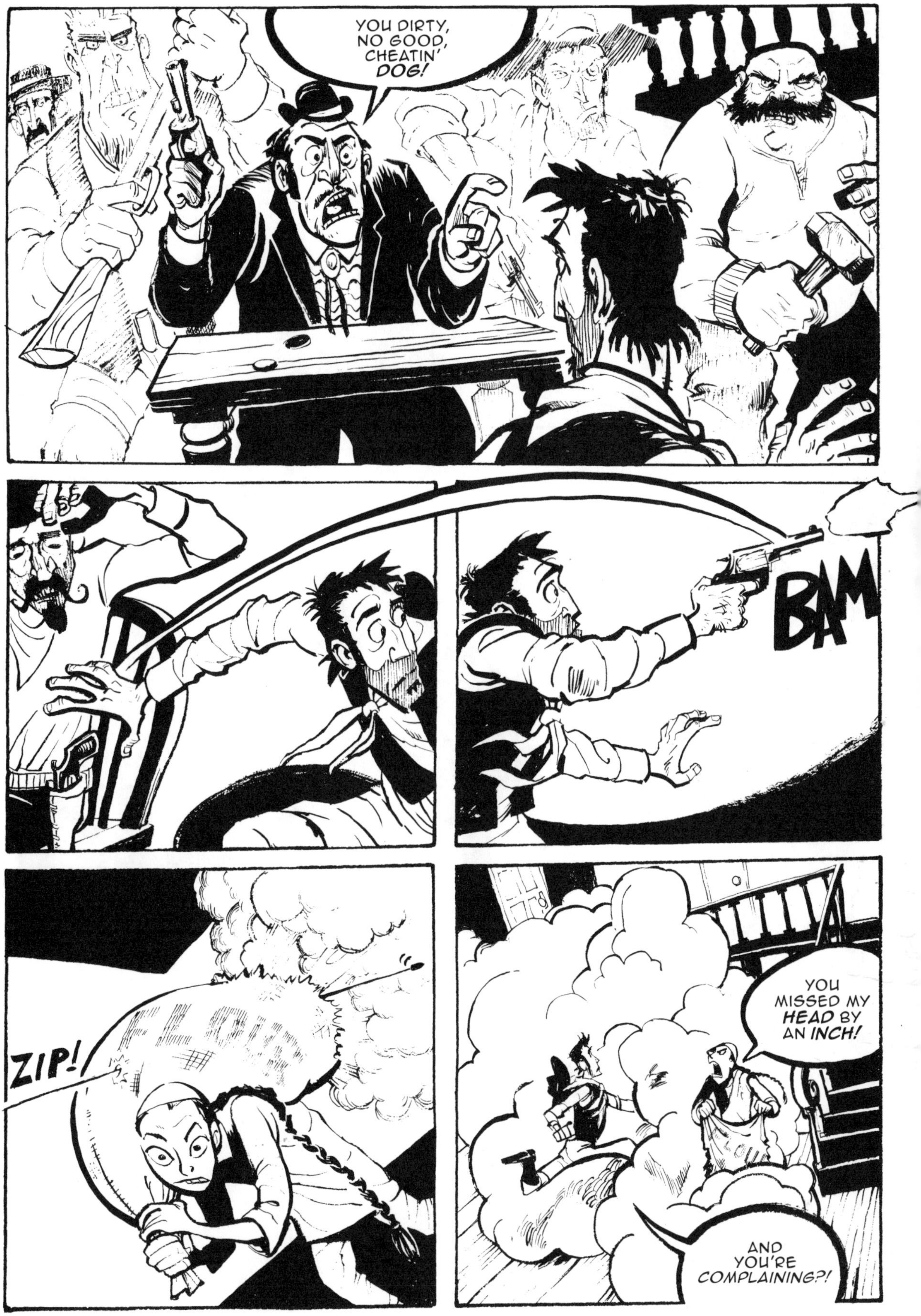
YOU DIRTY, NO GOOD, CHEATIN' DOG!
BAM
ZIP!
YOU MISSED MY HEAD BY AN INCH!
AND YOU'RE COMPLAINING?!

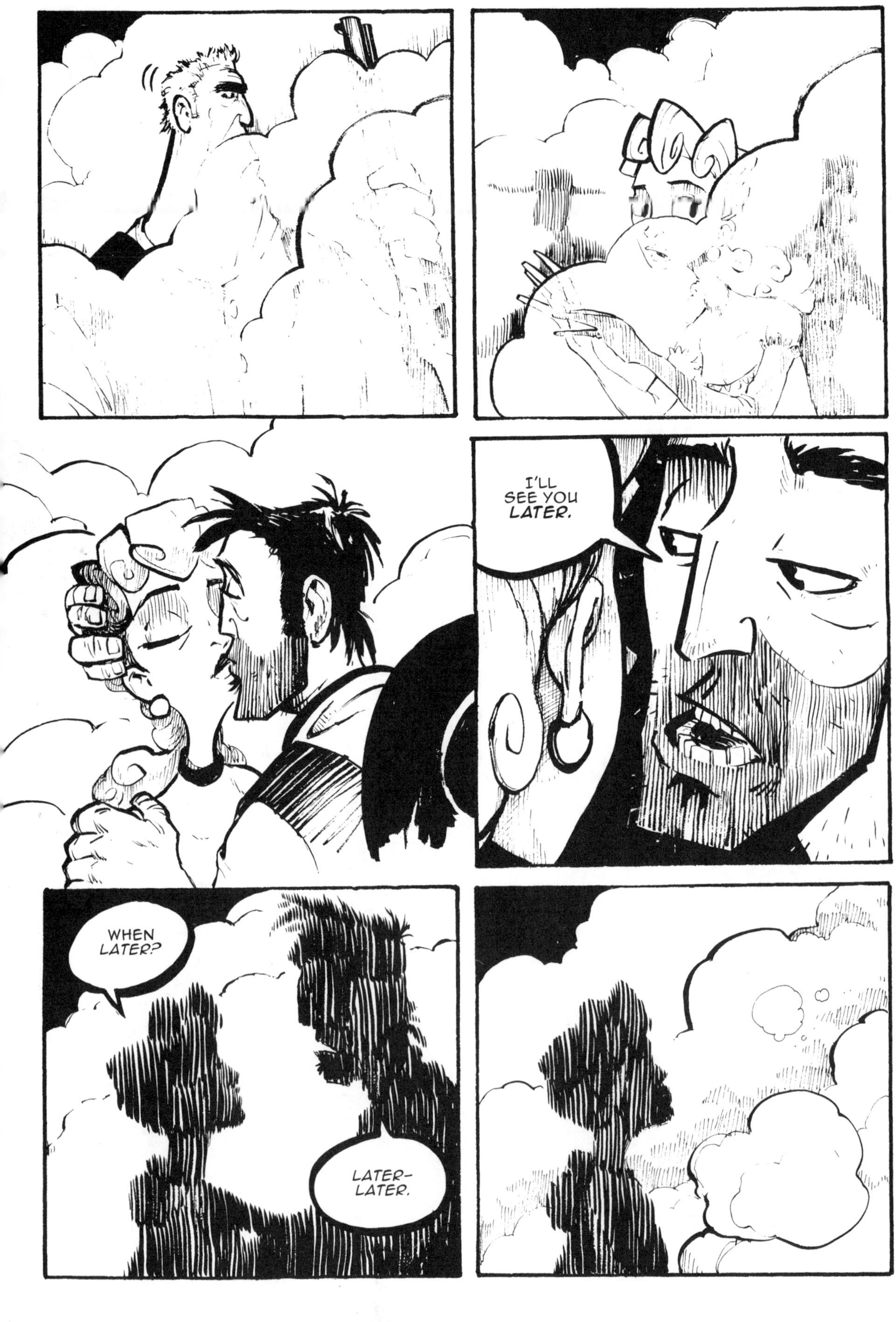
I'LL SEE YOU LATER.
WHEN LATER?
LATER-LATER.

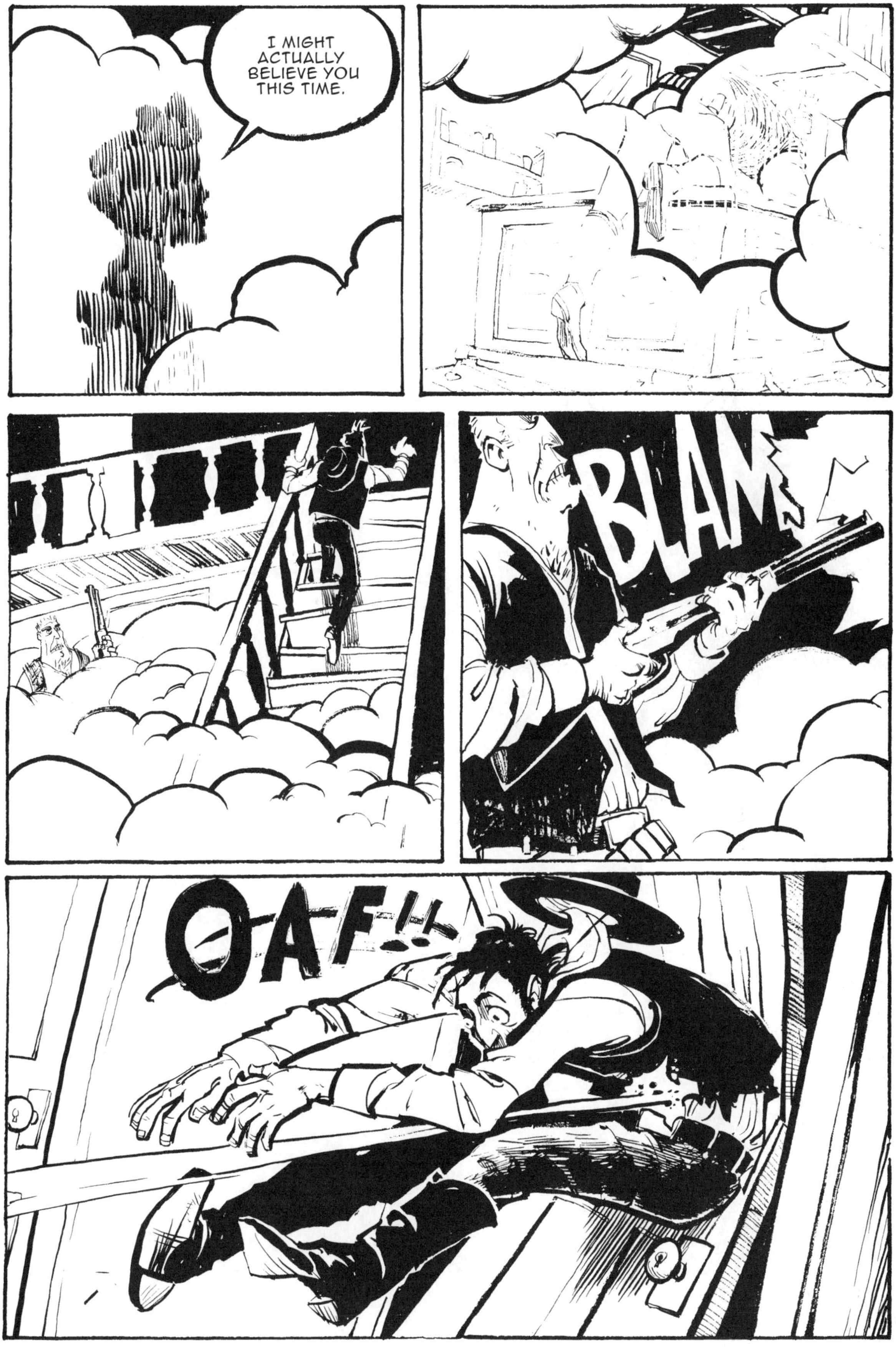
I MIGHT ACTUALLY BELIEVE YOU THIS TIME.
BLAM
OAF!!

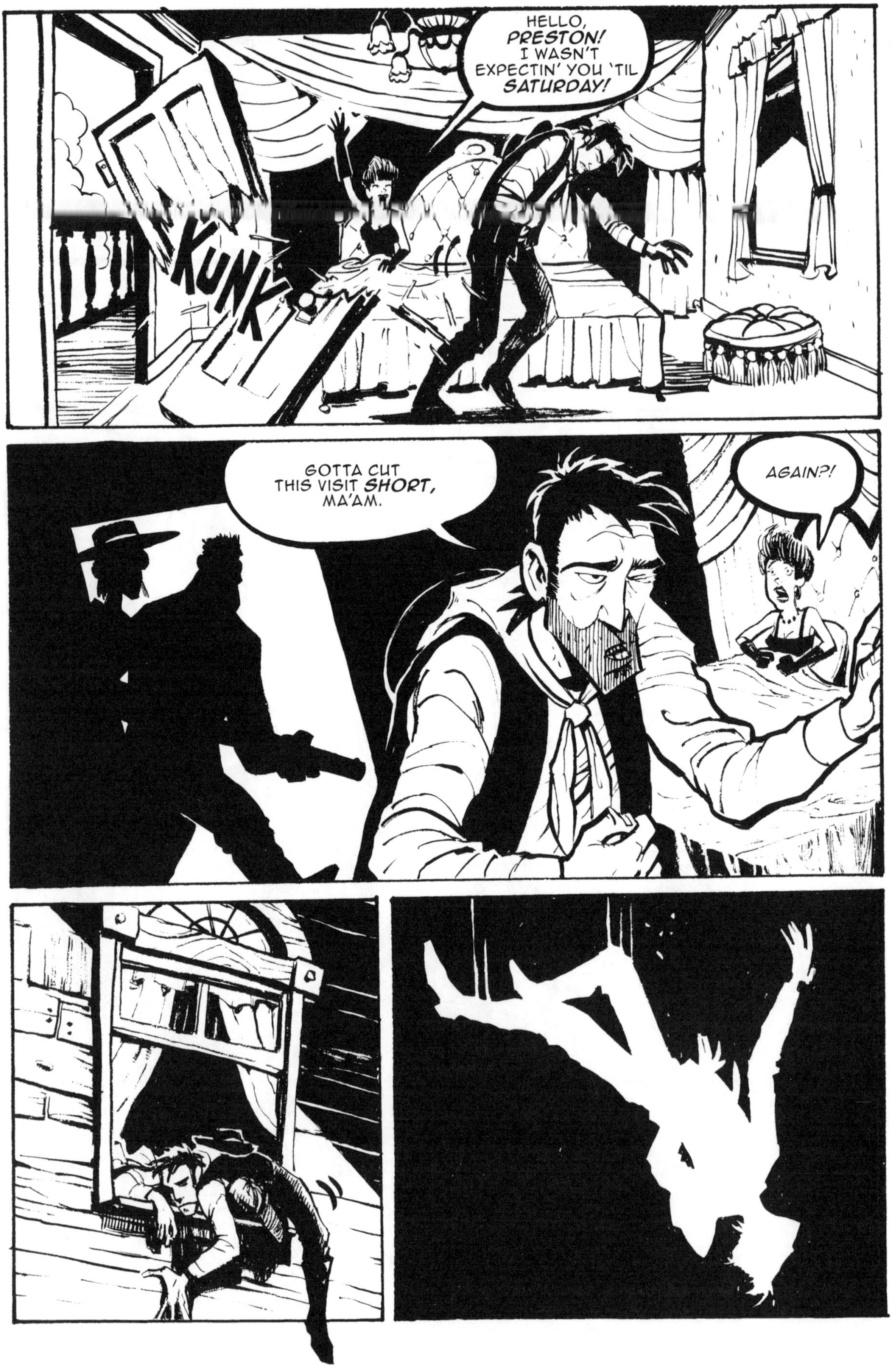
HELLO, PRESTON! I WASN'T EXPECTIN' YOU 'TIL SATURDAY!
KUNK
GOTTA CUT THIS VISIT SHORT, MA'AM.
AGAIN?!

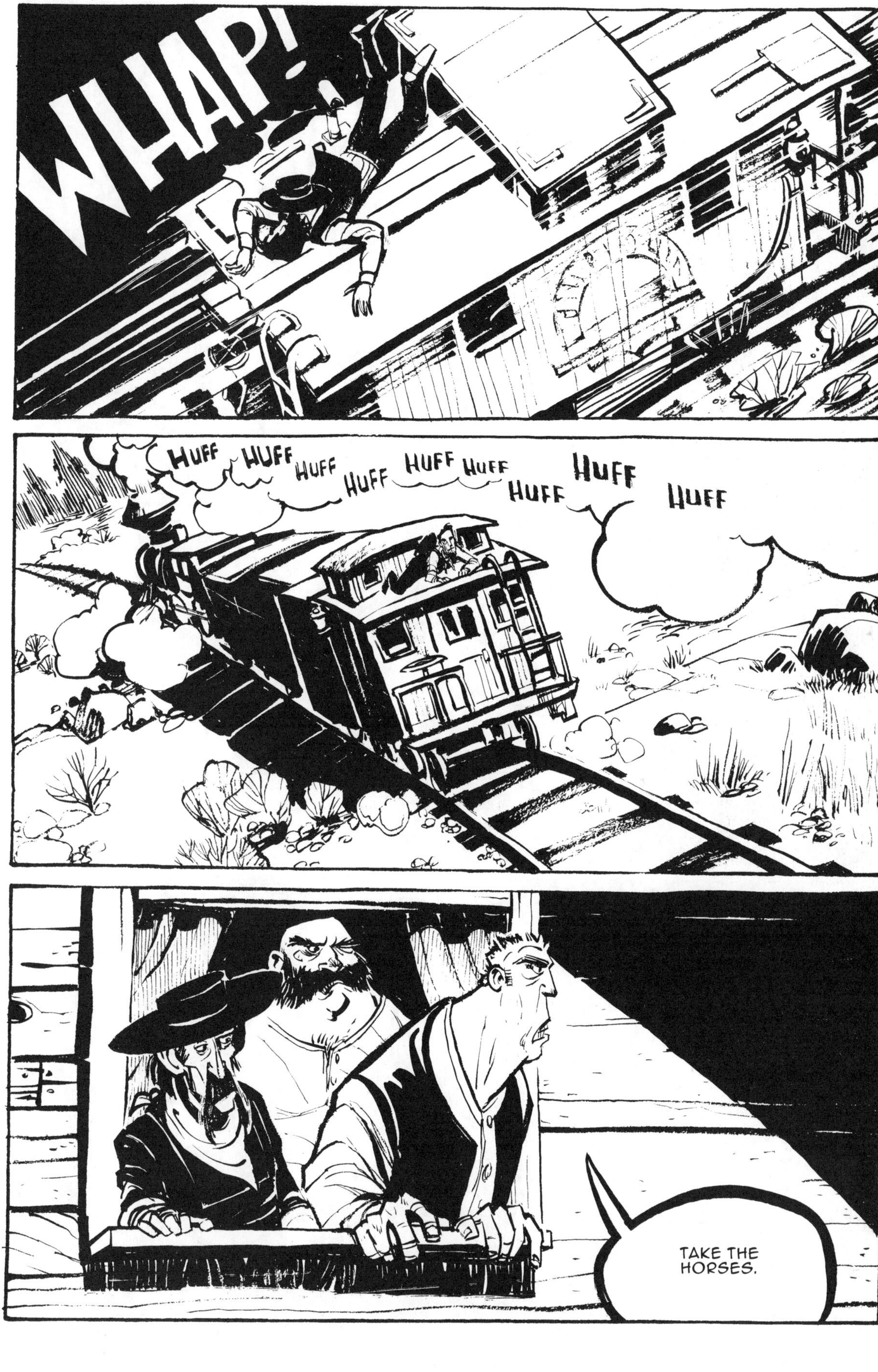
WHAP!
HUFF HUFF HUFF HUFF HUFF HUFF HUFF HUFF HUFF
TAKE THE HORSES.

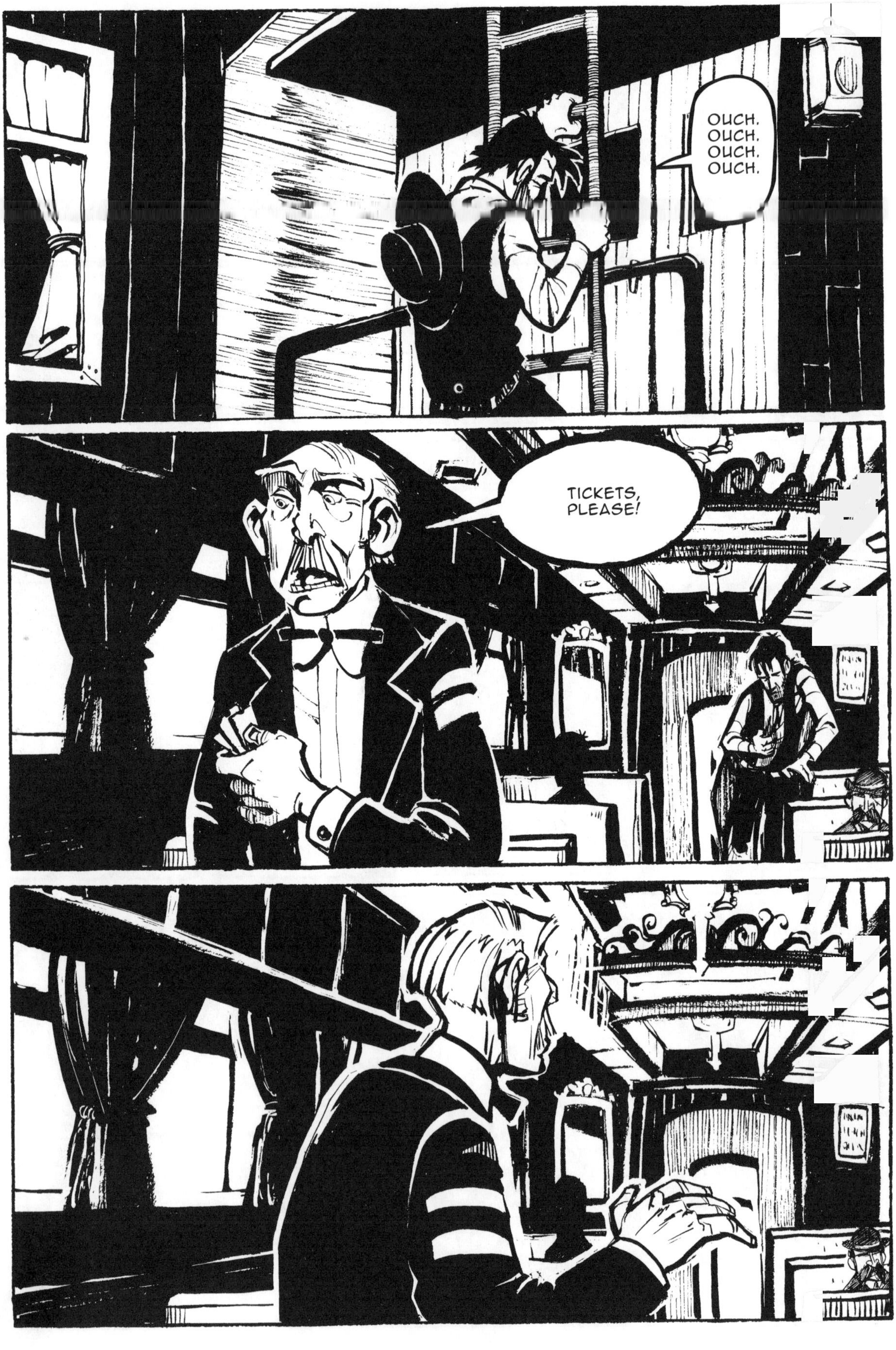
OUCH. OUCH. OUCH. OUCH.
TICKETS, PLEASE!

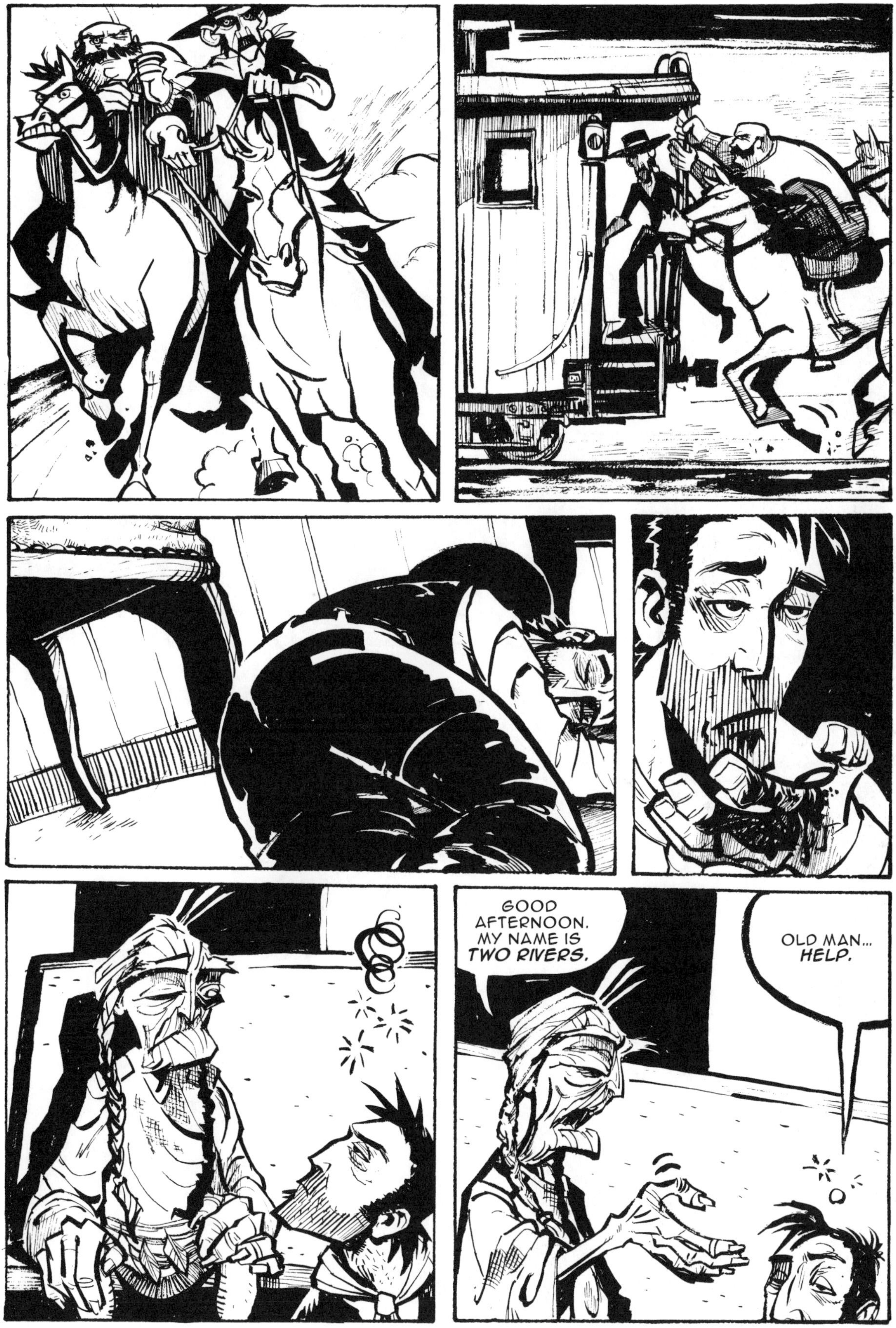
GOOD AFTERNOON. MY NAME IS TWO RIVERS.
OLD MAN... HELP.

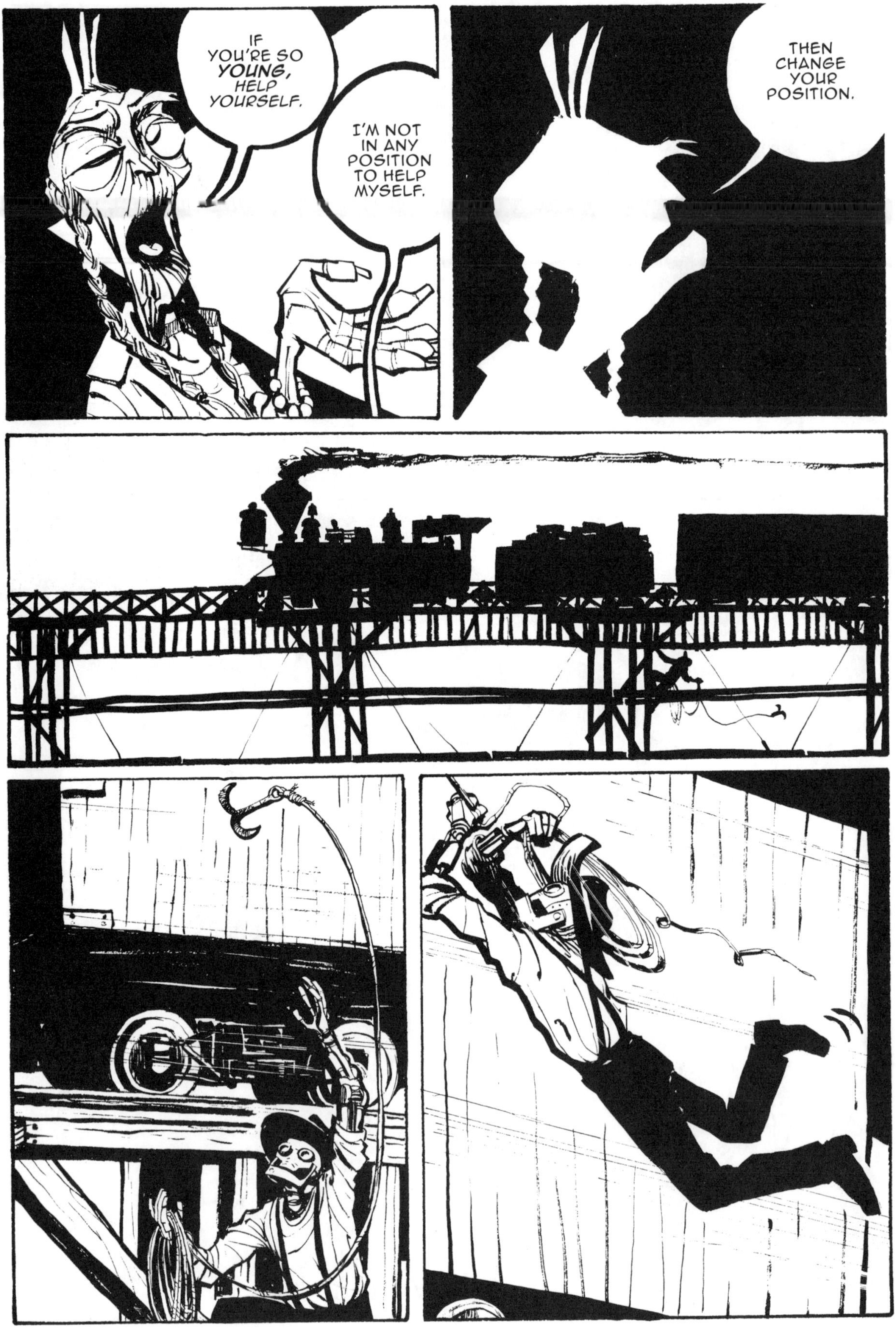
IF YOU'RE SO *YOUNG,* HELP YOURSELF.
I'M NOT IN ANY POSITION TO HELP MYSELF.
THEN CHANGE YOUR POSITION.

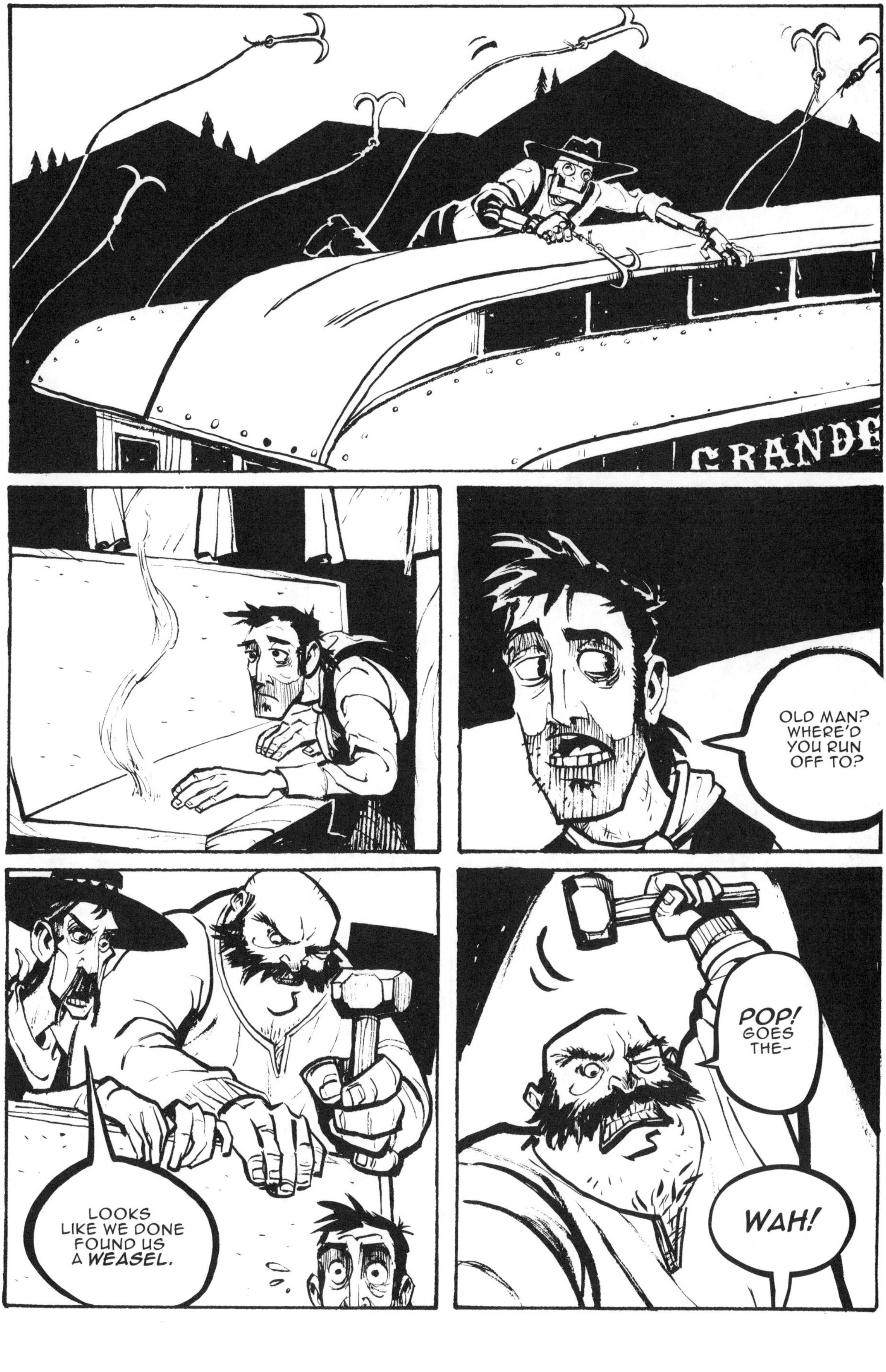
GRANDE
OLD MAN? WHERE'D YOU RUN OFF TO?
LOOKS LIKE WE DONE FOUND US A *WEASEL.*
POP! GOES THE-
WAH!

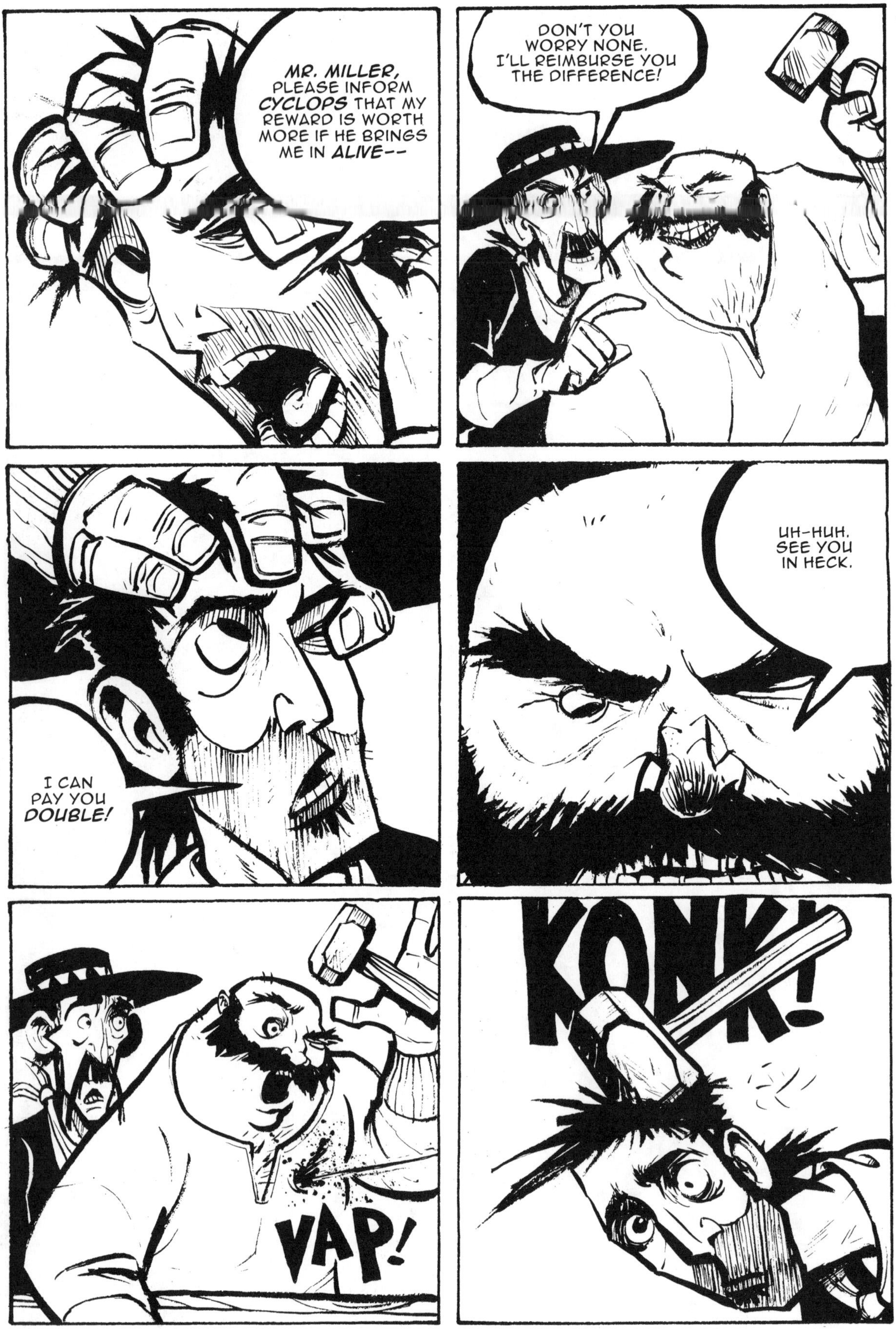

MR. MILLER, PLEASE INFORM CYCLOPS THAT MY REWARD IS WORTH MORE IF HE BRINGS ME IN ALIVE--
DON'T YOU WORRY NONE. I'LL REIMBURSE YOU THE DIFFERENCE!
I CAN PAY YOU DOUBLE!
UH-HUH. SEE YOU IN HECK.
VAP!
KONK!

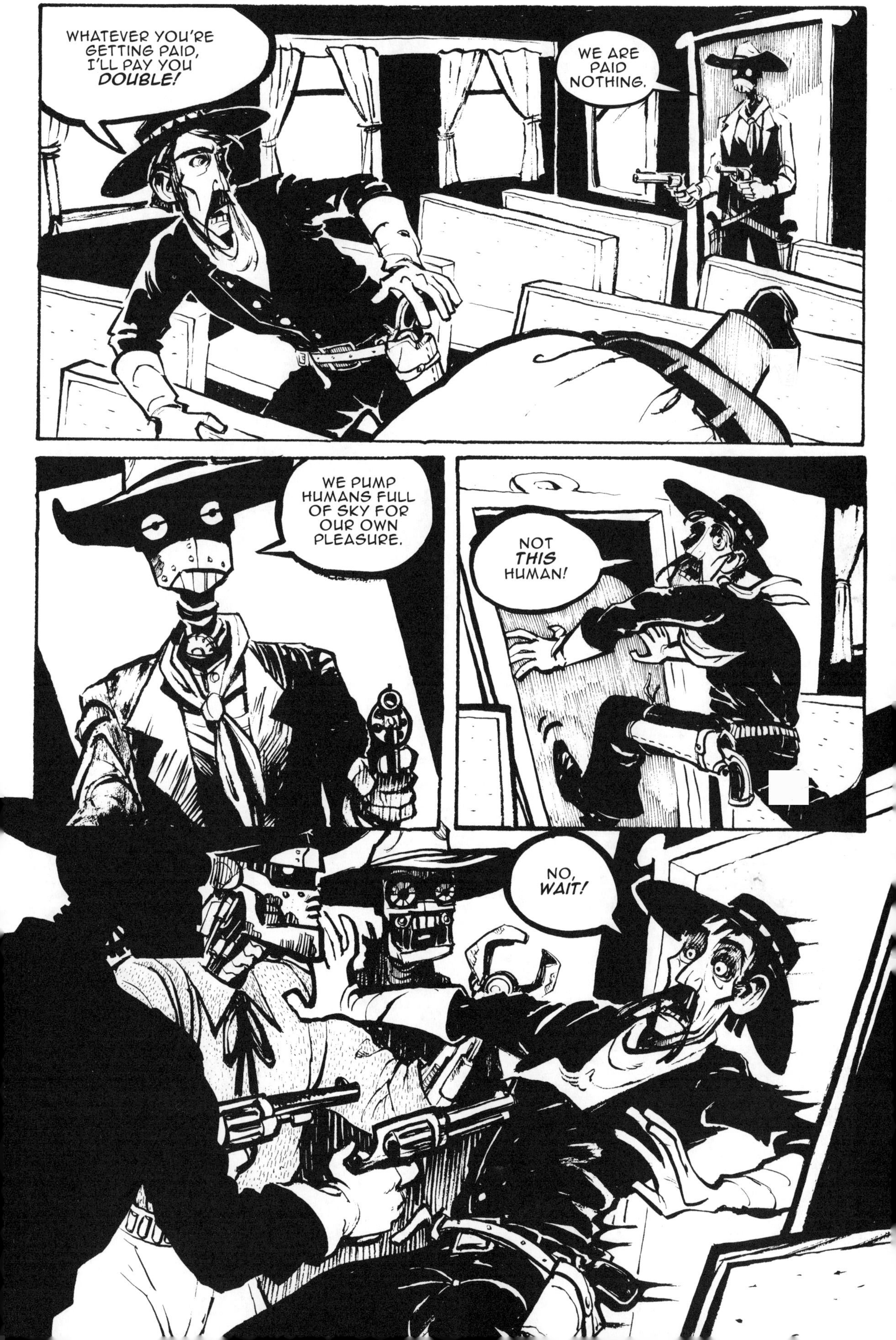
WHATEVER YOU'RE GETTING PAID, I'LL PAY YOU DOUBLE!
WE ARE PAID NOTHING.
WE PUMP HUMANS FULL OF SKY FOR OUR OWN PLEASURE.
NOT THIS HUMAN!
NO, WAIT!

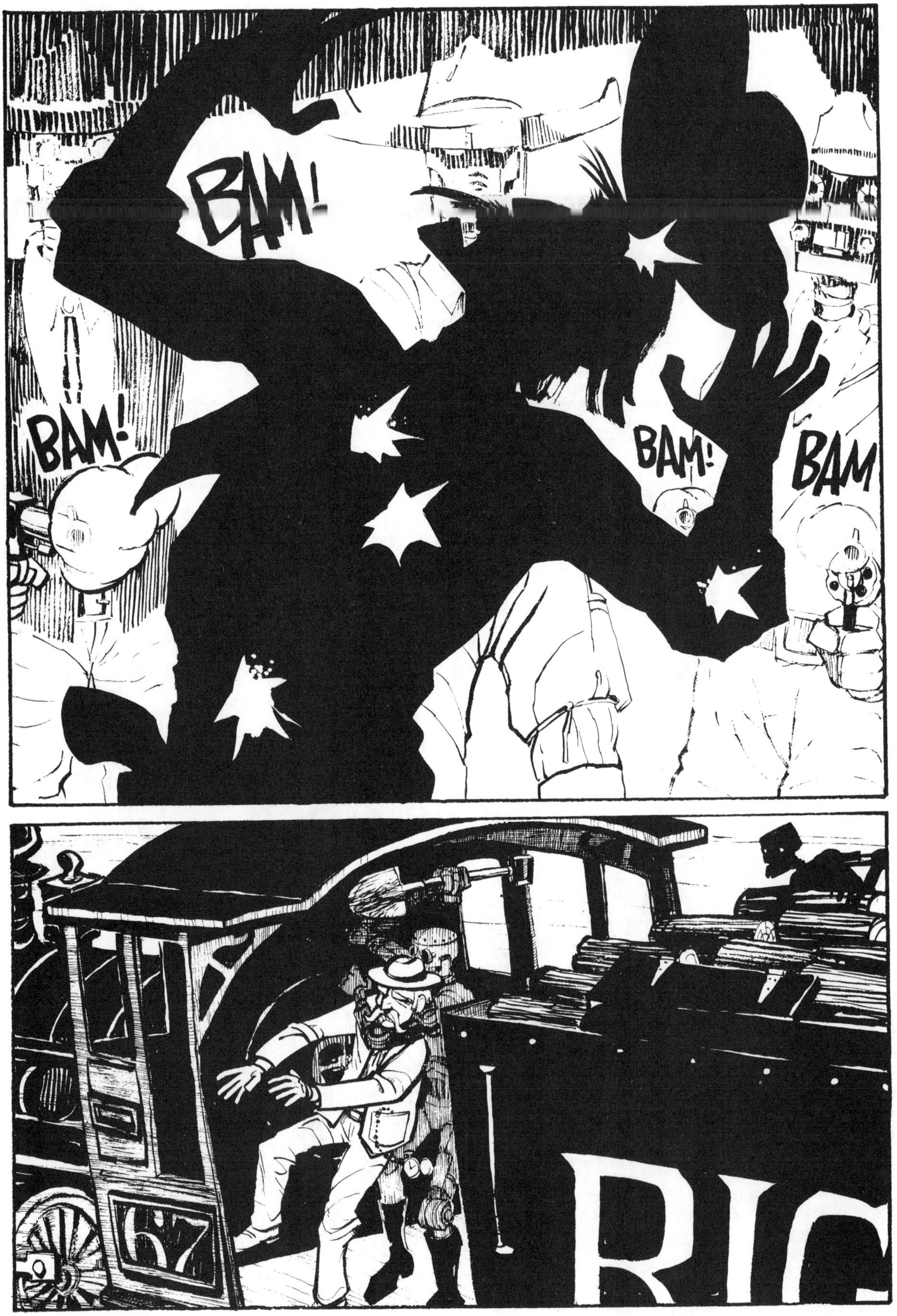
BAM!
BAM!
BAM!
BAM
67
RIC

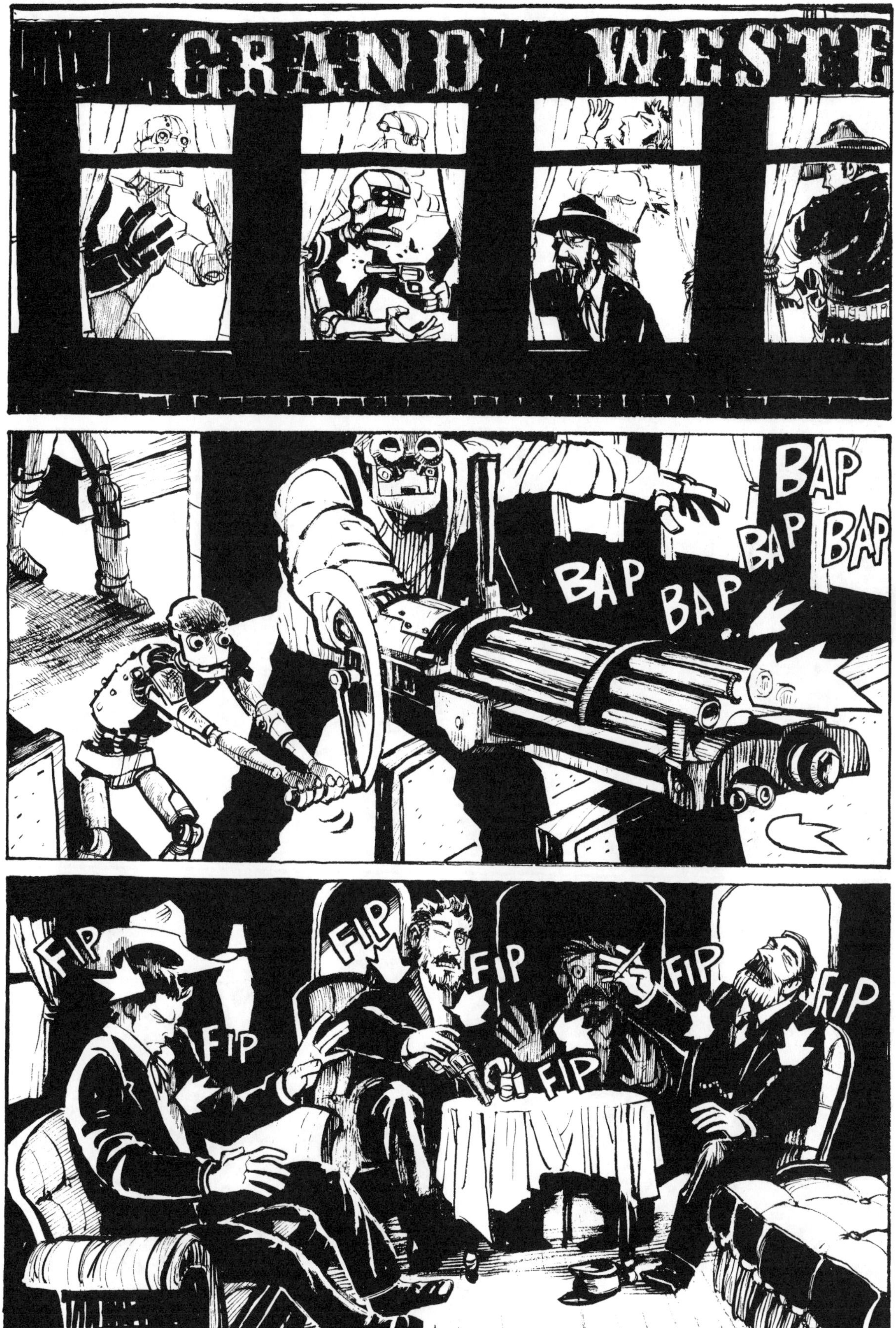
GRAND WESTE
BAP
BAP
BAP
BAP
BAP
BAP
FIP
FIP
FIP
FIP
FIP
FIP
FIP

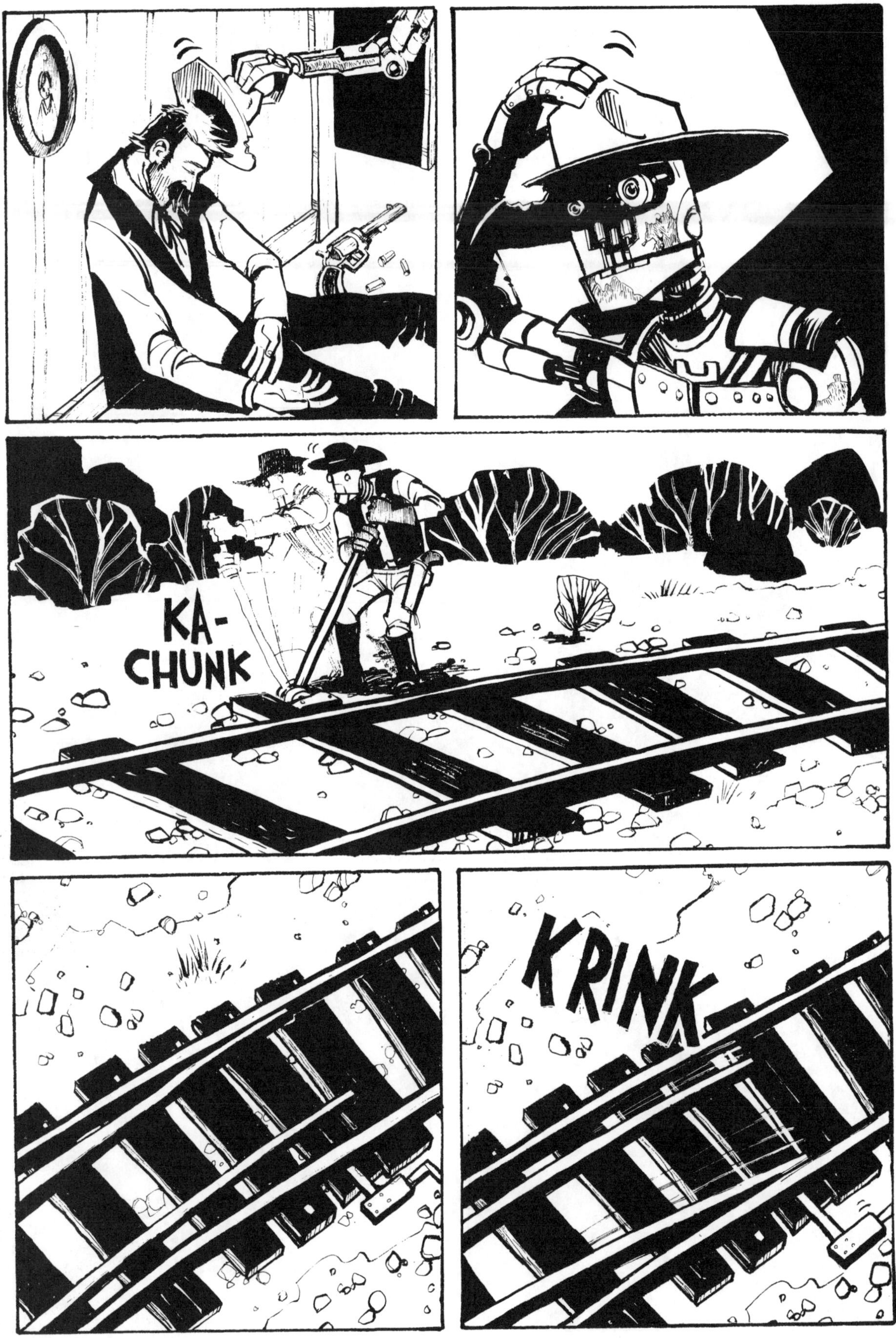
KA-
CHUNK
KRINK

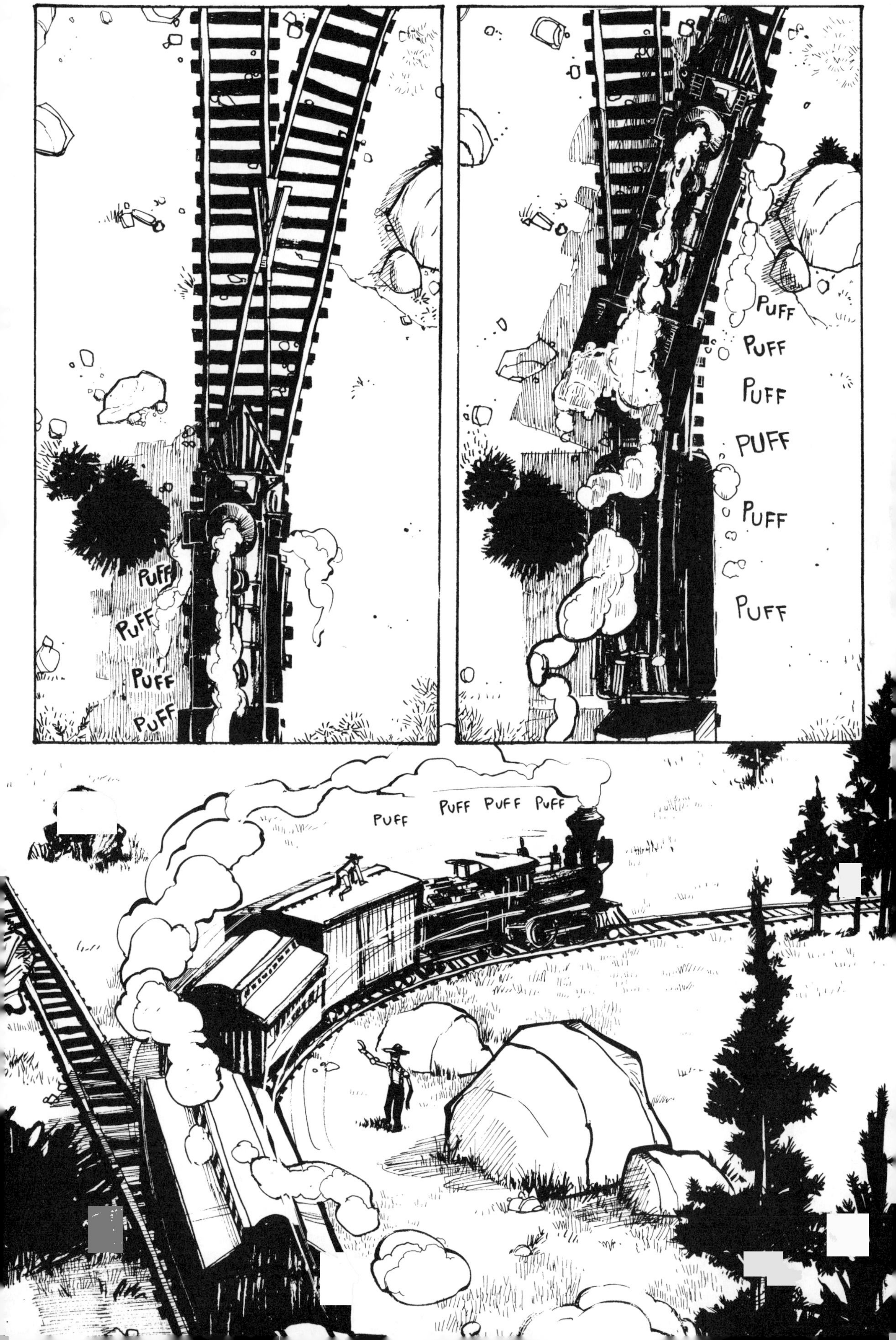
PUFF
PUFF
PUFF
PUFF
PUFF
PUFF
PUFF
PUFF
PUFF
PUFF
PUFF
PUFF PUFF PUFF

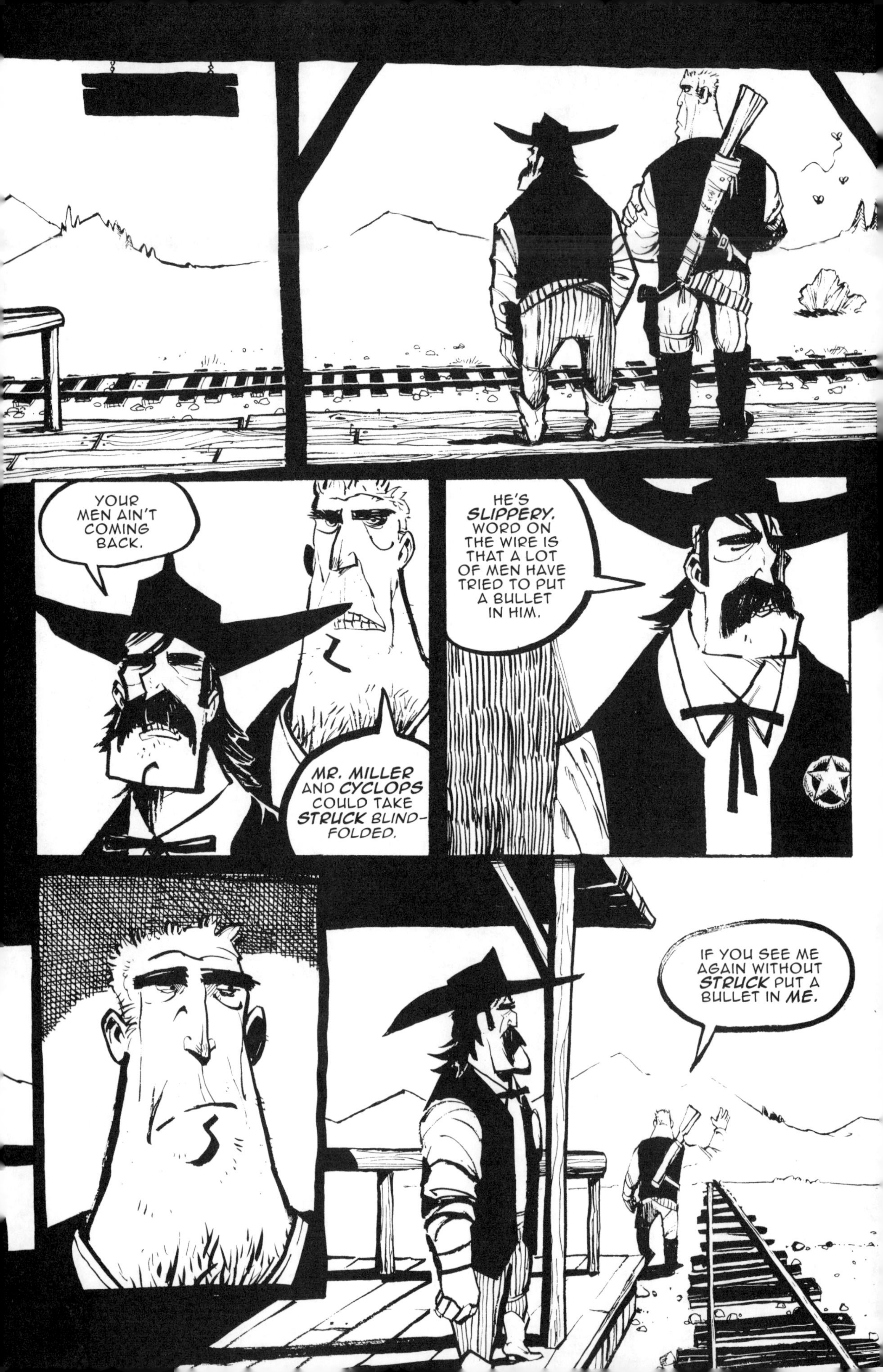
YOUR MEN AIN'T COMING BACK.
MR. MILLER AND CYCLOPS COULD TAKE STRUCK BLIND-FOLDED.
HE'S SLIPPERY. WORD ON THE WIRE IS THAT A LOT OF MEN HAVE TRIED TO PUT A BULLET IN HIM.
IF YOU SEE ME AGAIN WITHOUT STRUCK PUT A BULLET IN ME.

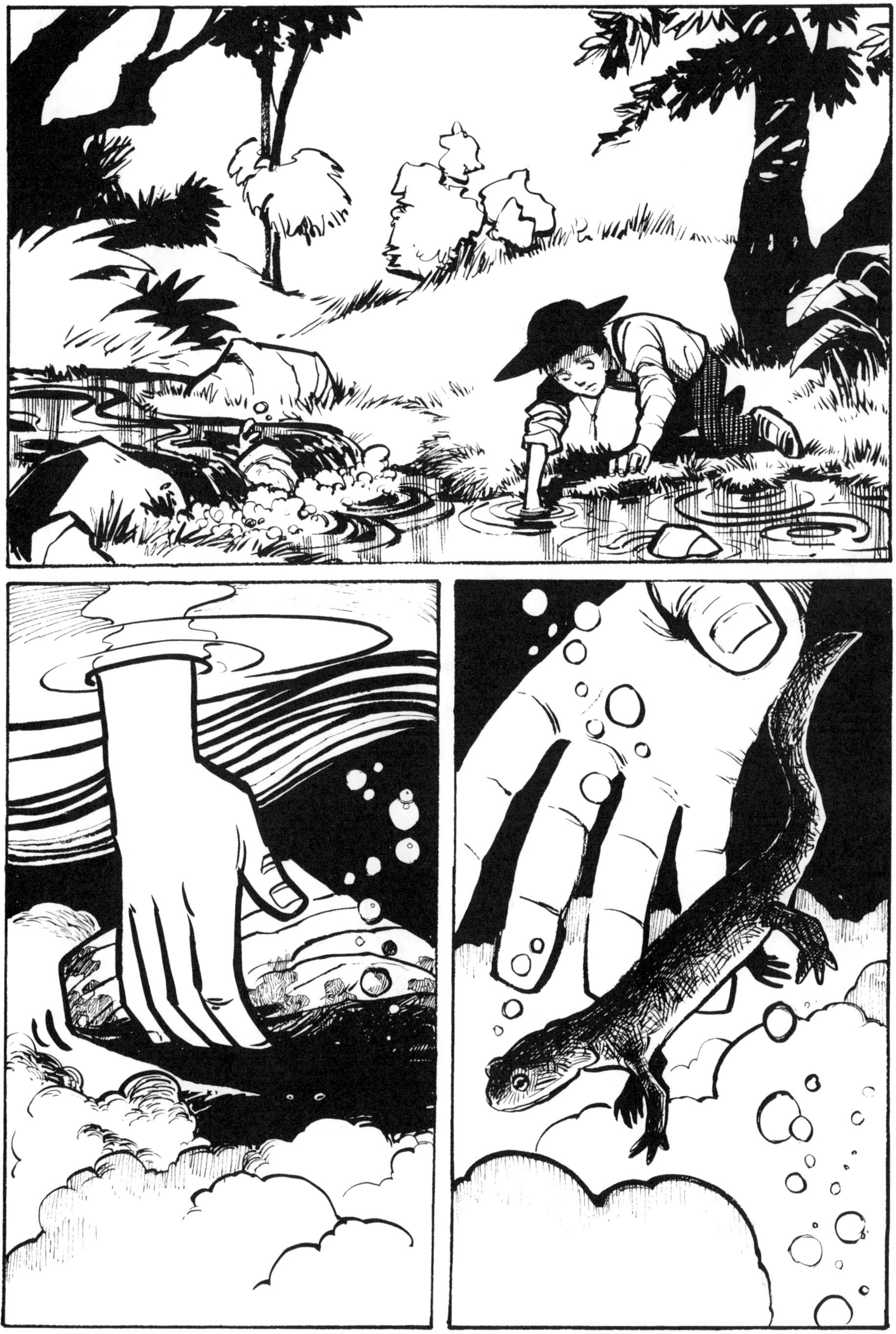

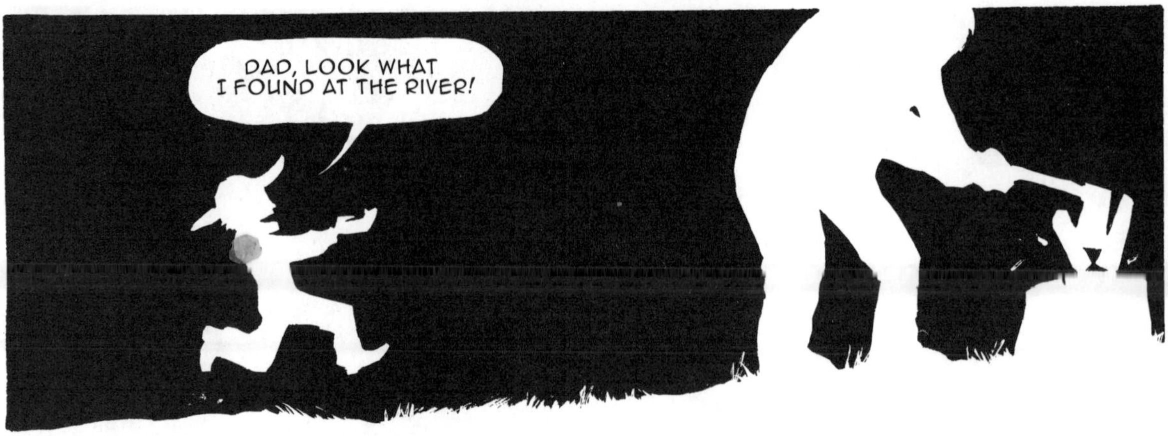
DAD, LOOK WHAT I FOUND AT THE RIVER!

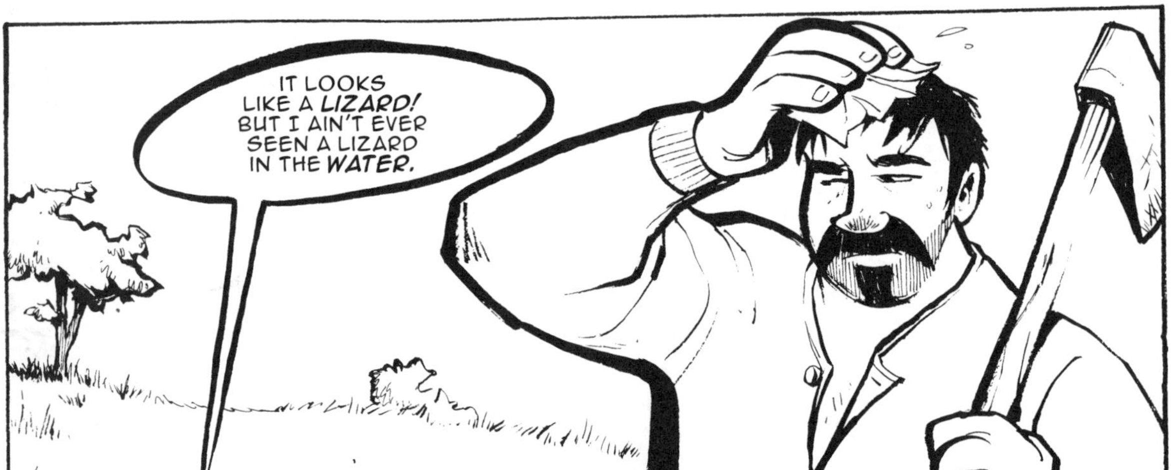
IT LOOKS LIKE A LIZARD! BUT I AIN'T EVER SEEN A LIZARD IN THE WATER.

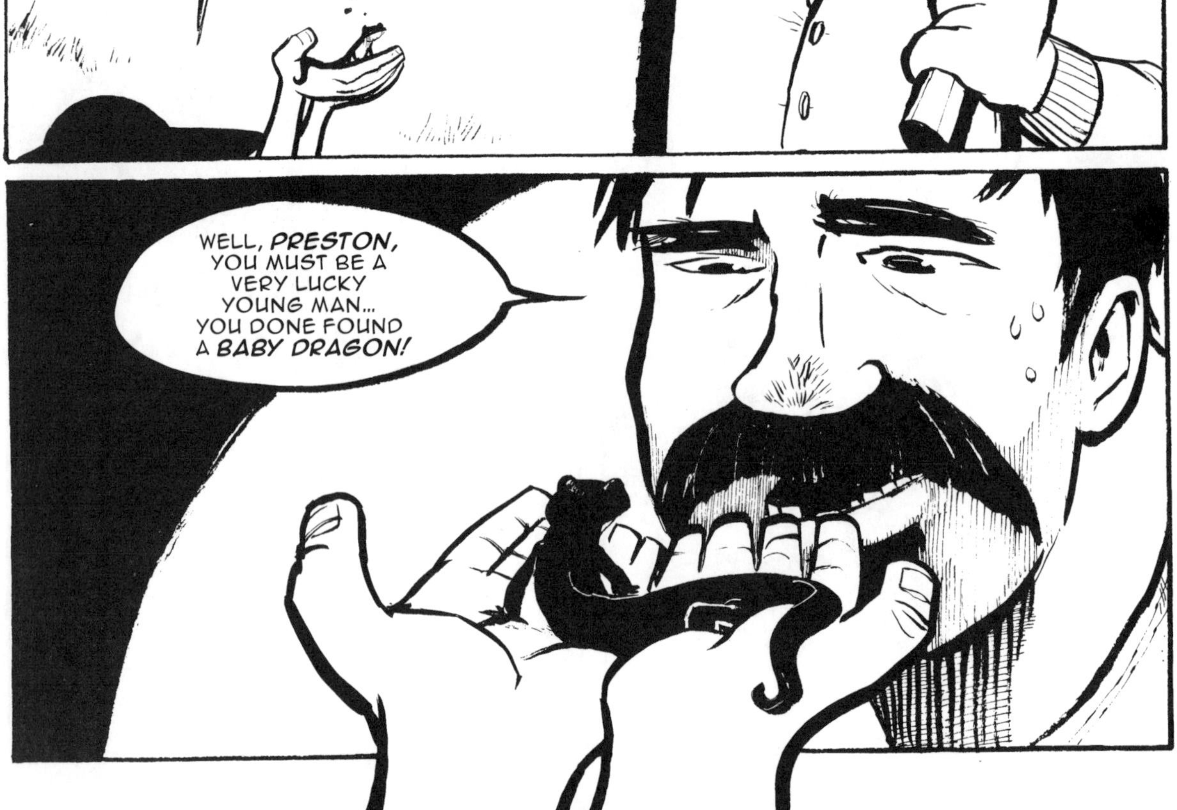
WELL, PRESTON, YOU MUST BE A VERY LUCKY YOUNG MAN... YOU DONE FOUND A BABY DRAGON!

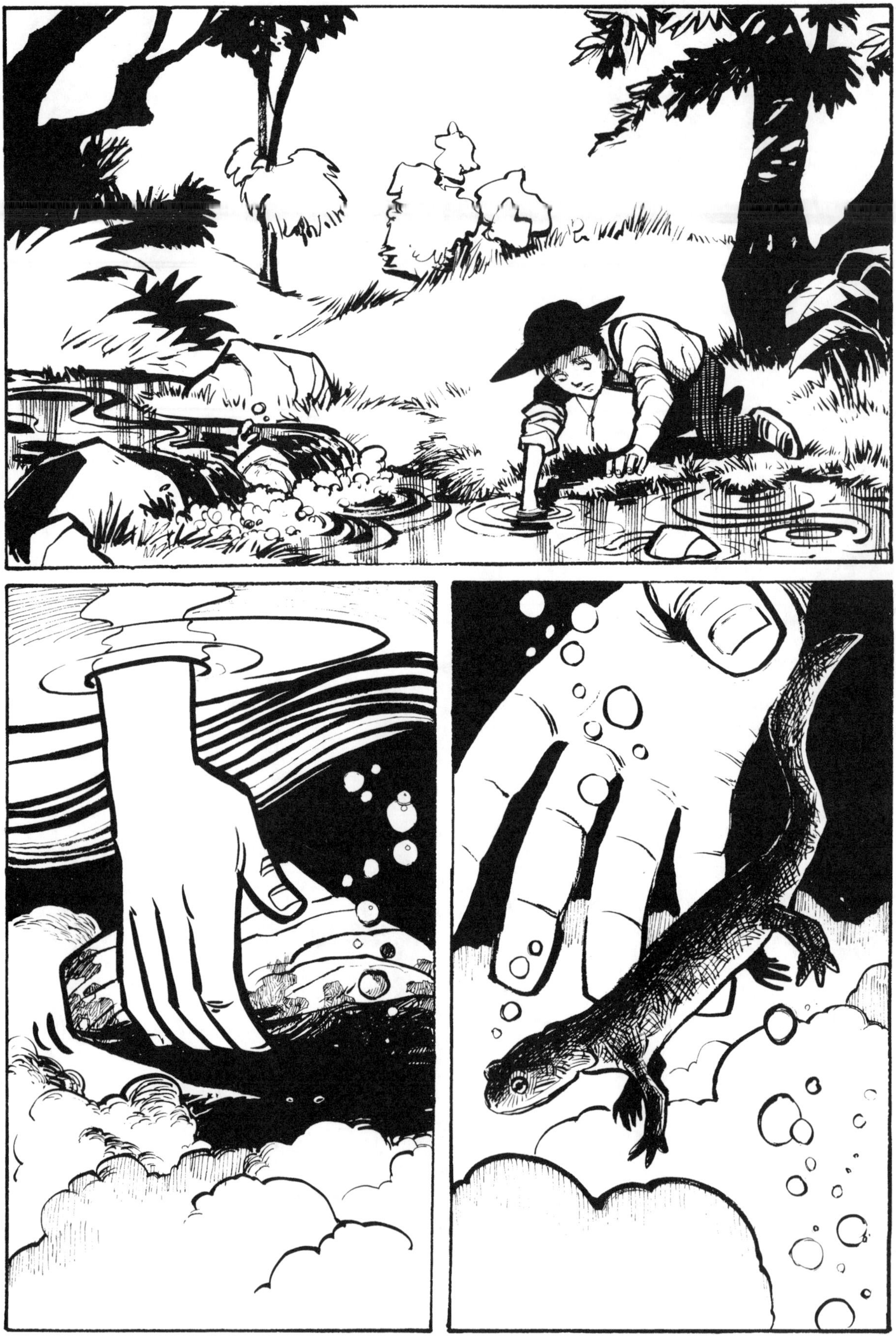

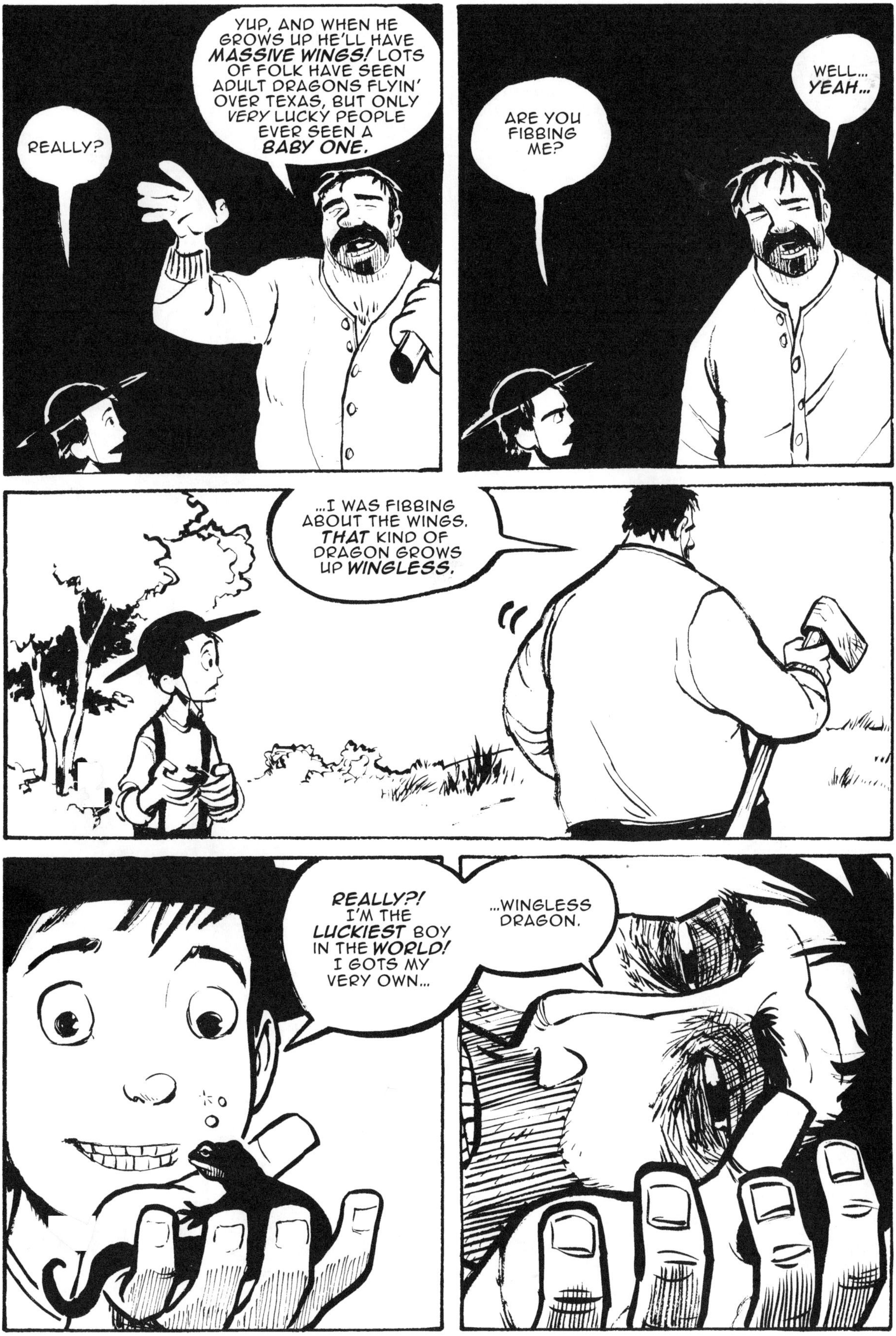
REALLY?
YUP, AND WHEN HE GROWS UP HE'LL HAVE MASSIVE WINGS! LOTS OF FOLK HAVE SEEN ADULT DRAGONS FLYIN' OVER TEXAS, BUT ONLY VERY LUCKY PEOPLE EVER SEEN A BABY ONE.
ARE YOU FIBBING ME?
WELL... YEAH...
...I WAS FIBBING ABOUT THE WINGS. THAT KIND OF DRAGON GROWS UP WINGLESS.
REALLY?! I'M THE LUCKIEST BOY IN THE WORLD! I GOTS MY VERY OWN...
...WINGLESS DRAGON.

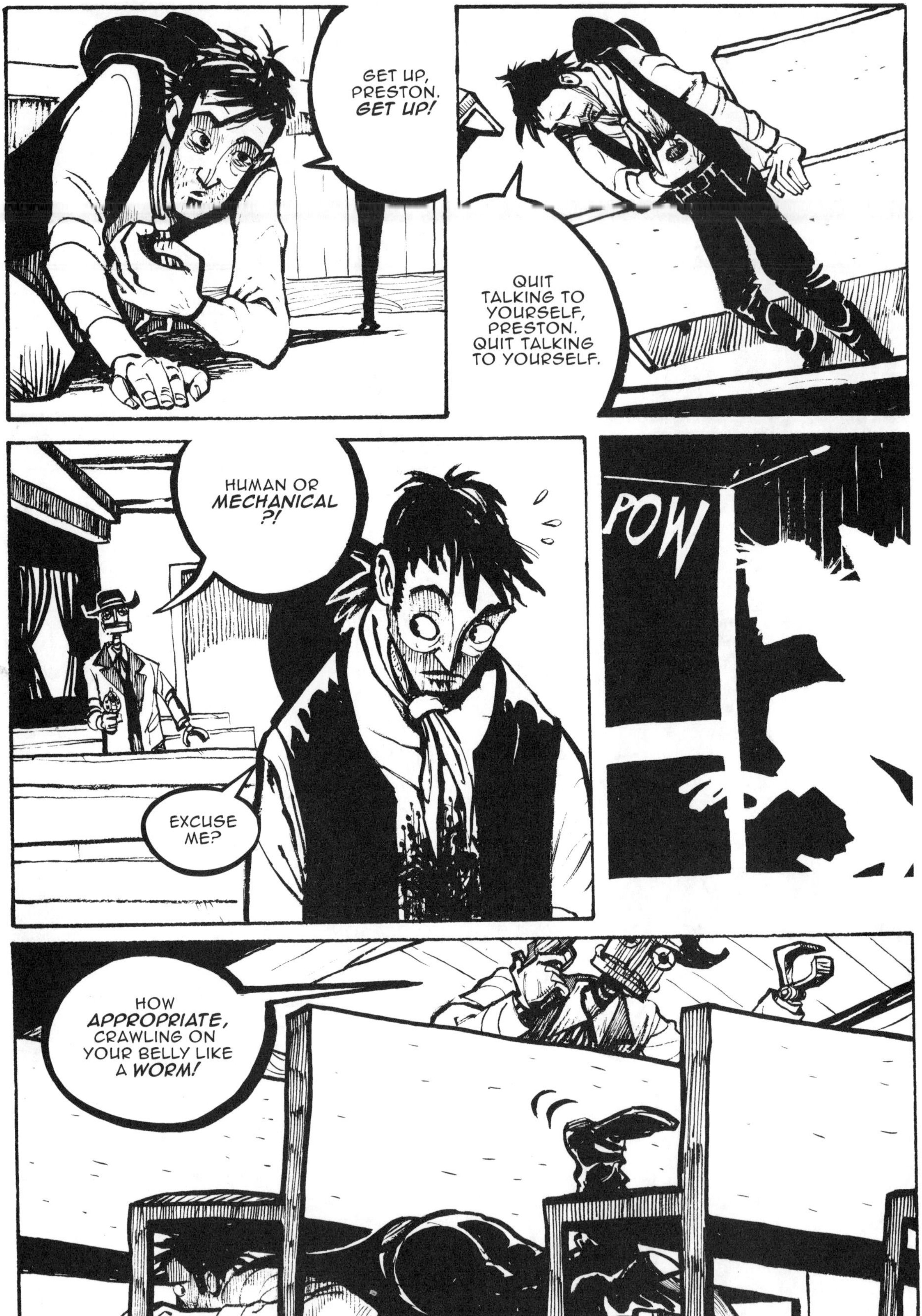
GET UP, PRESTON. GET UP!
QUIT TALKING TO YOURSELF, PRESTON. QUIT TALKING TO YOURSELF.
HUMAN OR MECHANICAL ?!
EXCUSE ME?
POW
HOW APPROPRIATE, CRAWLING ON YOUR BELLY LIKE A WORM!

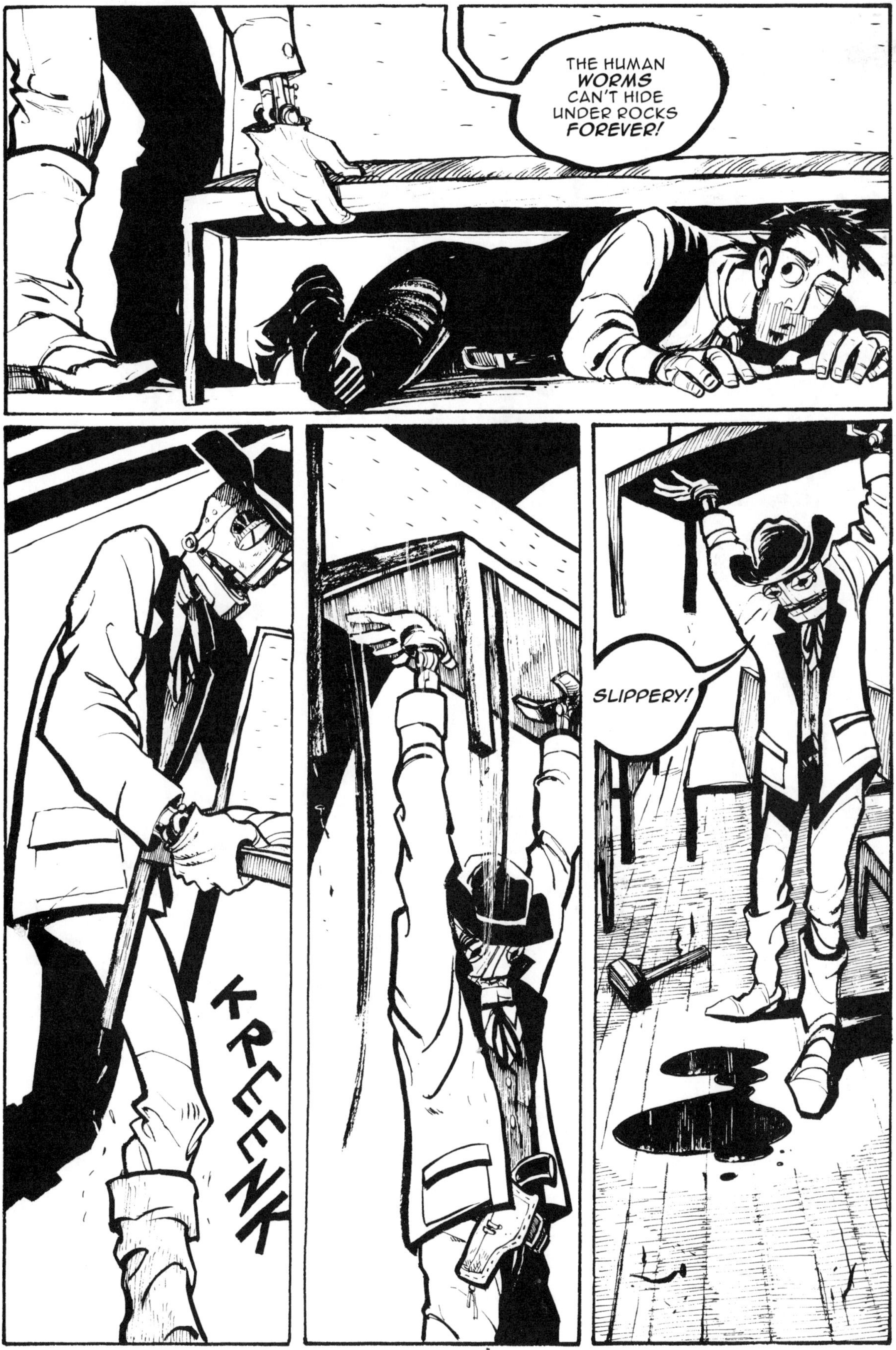
THE HUMAN WORMS CAN'T HIDE UNDER ROCKS FOREVER!
KREENK
SLIPPERY!

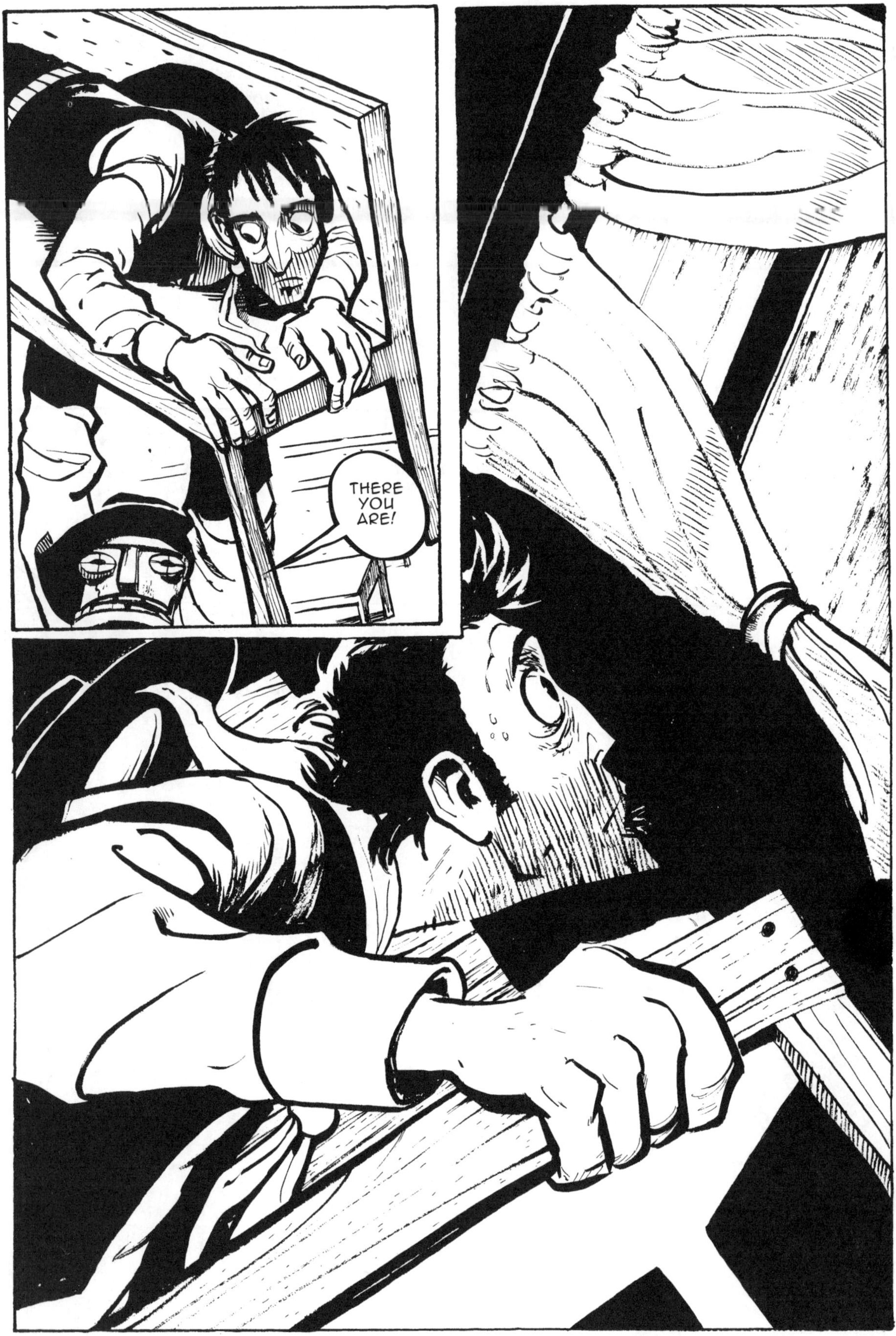
THERE YOU ARE!

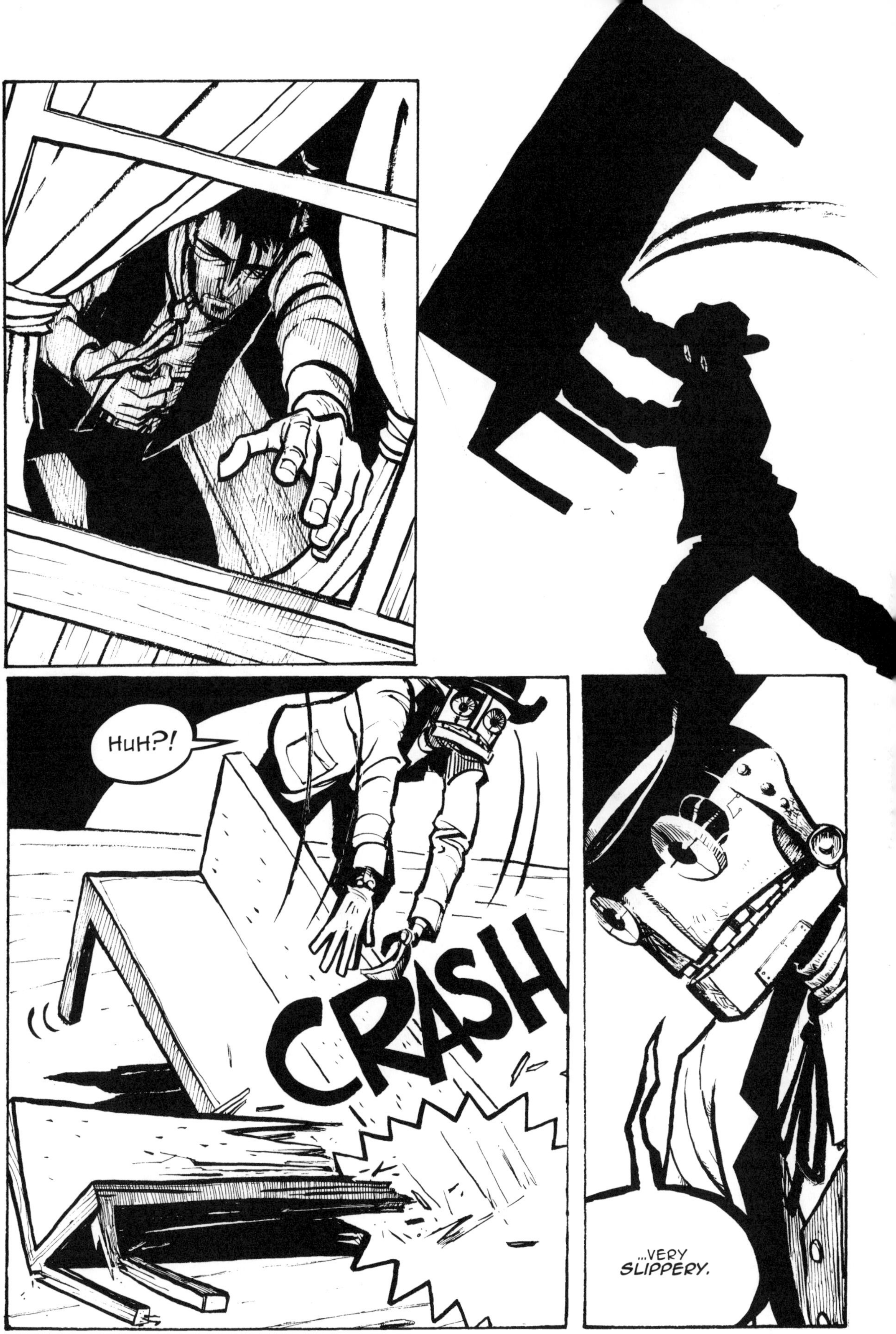
HuH?!
CRASH
...VERY
SLIPPERY.

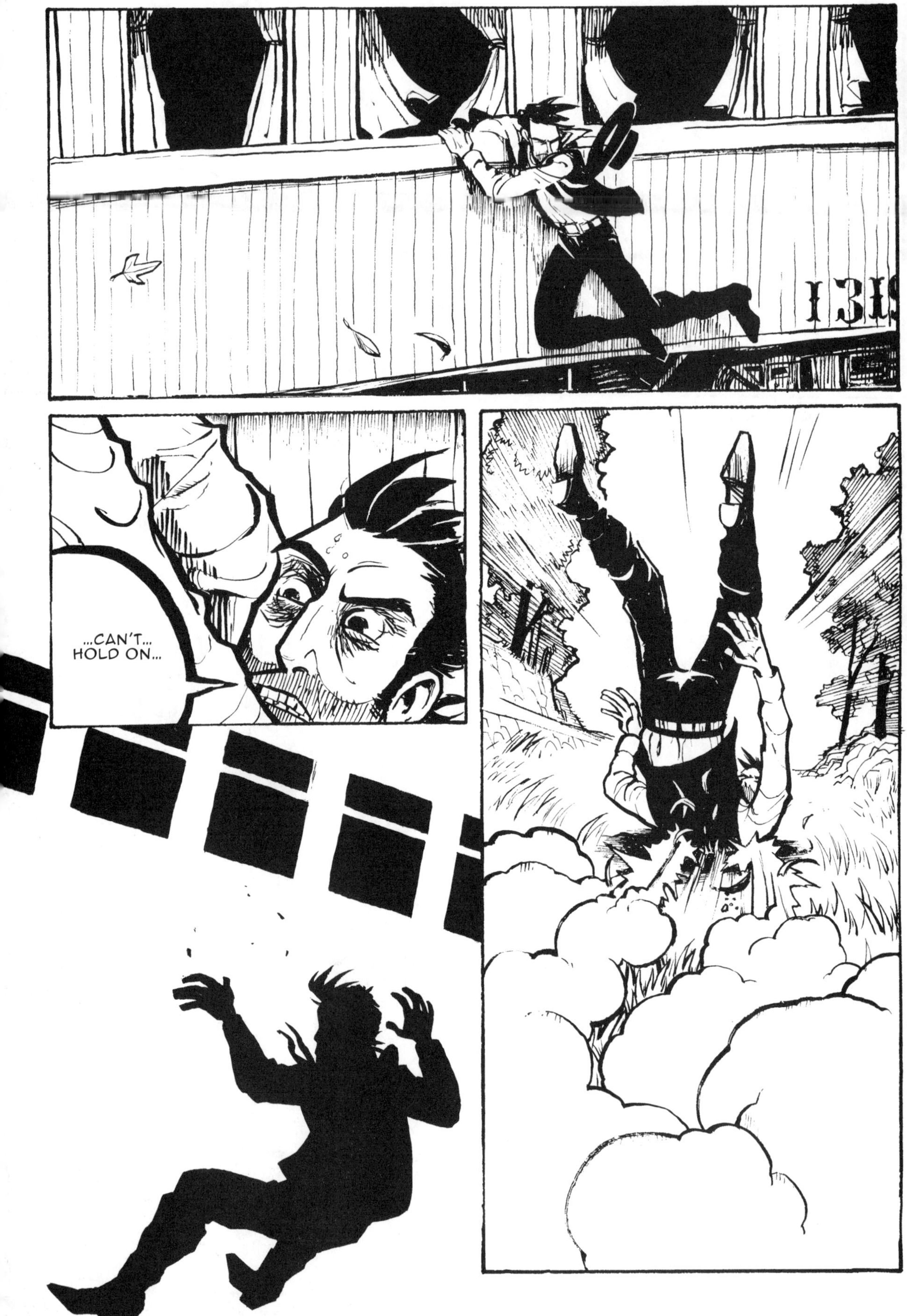
1319
...CAN'T...
HOLD ON...

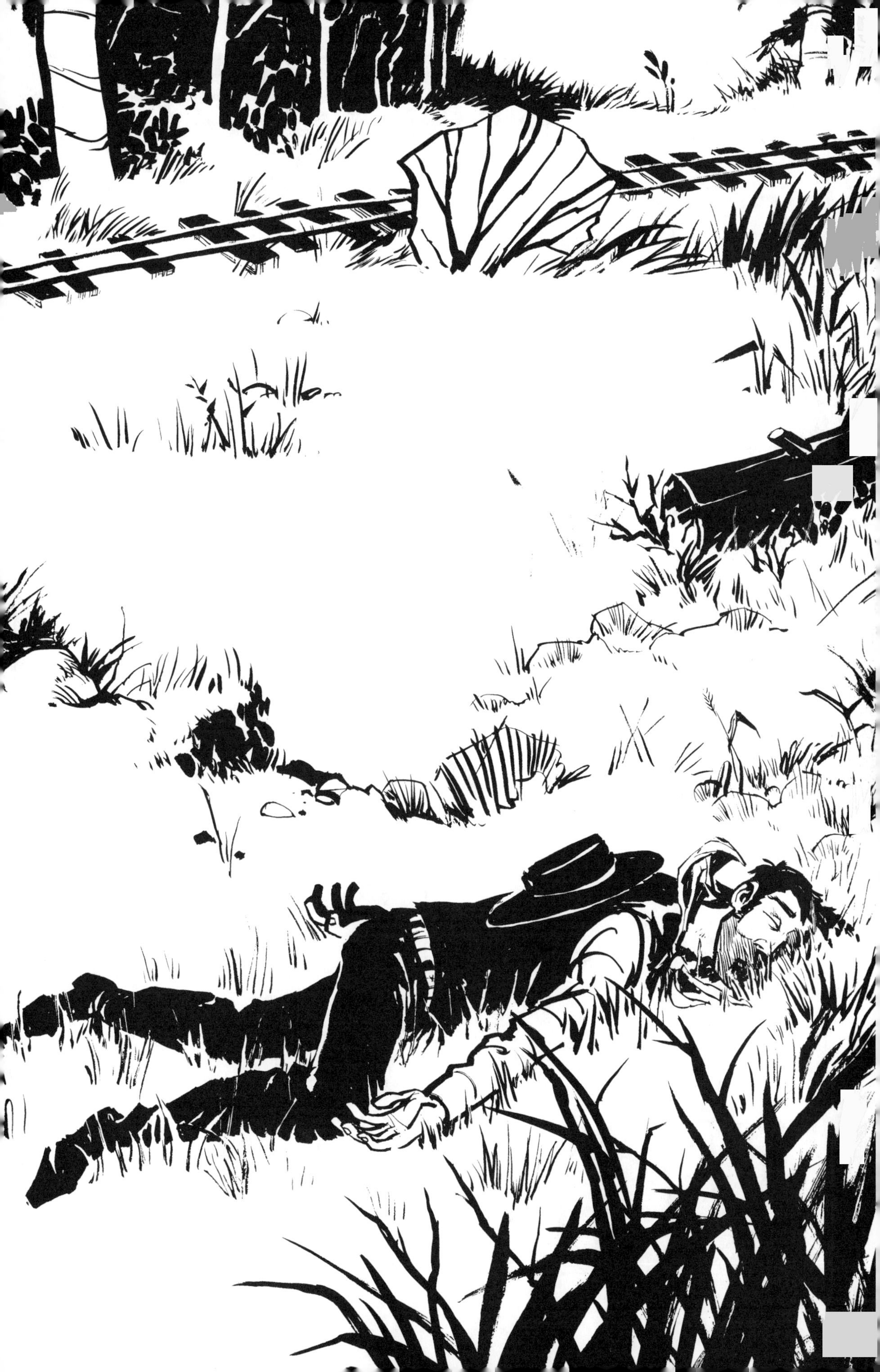

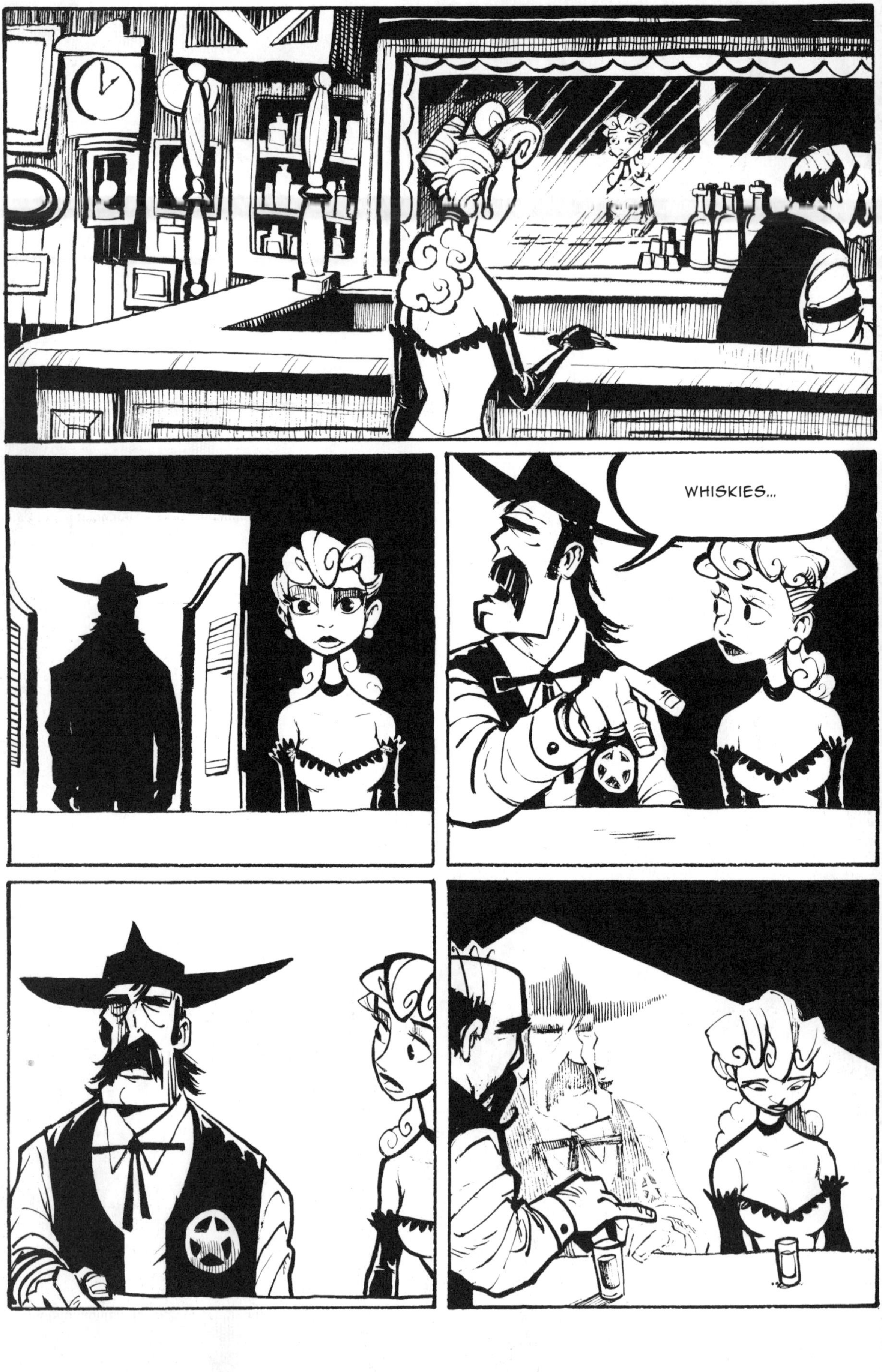
WHISKIES...

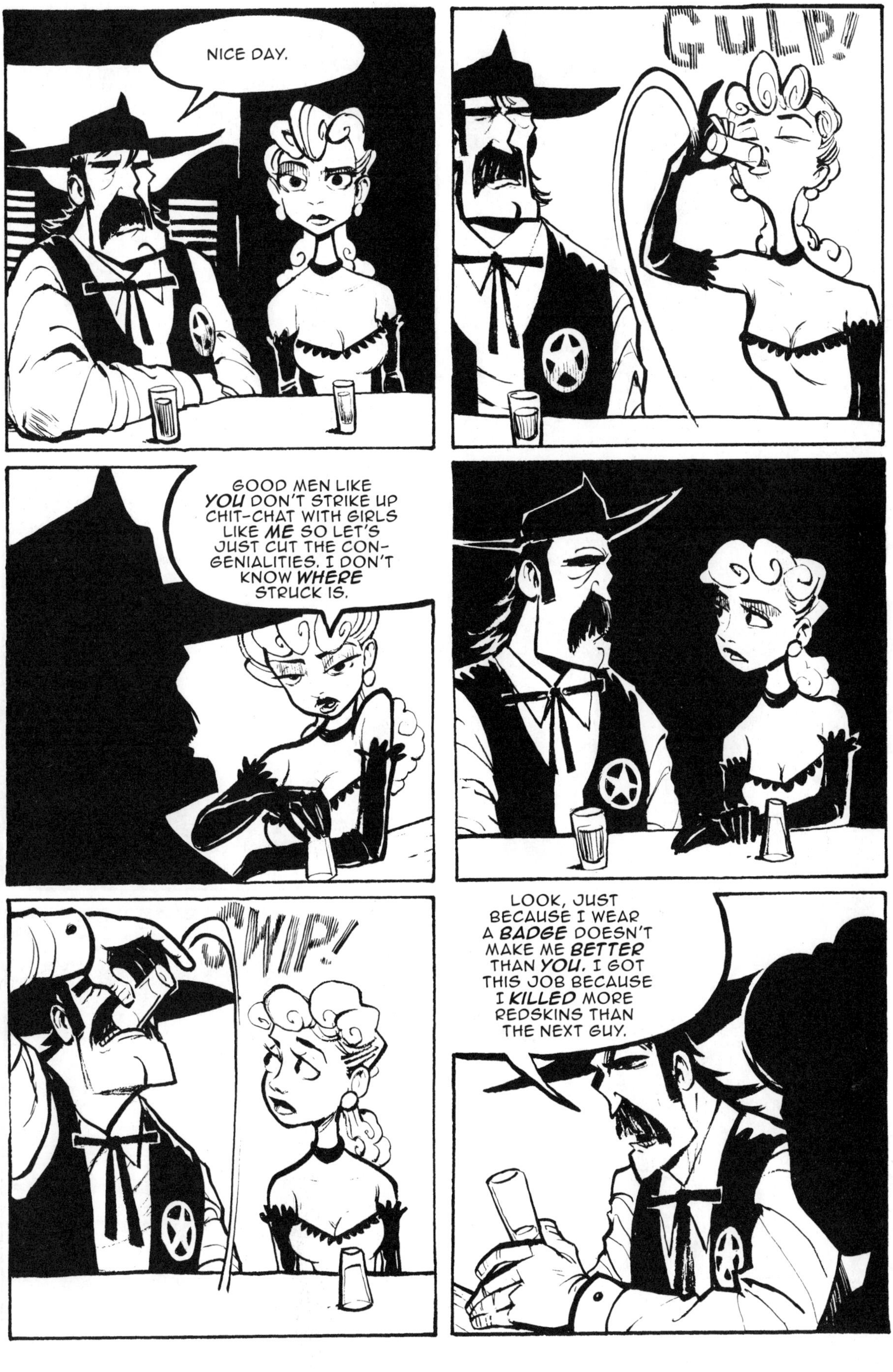
NICE DAY.
GULP!
GOOD MEN LIKE YOU DON'T STRIKE UP CHIT-CHAT WITH GIRLS LIKE ME SO LET'S JUST CUT THE CON-GENIALITIES. I DON'T KNOW WHERE STRUCK IS.
WIP!
LOOK, JUST BECAUSE I WEAR A BADGE DOESN'T MAKE ME BETTER THAN YOU. I GOT THIS JOB BECAUSE I KILLED MORE REDSKINS THAN THE NEXT GUY.

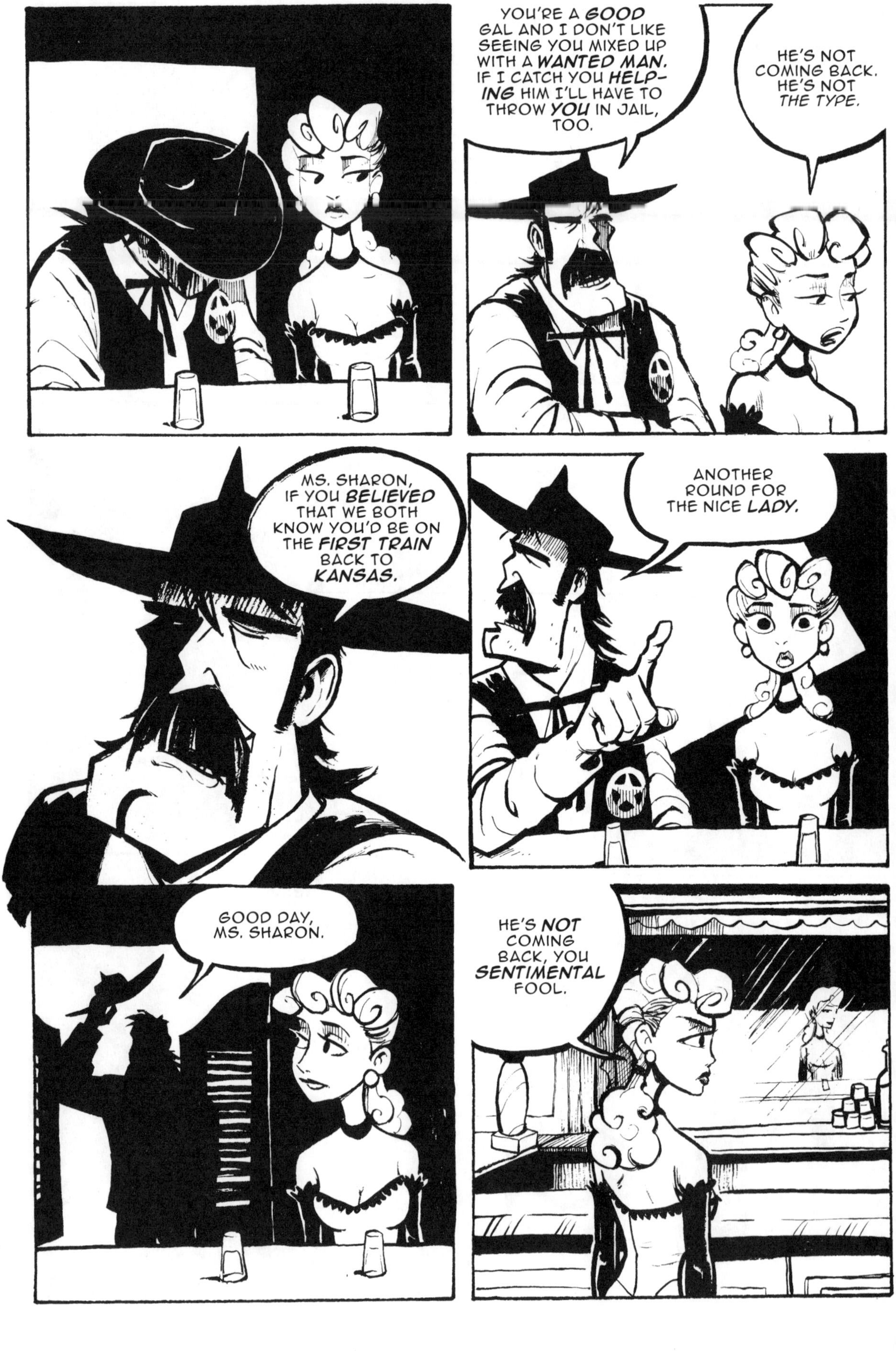
YOU'RE A GOOD GAL AND I DON'T LIKE SEEING YOU MIXED UP WITH A WANTED MAN. IF I CATCH YOU HELPING HIM I'LL HAVE TO THROW YOU IN JAIL, TOO.
HE'S NOT COMING BACK. HE'S NOT THE TYPE.
MS. SHARON, IF YOU BELIEVED THAT WE BOTH KNOW YOU'D BE ON THE FIRST TRAIN BACK TO KANSAS.
ANOTHER ROUND FOR THE NICE LADY.
GOOD DAY, MS. SHARON.
HE'S NOT COMING BACK, YOU SENTIMENTAL FOOL.

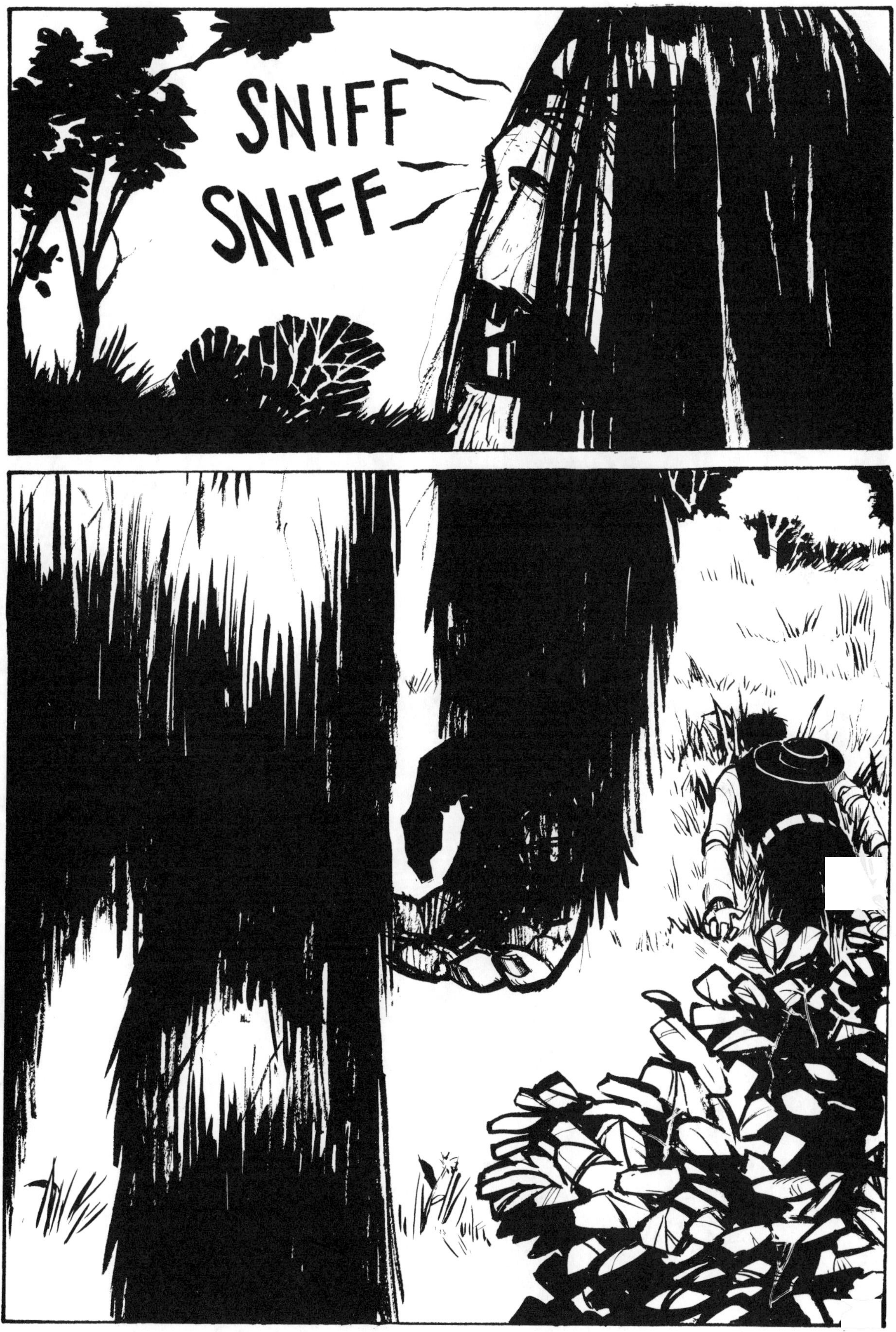
SNIFF
SNIFF

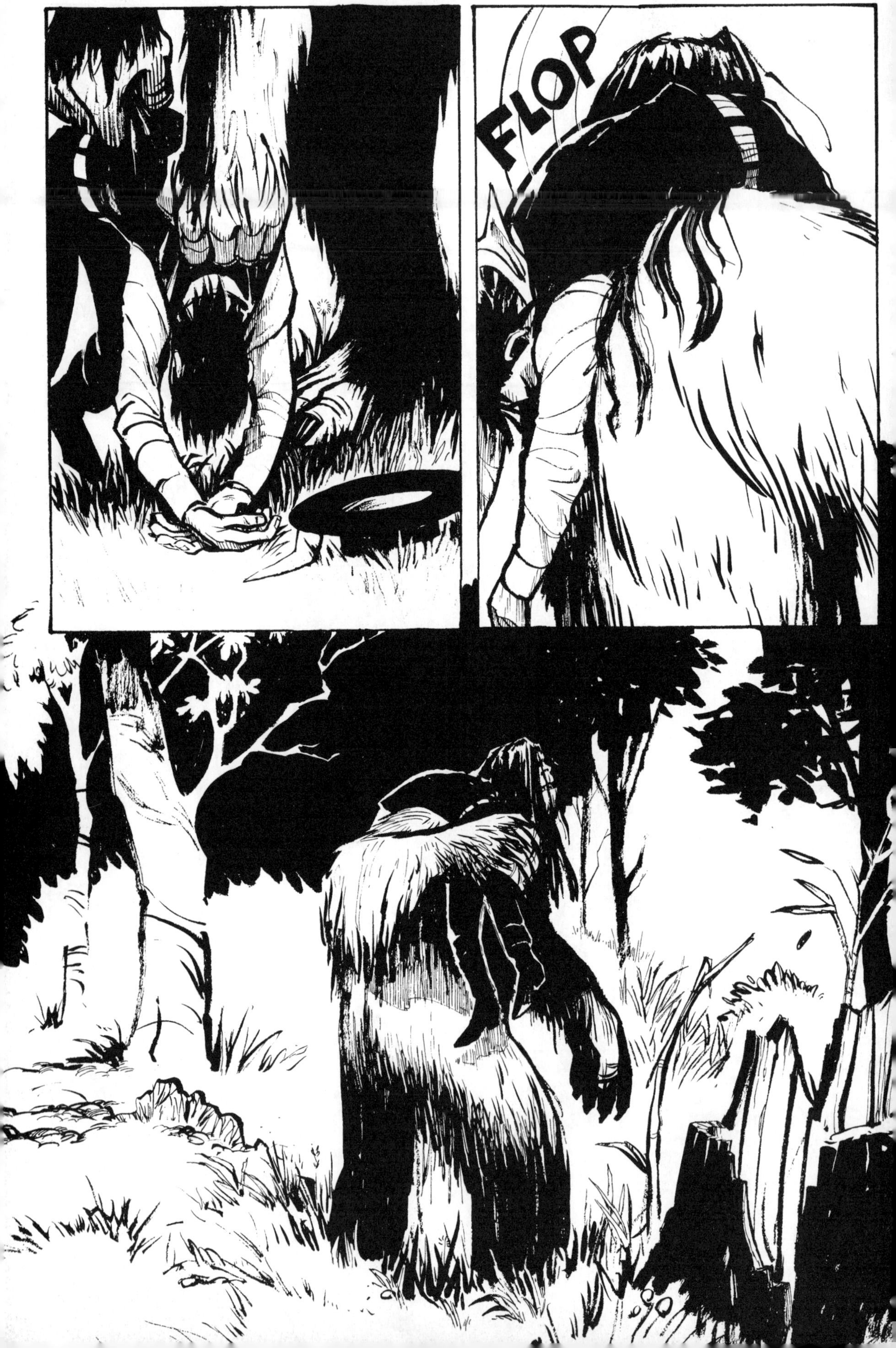
FLOP

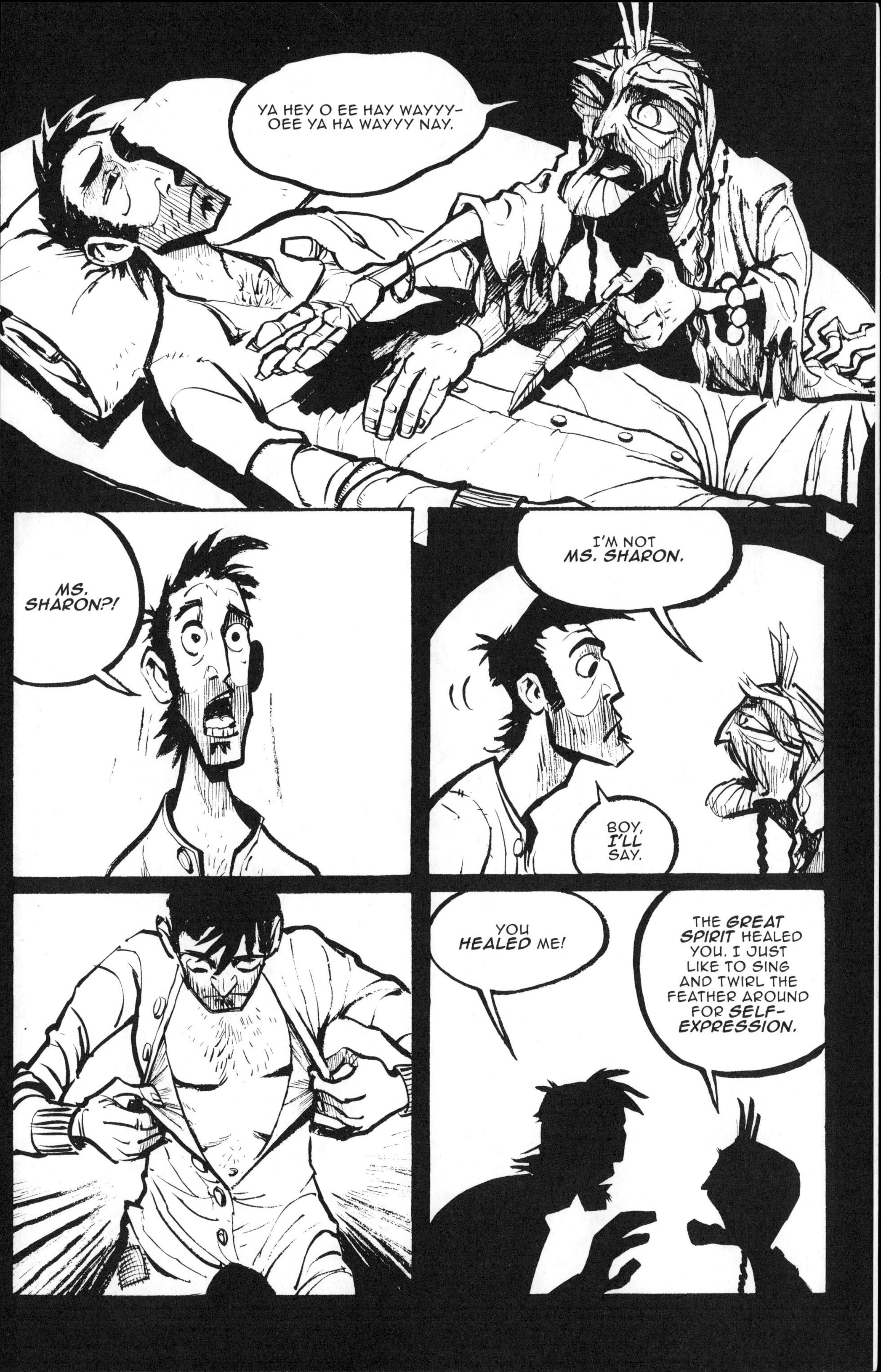
YA HEY O EE HAY WAYYY-OEE YA HA WAYYY NAY.
MS. SHARON?!
I'M NOT MS. SHARON.
BOY, I'LL SAY.
YOU HEALED ME!
THE GREAT SPIRIT HEALED YOU. I JUST LIKE TO SING AND TWIRL THE FEATHER AROUND FOR SELF-EXPRESSION.

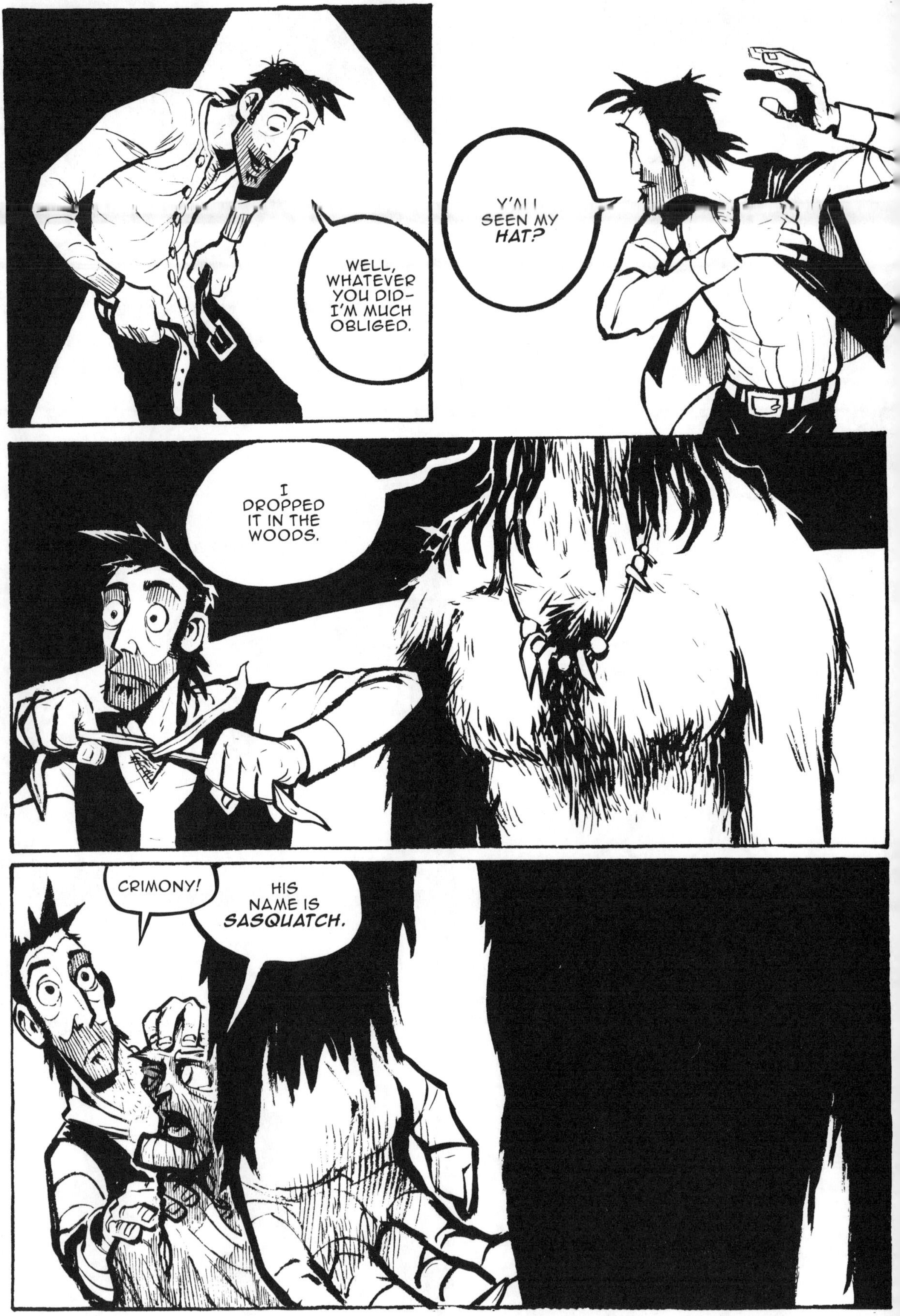
WELL, WHATEVER YOU DID- I'M MUCH OBLIGED.
Y'ALL SEEN MY HAT?
I DROPPED IT IN THE WOODS.
CRIMONY!
HIS NAME IS SASQUATCH.

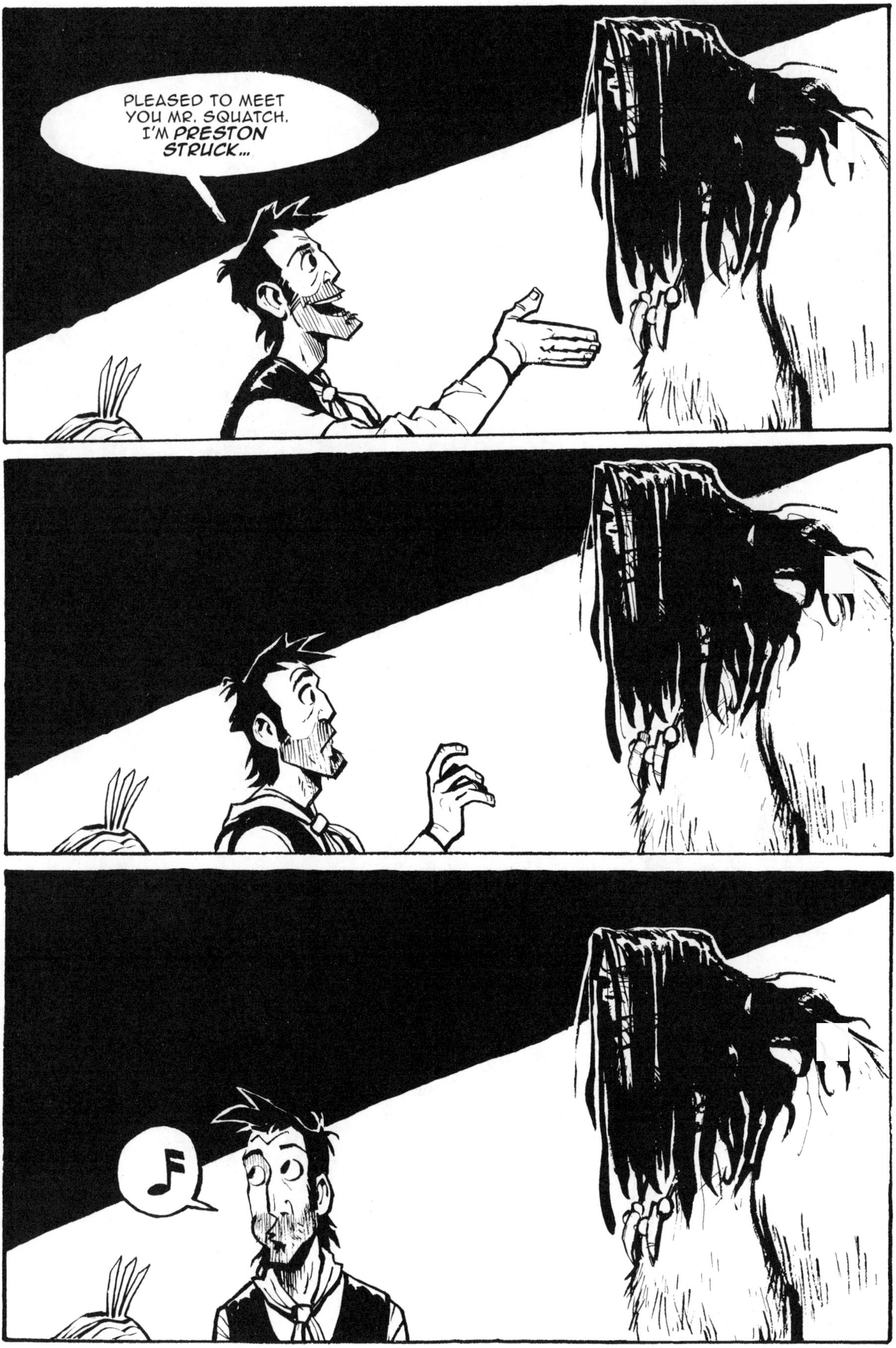
PLEASED TO MEET YOU MR. SQUATCH. I'M PRESTON STRUCK...

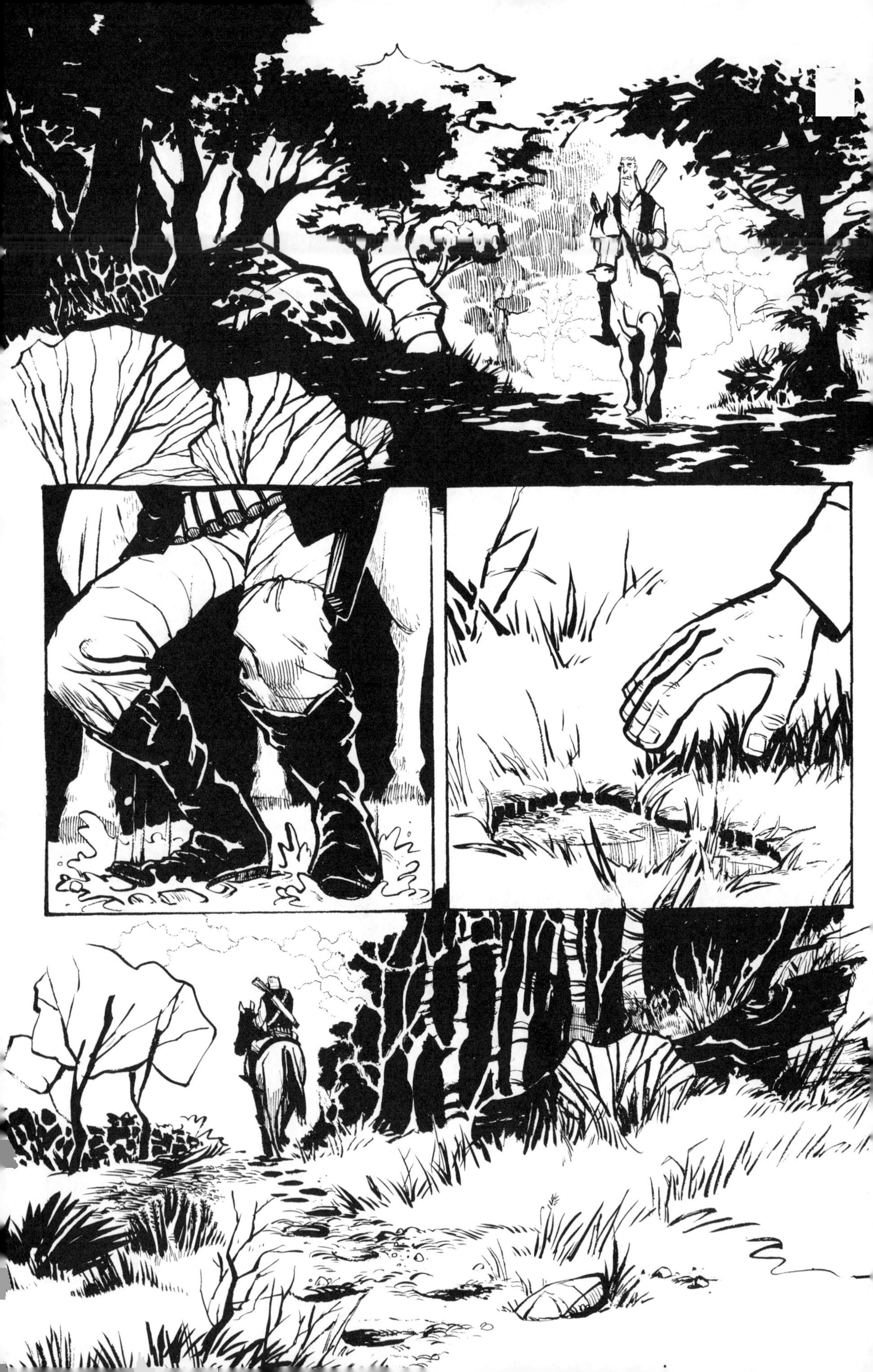

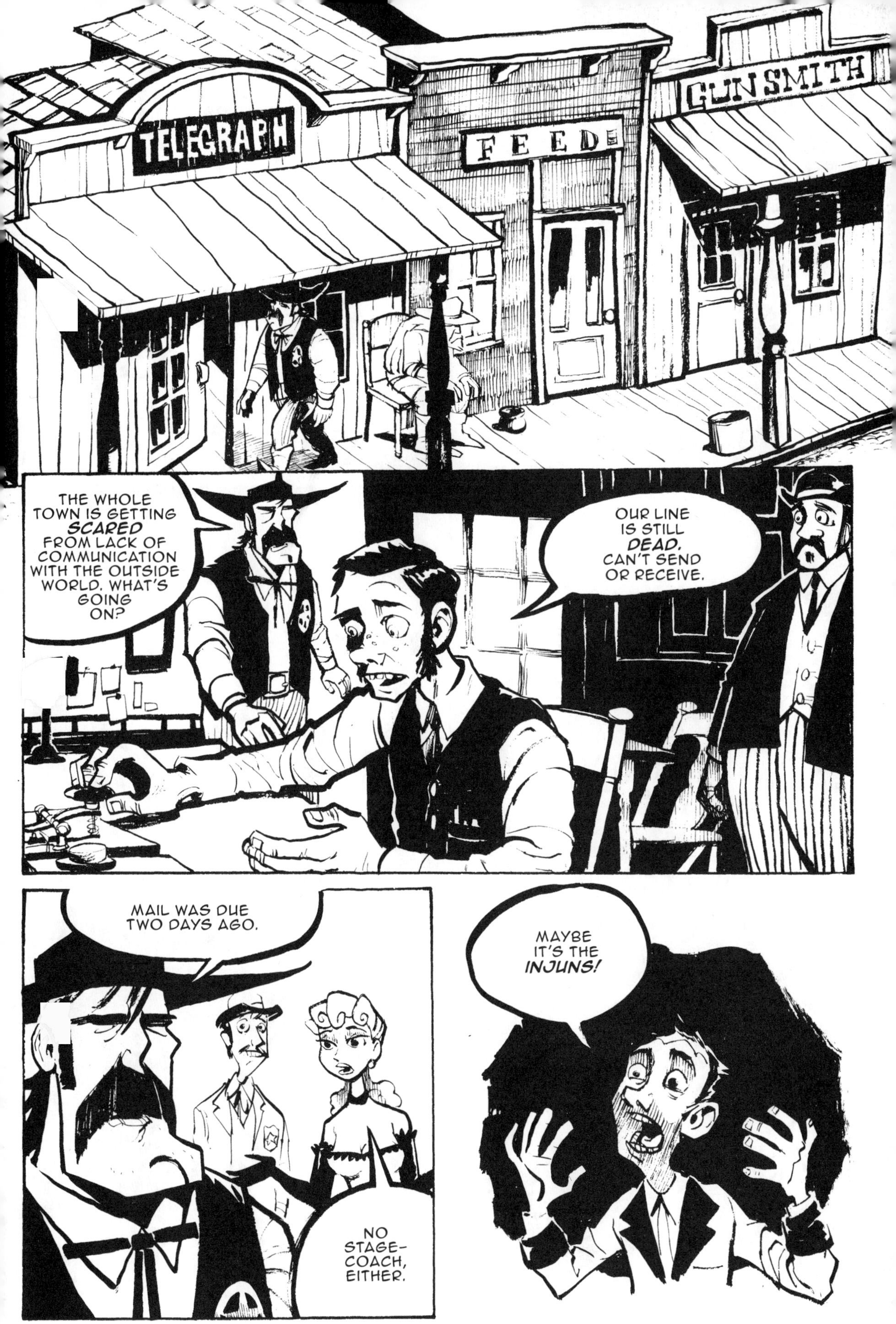
TELEGRAPH
FEED
GUNSMITH
THE WHOLE TOWN IS GETTING SCARED FROM LACK OF COMMUNICATION WITH THE OUTSIDE WORLD. WHAT'S GOING ON?
OUR LINE IS STILL DEAD. CAN'T SEND OR RECEIVE.
MAIL WAS DUE TWO DAYS AGO.
NO STAGE-COACH, EITHER.
MAYBE IT'S THE INJUNS!

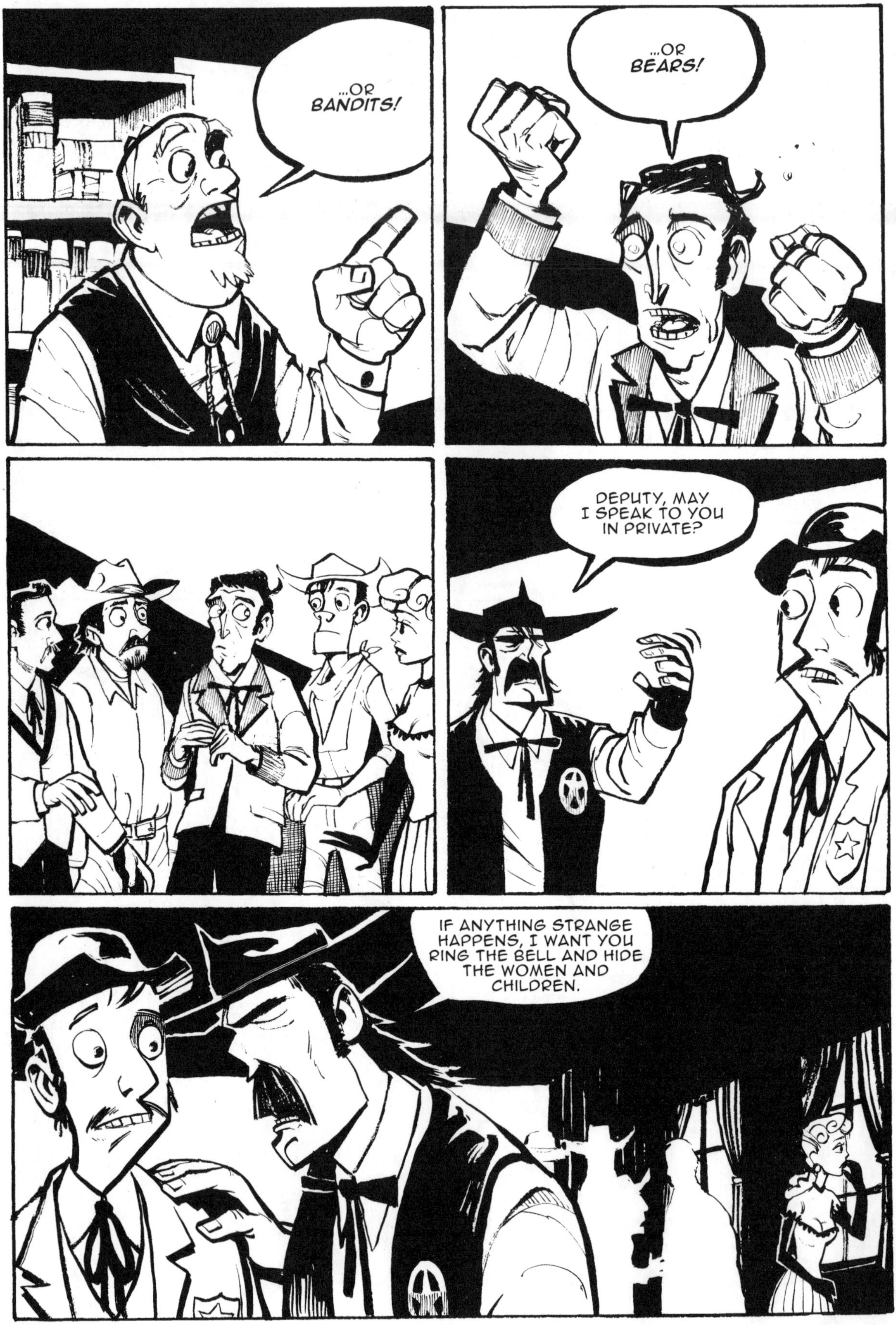
...OR BANDITS!
...OR BEARS!
DEPUTY, MAY I SPEAK TO YOU IN PRIVATE?
IF ANYTHING STRANGE HAPPENS, I WANT YOU RING THE BELL AND HIDE THE WOMEN AND CHILDREN.

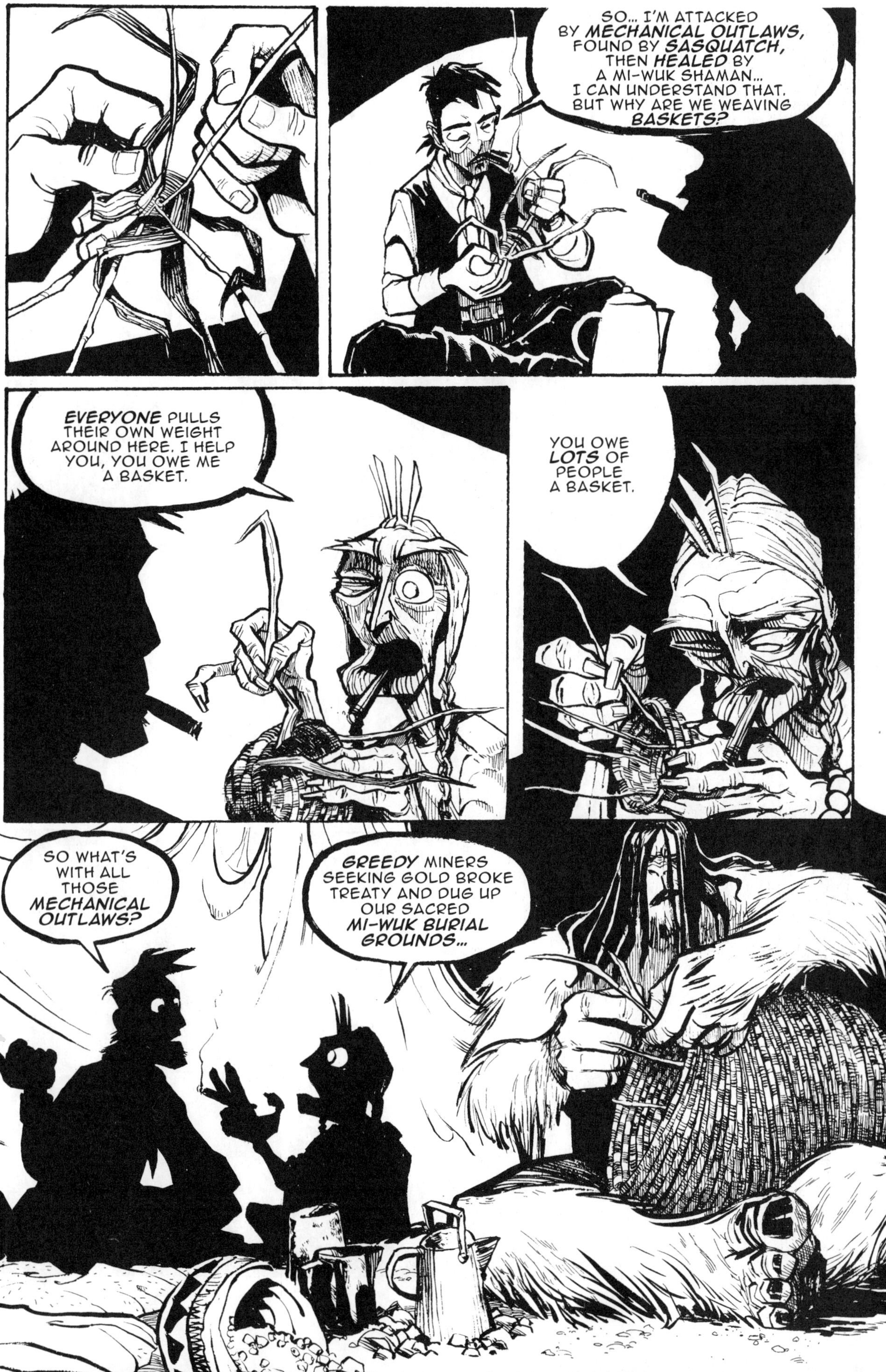
SO... I'M ATTACKED BY MECHANICAL OUTLAWS, FOUND BY SASQUATCH, THEN HEALED BY A MI-WUK SHAMAN... I CAN UNDERSTAND THAT. BUT WHY ARE WE WEAVING BASKETS?
EVERYONE PULLS THEIR OWN WEIGHT AROUND HERE. I HELP YOU, YOU OWE ME A BASKET.
YOU OWE LOTS OF PEOPLE A BASKET.
SO WHAT'S WITH ALL THOSE MECHANICAL OUTLAWS?
GREEDY MINERS SEEKING GOLD BROKE TREATY AND DUG UP OUR SACRED MI-WUK BURIAL GROUNDS...

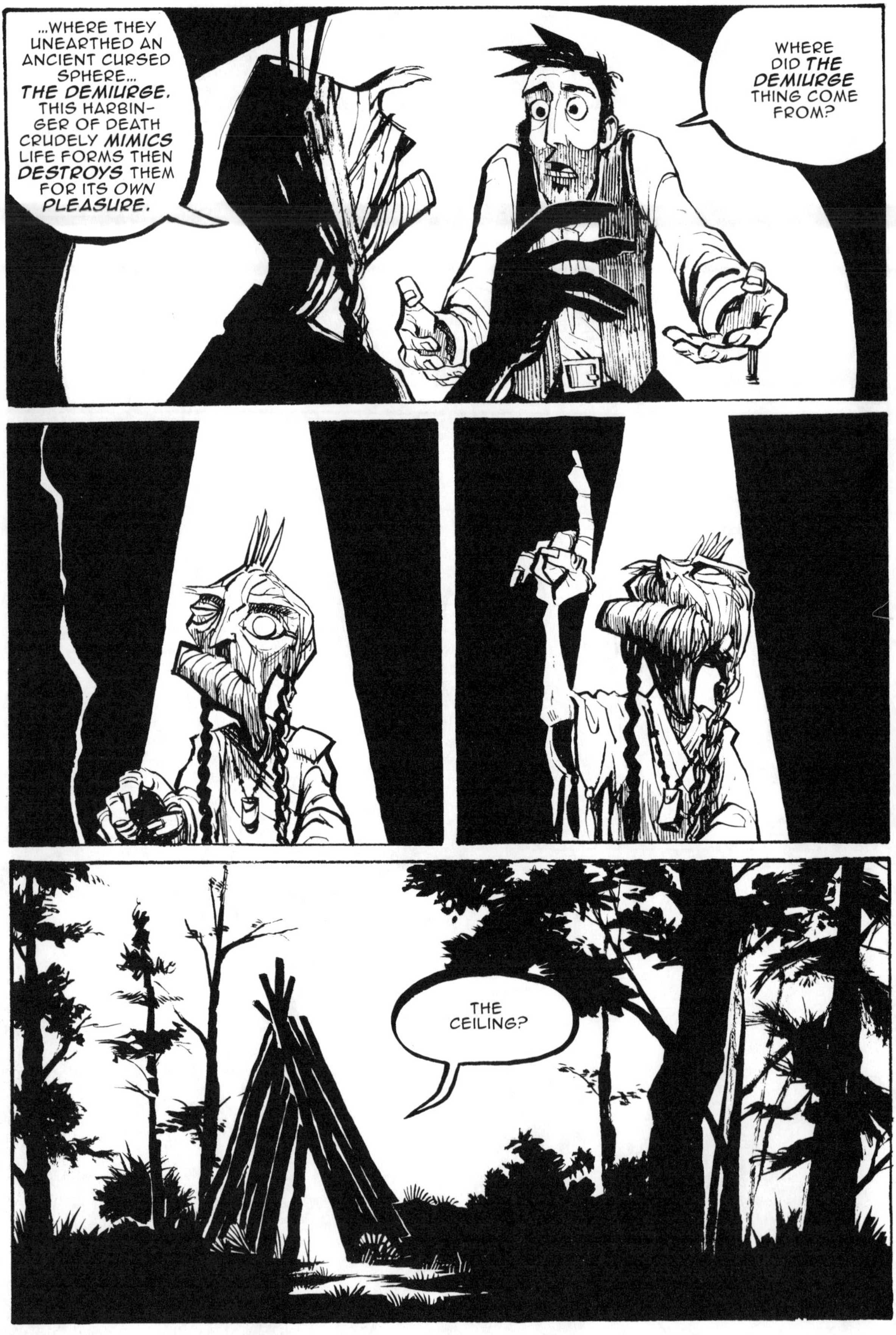
...WHERE THEY UNEARTHED AN ANCIENT CURSED SPHERE... THE DEMIURGE. THIS HARBIN-GER OF DEATH CRUDELY MIMICS LIFE FORMS THEN DESTROYS THEM FOR ITS OWN PLEASURE.
WHERE DID THE DEMIURGE THING COME FROM?
THE CEILING?

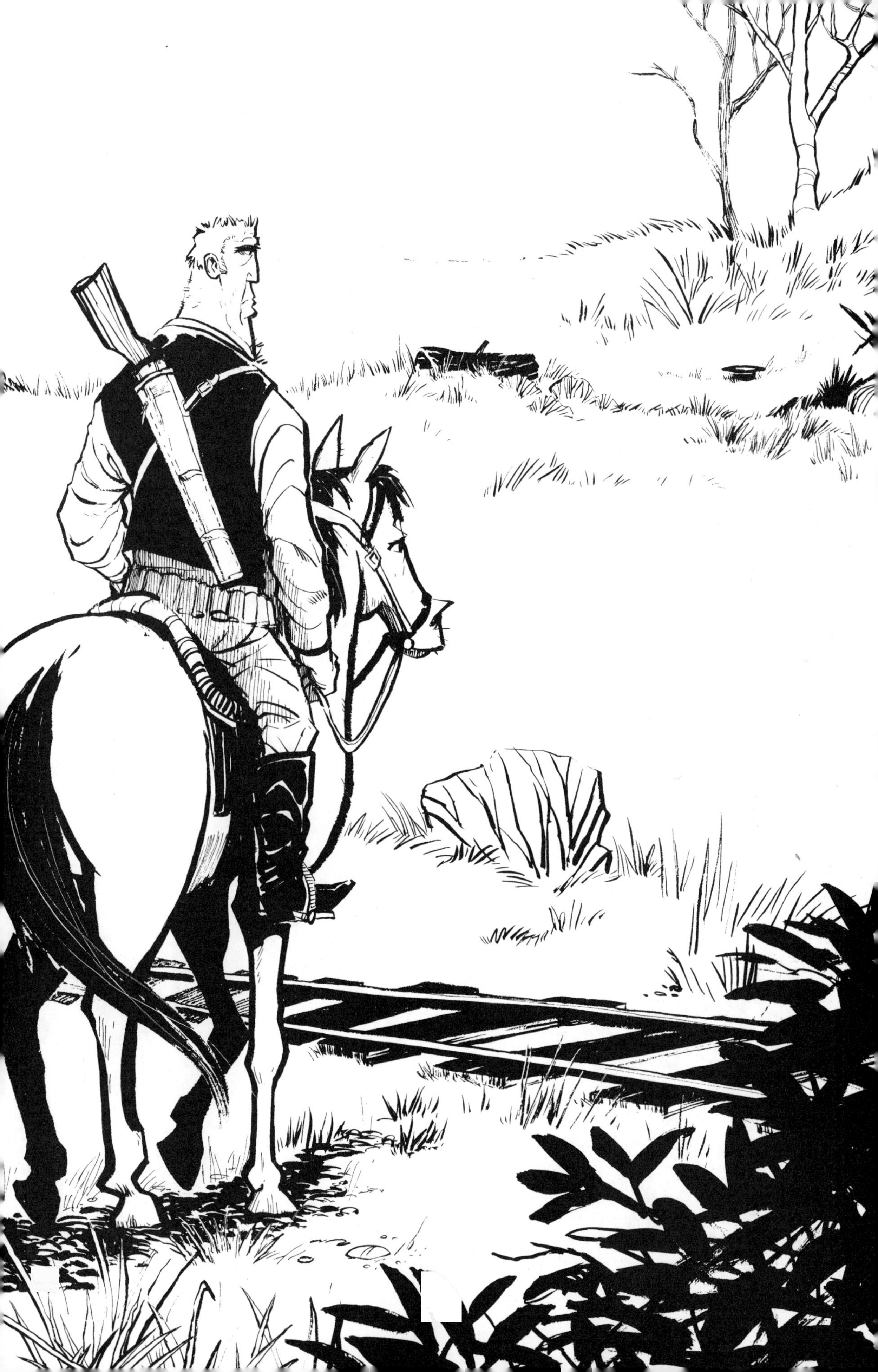

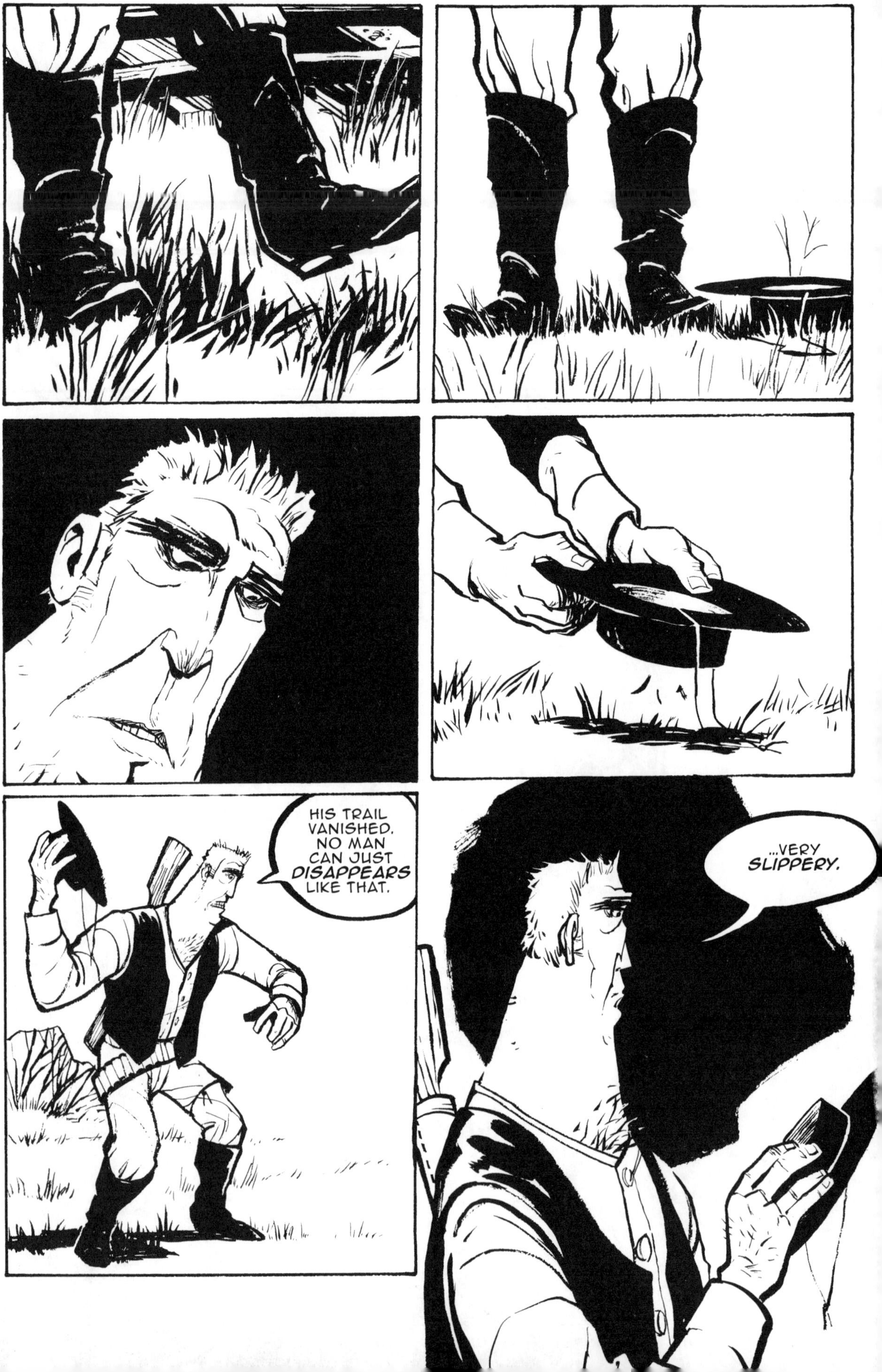
HIS TRAIL VANISHED. NO MAN CAN JUST DISAPPEARS LIKE THAT.
...VERY SLIPPERY.

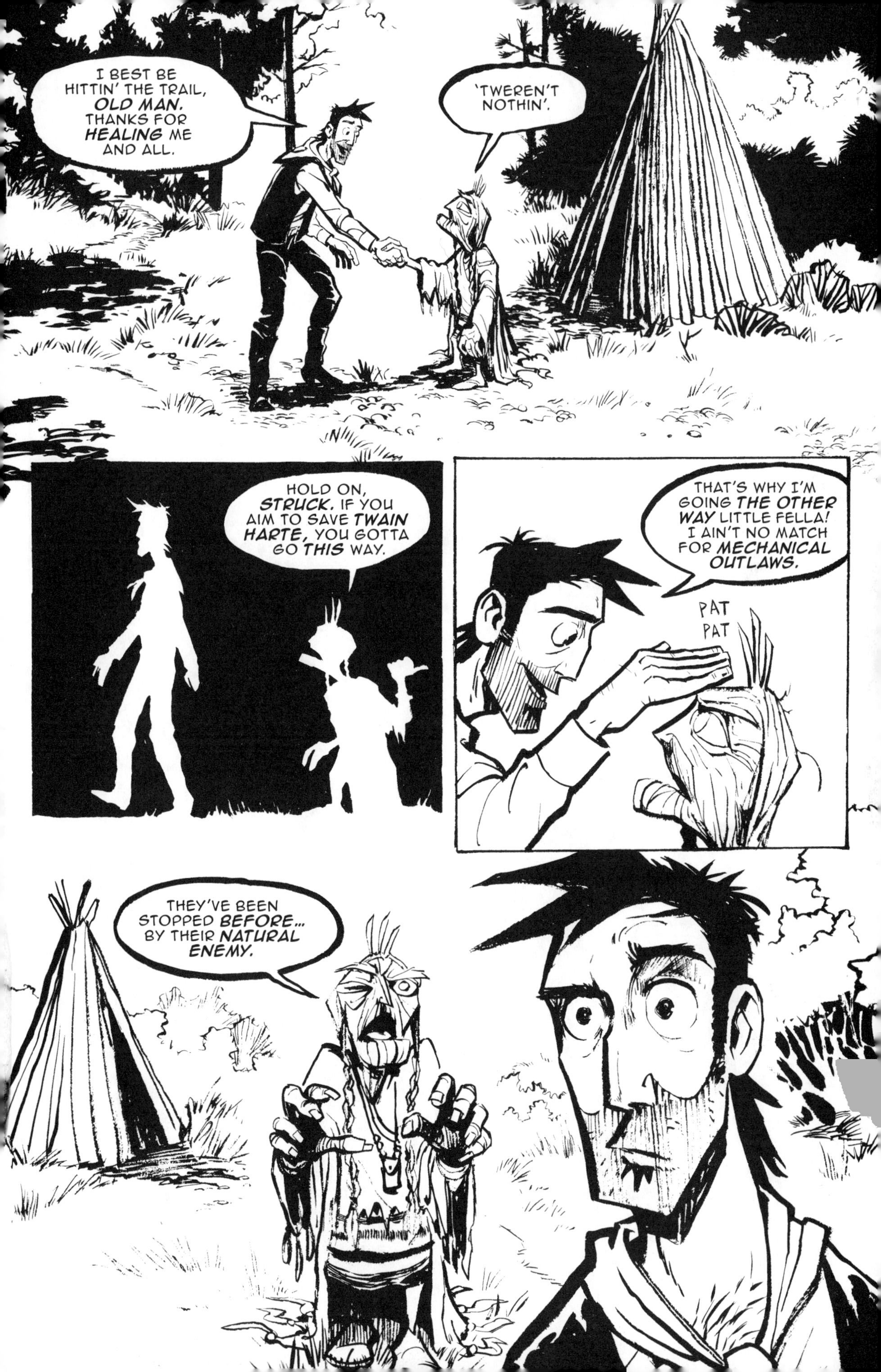
I BEST BE HITTIN' THE TRAIL, **OLD MAN.** THANKS FOR **HEALING** ME AND ALL.
'TWEREN'T NOTHIN'.
HOLD ON, **STRUCK.** IF YOU AIM TO SAVE **TWAIN HARTE,** YOU GOTTA GO **THIS** WAY.
THAT'S WHY I'M GOING **THE OTHER WAY** LITTLE FELLA! I AIN'T NO MATCH FOR **MECHANICAL OUTLAWS.**
PAT PAT
THEY'VE BEEN STOPPED **BEFORE**... BY THEIR **NATURAL ENEMY.**

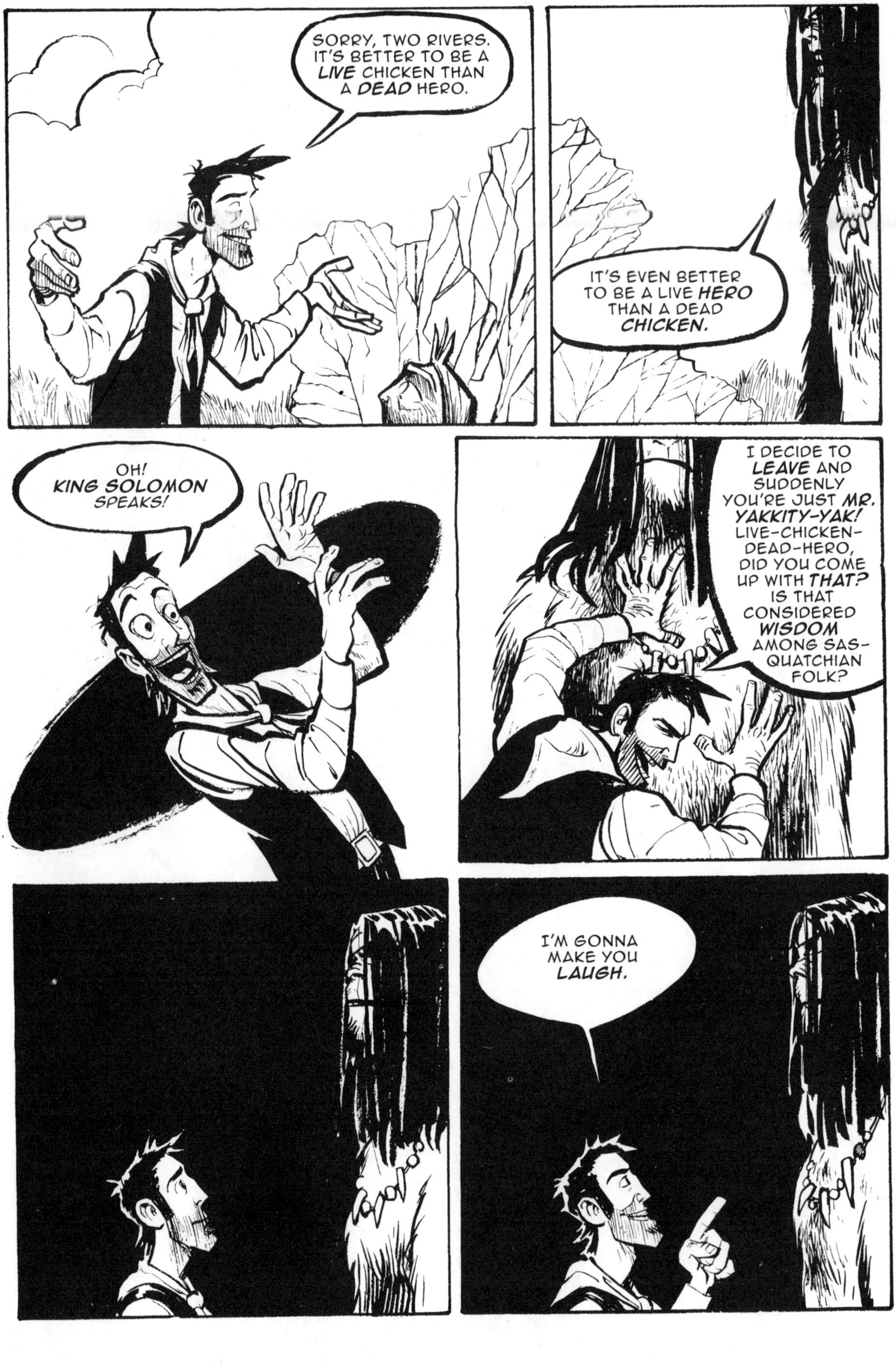
SORRY, TWO RIVERS. IT'S BETTER TO BE A LIVE CHICKEN THAN A DEAD HERO.
IT'S EVEN BETTER TO BE A LIVE HERO THAN A DEAD CHICKEN.
OH! KING SOLOMON SPEAKS!
I DECIDE TO LEAVE AND SUDDENLY YOU'RE JUST MR. YAKKITY-YAK! LIVE-CHICKEN-DEAD-HERO, DID YOU COME UP WITH THAT? IS THAT CONSIDERED WISDOM AMONG SAS-QUATCHIAN FOLK?
I'M GONNA MAKE YOU LAUGH.

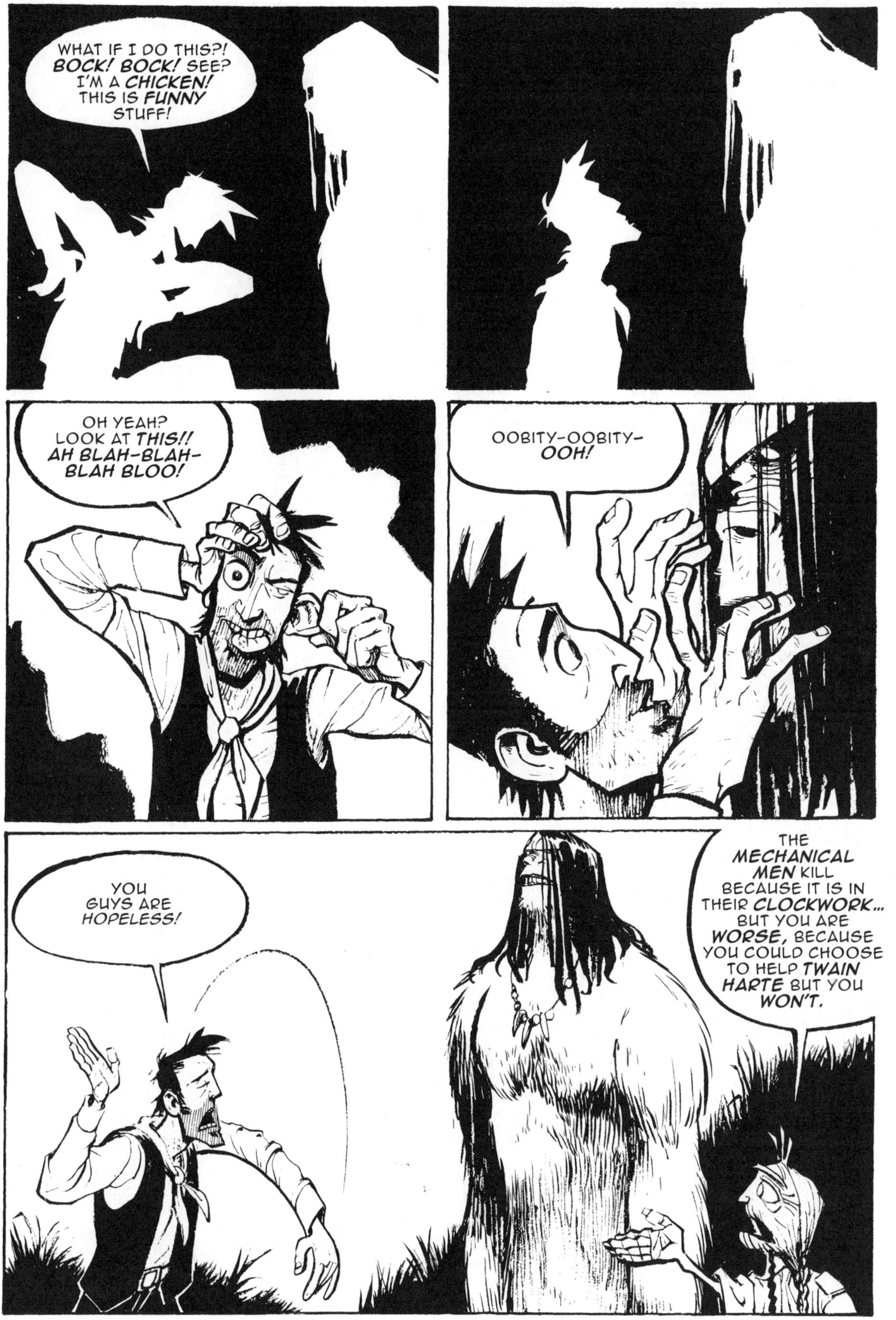

WHAT IF I DO THIS?! BOCK! BOCK! SEE? I'M A CHICKEN! THIS IS FUNNY STUFF!
OH YEAH? LOOK AT THIS!! AH BLAH-BLAH-BLAH BLOO!
OOBITY-OOBITY-OOH!
YOU GUYS ARE HOPELESS!
THE MECHANICAL MEN KILL BECAUSE IT IS IN THEIR CLOCKWORK... BUT YOU ARE WORSE, BECAUSE YOU COULD CHOOSE TO HELP TWAIN HARTE BUT YOU WON'T.

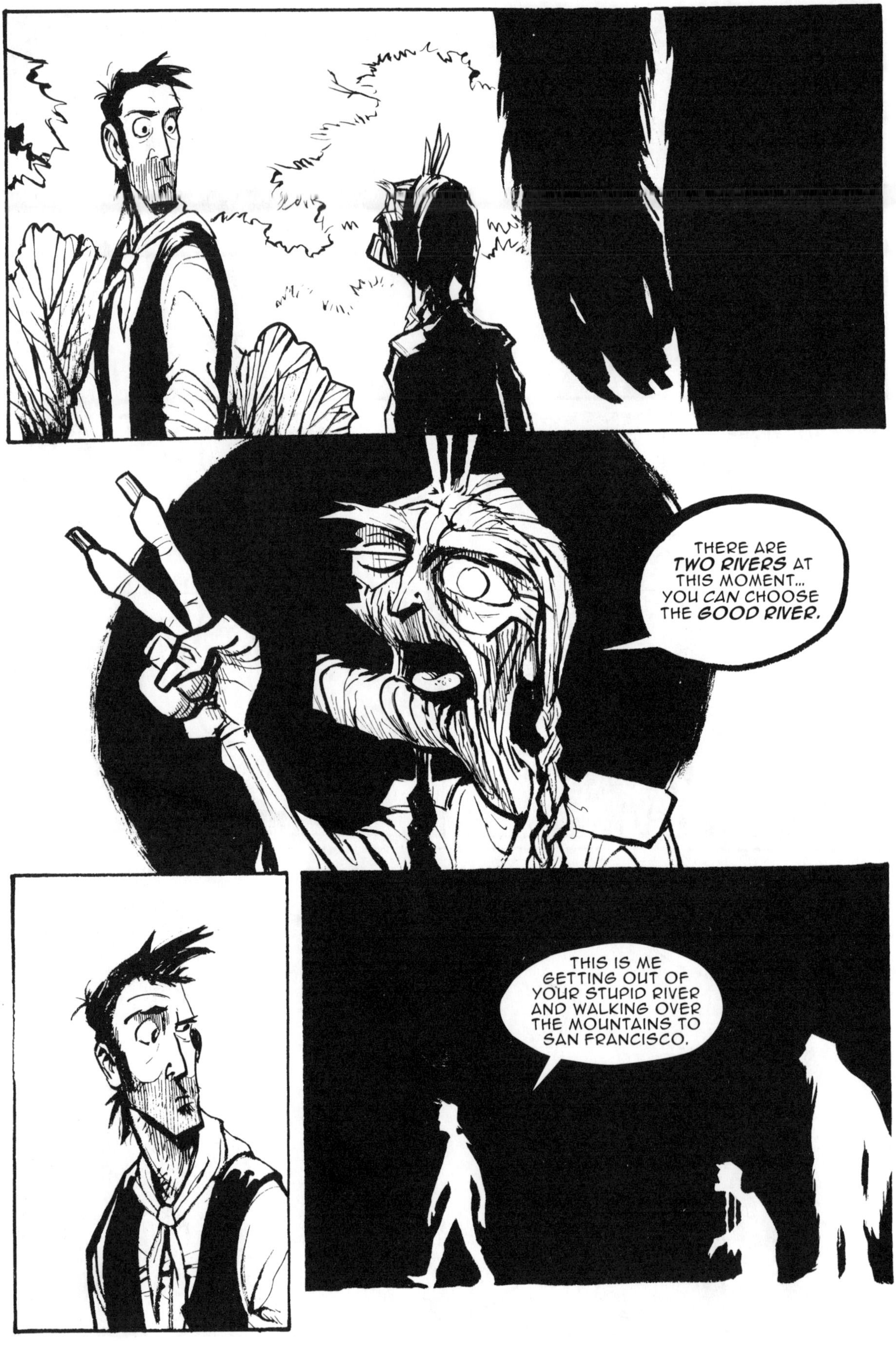
THERE ARE TWO RIVERS AT THIS MOMENT... YOU CAN CHOOSE THE GOOD RIVER.
THIS IS ME GETTING OUT OF YOUR STUPID RIVER AND WALKING OVER THE MOUNTAINS TO SAN FRANCISCO.

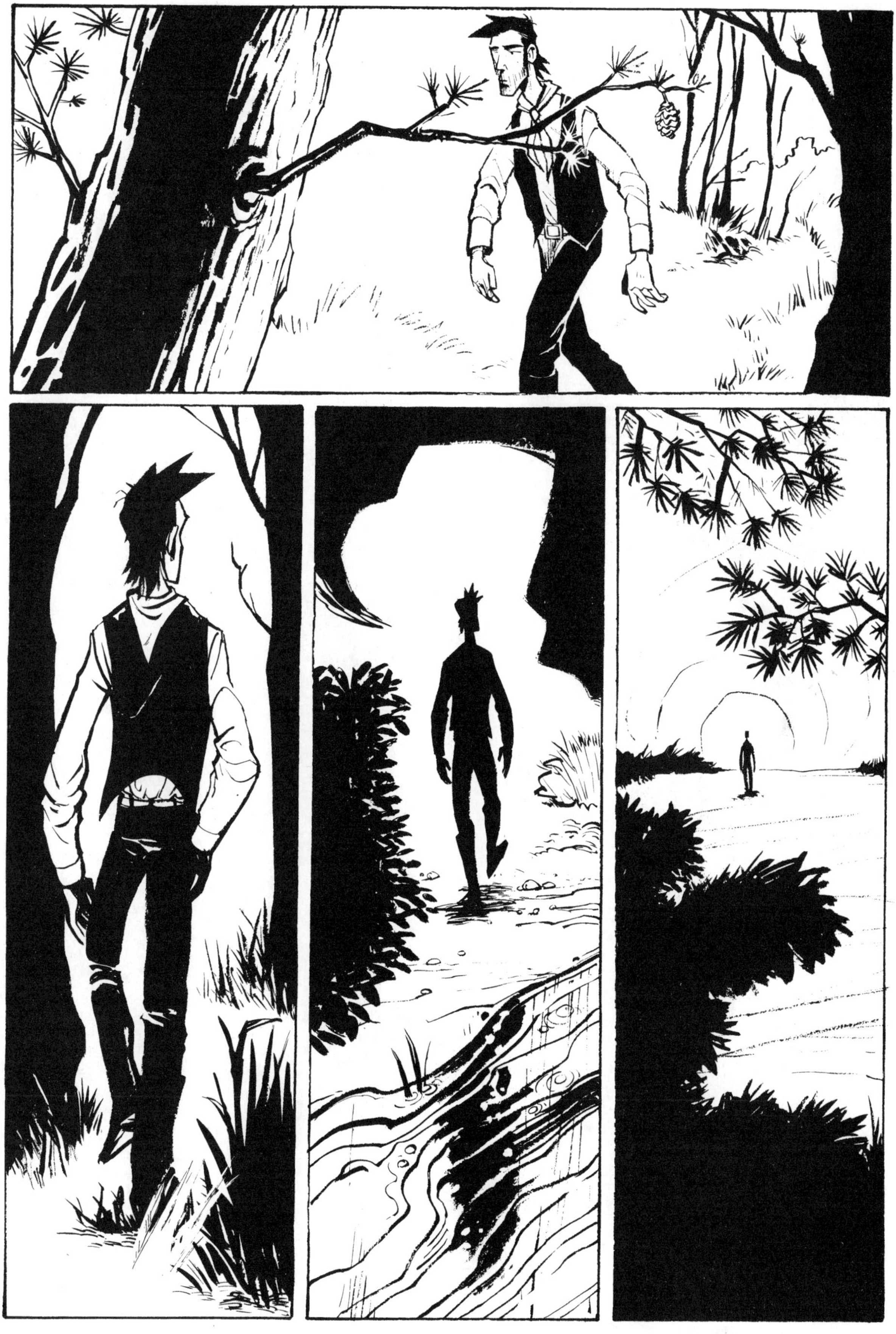

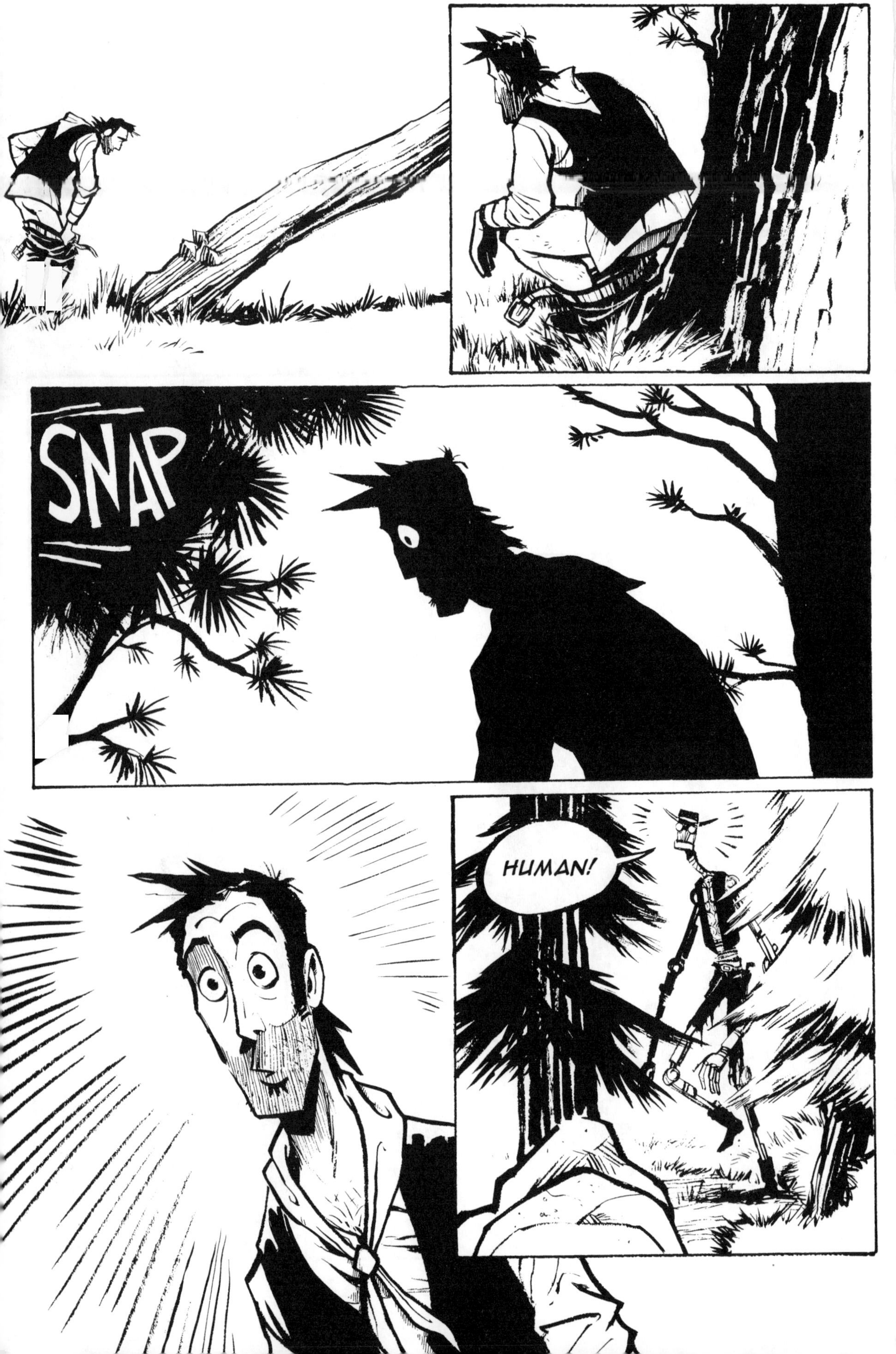
SNAP
HUMAN!

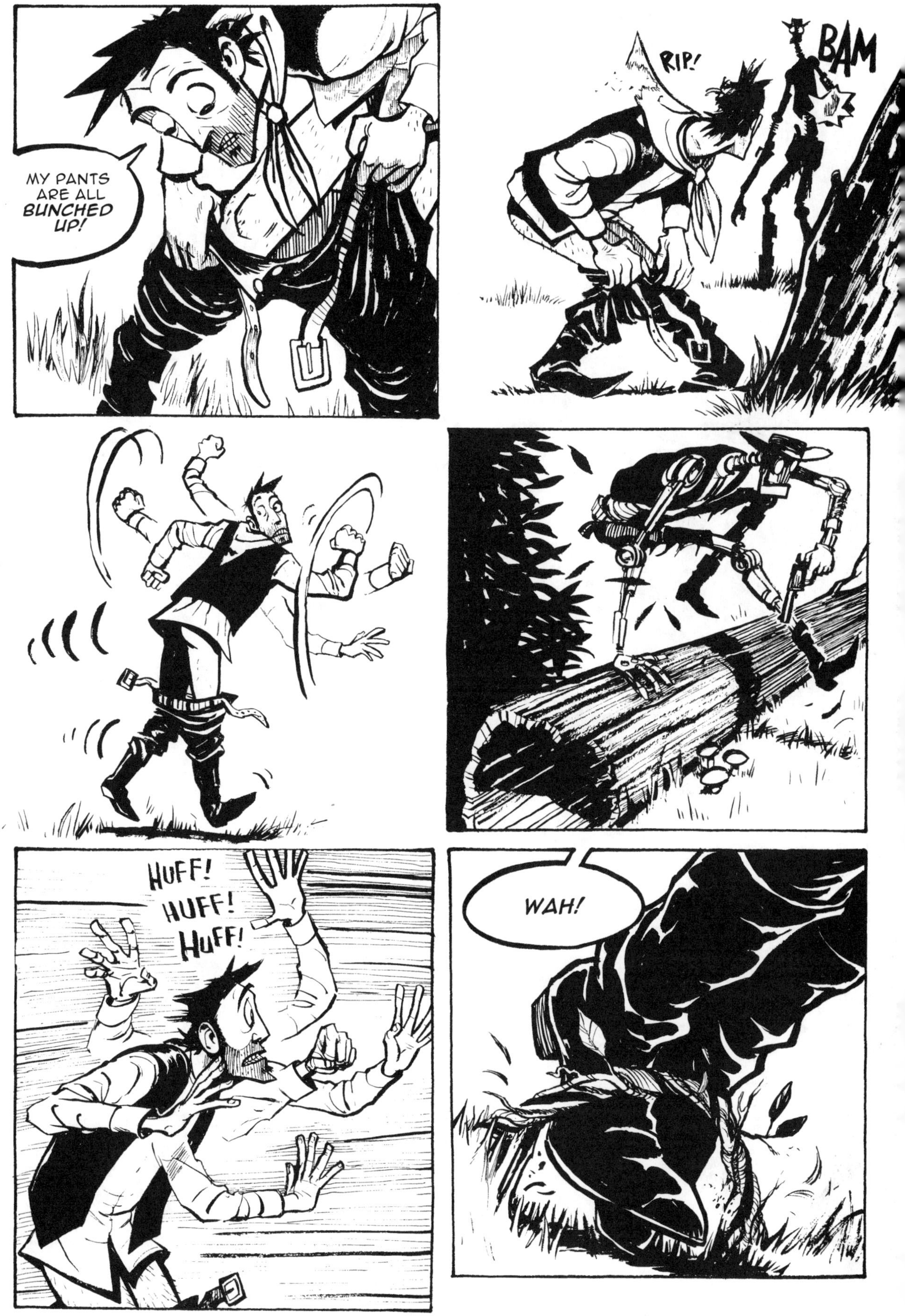
MY PANTS ARE ALL BUNCHED UP!
RIP!
BAM
HUFF!
HUFF!
HUFF!
WAH!

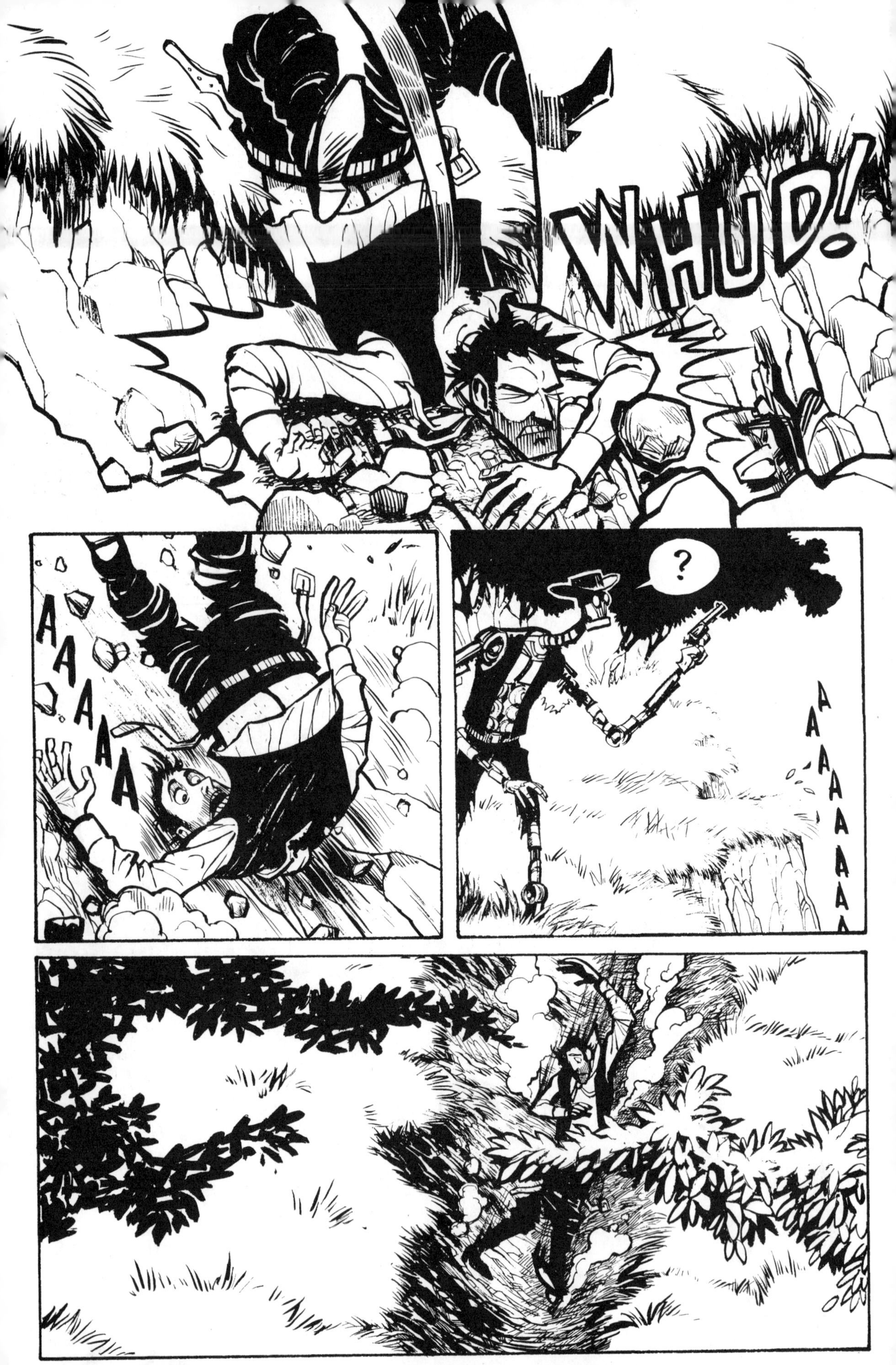
WHUD!
AAAAAA
?
AAAAAAAAA

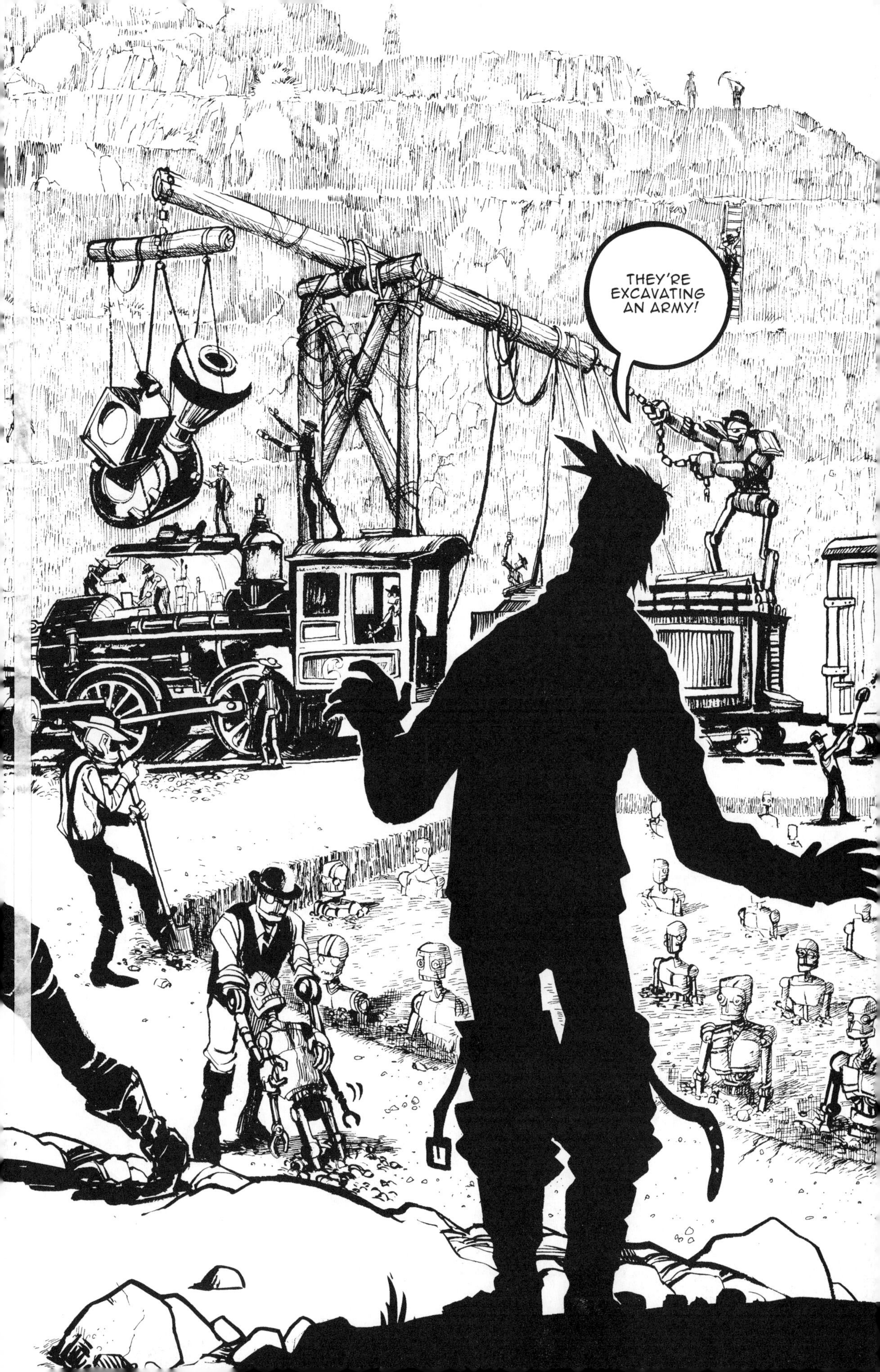
THEY'RE EXCAVATING AN ARMY!

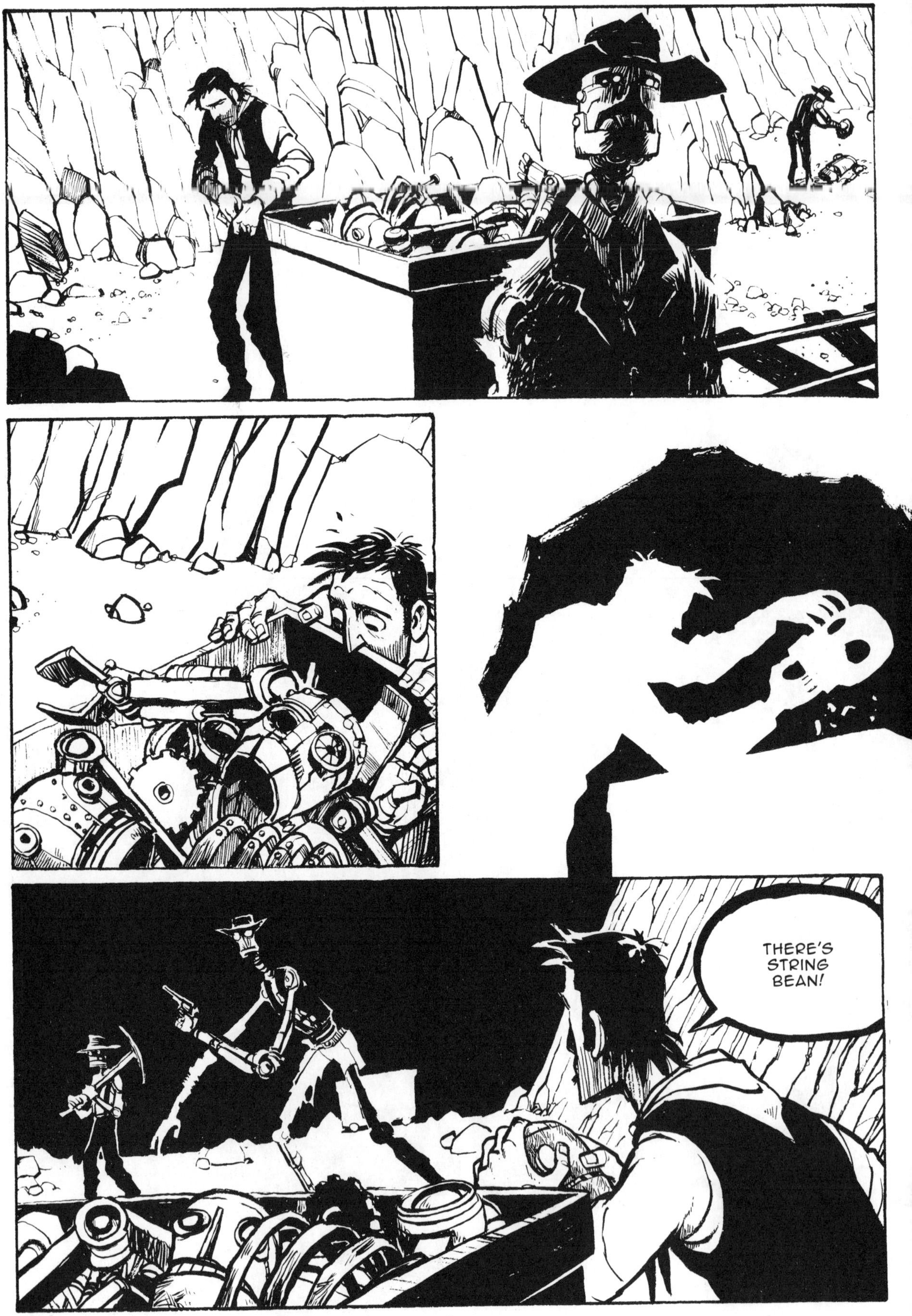
THERE'S
STRING
BEAN!

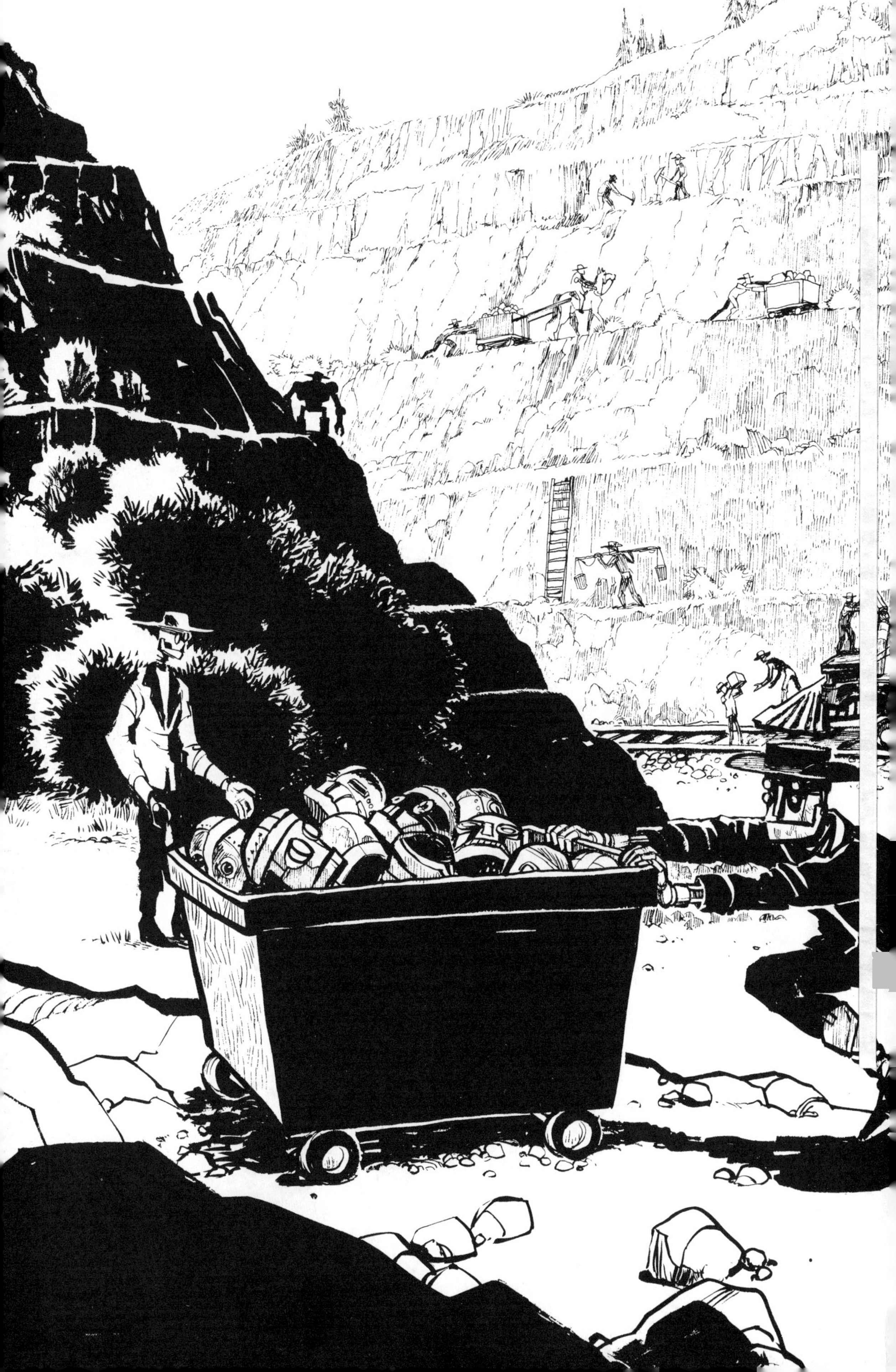

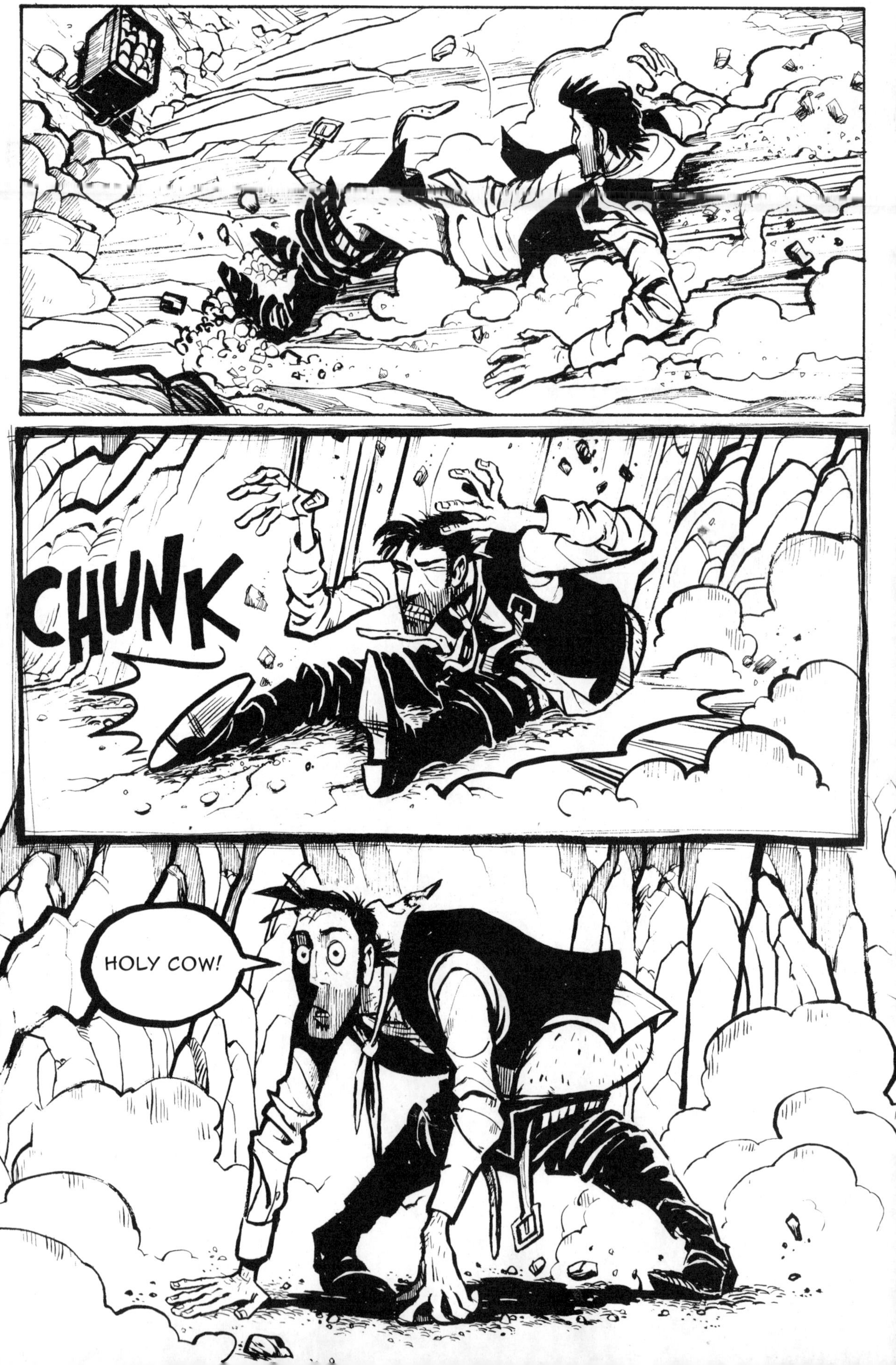
CHUNK
HOLY COW!

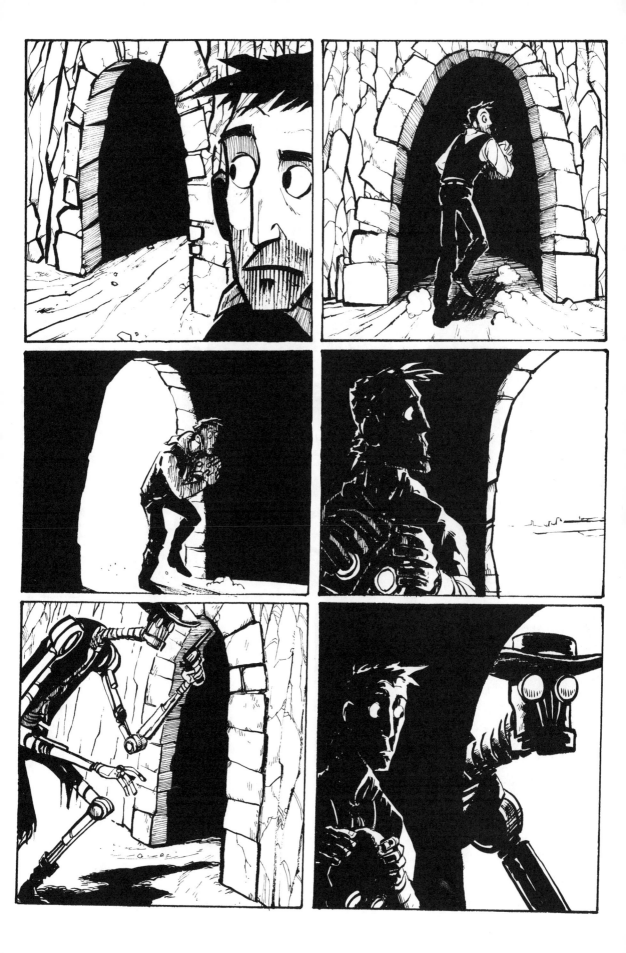

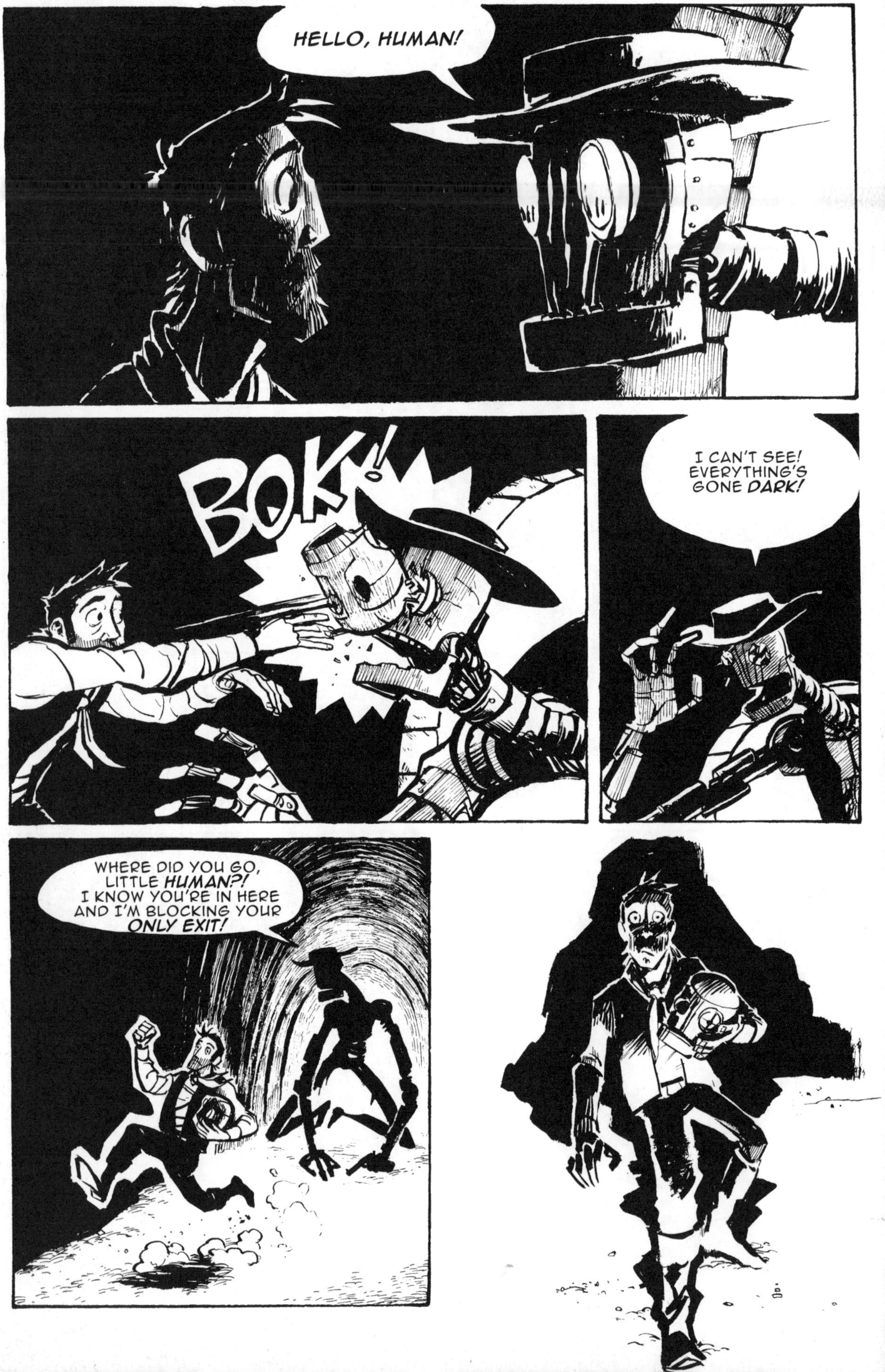
HELLO, HUMAN!
BOK!
I CAN'T SEE! EVERYTHING'S GONE DARK!
WHERE DID YOU GO, LITTLE HUMAN?! I KNOW YOU'RE IN HERE AND I'M BLOCKING YOUR ONLY EXIT!

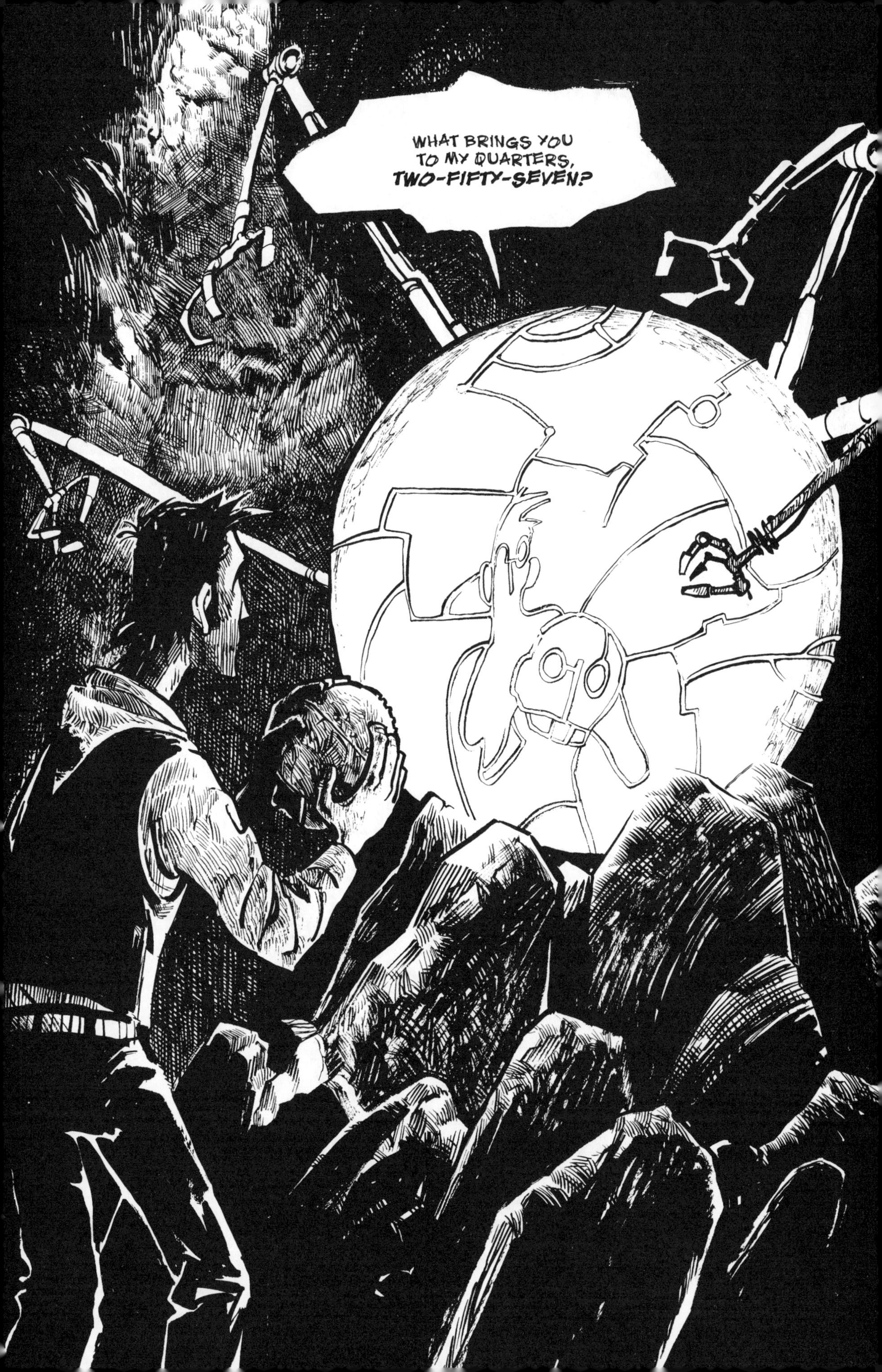
WHAT BRINGS YOU TO MY QUARTERS, TWO-FIFTY-SEVEN?

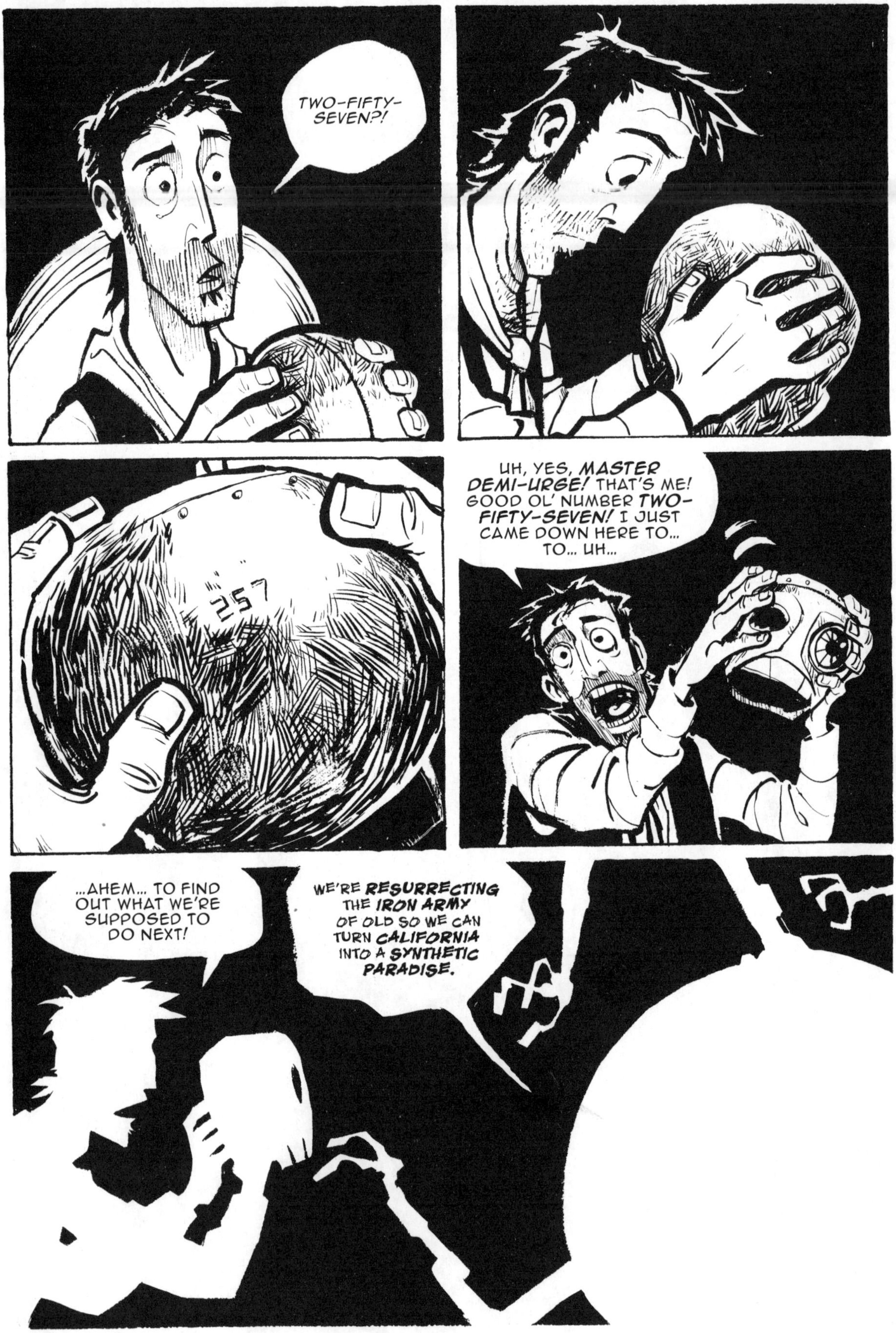
TWO-FIFTY-SEVEN?!
257
UH, YES, MASTER DEMI-URGE! THAT'S ME! GOOD OL' NUMBER TWO-FIFTY-SEVEN! I JUST CAME DOWN HERE TO... TO... UH...
...AHEM... TO FIND OUT WHAT WE'RE SUPPOSED TO DO NEXT!
WE'RE RESURRECTING THE IRON ARMY OF OLD SO WE CAN TURN CALIFORNIA INTO A SYNTHETIC PARADISE.

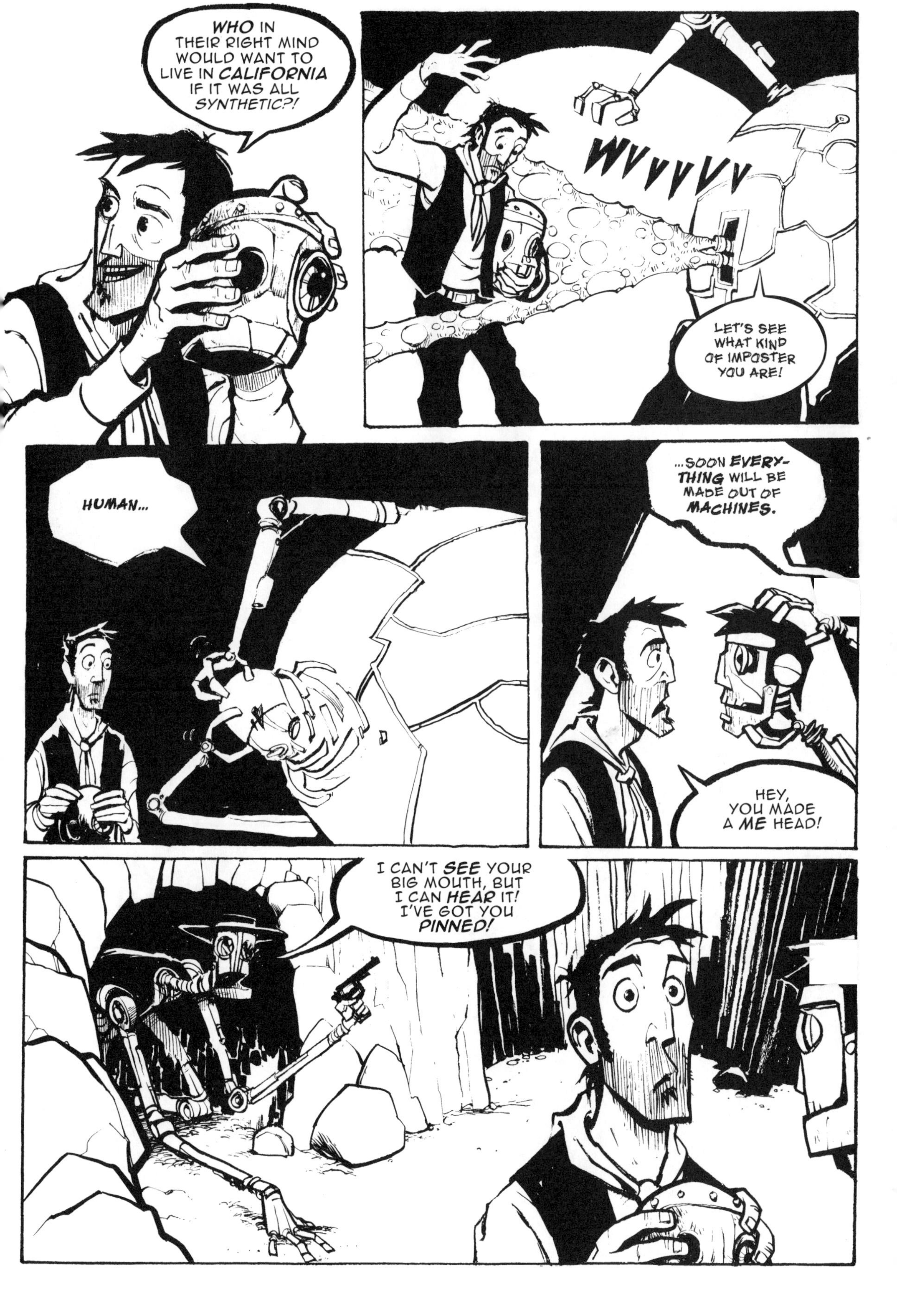
WHO IN THEIR RIGHT MIND WOULD WANT TO LIVE IN CALIFORNIA IF IT WAS ALL SYNTHETIC?!
WVVVVV
LET'S SEE WHAT KIND OF IMPOSTER YOU ARE!
HUMAN...
...SOON EVERYTHING WILL BE MADE OUT OF MACHINES.
HEY, YOU MADE A ME HEAD!
I CAN'T SEE YOUR BIG MOUTH, BUT I CAN HEAR IT! I'VE GOT YOU PINNED!

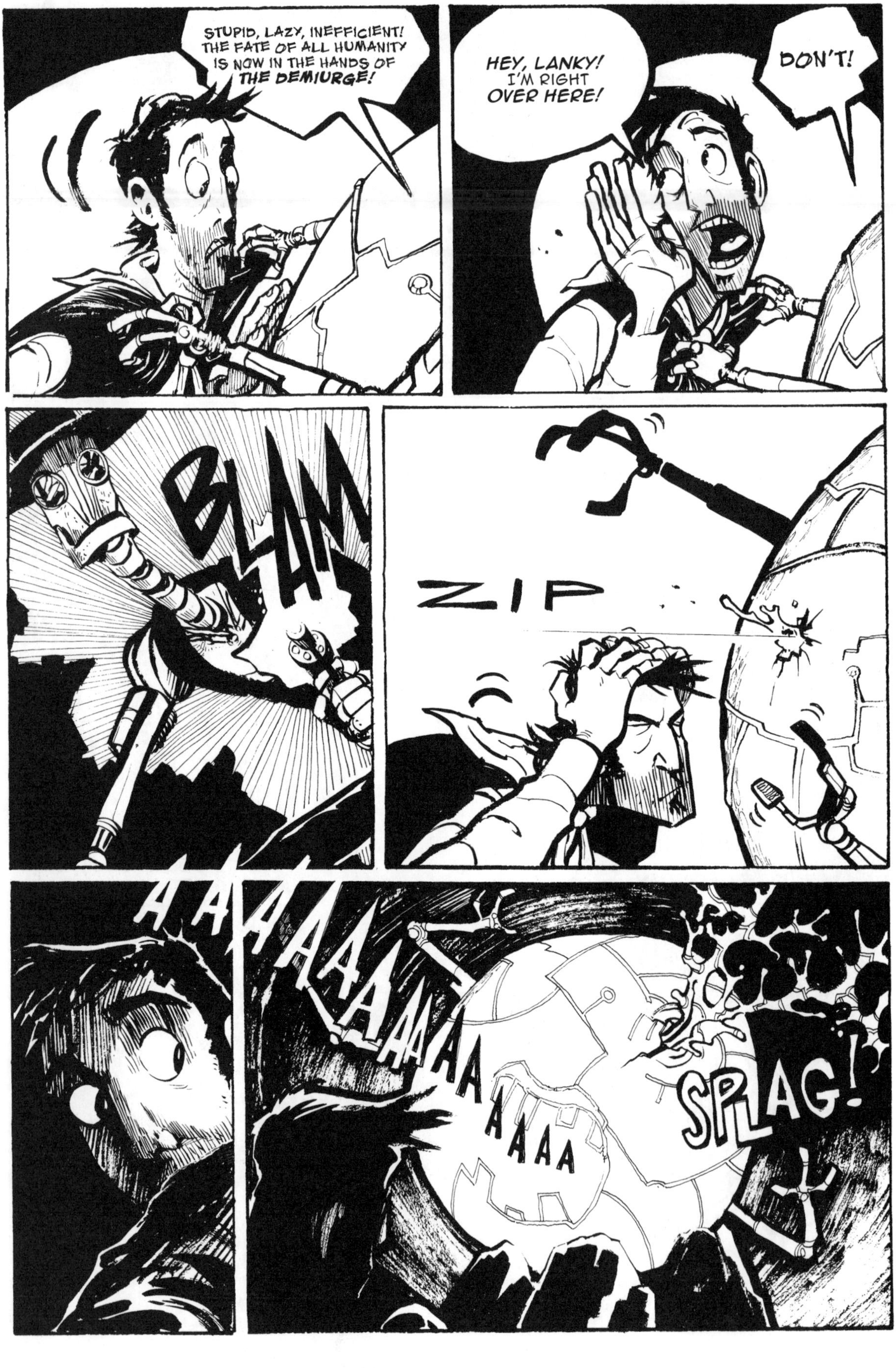
STUPID, LAZY, INEFFICIENT! THE FATE OF ALL HUMANITY IS NOW IN THE HANDS OF THE DEMIURGE!
HEY, LANKY! I'M RIGHT OVER HERE!
DON'T!
BLAM
ZIP
AAAAAAAAAAAAAAAAAAA
SPLAG!

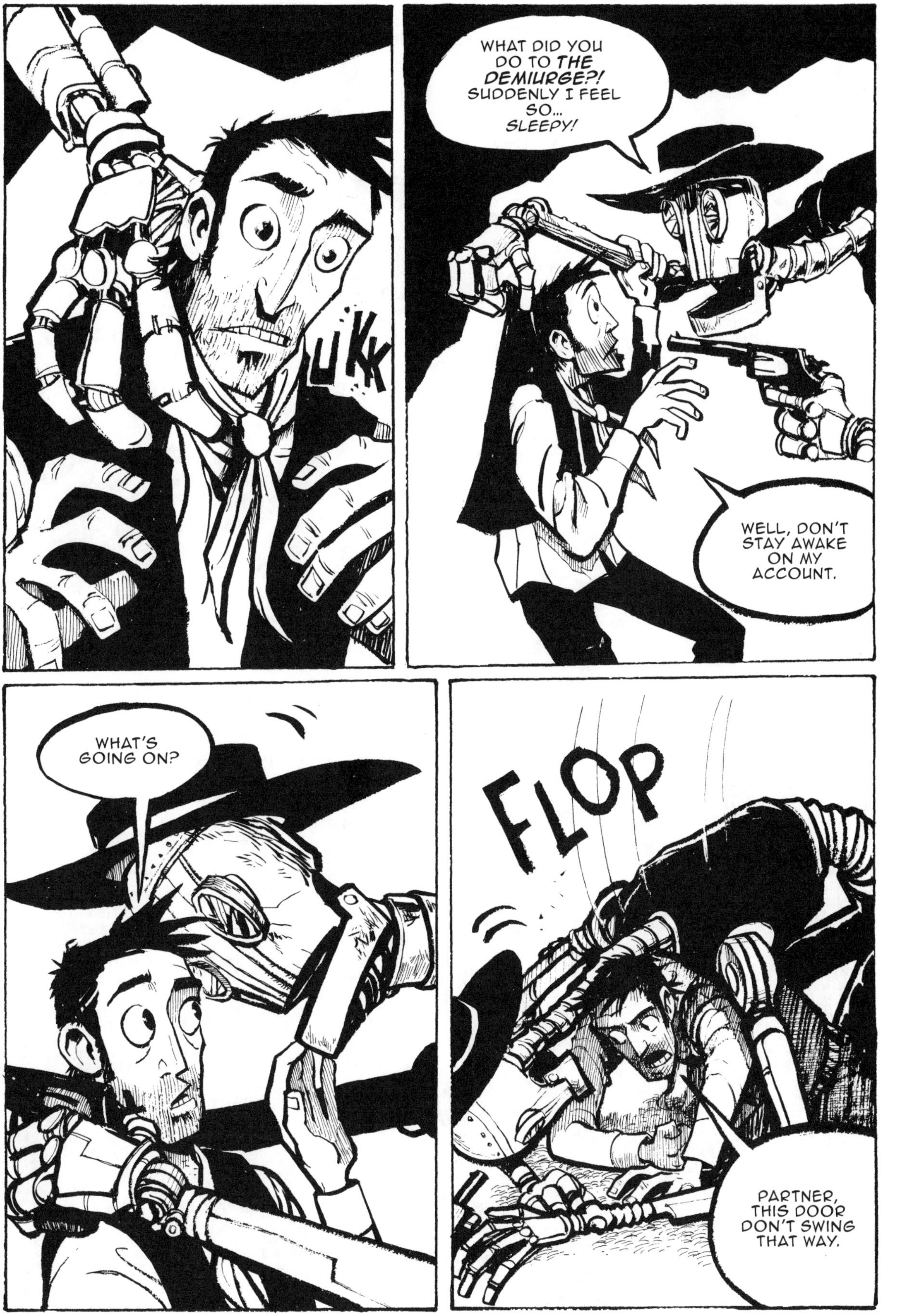
UKK
WHAT DID YOU DO TO THE DEMIURGE?! SUDDENLY I FEEL SO... SLEEPY!
WELL, DON'T STAY AWAKE ON MY ACCOUNT.
WHAT'S GOING ON?
FLOP
PARTNER, THIS DOOR DON'T SWING THAT WAY.

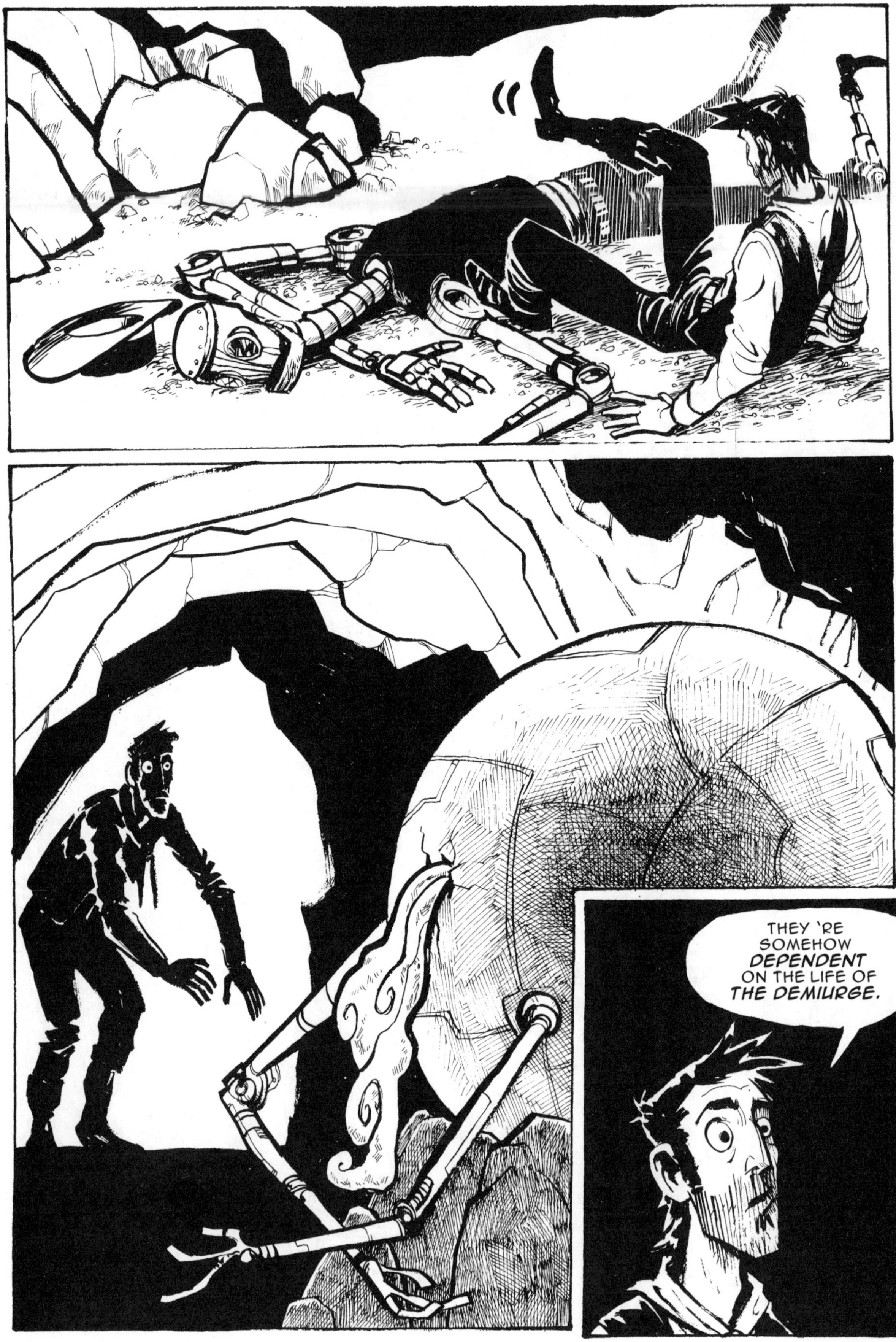
THEY 'RE SOMEHOW DEPENDENT ON THE LIFE OF THE DEMIURGE.

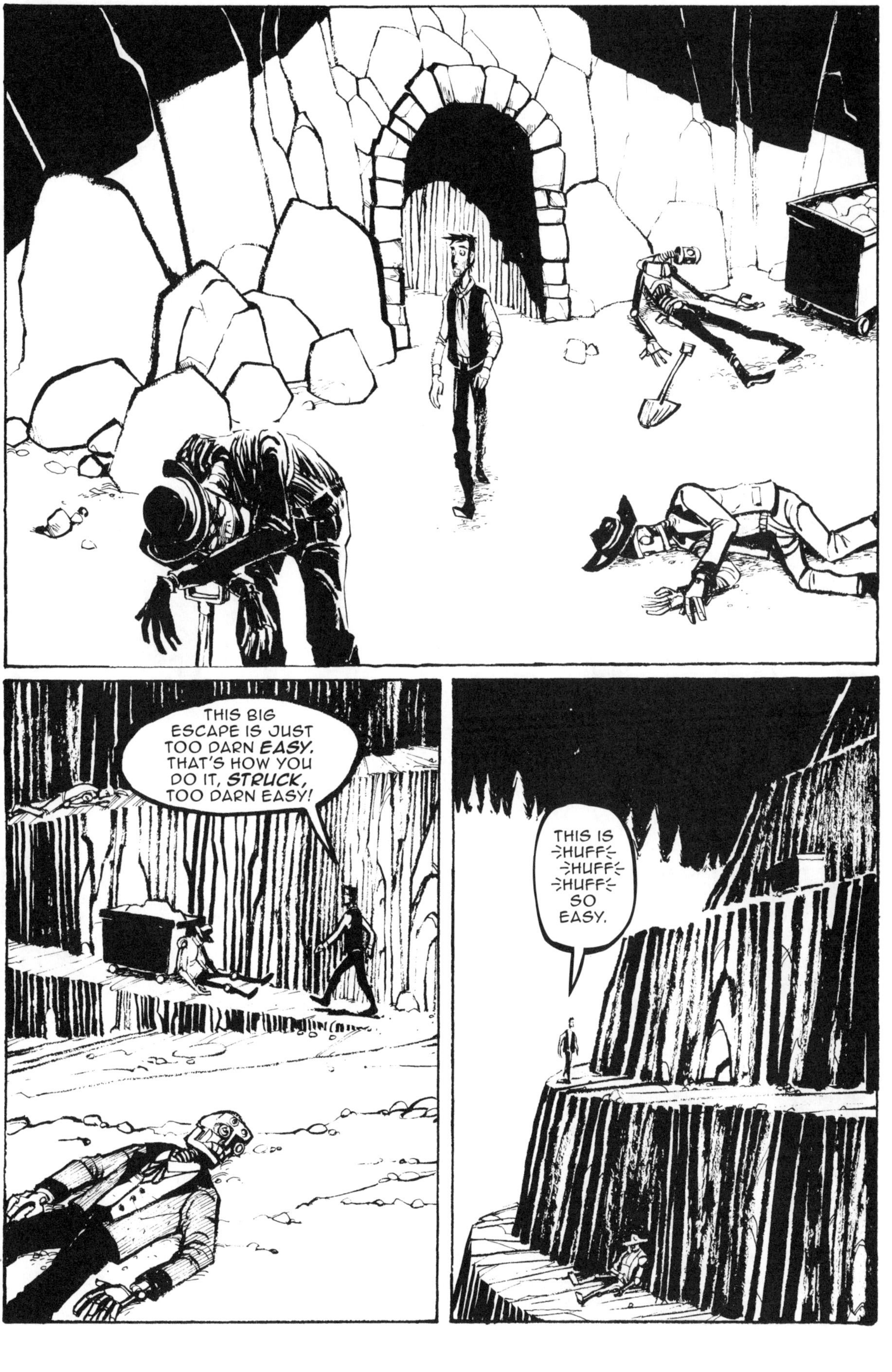
THIS BIG ESCAPE IS JUST TOO DARN *EASY.* THAT'S HOW YOU DO IT, *STRUCK,* TOO DARN EASY!
THIS IS HUFF HUFF HUFF SO EASY.

GASP!

...NOT SO EASY!

MIND IF I PULL UP A ROCK WHILE I CATCH MY BREATH?

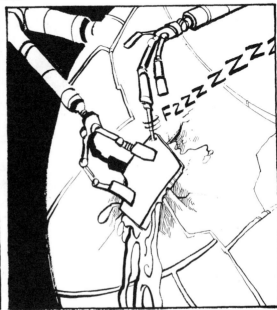

NICE DAY.

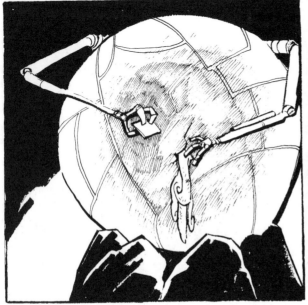

FZZZZZZZZ

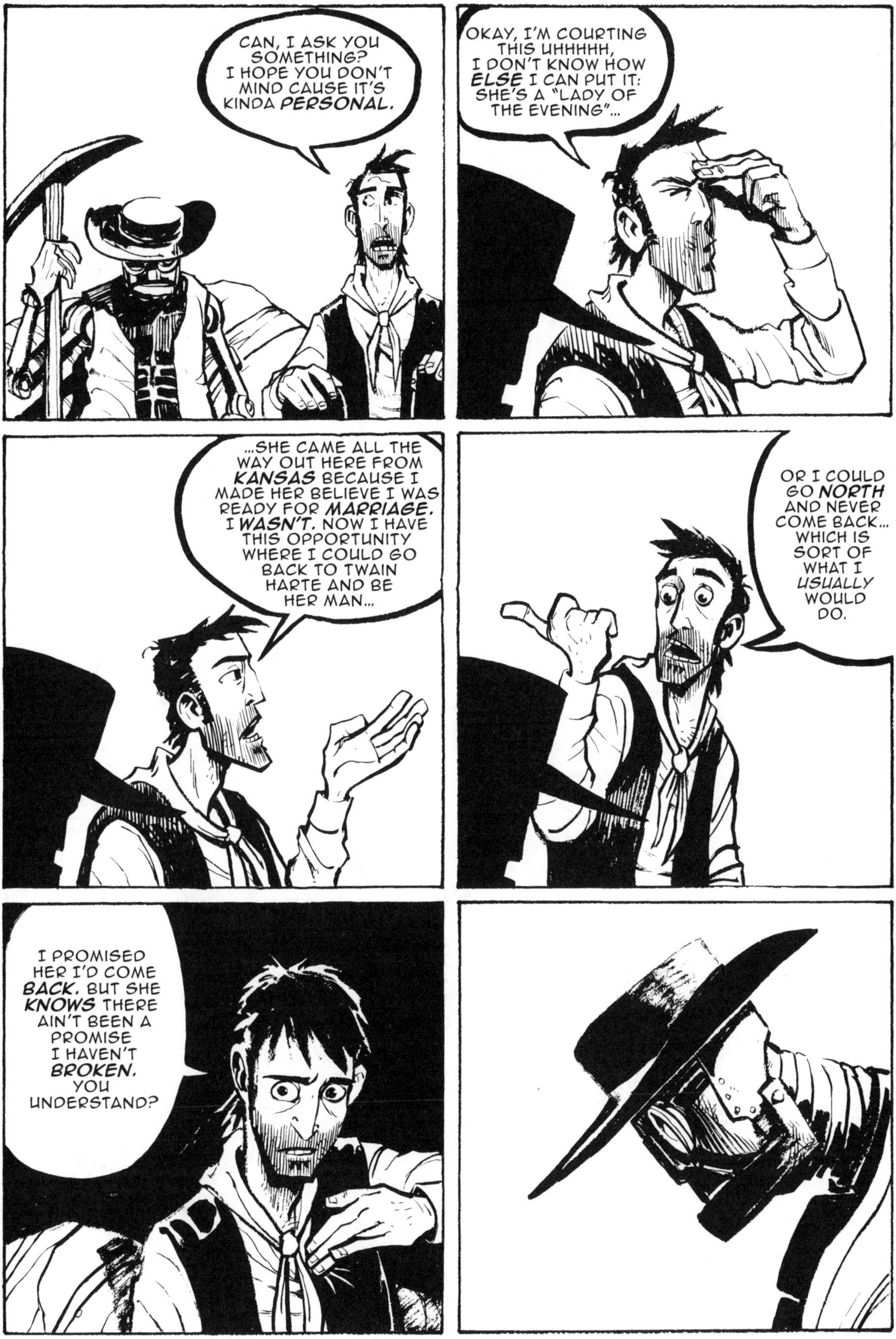

CAN, I ASK YOU SOMETHING? I HOPE YOU DON'T MIND CAUSE IT'S KINDA PERSONAL.
OKAY, I'M COURTING THIS UHHHHH, I DON'T KNOW HOW ELSE I CAN PUT IT: SHE'S A "LADY OF THE EVENING"...
...SHE CAME ALL THE WAY OUT HERE FROM KANSAS BECAUSE I MADE HER BELIEVE I WAS READY FOR MARRIAGE. I WASN'T. NOW I HAVE THIS OPPORTUNITY WHERE I COULD GO BACK TO TWAIN HARTE AND BE HER MAN...
OR I COULD GO NORTH AND NEVER COME BACK... WHICH IS SORT OF WHAT I USUALLY WOULD DO.
I PROMISED HER I'D COME BACK. BUT SHE KNOWS THERE AIN'T BEEN A PROMISE I HAVEN'T BROKEN. YOU UNDERSTAND?

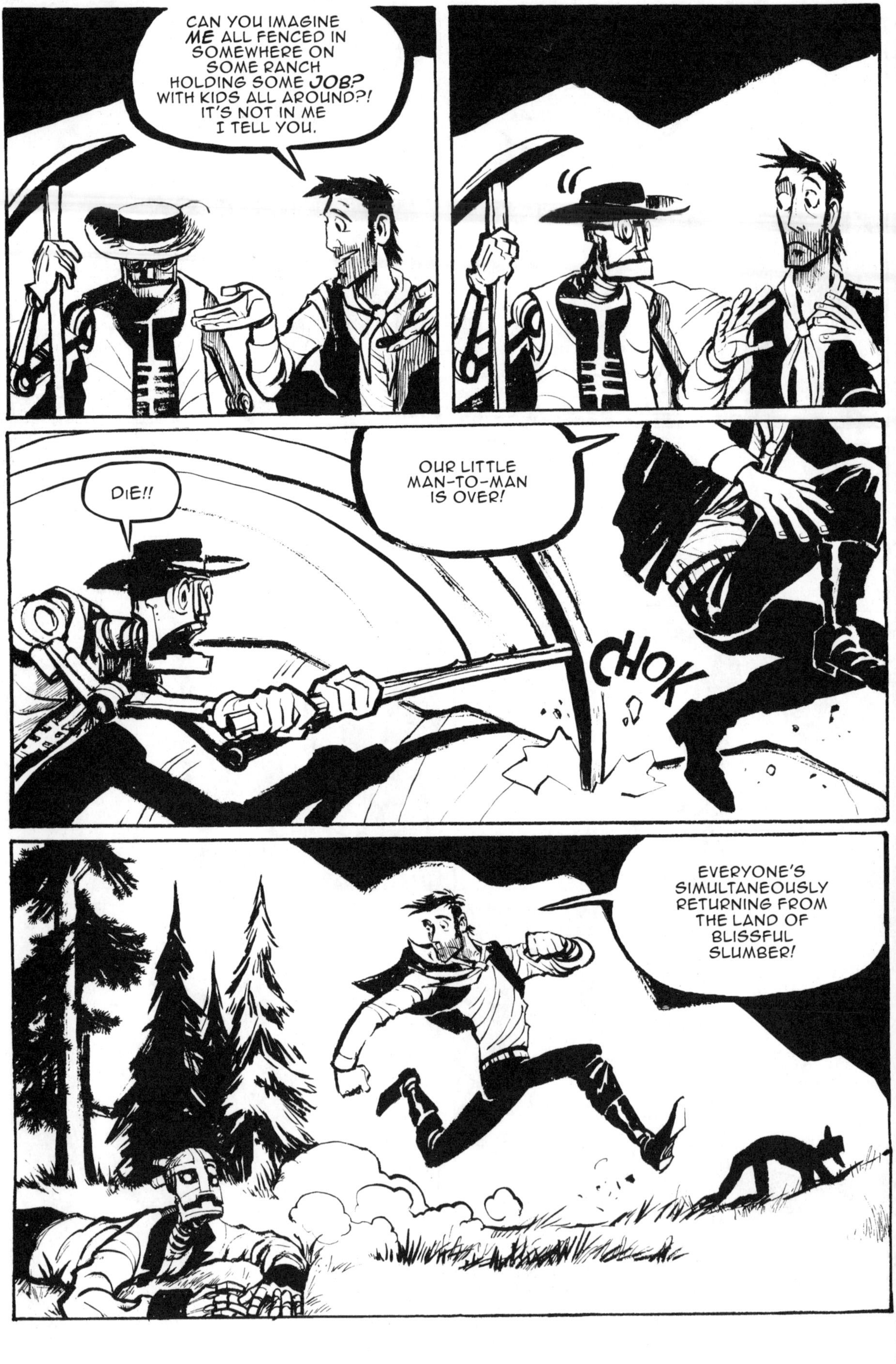
CAN YOU IMAGINE ME ALL FENCED IN SOMEWHERE ON SOME RANCH HOLDING SOME JOB? WITH KIDS ALL AROUND?! IT'S NOT IN ME I TELL YOU.
DIE!!
OUR LITTLE MAN-TO-MAN IS OVER!
CHOK
EVERYONE'S SIMULTANEOUSLY RETURNING FROM THE LAND OF BLISSFUL SLUMBER!

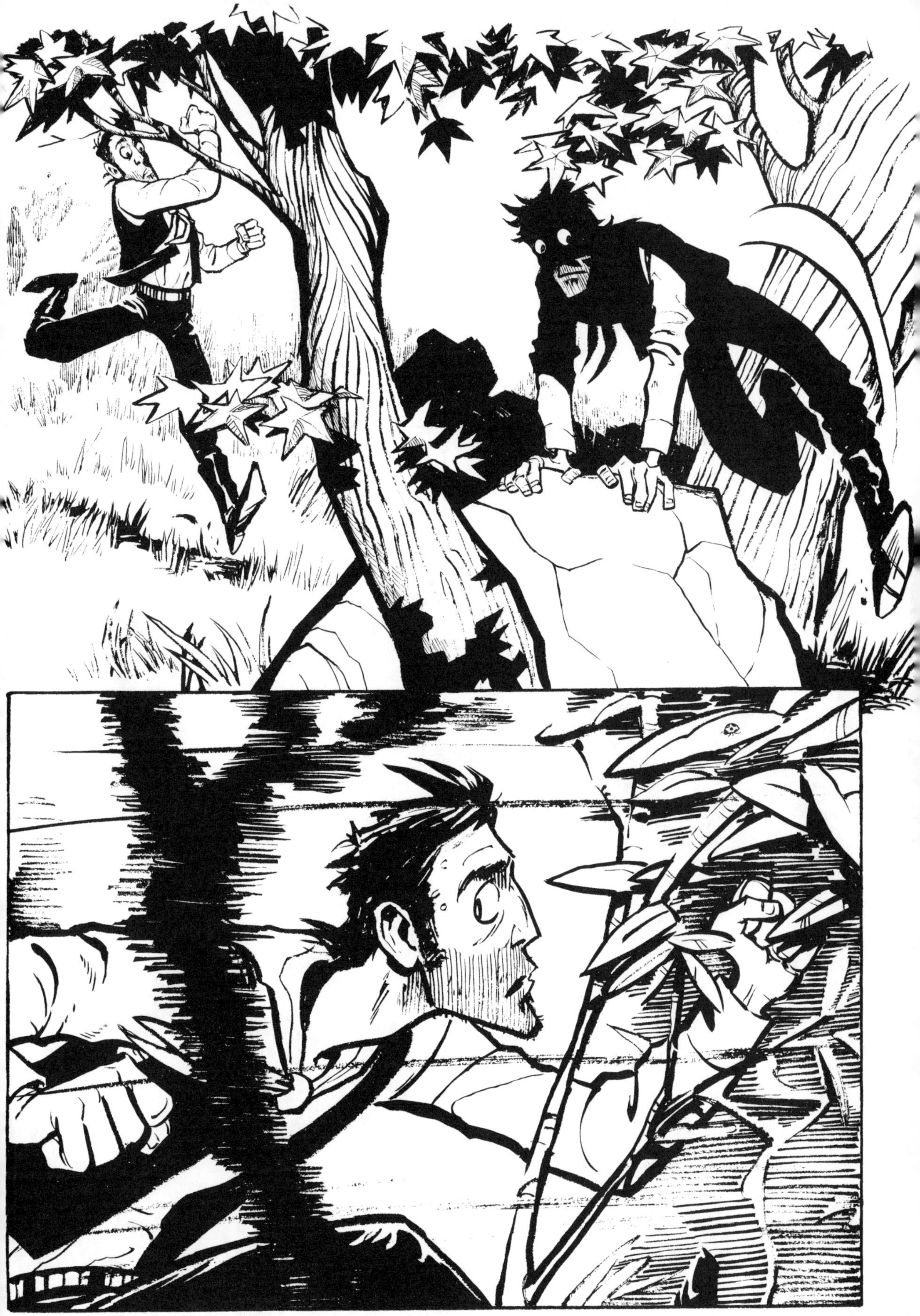

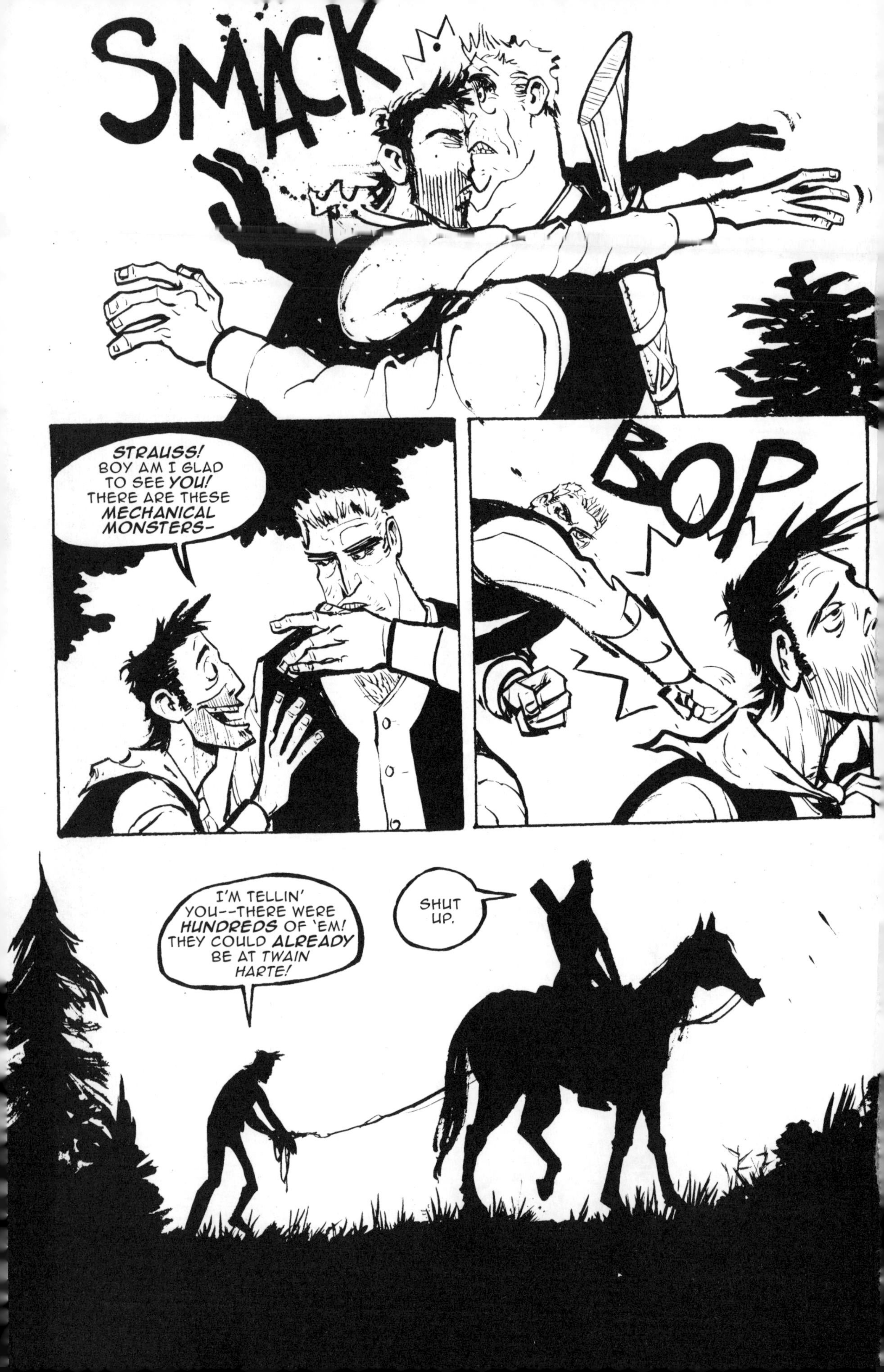
SMACK
STRAUSS! BOY AM I GLAD TO SEE YOU! THERE ARE THESE MECHANICAL MONSTERS-
BOP
I'M TELLIN' YOU--THERE WERE HUNDREDS OF 'EM! THEY COULD ALREADY BE AT TWAIN HARTE!
SHUT UP.

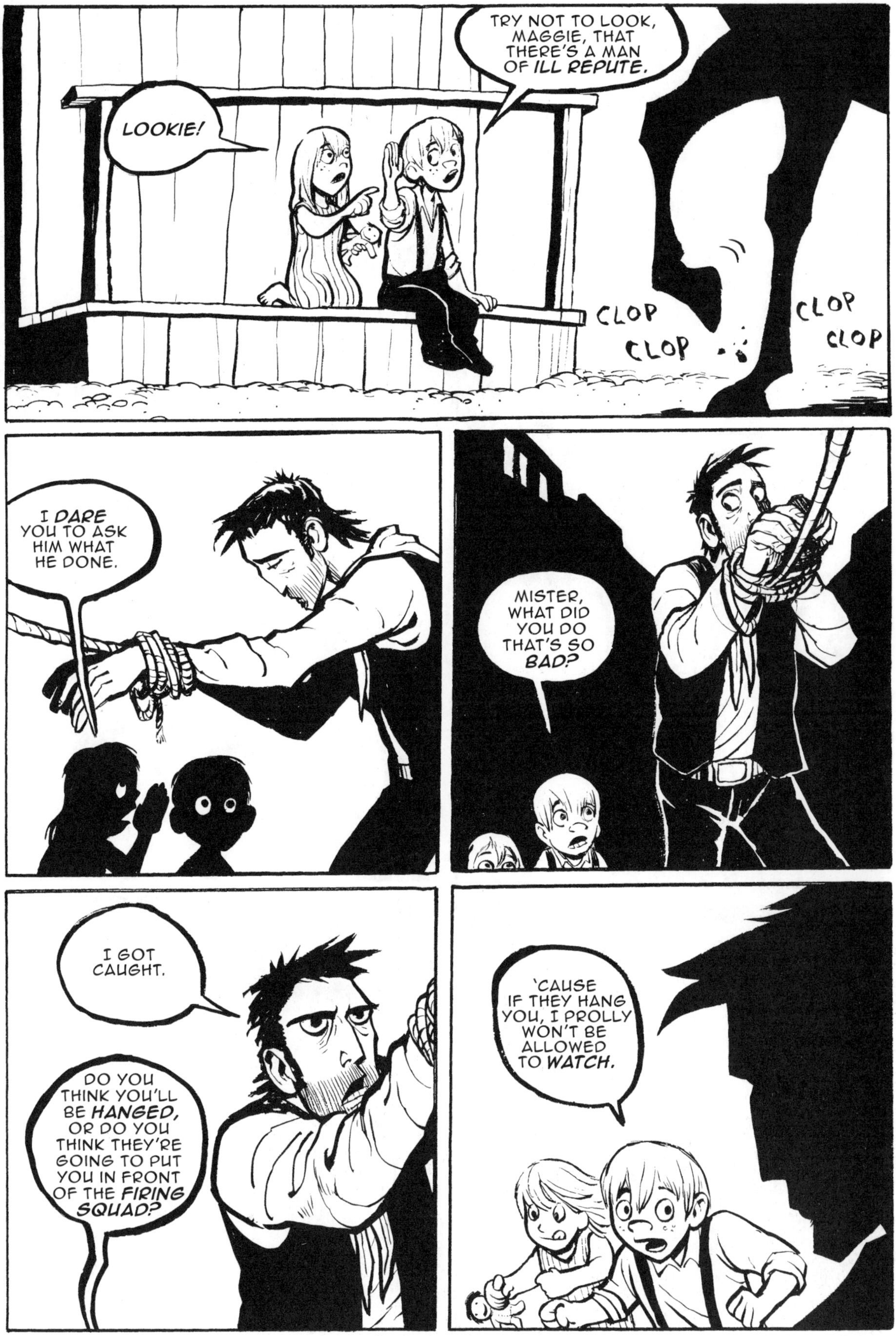

LOOKIE!
TRY NOT TO LOOK, MAGGIE, THAT THERE'S A MAN OF ILL REPUTE.
CLOP
CLOP
CLOP
CLOP
I DARE YOU TO ASK HIM WHAT HE DONE.
MISTER, WHAT DID YOU DO THAT'S SO BAD?
I GOT CAUGHT.
DO YOU THINK YOU'LL BE HANGED, OR DO YOU THINK THEY'RE GOING TO PUT YOU IN FRONT OF THE FIRING SQUAD?
'CAUSE IF THEY HANG YOU, I PROLLY WON'T BE ALLOWED TO WATCH.

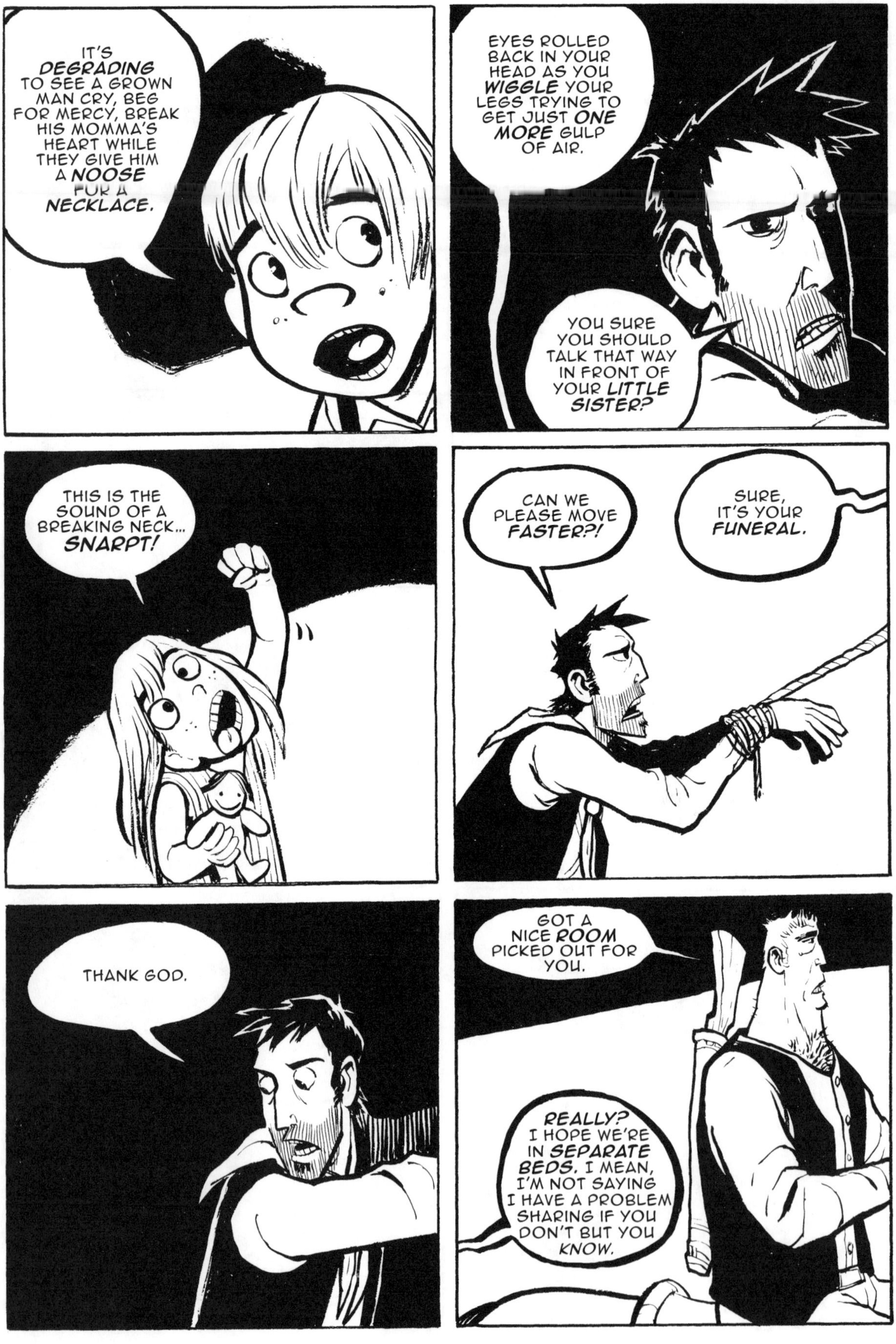
IT'S DEGRADING TO SEE A GROWN MAN CRY, BEG FOR MERCY, BREAK HIS MOMMA'S HEART WHILE THEY GIVE HIM A NOOSE FOR A NECKLACE.
EYES ROLLED BACK IN YOUR HEAD AS YOU WIGGLE YOUR LEGS TRYING TO GET JUST ONE MORE GULP OF AIR.
YOU SURE YOU SHOULD TALK THAT WAY IN FRONT OF YOUR LITTLE SISTER?
THIS IS THE SOUND OF A BREAKING NECK... SNARPT!
CAN WE PLEASE MOVE FASTER?!
SURE, IT'S YOUR FUNERAL.
THANK GOD.
GOT A NICE ROOM PICKED OUT FOR YOU.
REALLY? I HOPE WE'RE IN SEPARATE BEDS. I MEAN, I'M NOT SAYING I HAVE A PROBLEM SHARING IF YOU DON'T BUT YOU KNOW.

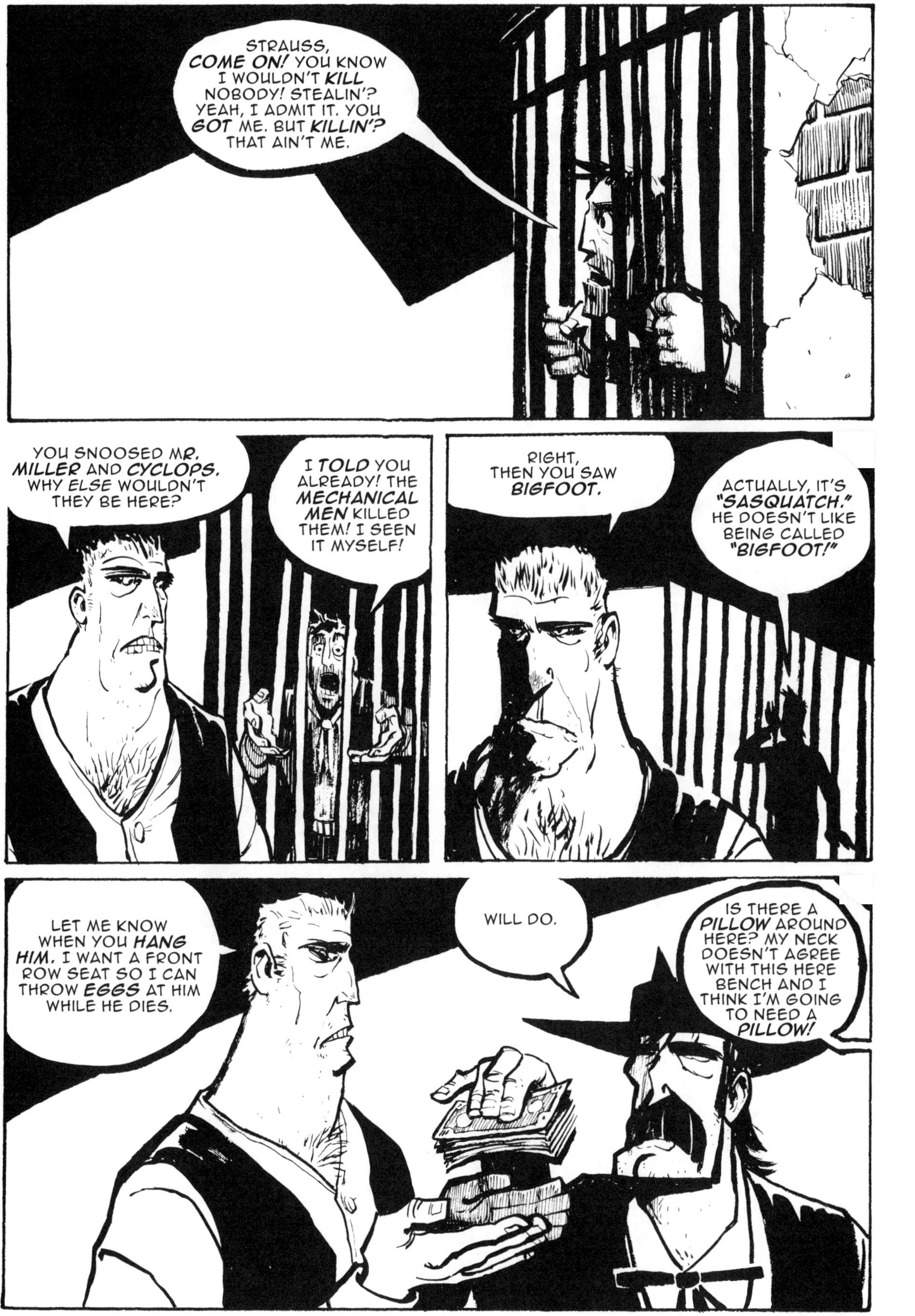
STRAUSS, **COME ON!** YOU KNOW I WOULDN'T **KILL** NOBODY! STEALIN'? YEAH, I ADMIT IT. YOU **GOT** ME. BUT **KILLIN'?** THAT AIN'T ME.
YOU SNOOSED MR. **MILLER** AND **CYCLOPS.** WHY *ELSE* WOULDN'T THEY BE HERE?
I **TOLD** YOU ALREADY! THE **MECHANICAL MEN** KILLED THEM! I SEEN IT MYSELF!
RIGHT, THEN YOU SAW **BIGFOOT.**
ACTUALLY, IT'S **"SASQUATCH."** HE DOESN'T LIKE BEING CALLED **"BIGFOOT!"**
LET ME KNOW WHEN YOU **HANG HIM.** I WANT A FRONT ROW SEAT SO I CAN THROW **EGGS** AT HIM WHILE HE DIES.
WILL DO.
IS THERE A **PILLOW** AROUND HERE? MY NECK DOESN'T AGREE WITH THIS HERE BENCH AND I THINK I'M GOING TO NEED A **PILLOW!**

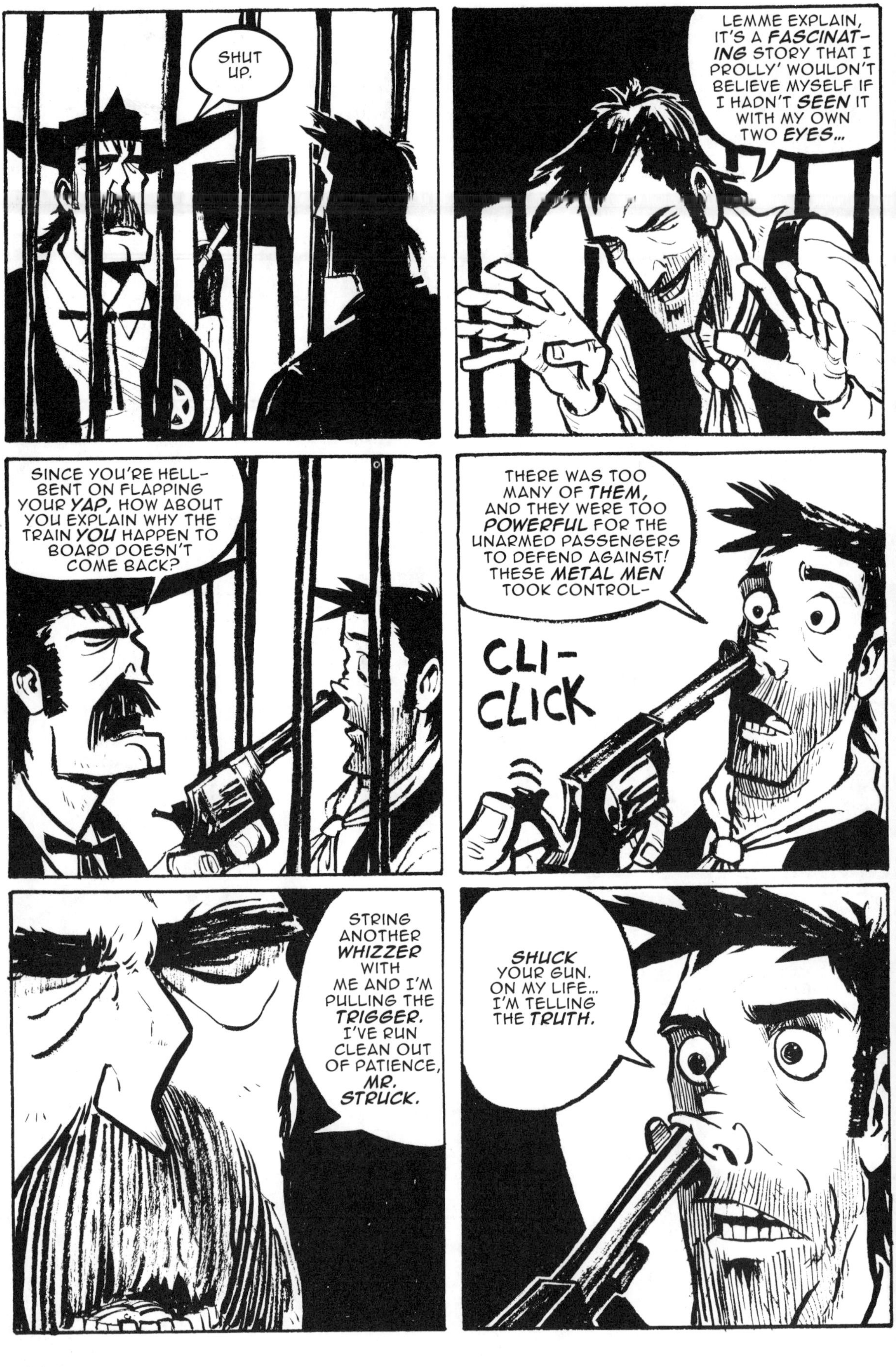
SHUT UP.
LEMME EXPLAIN, IT'S A FASCINATING STORY THAT I PROLLY' WOULDN'T BELIEVE MYSELF IF I HADN'T SEEN IT WITH MY OWN TWO EYES...
SINCE YOU'RE HELL-BENT ON FLAPPING YOUR YAP, HOW ABOUT YOU EXPLAIN WHY THE TRAIN YOU HAPPEN TO BOARD DOESN'T COME BACK?
THERE WAS TOO MANY OF THEM, AND THEY WERE TOO POWERFUL FOR THE UNARMED PASSENGERS TO DEFEND AGAINST! THESE METAL MEN TOOK CONTROL-
CLI-CLICK
STRING ANOTHER WHIZZER WITH ME AND I'M PULLING THE TRIGGER. I'VE RUN CLEAN OUT OF PATIENCE, MR. STRUCK.
SHUCK YOUR GUN. ON MY LIFE... I'M TELLING THE TRUTH.

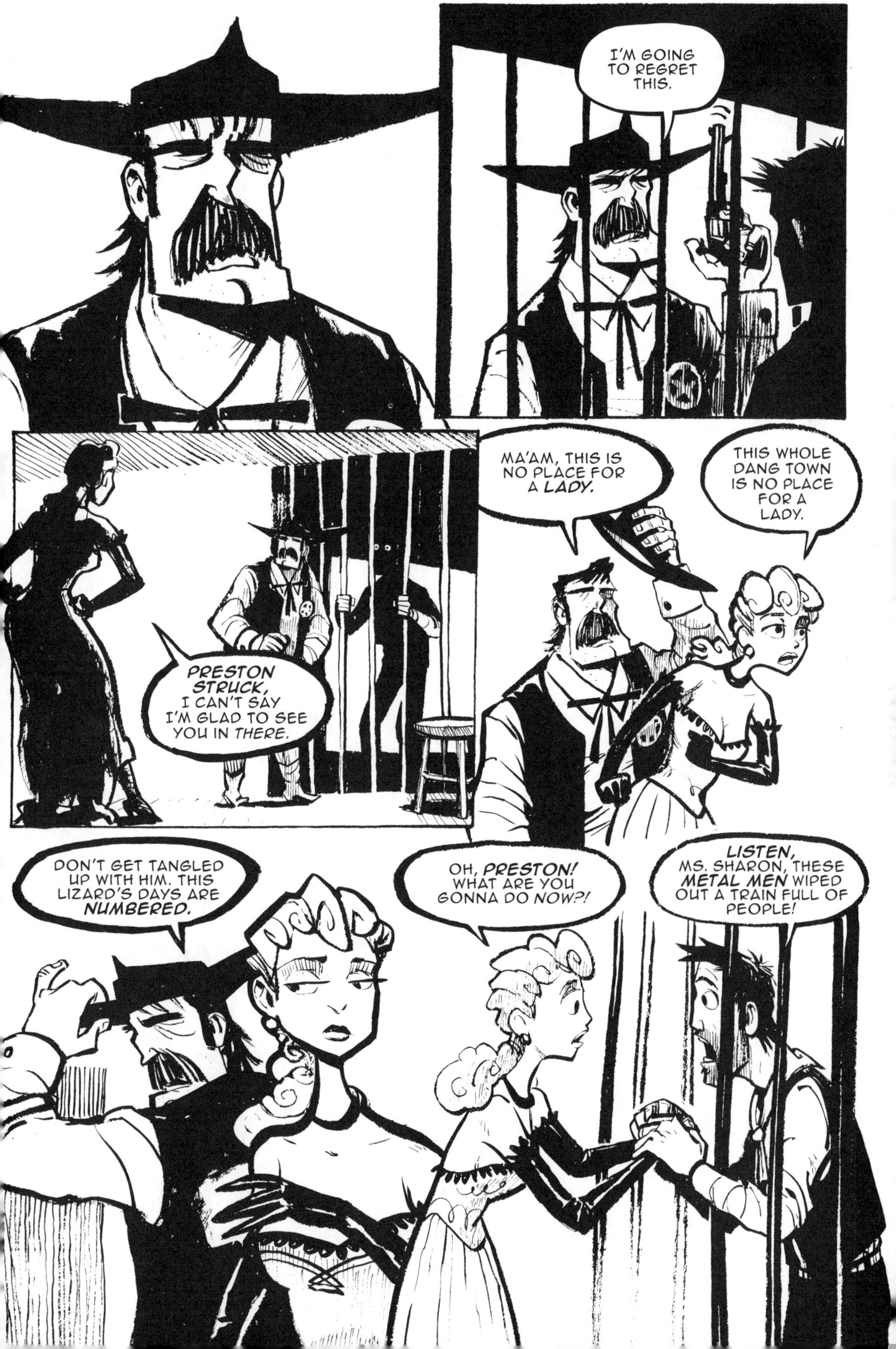
I'M GOING TO REGRET THIS.
PRESTON STRUCK, I CAN'T SAY I'M GLAD TO SEE YOU IN THERE.
MA'AM, THIS IS NO PLACE FOR A LADY.
THIS WHOLE DANG TOWN IS NO PLACE FOR A LADY.
DON'T GET TANGLED UP WITH HIM. THIS LIZARD'S DAYS ARE NUMBERED.
OH, PRESTON! WHAT ARE YOU GONNA DO NOW?!
LISTEN, MS. SHARON, THESE METAL MEN WIPED OUT A TRAIN FULL OF PEOPLE!

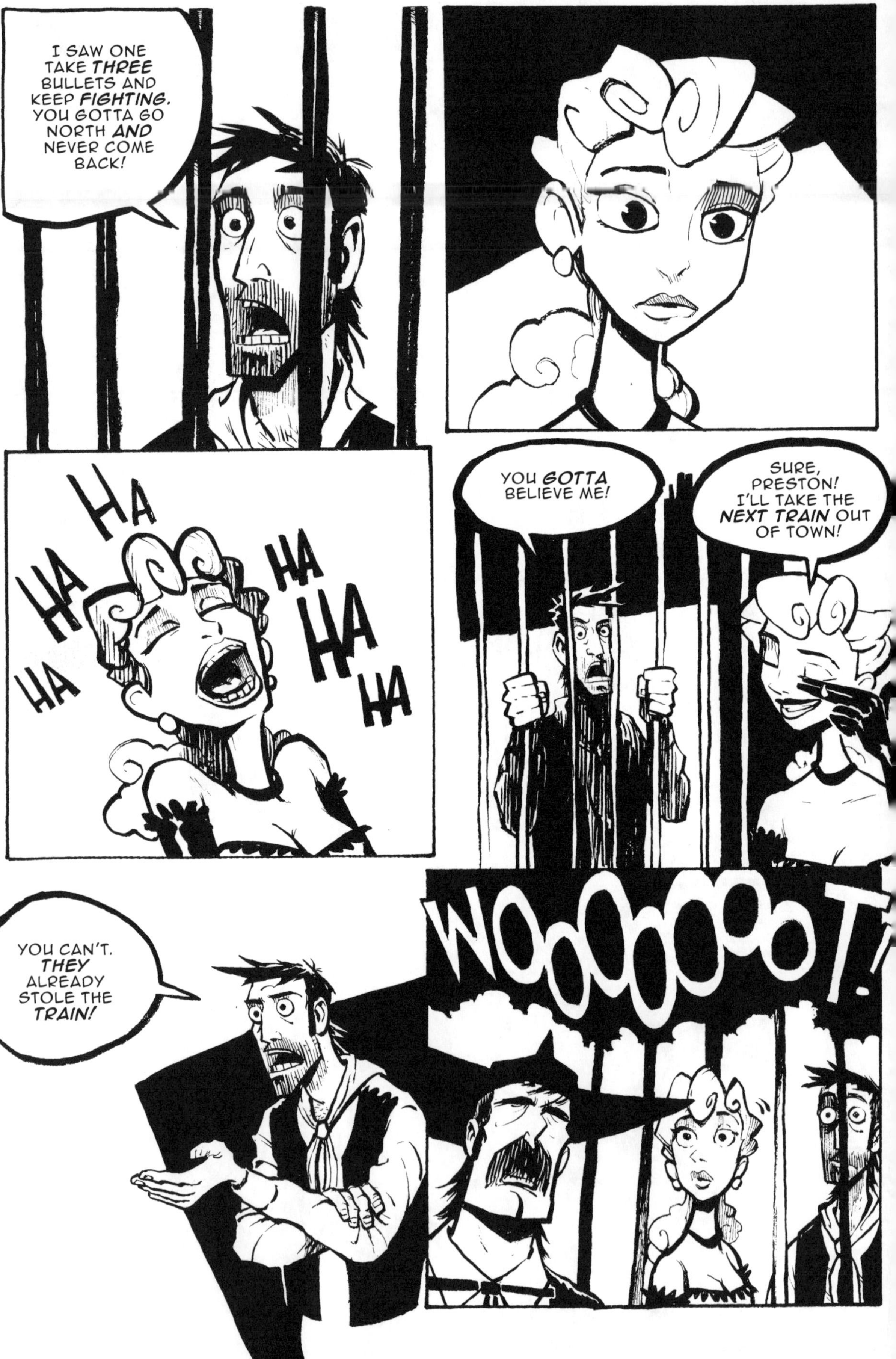
I SAW ONE TAKE THREE BULLETS AND KEEP FIGHTING. YOU GOTTA GO NORTH AND NEVER COME BACK!
HA HA HA HA HA HA HA HA
YOU GOTTA BELIEVE ME!
SURE, PRESTON! I'LL TAKE THE NEXT TRAIN OUT OF TOWN!
YOU CAN'T. THEY ALREADY STOLE THE TRAIN!
WOOOOOOOT!!

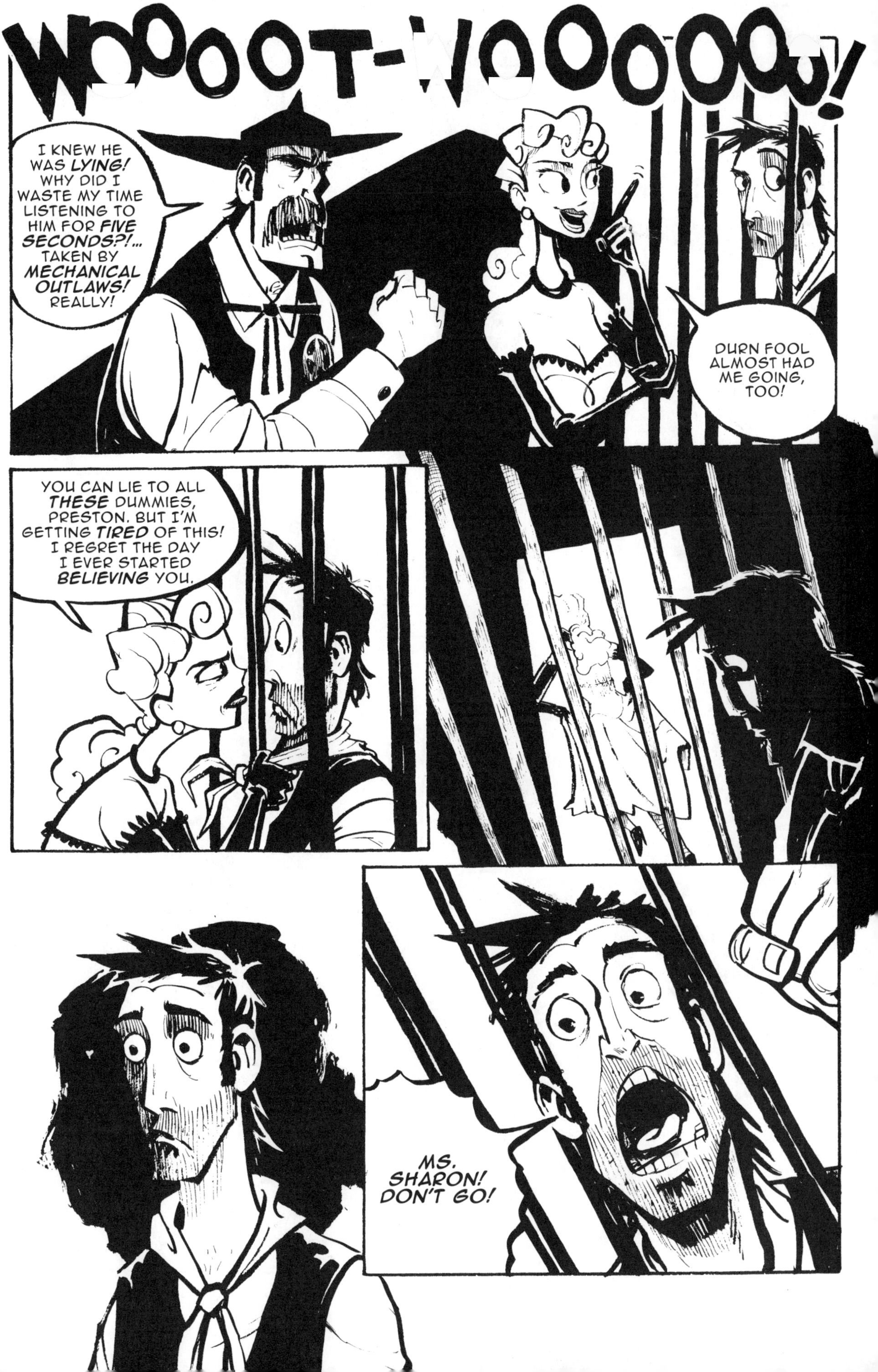
WOOOOT-WOOOOOOW!
I KNEW HE WAS LYING! WHY DID I WASTE MY TIME LISTENING TO HIM FOR FIVE SECONDS?!... TAKEN BY MECHANICAL OUTLAWS! REALLY!
DURN FOOL ALMOST HAD ME GOING, TOO!
YOU CAN LIE TO ALL THESE DUMMIES, PRESTON. BUT I'M GETTING TIRED OF THIS! I REGRET THE DAY I EVER STARTED BELIEVING YOU.
MS. SHARON! DON'T GO!

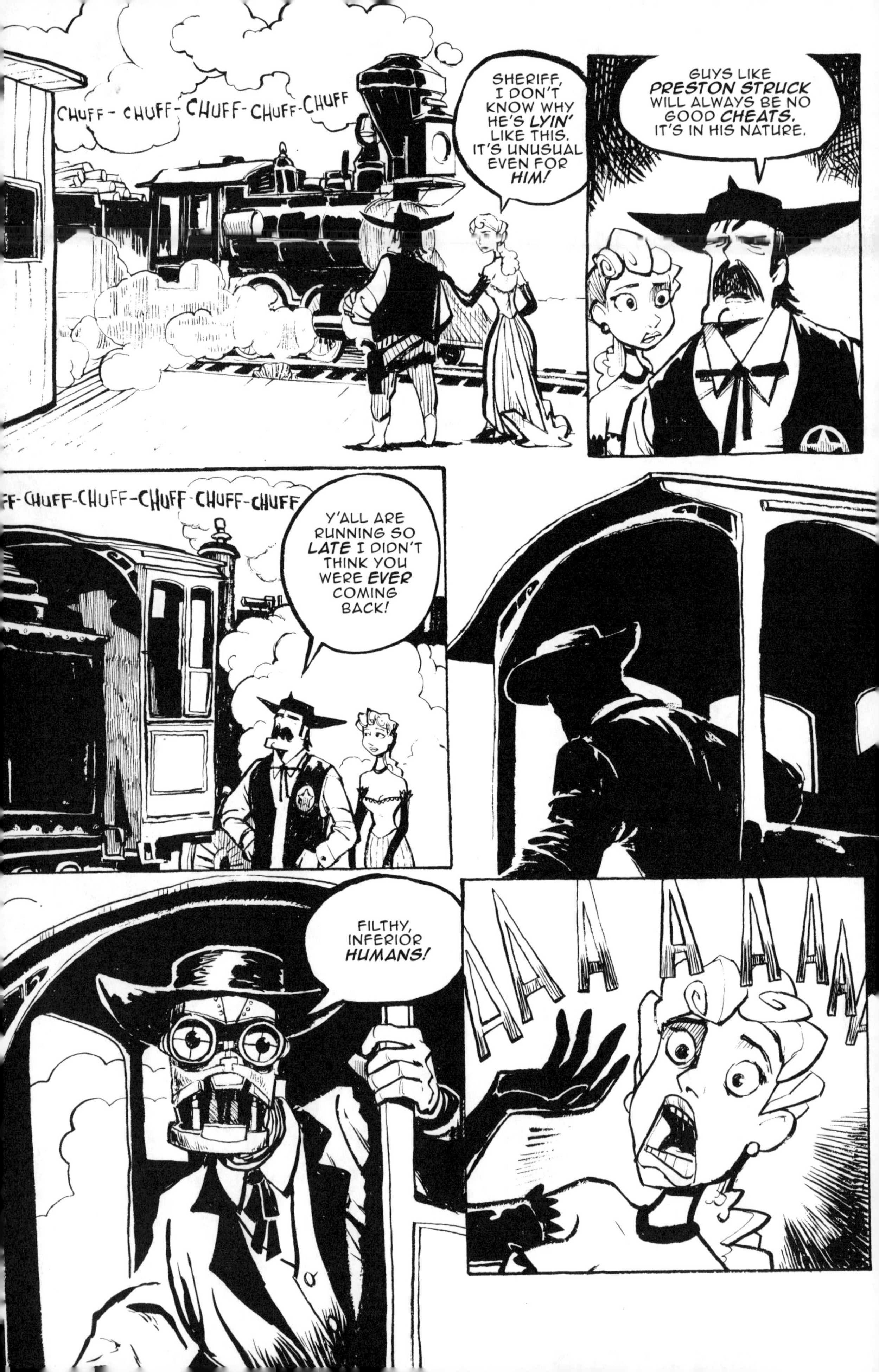
CHUFF - CHUFF - CHUFF - CHUFF - CHUFF
SHERIFF, I DON'T KNOW WHY HE'S LYIN' LIKE THIS. IT'S UNUSUAL EVEN FOR HIM!
GUYS LIKE PRESTON STRUCK WILL ALWAYS BE NO GOOD CHEATS. IT'S IN HIS NATURE.
FF-CHUFF-CHUFF-CHUFF-CHUFF-CHUFF
Y'ALL ARE RUNNING SO LATE I DIDN'T THINK YOU WERE EVER COMING BACK!
FILTHY, INFERIOR HUMANS!
AAAAAAAAA

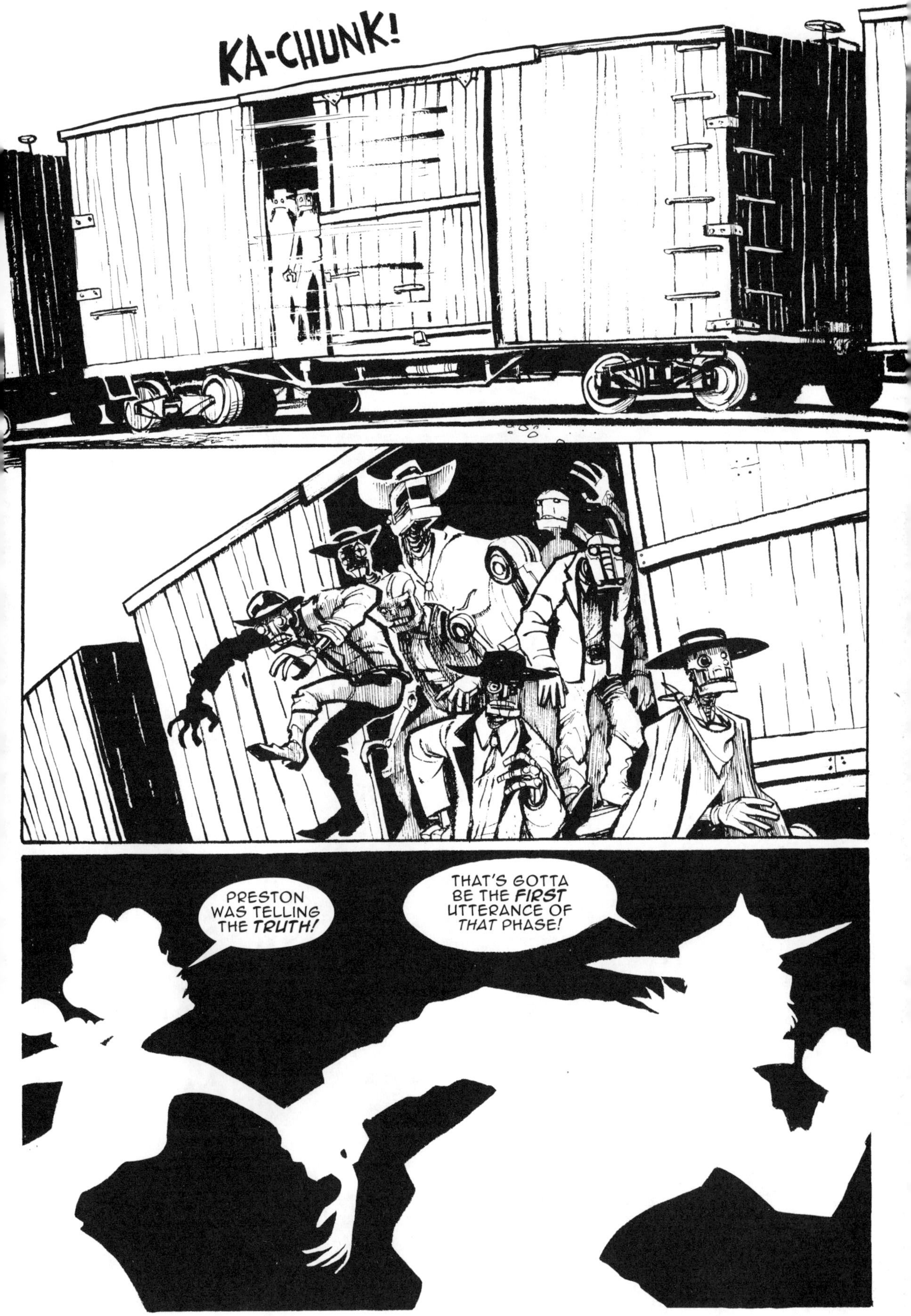
KA-CHUNK!
PRESTON WAS TELLING THE *TRUTH!*
THAT'S GOTTA BE THE *FIRST* UTTERANCE OF *THAT* PHASE!

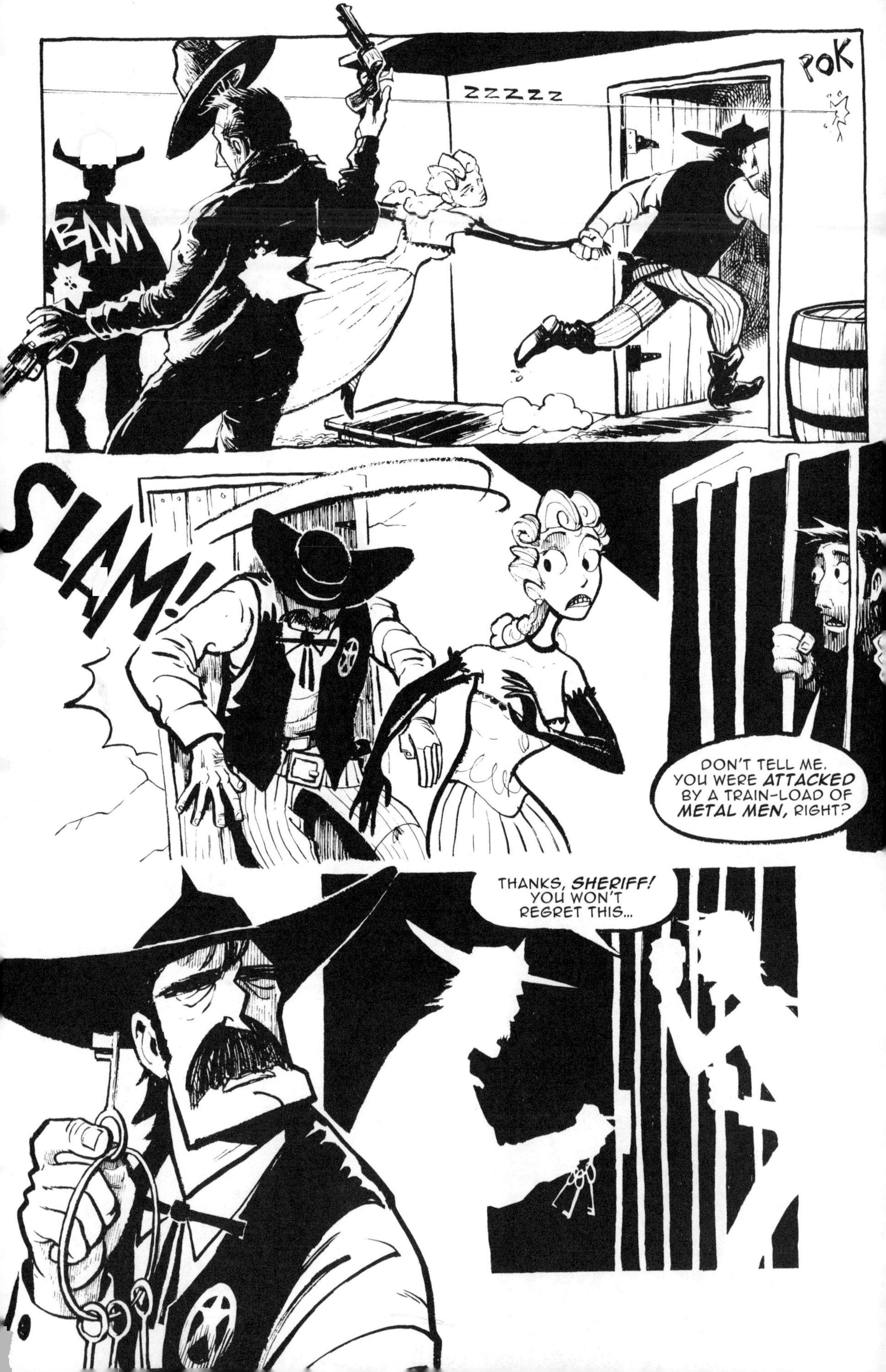
POK
ZZZZZ
BAM
SLAM!
DON'T TELL ME. YOU WERE ATTACKED BY A TRAIN-LOAD OF METAL MEN, RIGHT?
THANKS, SHERIFF! YOU WON'T REGRET THIS...

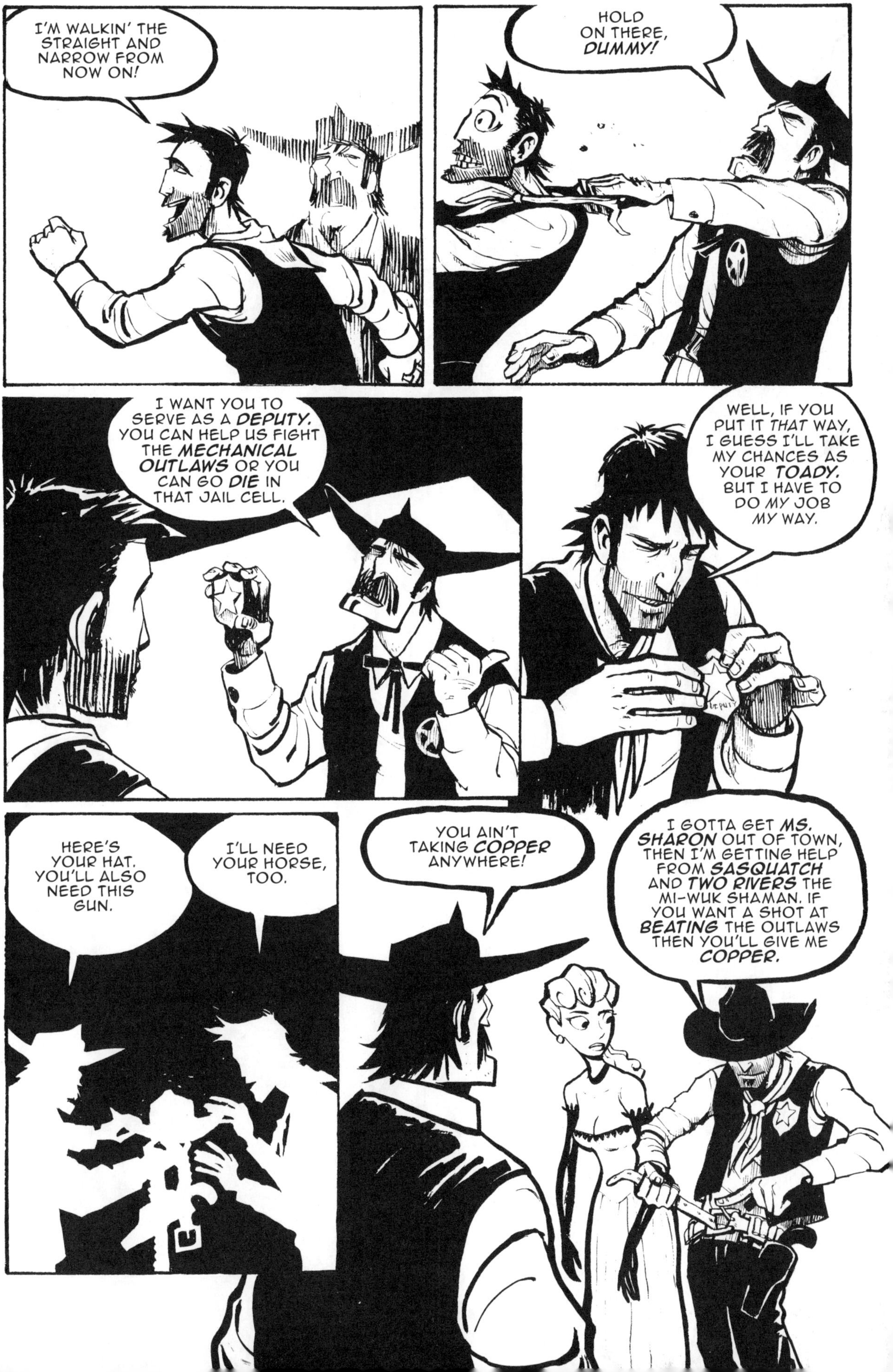
I'M WALKIN' THE STRAIGHT AND NARROW FROM NOW ON!
HOLD ON THERE, DUMMY!
I WANT YOU TO SERVE AS A DEPUTY. YOU CAN HELP US FIGHT THE MECHANICAL OUTLAWS OR YOU CAN GO DIE IN THAT JAIL CELL.
WELL, IF YOU PUT IT THAT WAY, I GUESS I'LL TAKE MY CHANCES AS YOUR TOADY. BUT I HAVE TO DO MY JOB MY WAY.
DEPUTY
HERE'S YOUR HAT. YOU'LL ALSO NEED THIS GUN.
I'LL NEED YOUR HORSE, TOO.
YOU AIN'T TAKING COPPER ANYWHERE!
I GOTTA GET MS. SHARON OUT OF TOWN, THEN I'M GETTING HELP FROM SASQUATCH AND TWO RIVERS THE MI-WUK SHAMAN. IF YOU WANT A SHOT AT BEATING THE OUTLAWS THEN YOU'LL GIVE ME COPPER.

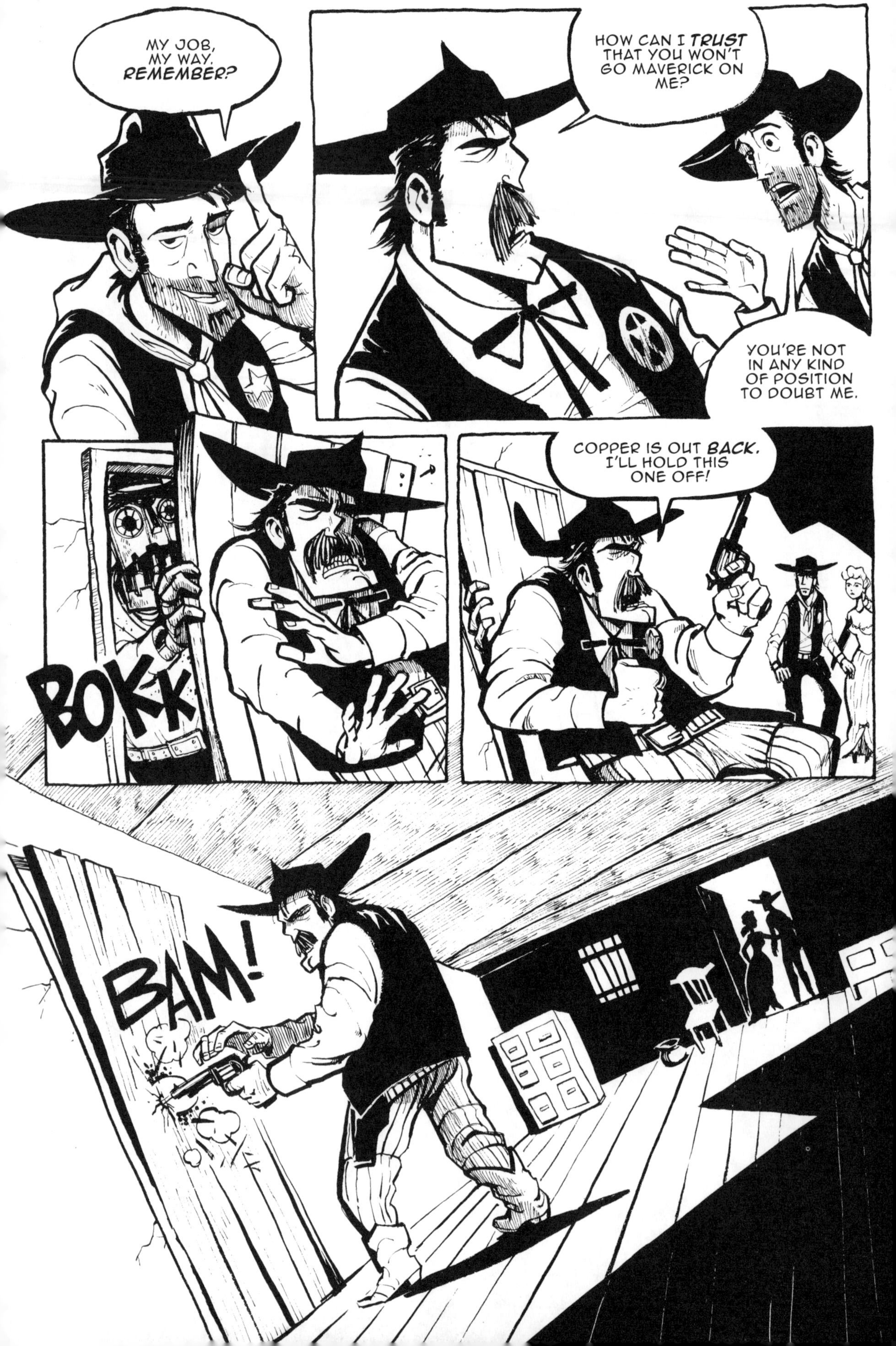
MY JOB, MY WAY. REMEMBER?
HOW CAN I TRUST THAT YOU WON'T GO MAVERICK ON ME?
YOU'RE NOT IN ANY KIND OF POSITION TO DOUBT ME.
BOKK
COPPER IS OUT BACK. I'LL HOLD THIS ONE OFF!
BAM!

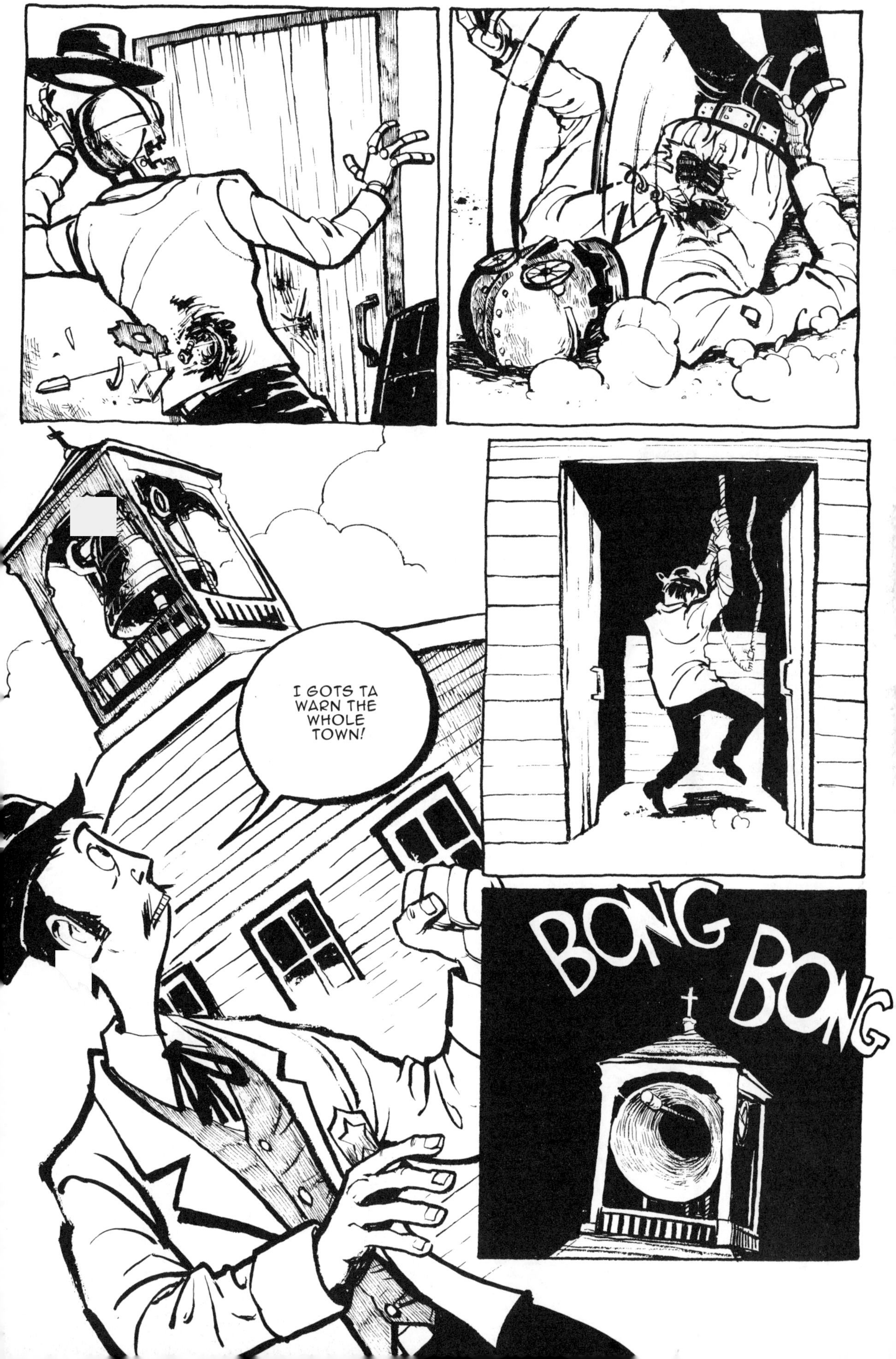
I GOTS TA WARN THE WHOLE TOWN!
BONG
BONG

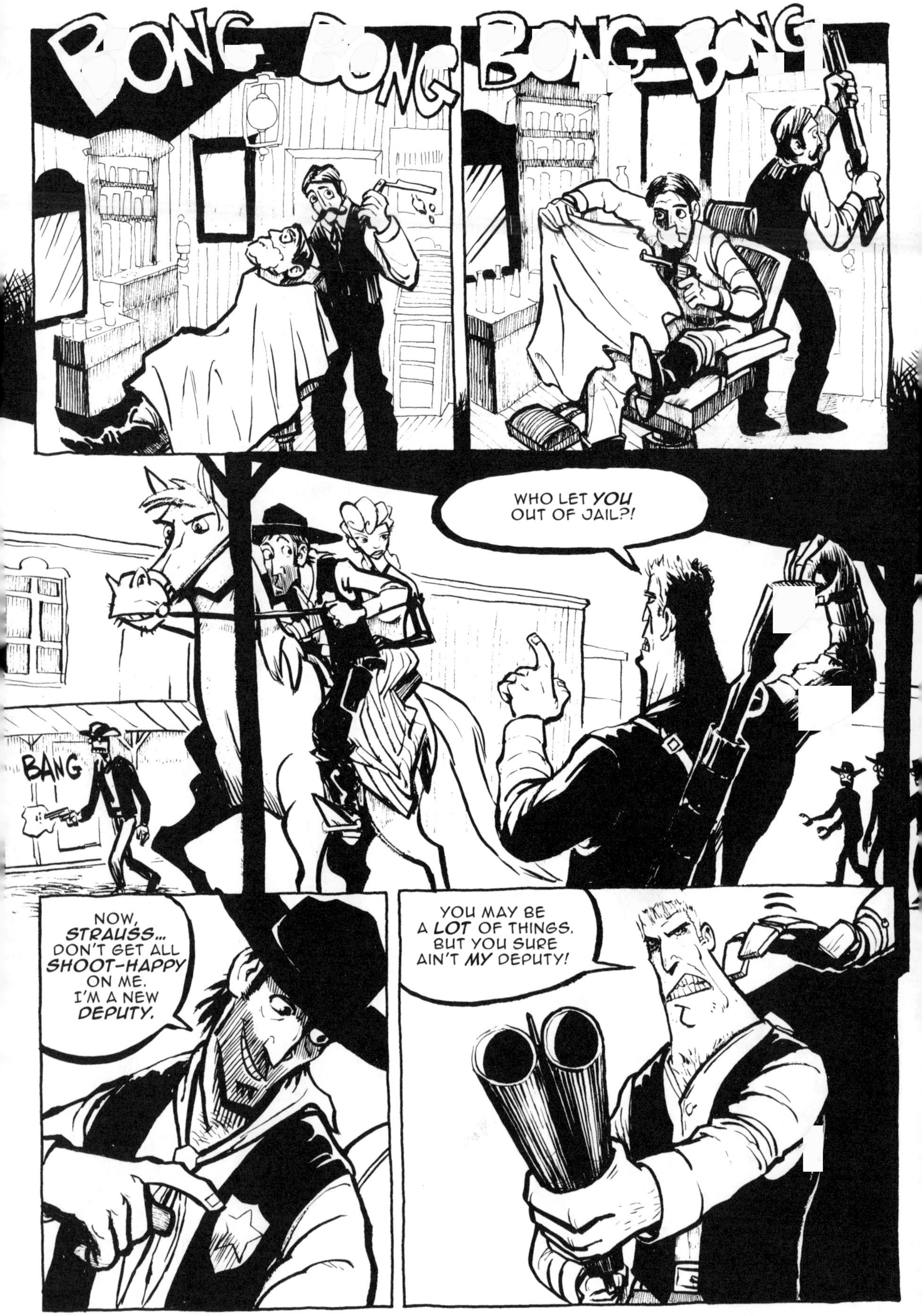
BONG BONG BONG BONG
BANG
WHO LET YOU OUT OF JAIL?!
NOW, STRAUSS... DON'T GET ALL SHOOT-HAPPY ON ME. I'M A NEW DEPUTY.
YOU MAY BE A LOT OF THINGS. BUT YOU SURE AIN'T MY DEPUTY!

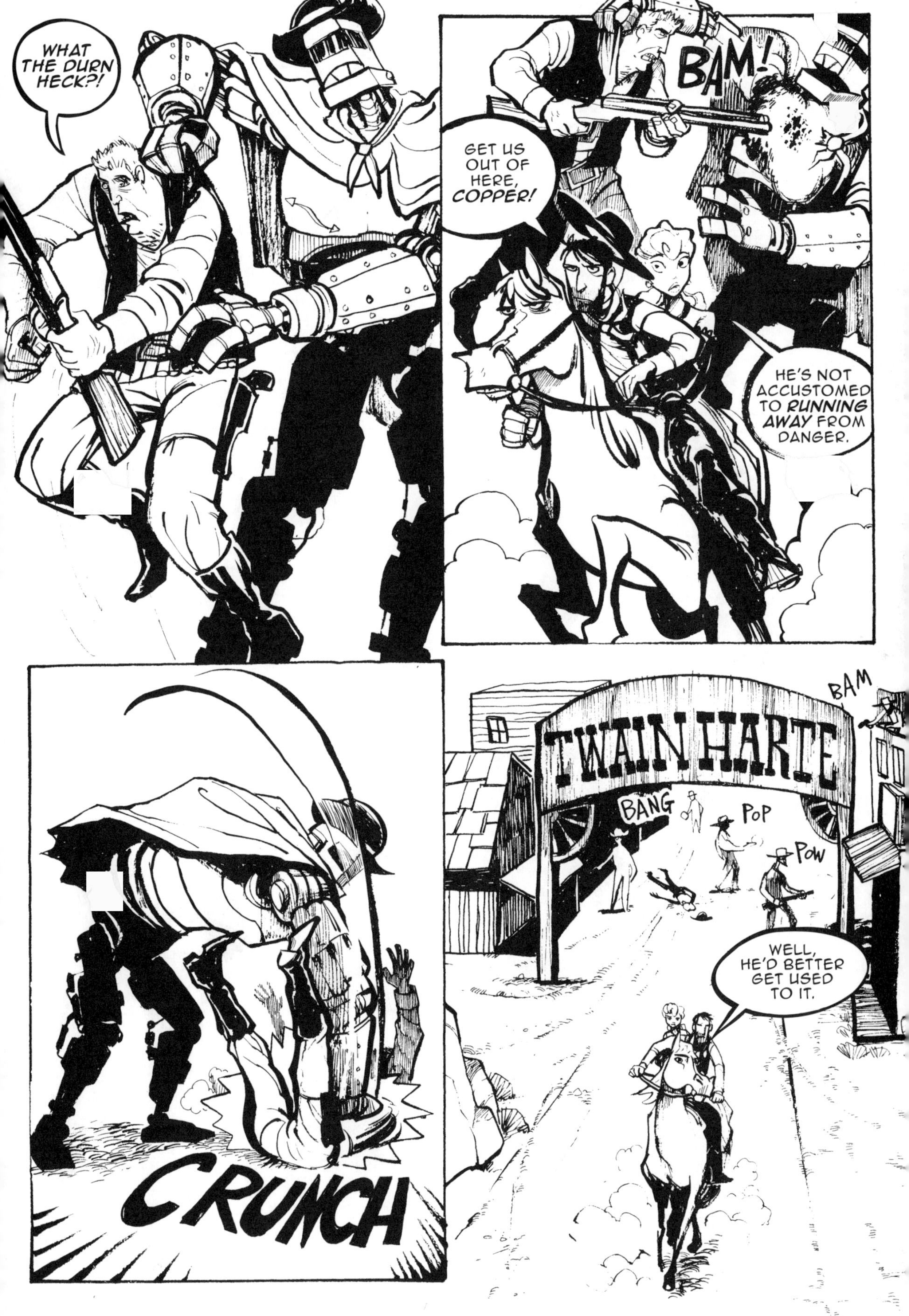
WHAT THE DURN HECK?!
BAM!
GET US OUT OF HERE, COPPER!
HE'S NOT ACCUSTOMED TO RUNNING AWAY FROM DANGER.
CRUNCH
TWAIN HARTE
BAM
BANG
POP
POW
WELL, HE'D BETTER GET USED TO IT.

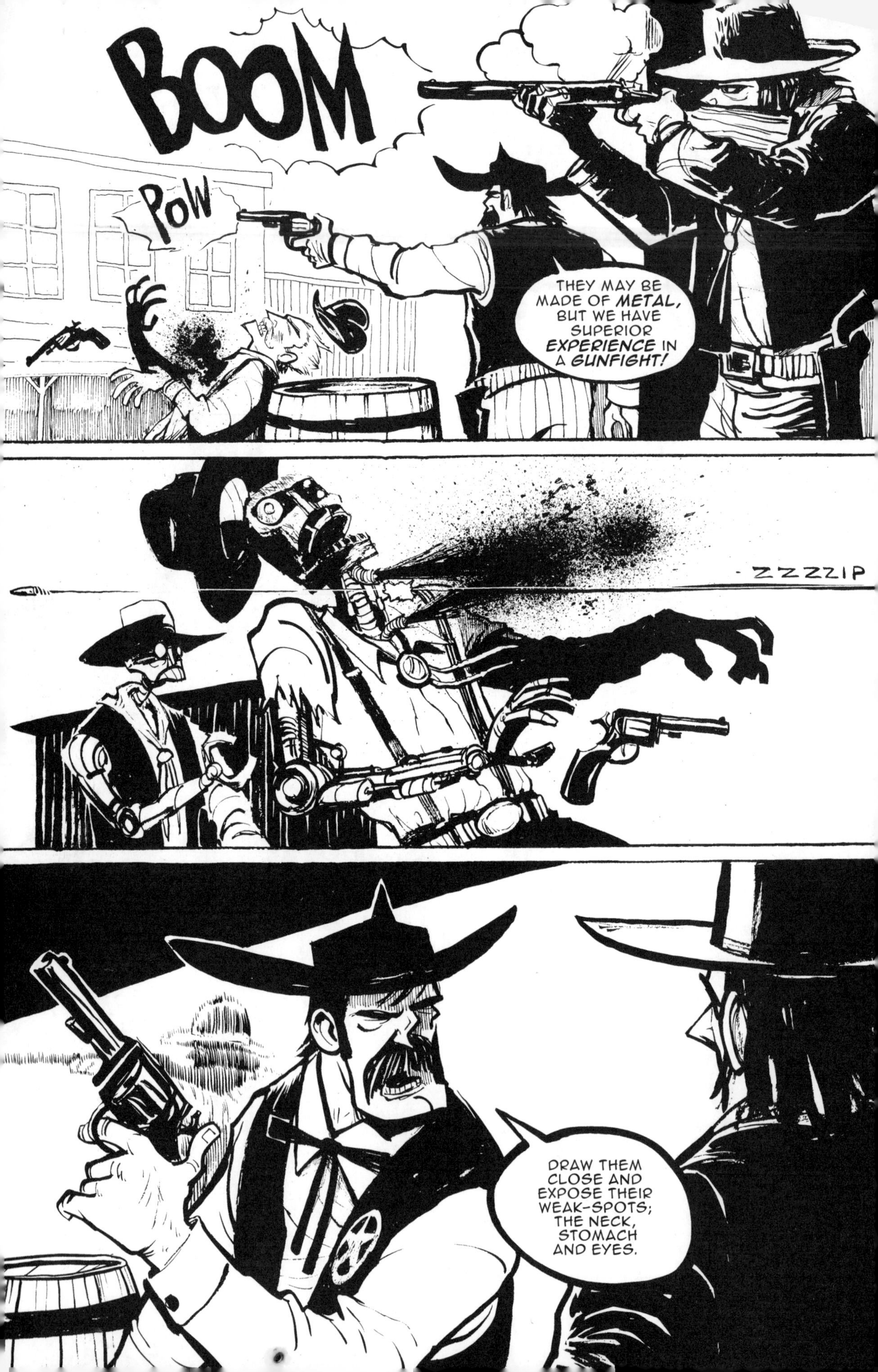
BOOM
POW
THEY MAY BE MADE OF METAL, BUT WE HAVE SUPERIOR EXPERIENCE IN A GUNFIGHT!
ZZZZIP
DRAW THEM CLOSE AND EXPOSE THEIR WEAK-SPOTS; THE NECK, STOMACH AND EYES.

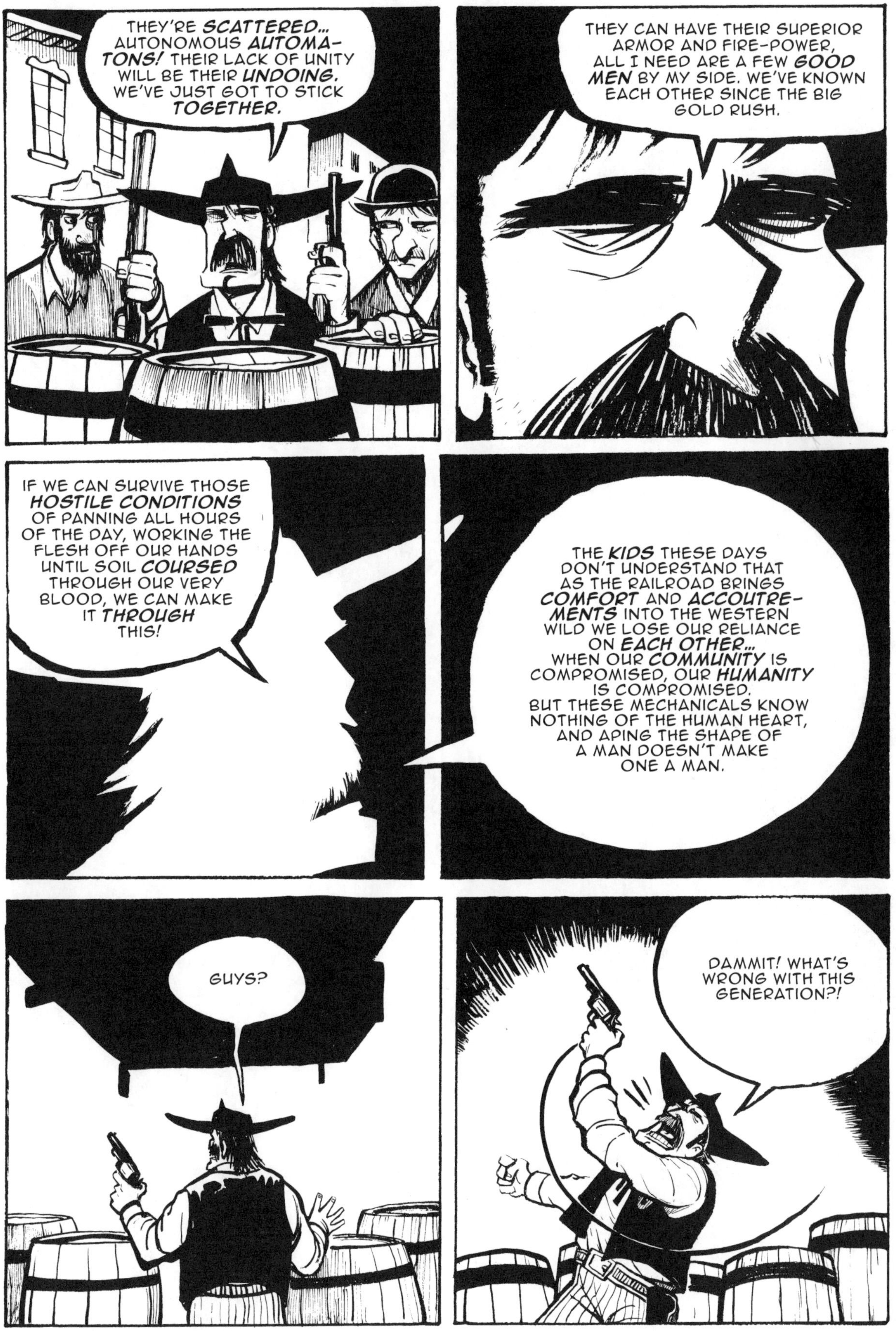
THEY'RE SCATTERED... AUTONOMOUS AUTOMATONS! THEIR LACK OF UNITY WILL BE THEIR UNDOING. WE'VE JUST GOT TO STICK TOGETHER.
THEY CAN HAVE THEIR SUPERIOR ARMOR AND FIRE-POWER, ALL I NEED ARE A FEW GOOD MEN BY MY SIDE. WE'VE KNOWN EACH OTHER SINCE THE BIG GOLD RUSH.
IF WE CAN SURVIVE THOSE HOSTILE CONDITIONS OF PANNING ALL HOURS OF THE DAY, WORKING THE FLESH OFF OUR HANDS UNTIL SOIL COURSED THROUGH OUR VERY BLOOD, WE CAN MAKE IT THROUGH THIS!
THE KIDS THESE DAYS DON'T UNDERSTAND THAT AS THE RAILROAD BRINGS COMFORT AND ACCOUTREMENTS INTO THE WESTERN WILD WE LOSE OUR RELIANCE ON EACH OTHER... WHEN OUR COMMUNITY IS COMPROMISED, OUR HUMANITY IS COMPROMISED. BUT THESE MECHANICALS KNOW NOTHING OF THE HUMAN HEART, AND APING THE SHAPE OF A MAN DOESN'T MAKE ONE A MAN.
GUYS?
DAMMIT! WHAT'S WRONG WITH THIS GENERATION?!

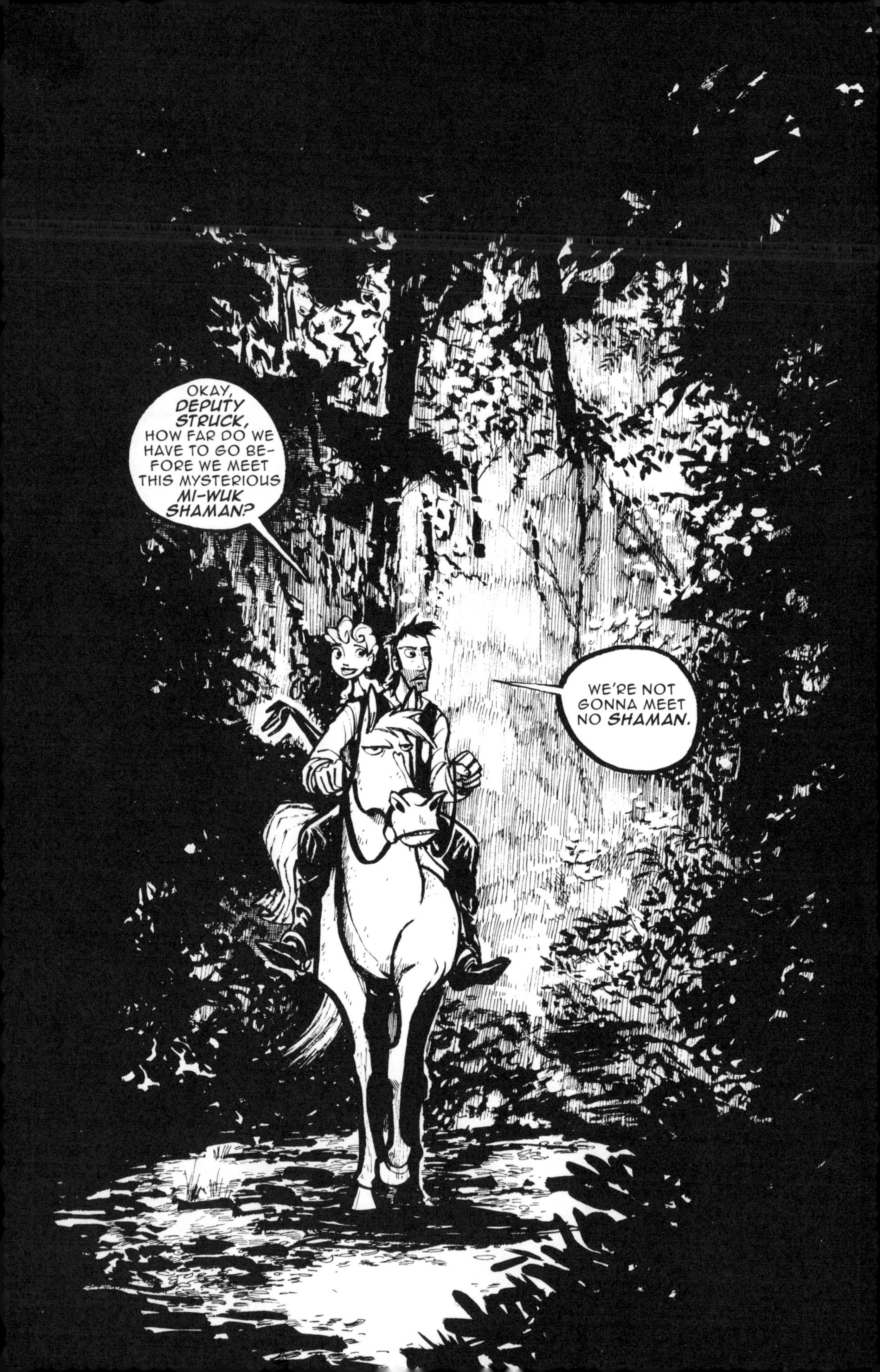
OKAY, DEPUTY STRUCK, HOW FAR DO WE HAVE TO GO BE-FORE WE MEET THIS MYSTERIOUS MI-WUK SHAMAN?
WE'RE NOT GONNA MEET NO SHAMAN.

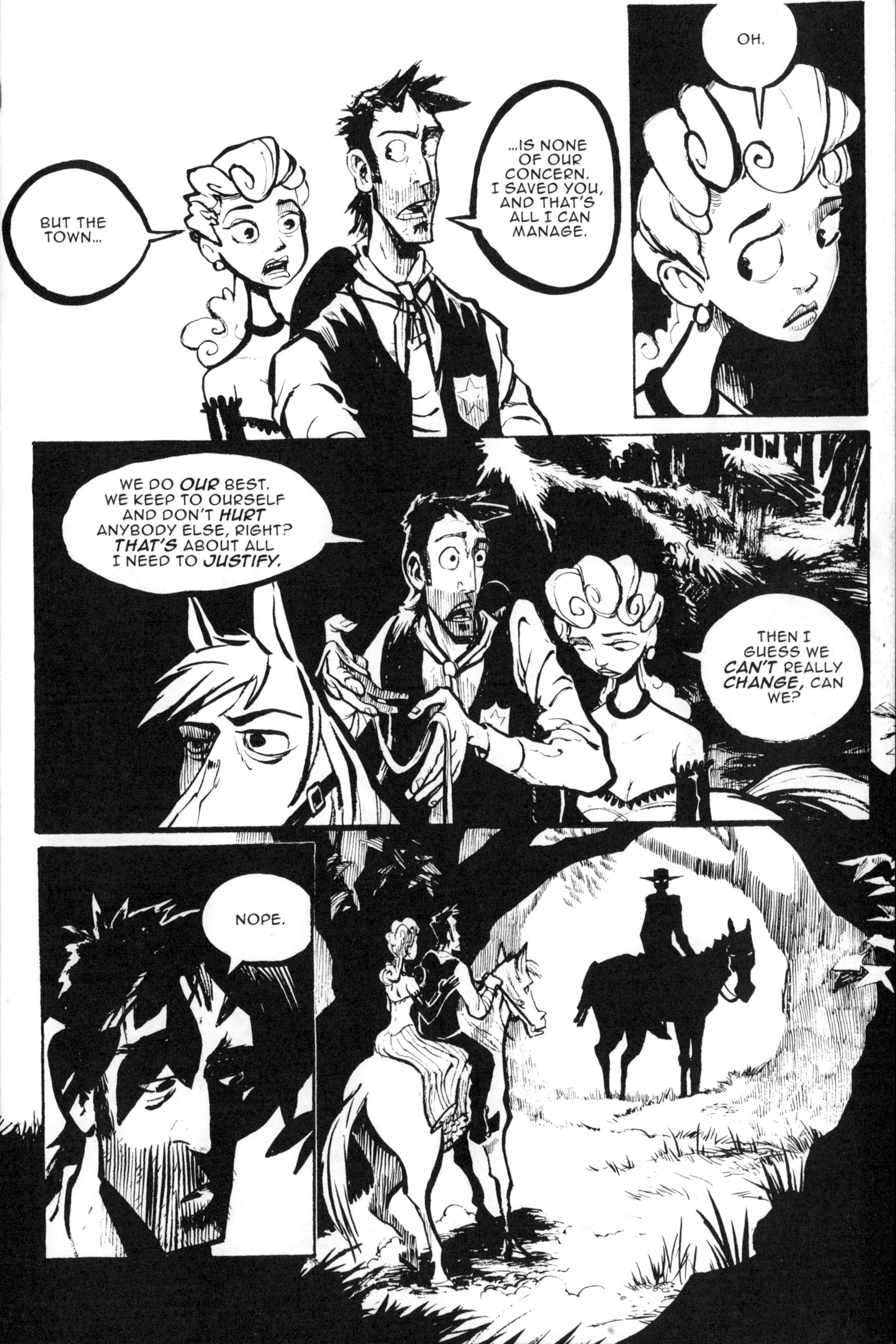
BUT THE TOWN...
...IS NONE OF OUR CONCERN. I SAVED YOU, AND THAT'S ALL I CAN MANAGE.
OH.
WE DO OUR BEST. WE KEEP TO OURSELF AND DON'T HURT ANYBODY ELSE, RIGHT? THAT'S ABOUT ALL I NEED TO JUSTIFY.
THEN I GUESS WE CAN'T REALLY CHANGE, CAN WE?
NOPE.

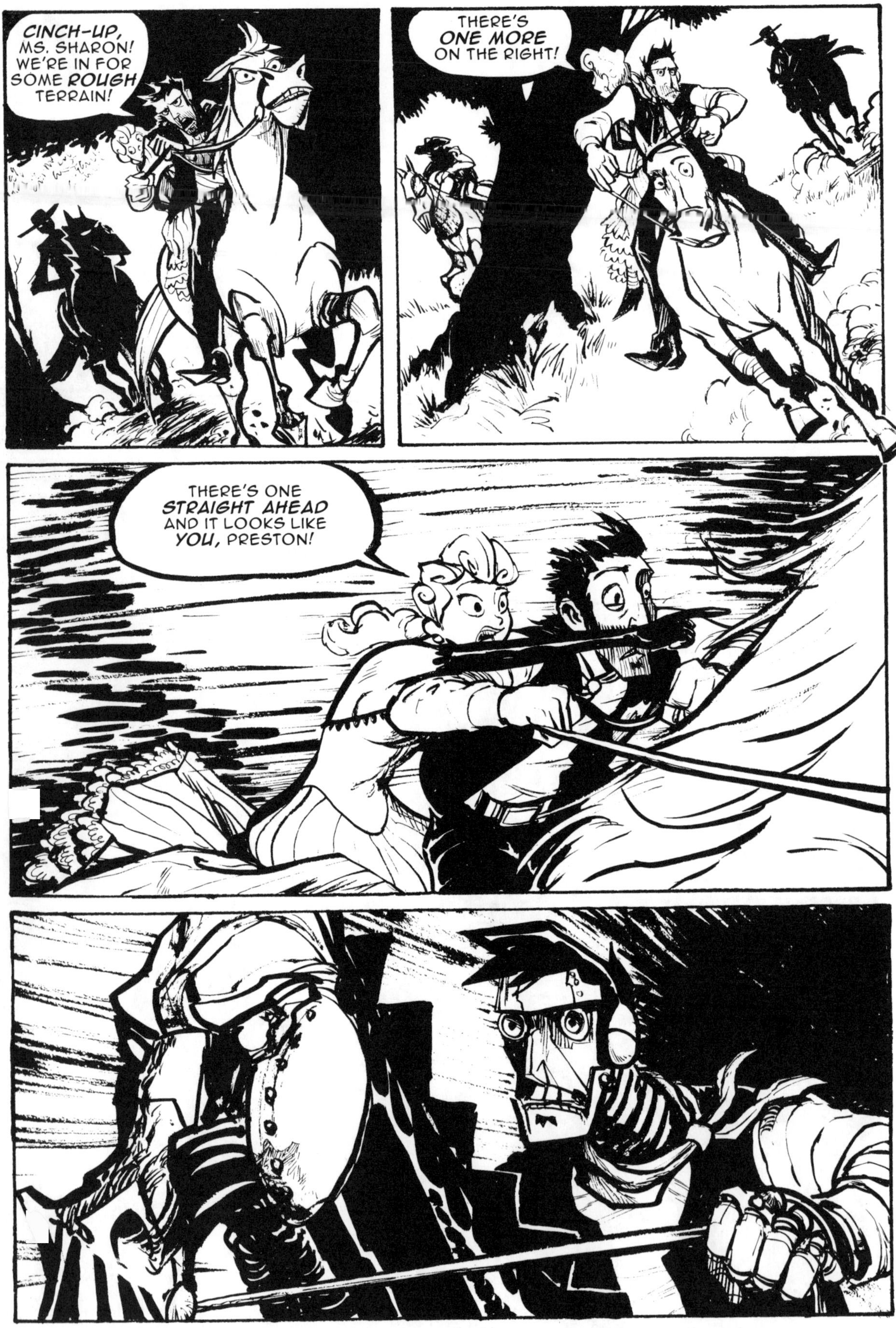
CINCH-UP, MS. SHARON! WE'RE IN FOR SOME ROUGH TERRAIN!
THERE'S ONE MORE ON THE RIGHT!
THERE'S ONE STRAIGHT AHEAD AND IT LOOKS LIKE YOU, PRESTON!

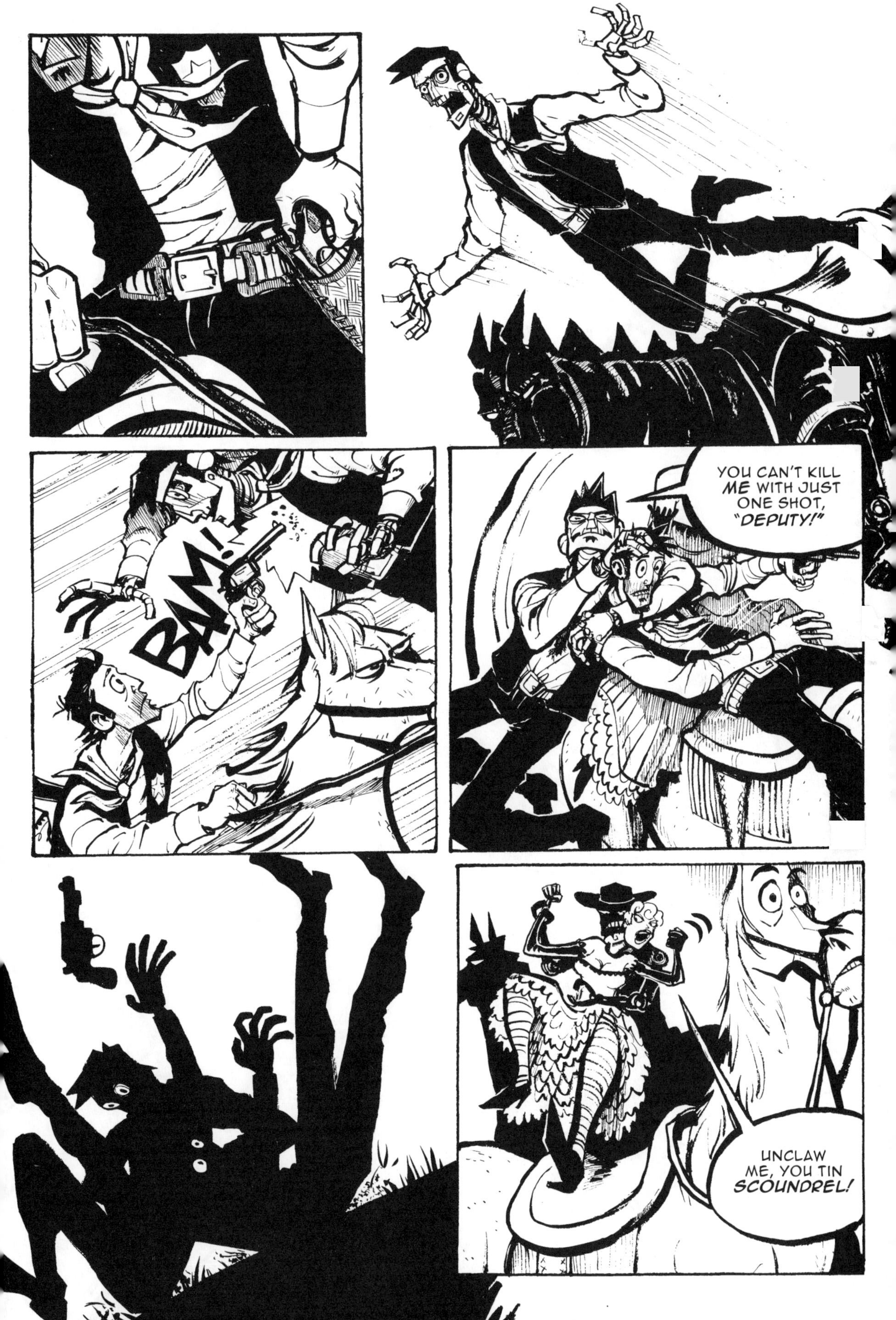
BAM!
YOU CAN'T KILL ME WITH JUST ONE SHOT, "DEPUTY!"
UNCLAW ME, YOU TIN SCOUNDREL!

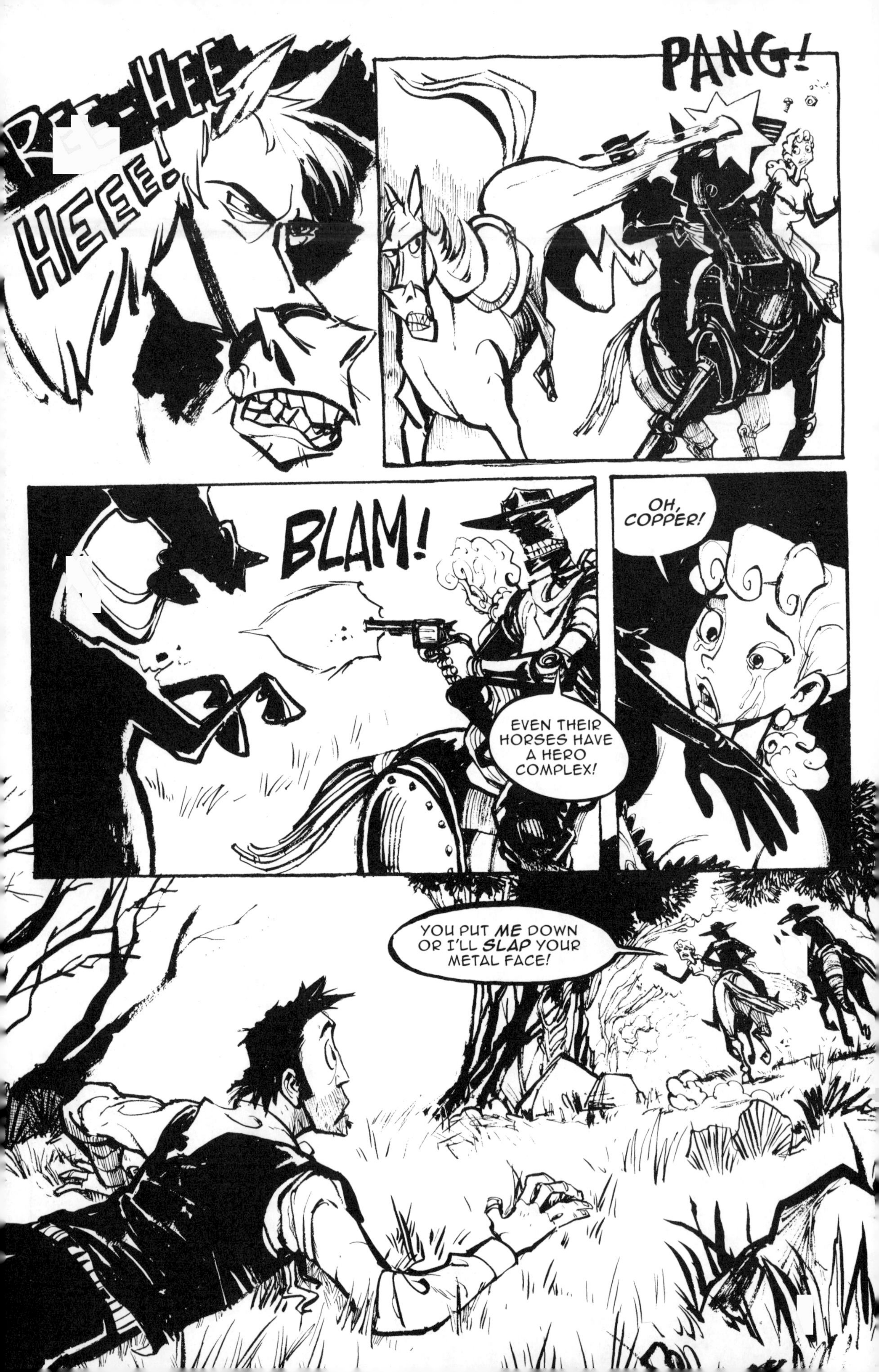
HEEEE!
PANG!
BLAM!
EVEN THEIR HORSES HAVE A HERO COMPLEX!
OH, COPPER!
YOU PUT *ME* DOWN OR I'LL *SLAP* YOUR METAL FACE!

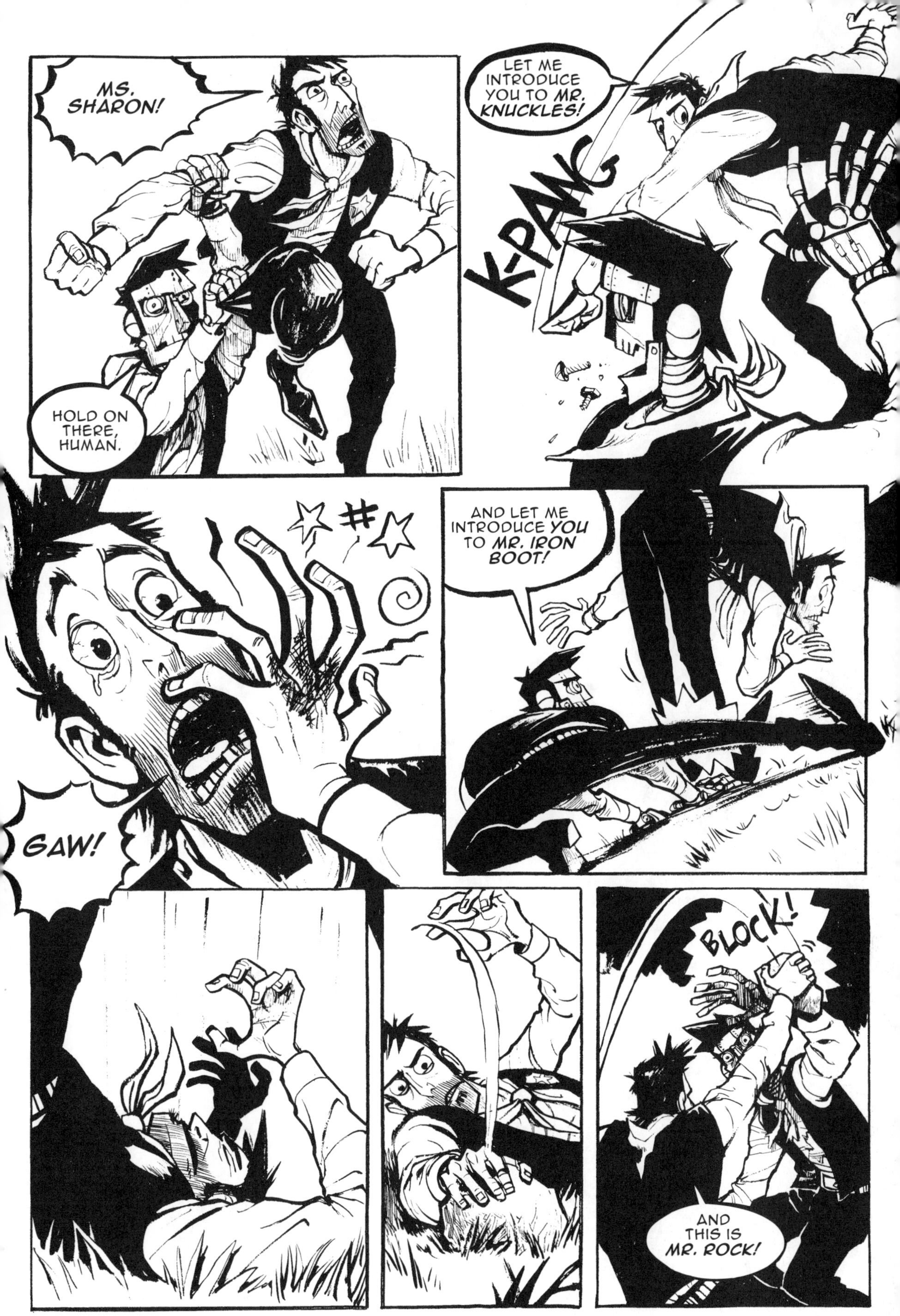
MS. SHARON!
HOLD ON THERE, HUMAN.
LET ME INTRODUCE YOU TO MR. KNUCKLES!
K-PANG
GAW!
AND LET ME INTRODUCE YOU TO MR. IRON BOOT!
BLOCK!
AND THIS IS MR. ROCK!

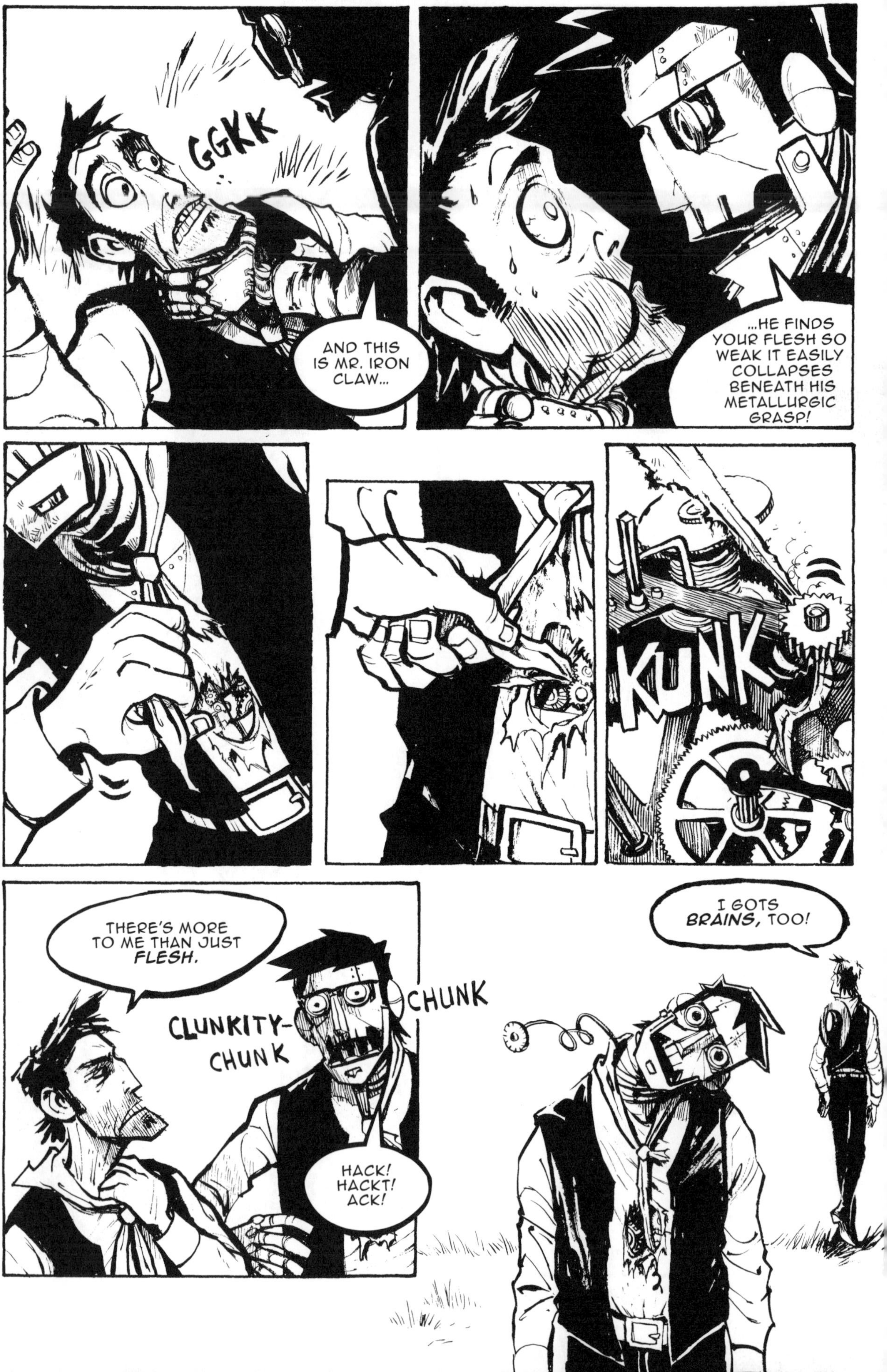
GGKK
AND THIS IS MR. IRON CLAW...
...HE FINDS YOUR FLESH SO WEAK IT EASILY COLLAPSES BENEATH HIS METALLURGIC GRASP!
KUNK
THERE'S MORE TO ME THAN JUST FLESH.
CLUNKITY-CHUNK
CHUNK
HACK! HACKT! ACK!
I GOTS BRAINS, TOO!

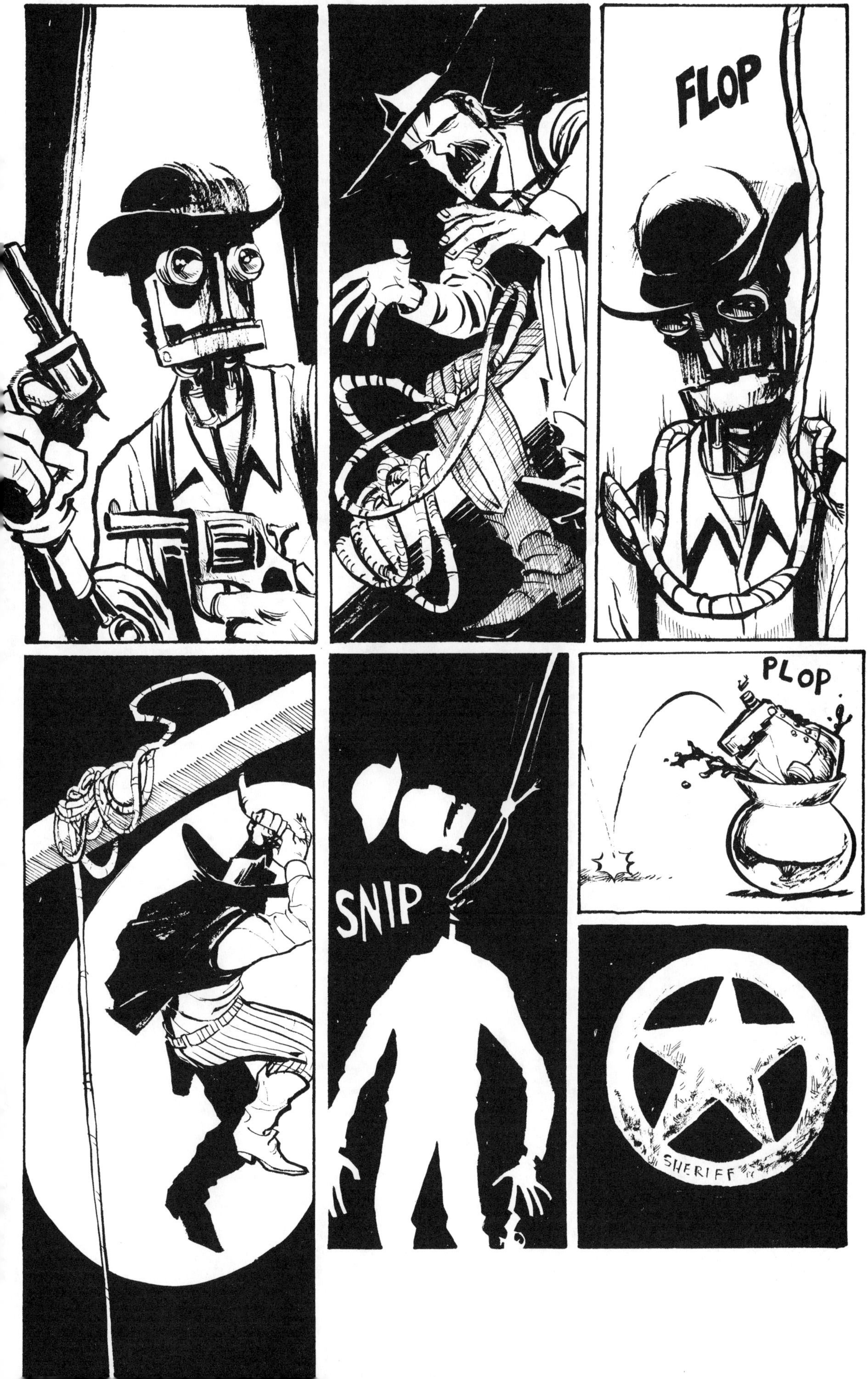
FLOP
SNIP
PLOP.
SHERIFF

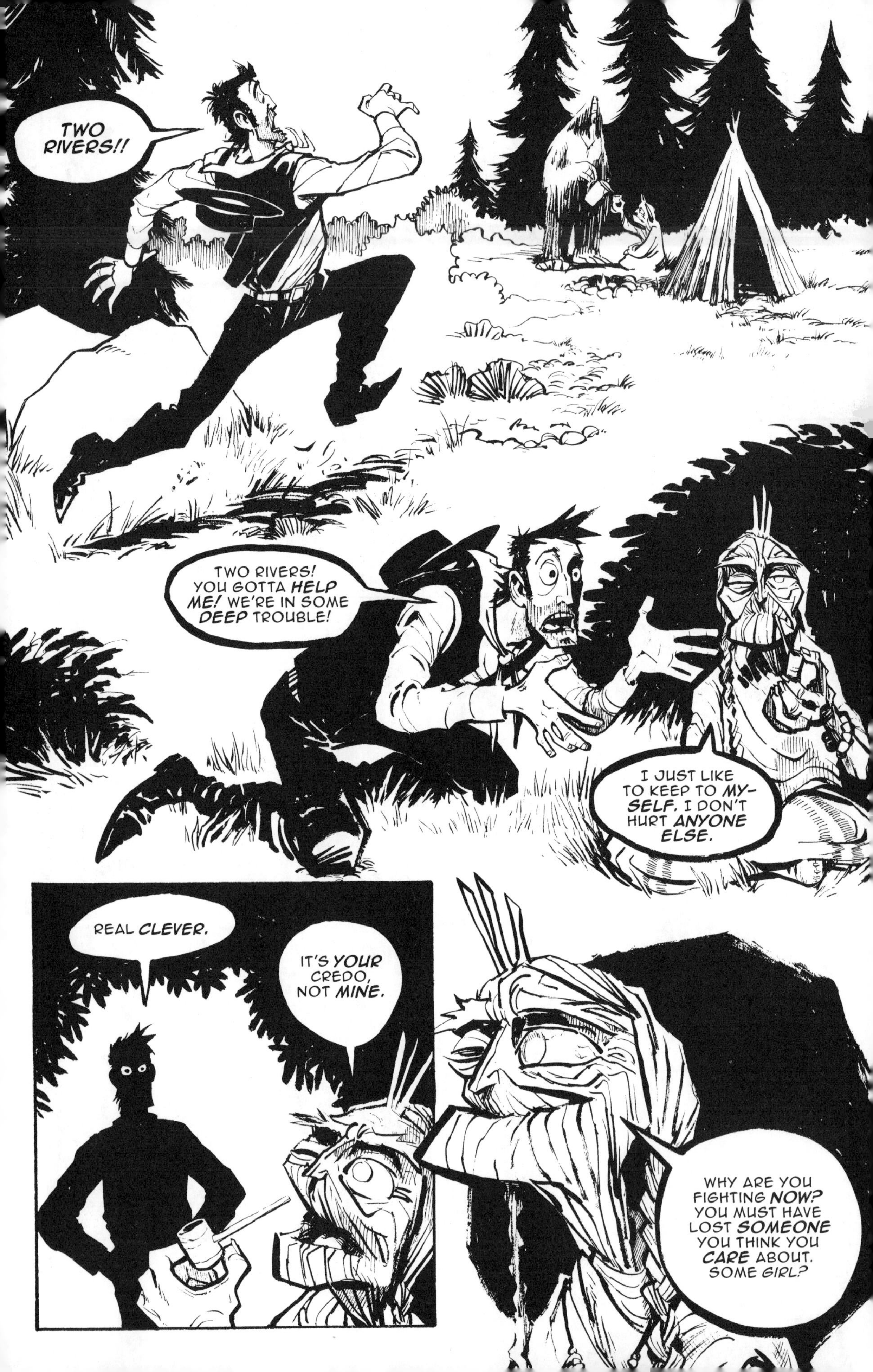
TWO RIVERS!!
TWO RIVERS! YOU GOTTA HELP ME! WE'RE IN SOME DEEP TROUBLE!
I JUST LIKE TO KEEP TO MY-SELF. I DON'T HURT ANYONE ELSE.
REAL CLEVER.
IT'S YOUR CREDO, NOT MINE.
WHY ARE YOU FIGHTING NOW? YOU MUST HAVE LOST SOMEONE YOU THINK YOU CARE ABOUT. SOME GIRL?

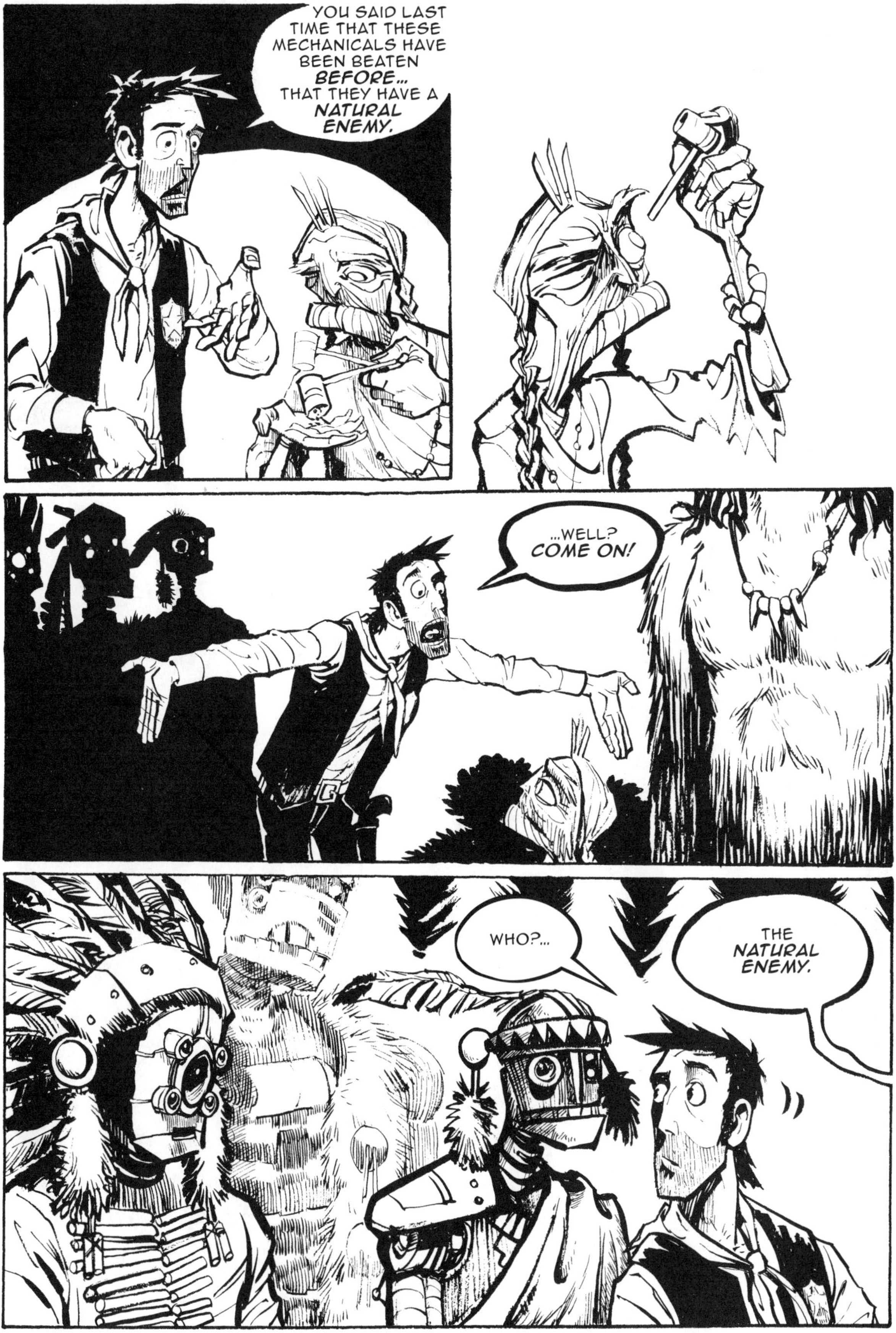
YOU SAID LAST TIME THAT THESE MECHANICALS HAVE BEEN BEATEN BEFORE... THAT THEY HAVE A NATURAL ENEMY.
...WELL? COME ON!
WHO?...
THE NATURAL ENEMY.

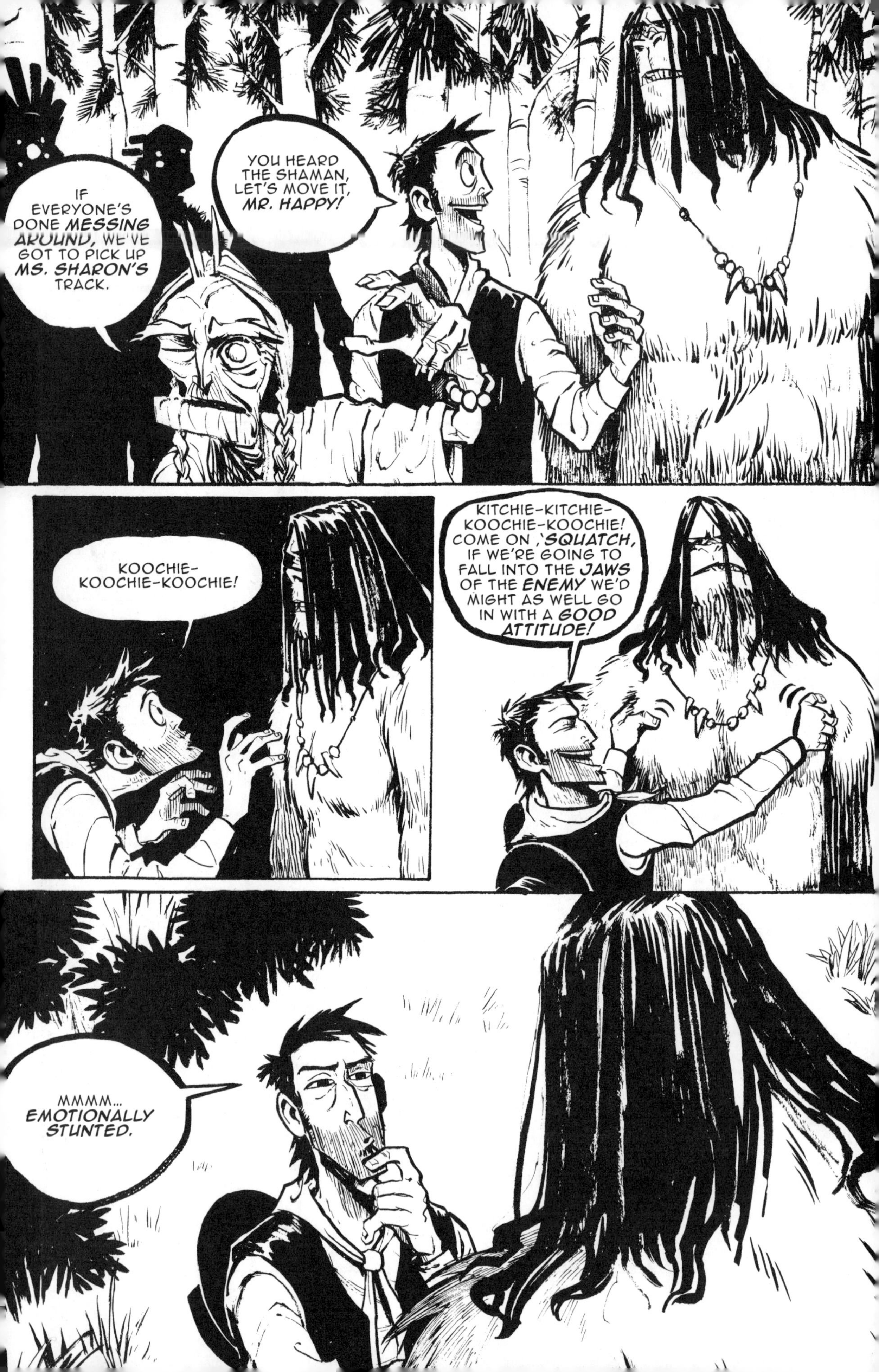
IF EVERYONE'S DONE MESSING AROUND, WE'VE GOT TO PICK UP MS. SHARON'S TRACK.
YOU HEARD THE SHAMAN, LET'S MOVE IT, MR. HAPPY!
KOOCHIE-KOOCHIE-KOOCHIE!
KITCHIE-KITCHIE-KOOCHIE-KOOCHIE! COME ON, 'SQUATCH, IF WE'RE GOING TO FALL INTO THE JAWS OF THE ENEMY WE'D MIGHT AS WELL GO IN WITH A GOOD ATTITUDE!
MMMM... EMOTIONALLY STUNTED.

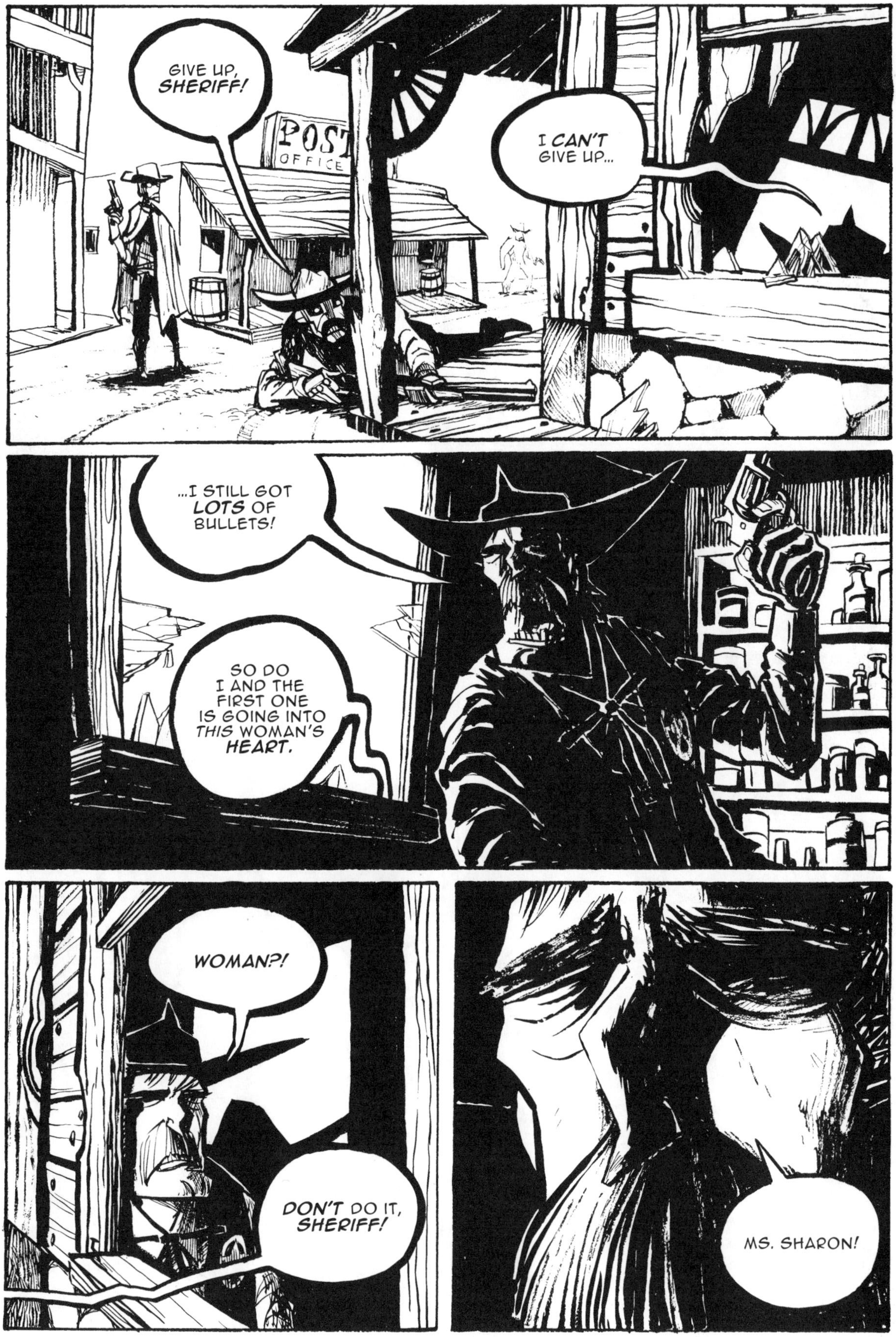
POST OFFICE
GIVE UP, SHERIFF!
I CAN'T GIVE UP...
...I STILL GOT LOTS OF BULLETS!
SO DO I AND THE FIRST ONE IS GOING INTO THIS WOMAN'S HEART.
WOMAN?!
DON'T DO IT, SHERIFF!
MS. SHARON!

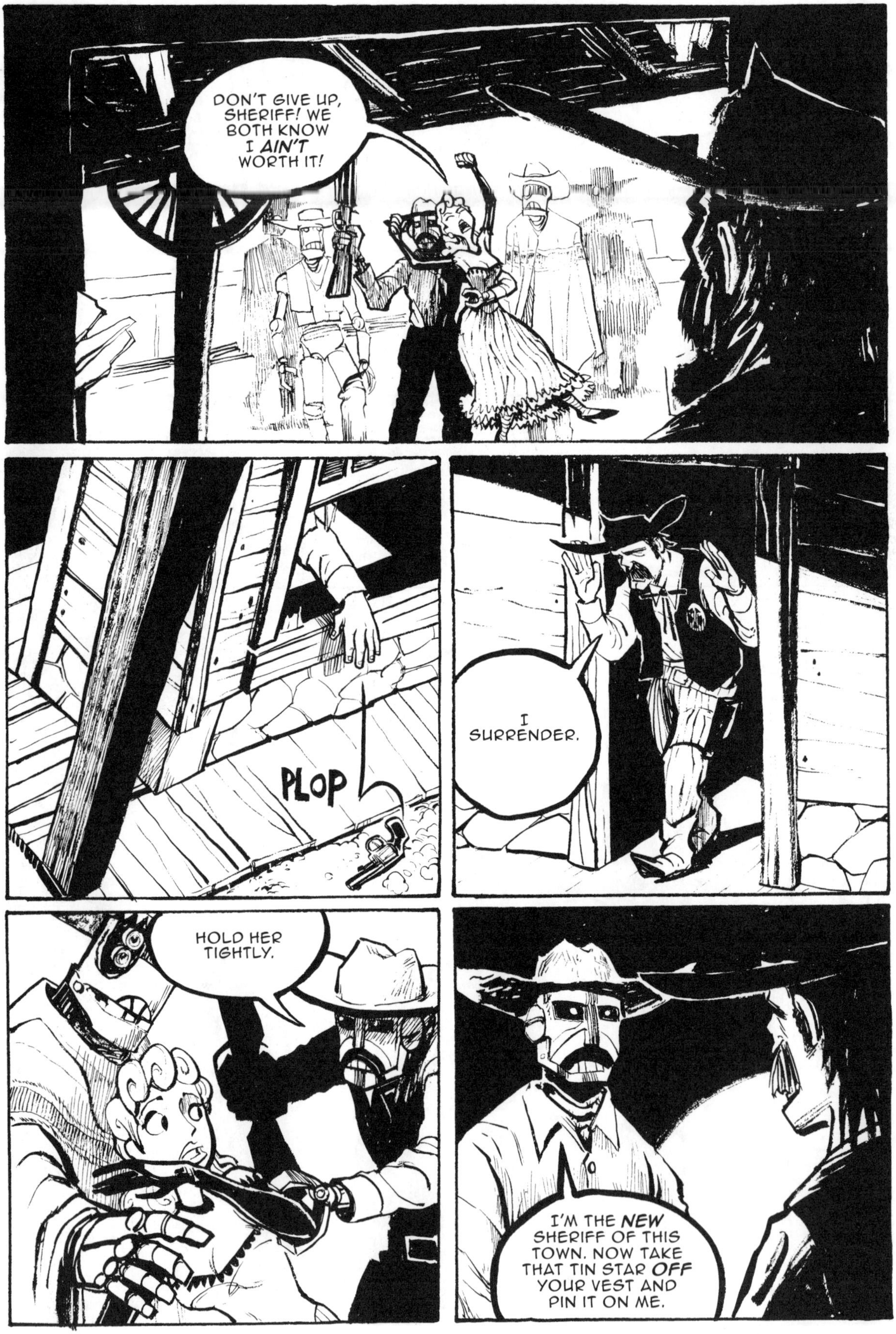
DON'T GIVE UP, SHERIFF! WE BOTH KNOW I AIN'T WORTH IT!
PLOP
I SURRENDER.
HOLD HER TIGHTLY.
I'M THE NEW SHERIFF OF THIS TOWN. NOW TAKE THAT TIN STAR OFF YOUR VEST AND PIN IT ON ME.

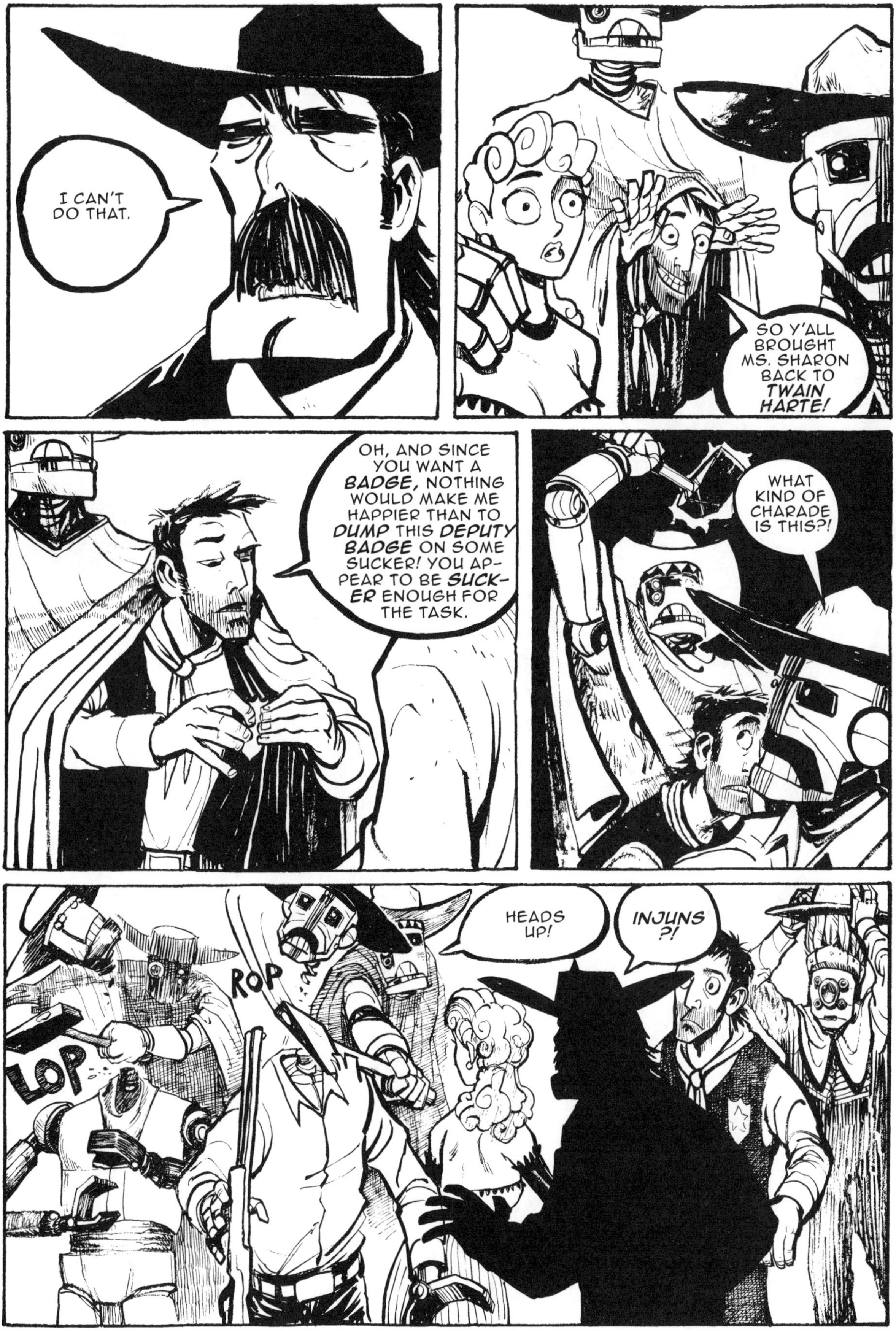
I CAN'T DO THAT.
SO Y'ALL BROUGHT MS. SHARON BACK TO TWAIN HARTE!
OH, AND SINCE YOU WANT A BADGE, NOTHING WOULD MAKE ME HAPPIER THAN TO DUMP THIS DEPUTY BADGE ON SOME SUCKER! YOU APPEAR TO BE SUCKER ENOUGH FOR THE TASK.
WHAT KIND OF CHARADE IS THIS?!
HEADS UP!
INJUNS ?!
ROP
LOP

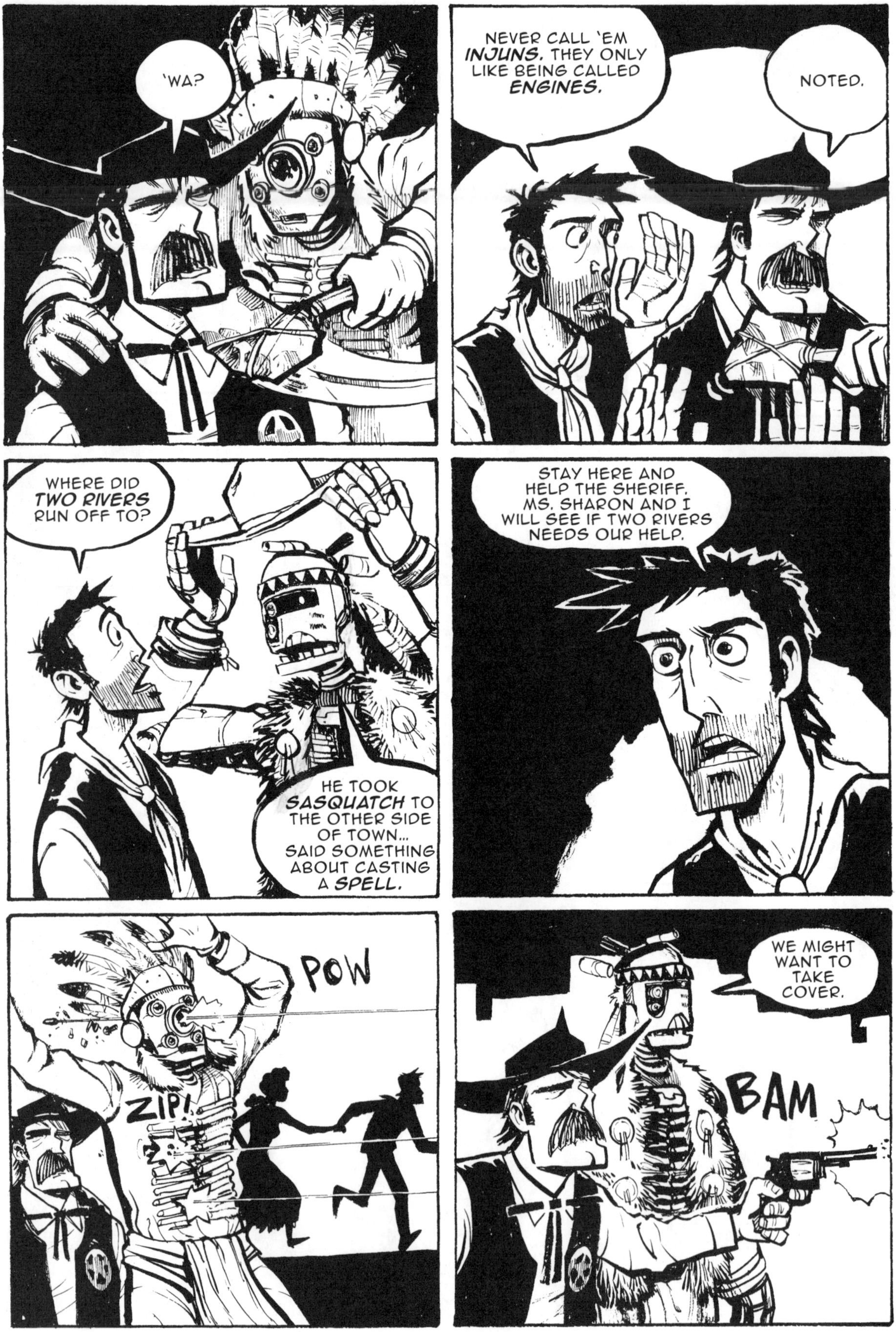
'WA?
NEVER CALL 'EM INJUNS. THEY ONLY LIKE BEING CALLED ENGINES.
NOTED.
WHERE DID TWO RIVERS RUN OFF TO?
HE TOOK SASQUATCH TO THE OTHER SIDE OF TOWN... SAID SOMETHING ABOUT CASTING A SPELL.
STAY HERE AND HELP THE SHERIFF. MS. SHARON AND I WILL SEE IF TWO RIVERS NEEDS OUR HELP.
POW
ZIP!
WE MIGHT WANT TO TAKE COVER.
BAM

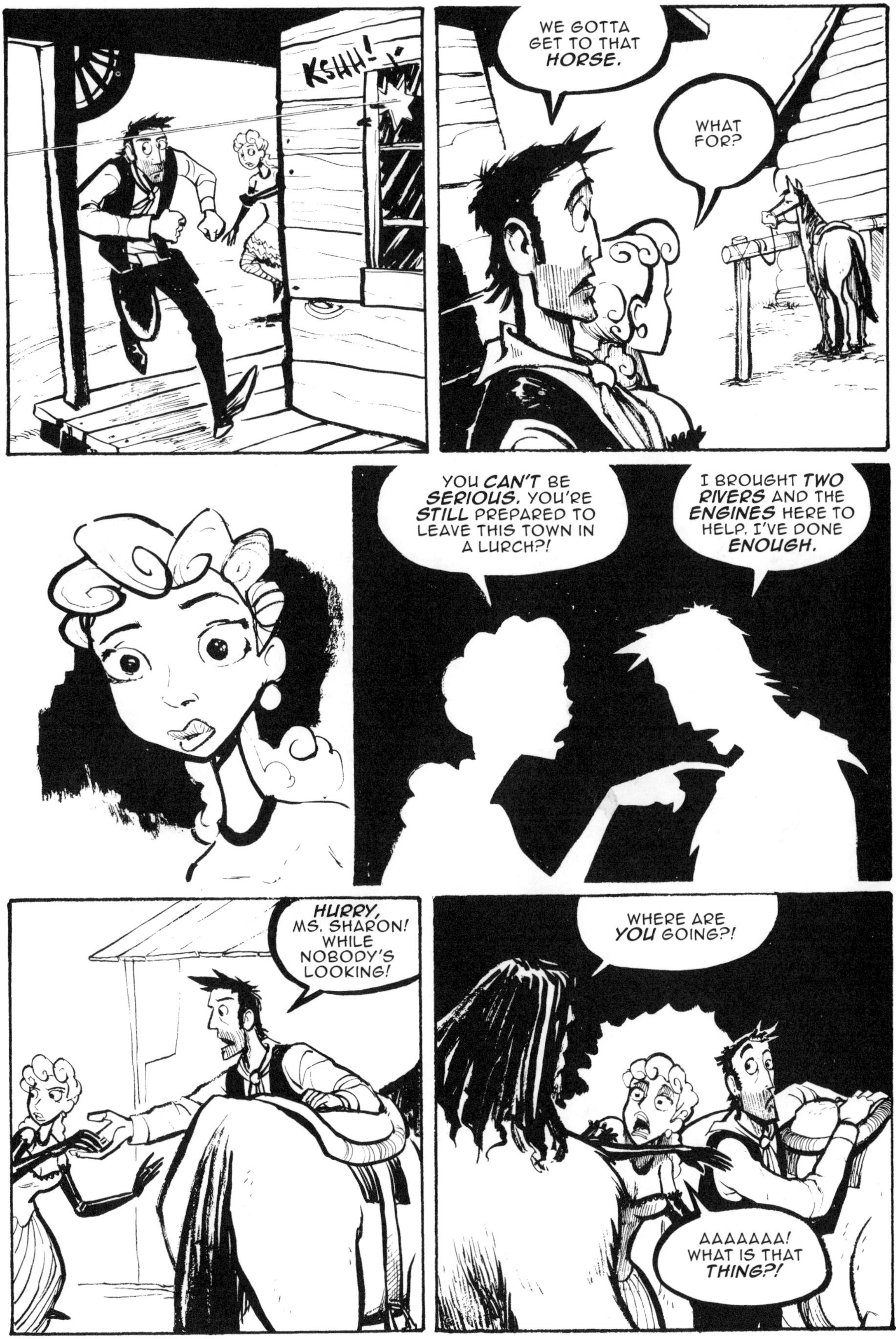
KSHH!
WE GOTTA GET TO THAT HORSE.
WHAT FOR?
YOU CAN'T BE SERIOUS. YOU'RE STILL PREPARED TO LEAVE THIS TOWN IN A LURCH?!
I BROUGHT TWO RIVERS AND THE ENGINES HERE TO HELP. I'VE DONE ENOUGH.
HURRY, MS. SHARON! WHILE NOBODY'S LOOKING!
WHERE ARE YOU GOING?!
AAAAAAA! WHAT IS THAT THING?!

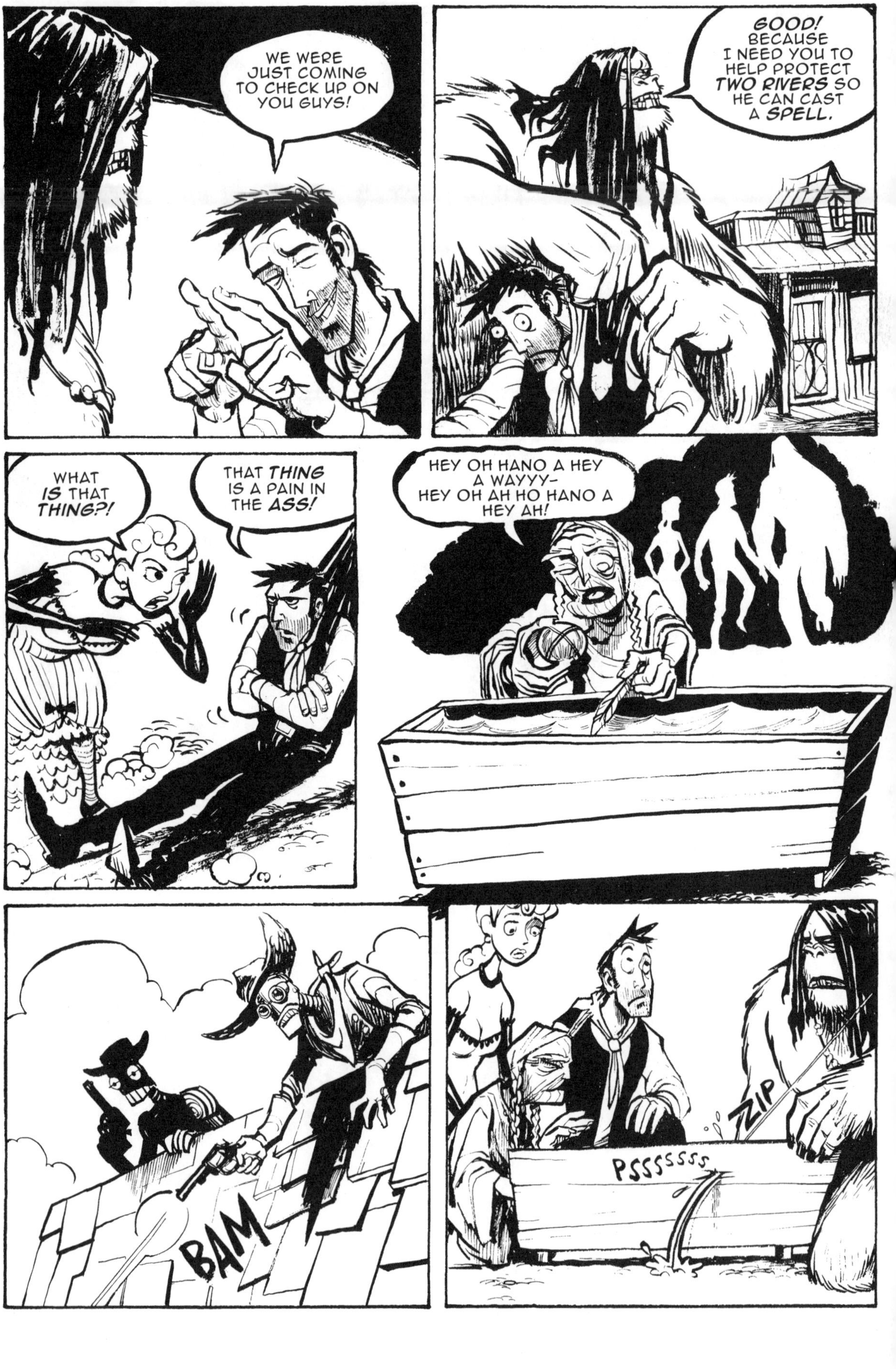
WE WERE JUST COMING TO CHECK UP ON YOU GUYS!
GOOD! BECAUSE I NEED YOU TO HELP PROTECT TWO RIVERS SO HE CAN CAST A SPELL.
WHAT IS THAT THING?!
THAT THING IS A PAIN IN THE ASS!
HEY OH HANO A HEY A WAYYY- HEY OH AH HO HANO A HEY AH!
BAM
ZIP
PSSSSSSS

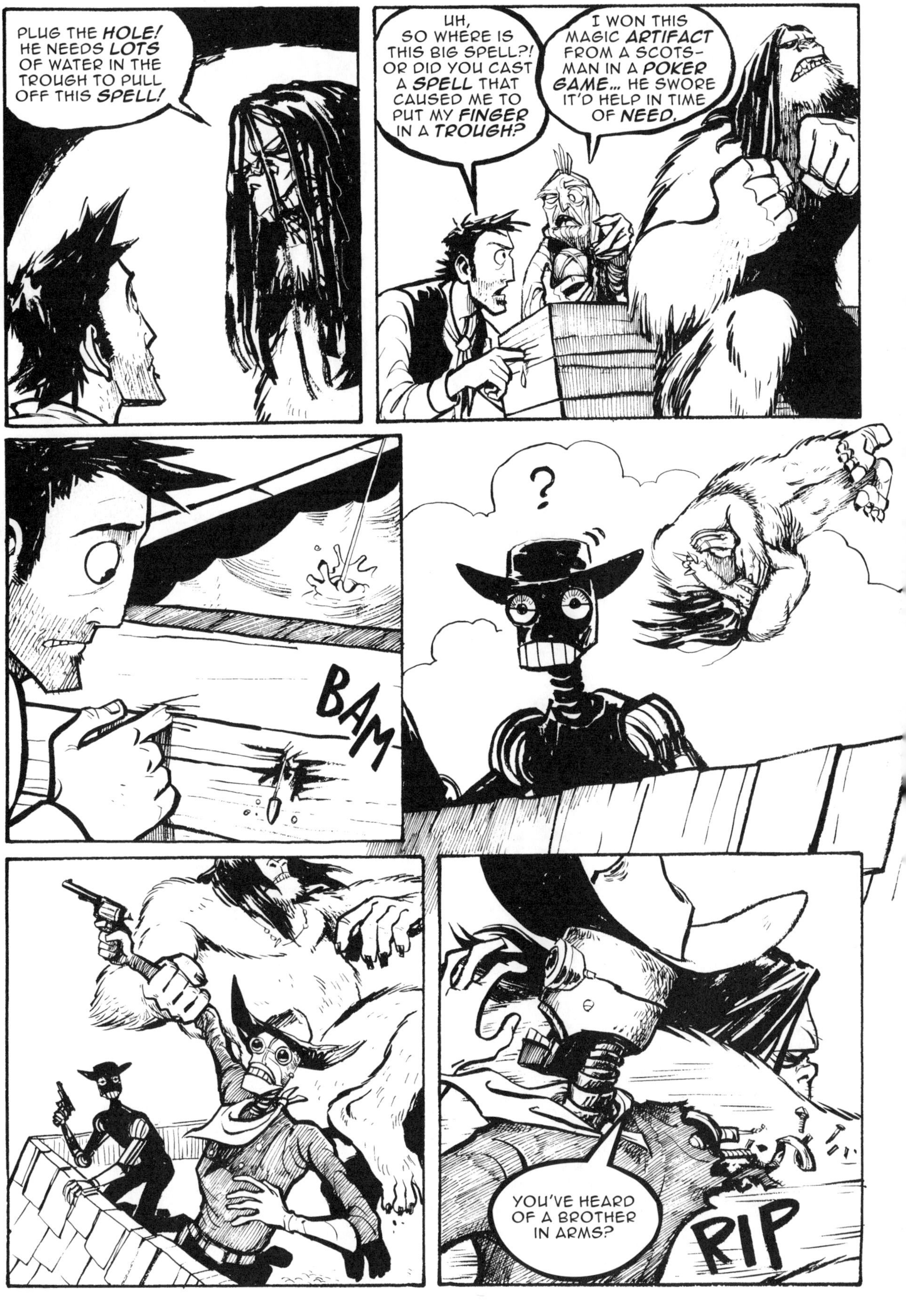
PLUG THE HOLE! HE NEEDS LOTS OF WATER IN THE TROUGH TO PULL OFF THIS SPELL!
UH, SO WHERE IS THIS BIG SPELL?! OR DID YOU CAST A SPELL THAT CAUSED ME TO PUT MY FINGER IN A TROUGH?
I WON THIS MAGIC ARTIFACT FROM A SCOTS-MAN IN A POKER GAME... HE SWORE IT'D HELP IN TIME OF NEED.
BAM
?
YOU'VE HEARD OF A BROTHER IN ARMS?
RIP

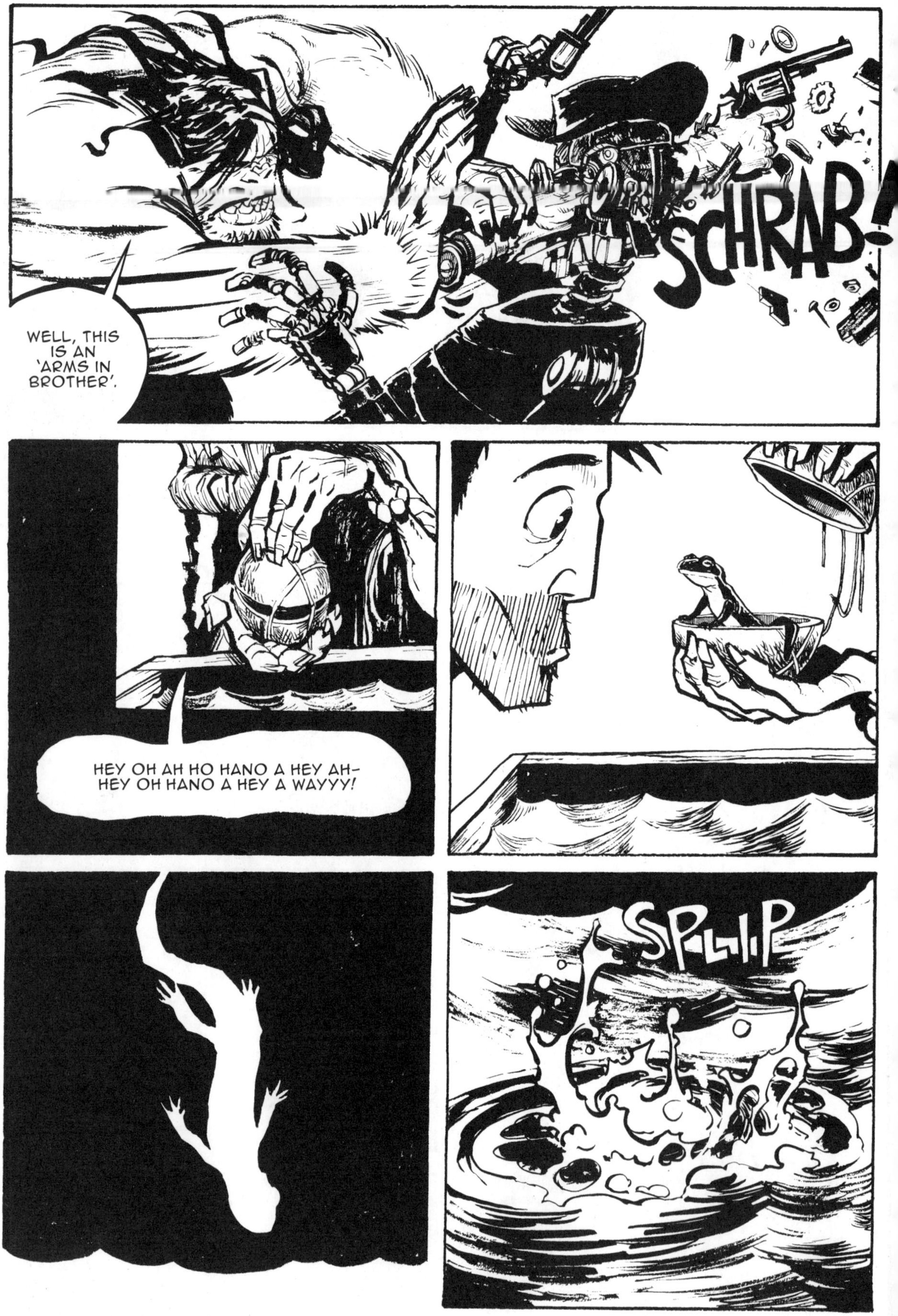
SCHRAB!
WELL, THIS IS AN 'ARMS IN BROTHER'.
HEY OH AH HO HANO A HEY AH-HEY OH HANO A HEY A WAYYY!
SPLIP

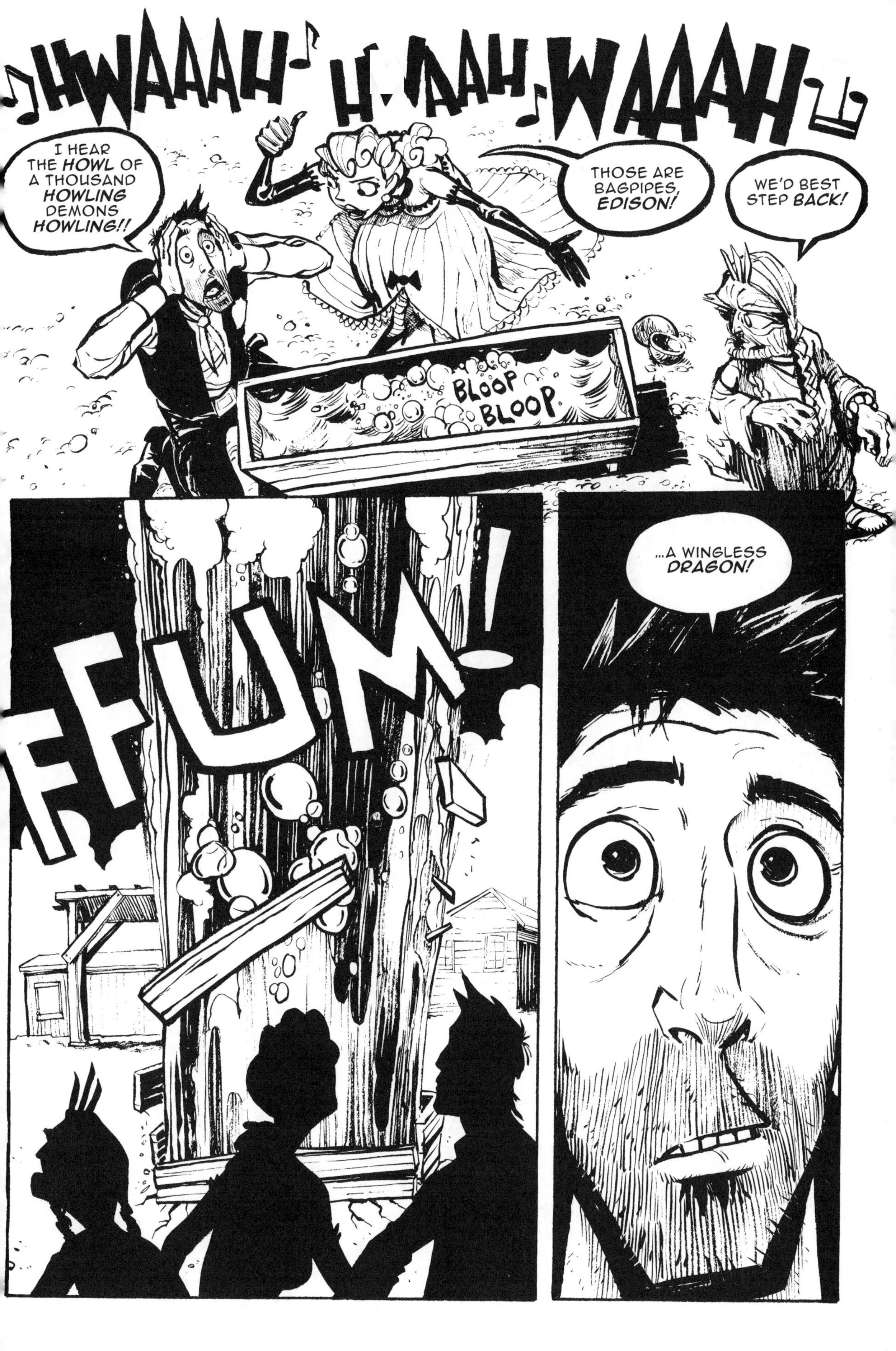
HWAAAH H WAAH WAAAH
I HEAR THE HOWL OF A THOUSAND HOWLING DEMONS HOWLING!!
THOSE ARE BAGPIPES, EDISON!
WE'D BEST STEP BACK!
BLOOP BLOOP
FFUM!
...A WINGLESS DRAGON!

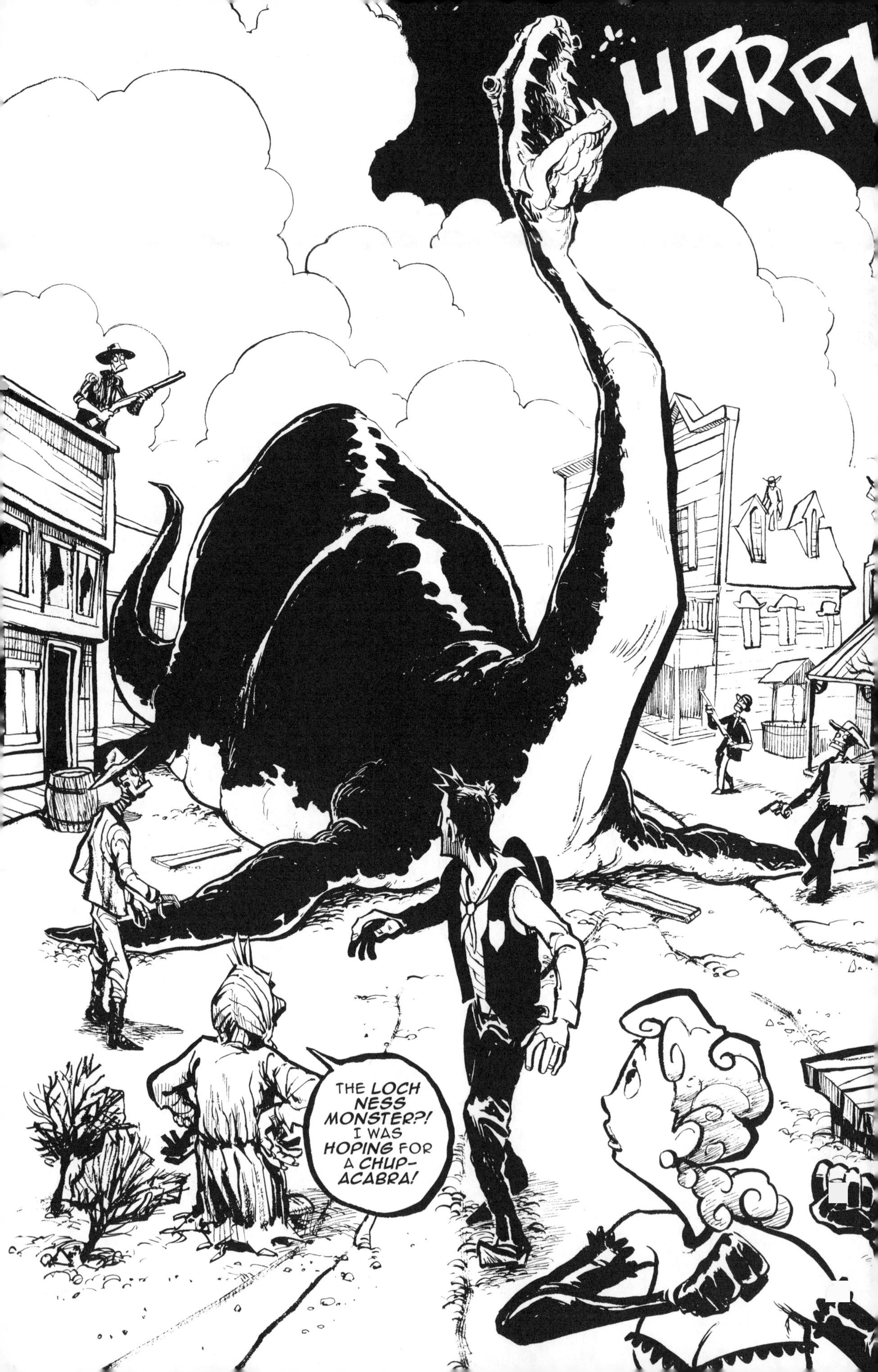
URRR
THE LOCH NESS MONSTER?! I WAS HOPING FOR A CHUP-ACABRA!

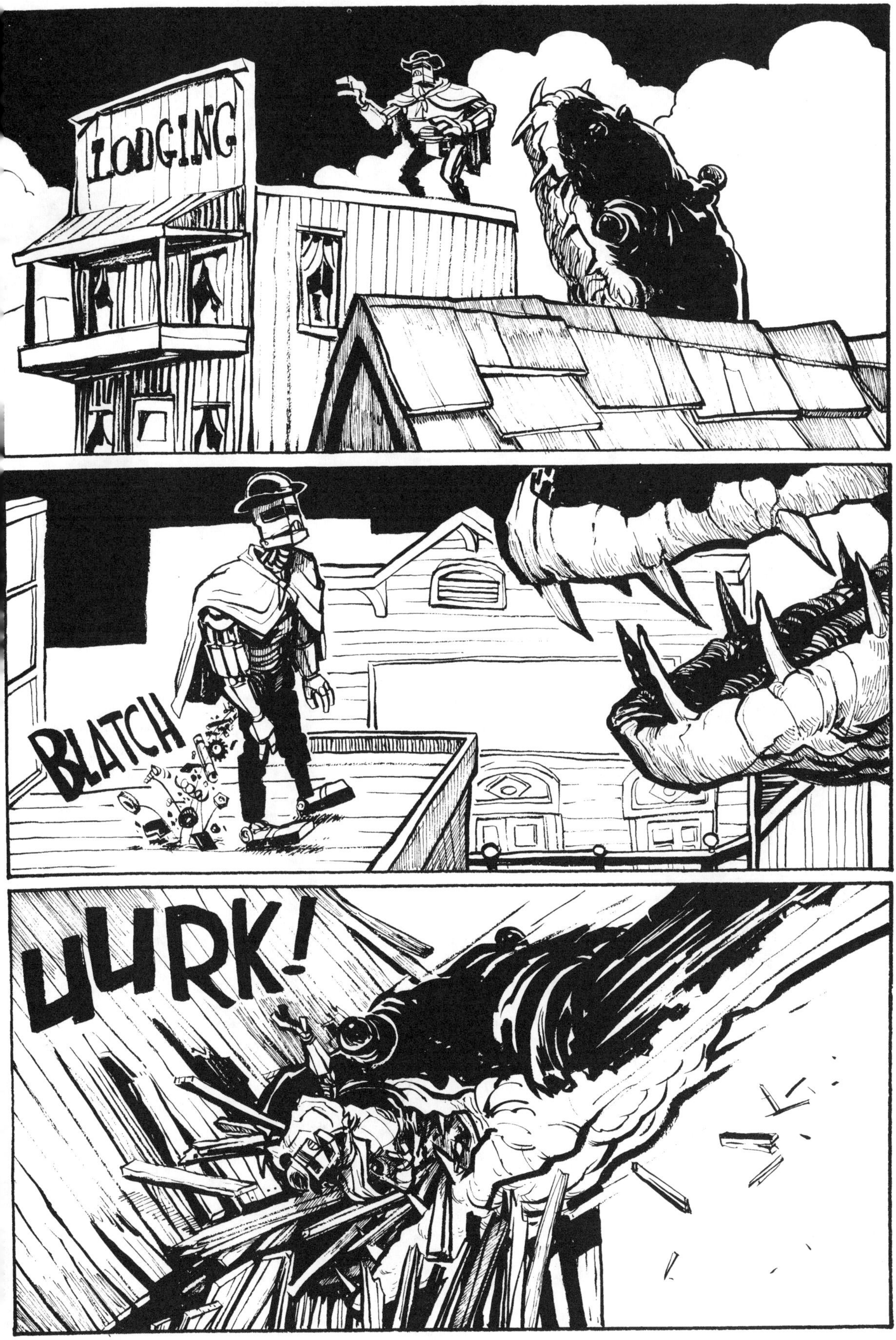
LODGING
BLATCH
UURK!

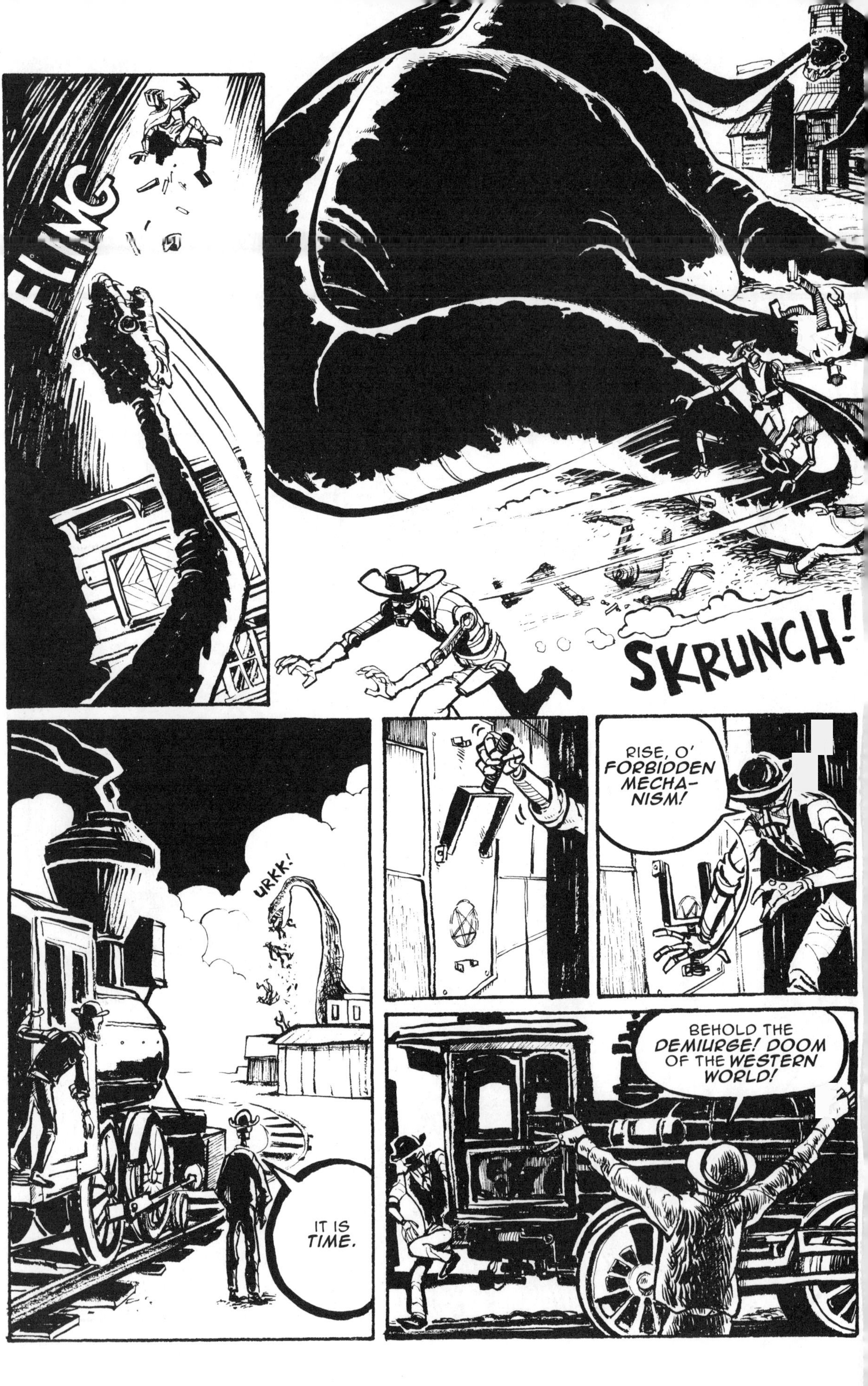
FLING
SKRUNCH!
URKK!
IT IS TIME.
RISE, O' FORBIDDEN MECHA-NISM!
BEHOLD THE DEMIURGE! DOOM OF THE WESTERN WORLD!

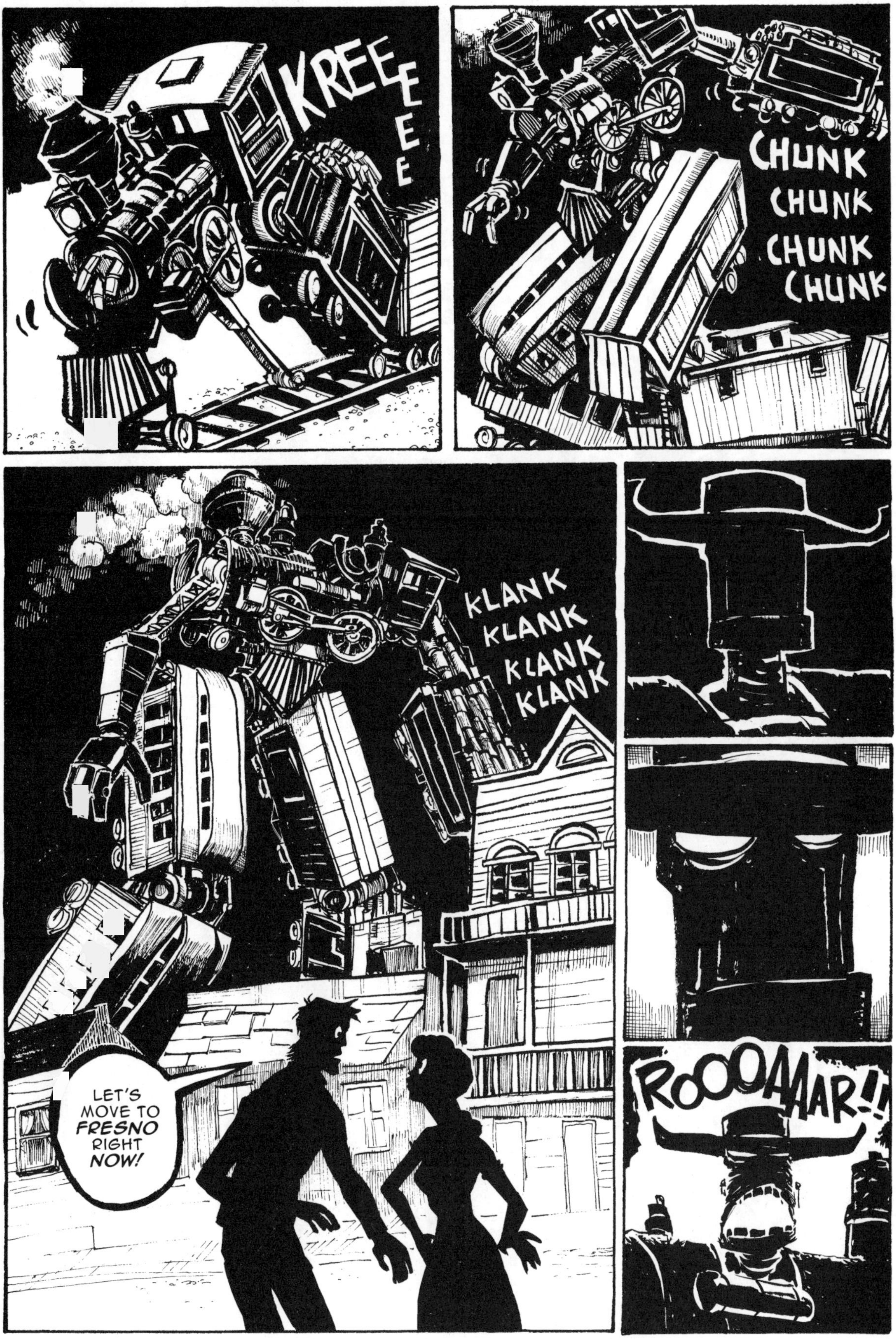
KREEEEE
CHUNK
CHUNK
CHUNK
CHUNK
KLANK
KLANK
KLANK
KLANK
LET'S MOVE TO FRESNO RIGHT NOW!
ROOOAAAR!!

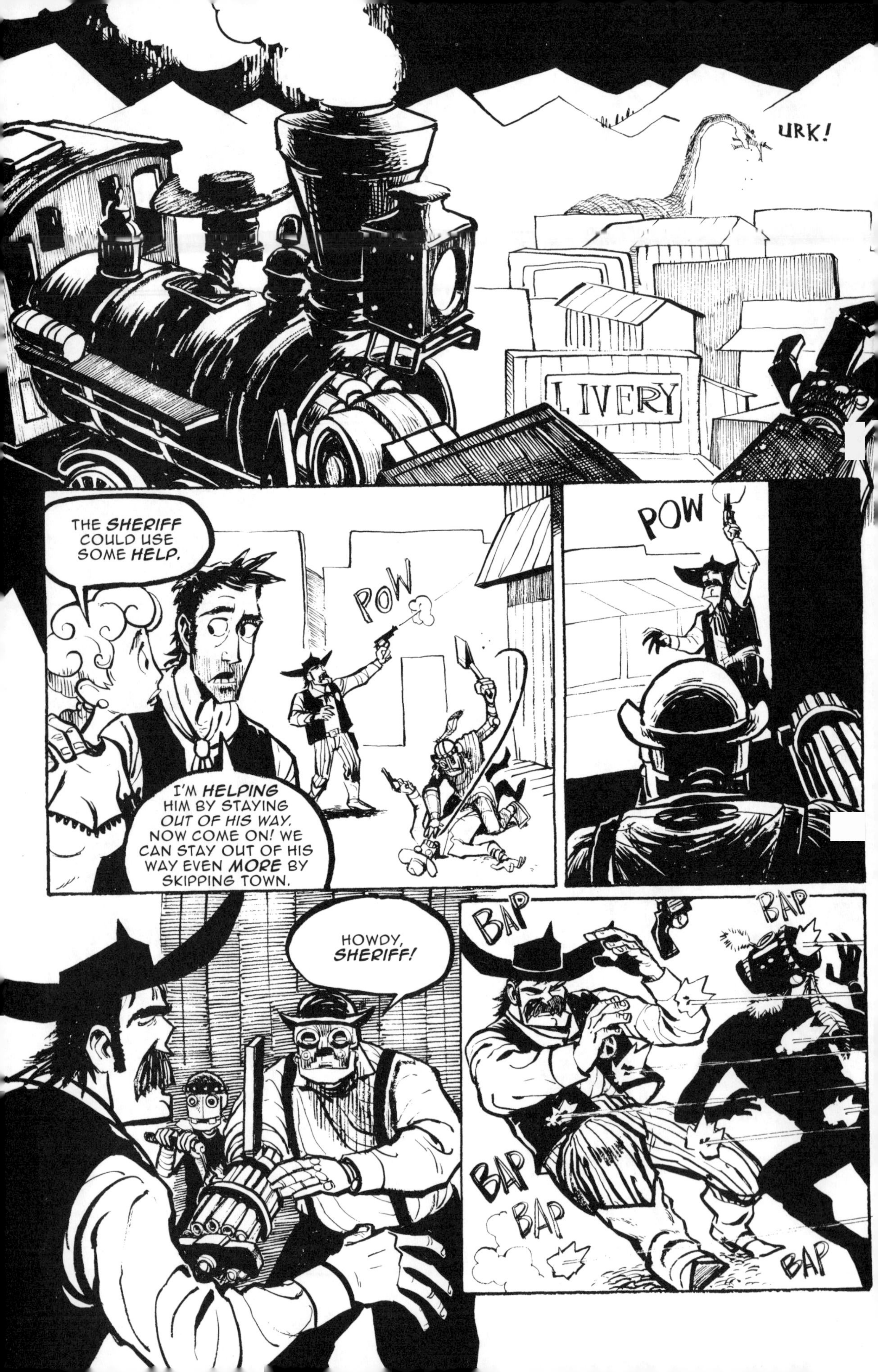
URK!
LIVERY
THE SHERIFF COULD USE SOME HELP.
POW
I'M HELPING HIM BY STAYING OUT OF HIS WAY. NOW COME ON! WE CAN STAY OUT OF HIS WAY EVEN MORE BY SKIPPING TOWN.
POW
HOWDY, SHERIFF!
BAP
BAP
BAP
BAP
BAP

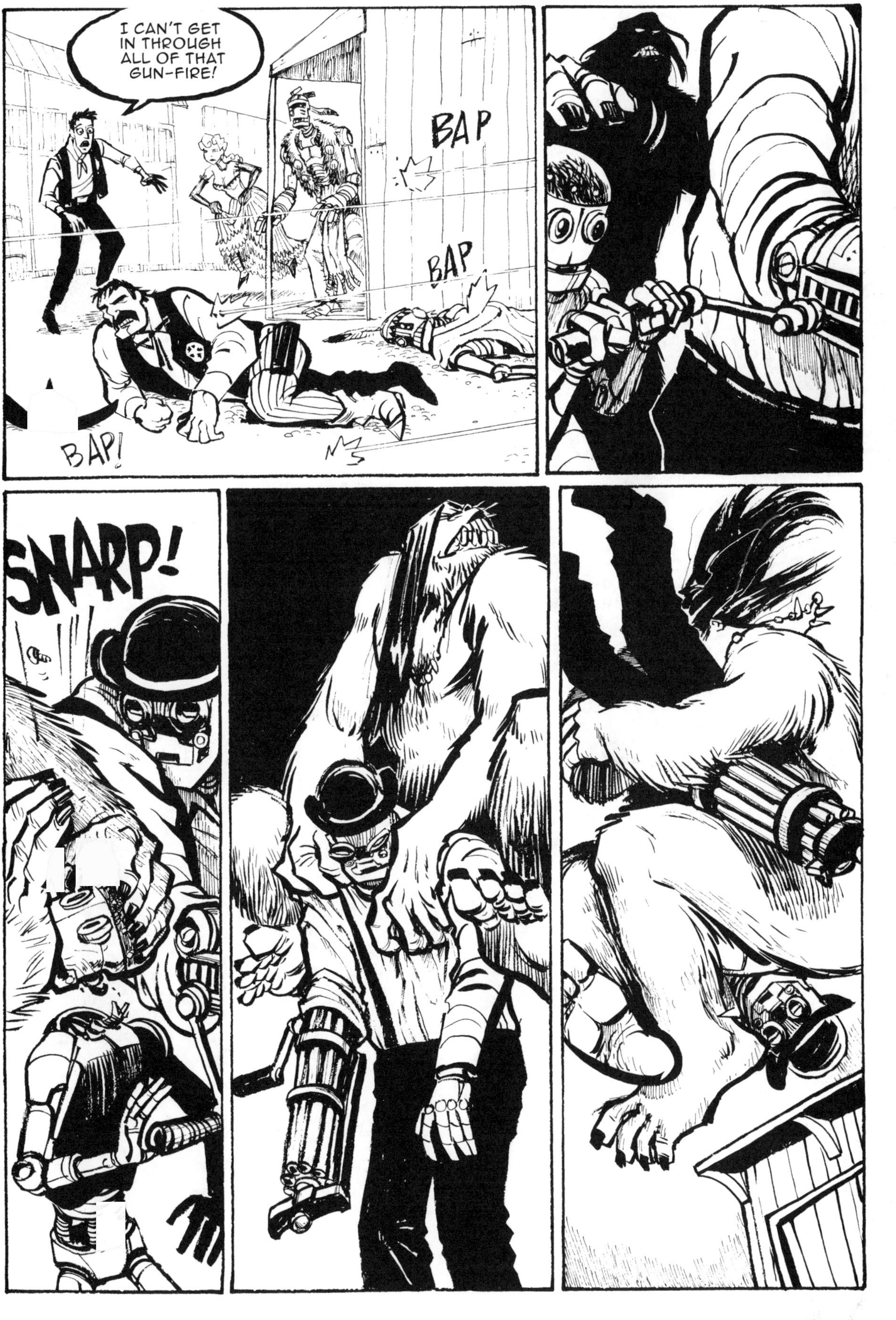
I CAN'T GET IN THROUGH ALL OF THAT GUN-FIRE!
BAP
BAP
BAP!
SNARP!

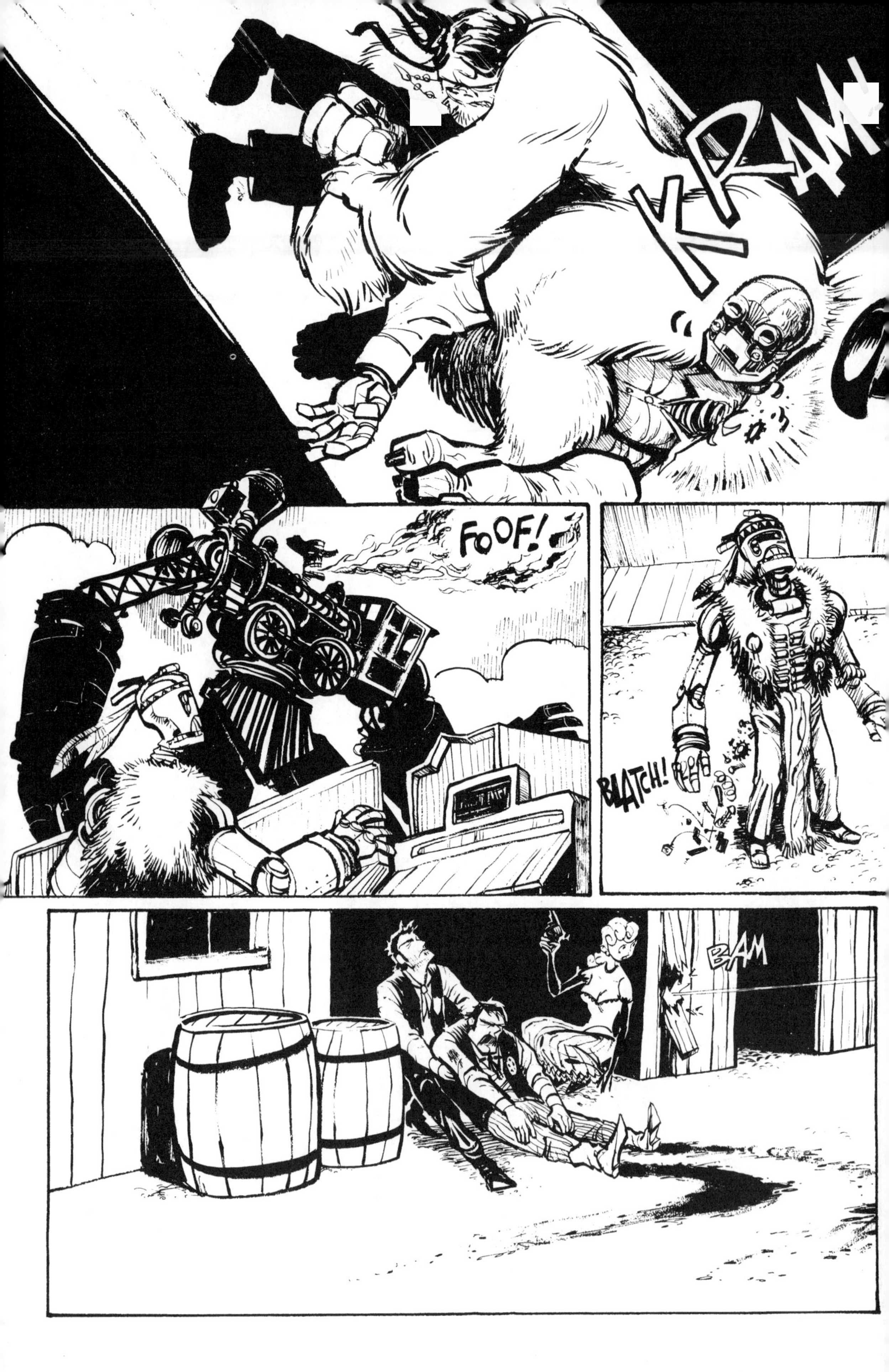

KRAM!
FOOF!
BLATCH!
BAM

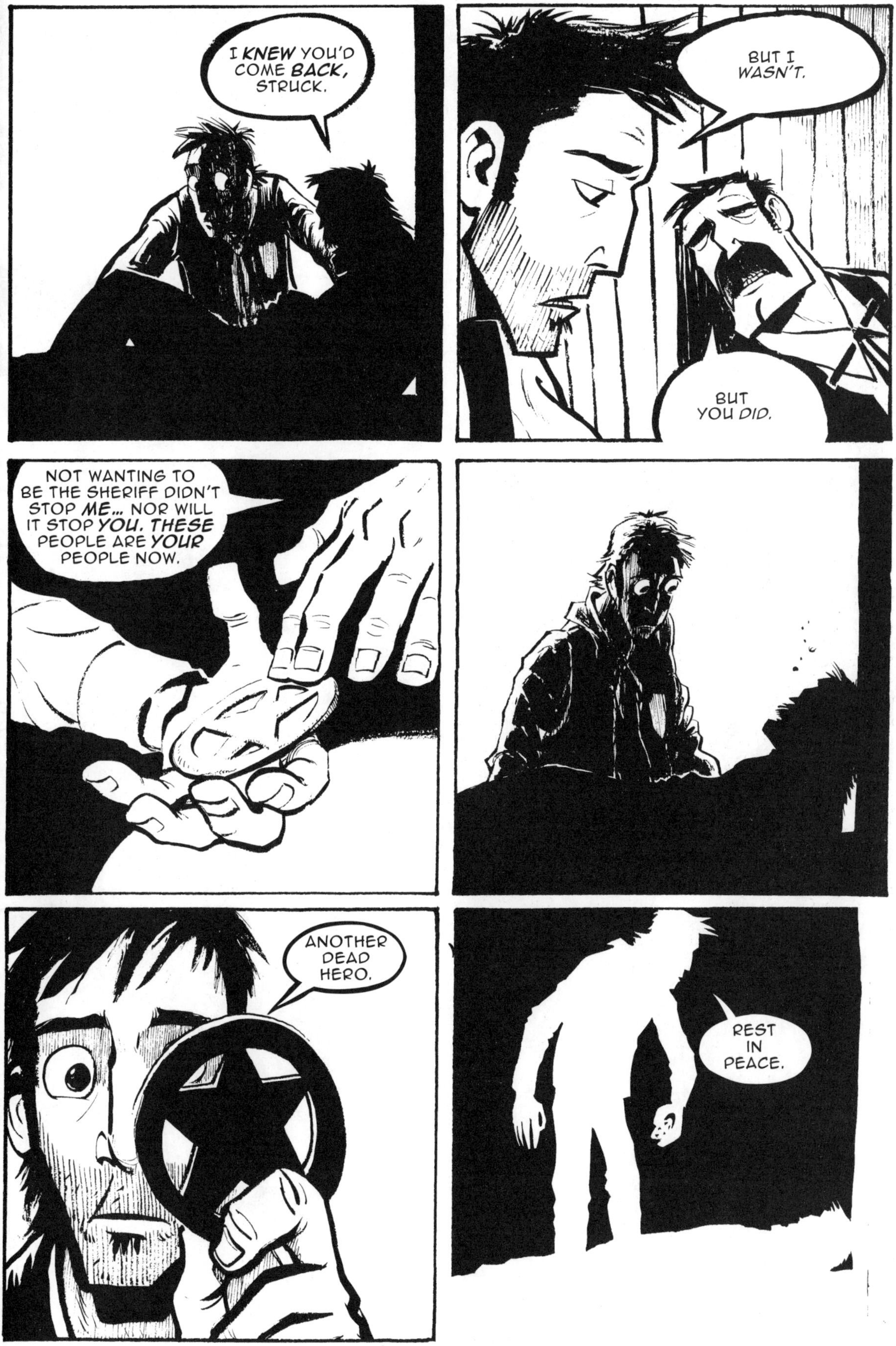
I KNEW YOU'D COME BACK, STRUCK.
BUT I WASN'T.
BUT YOU DID.
NOT WANTING TO BE THE SHERIFF DIDN'T STOP ME... NOR WILL IT STOP YOU. THESE PEOPLE ARE YOUR PEOPLE NOW.
ANOTHER DEAD HERO.
REST IN PEACE.

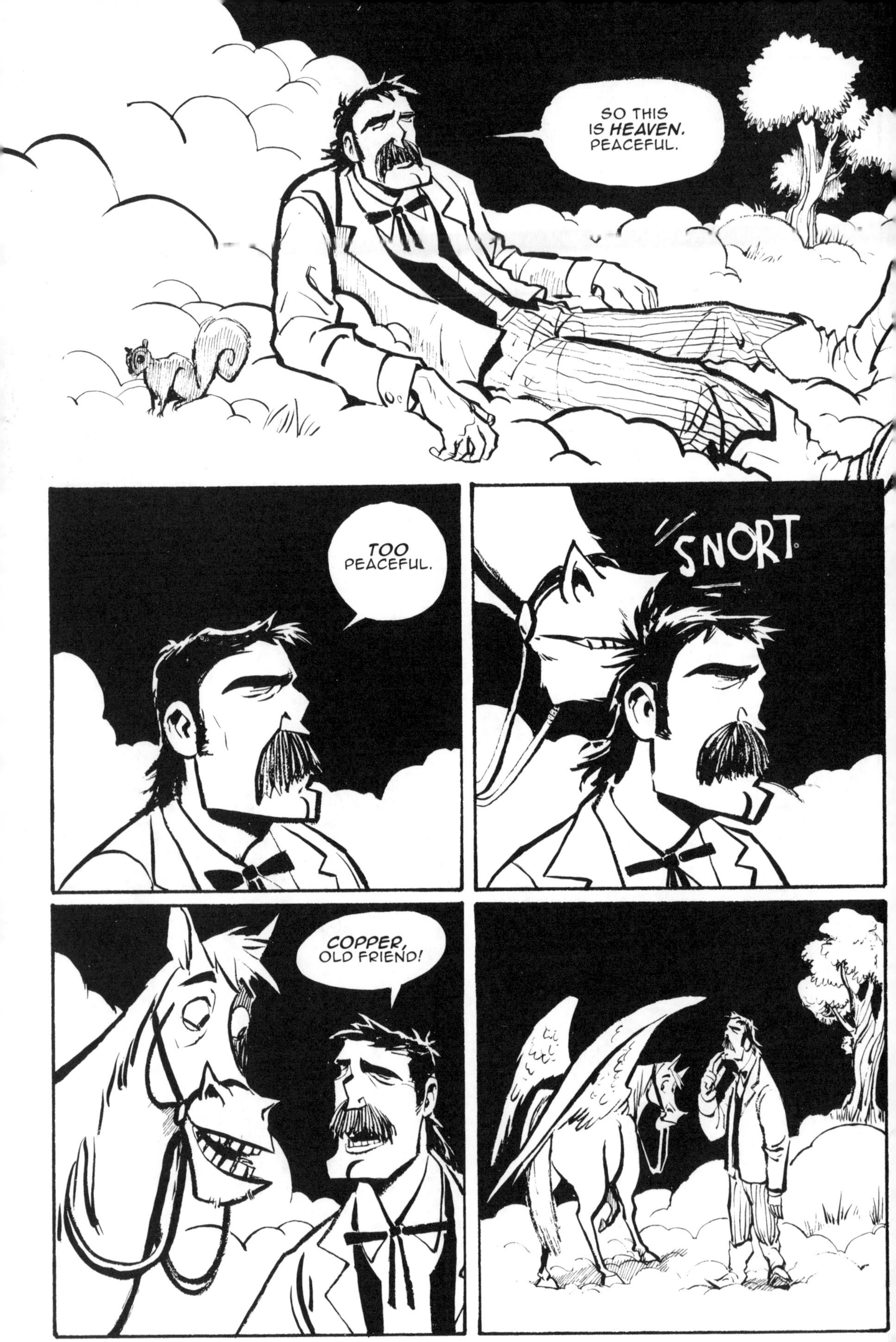
SO THIS IS HEAVEN. PEACEFUL.
TOO PEACEFUL.
SNORT.
COPPER, OLD FRIEND!

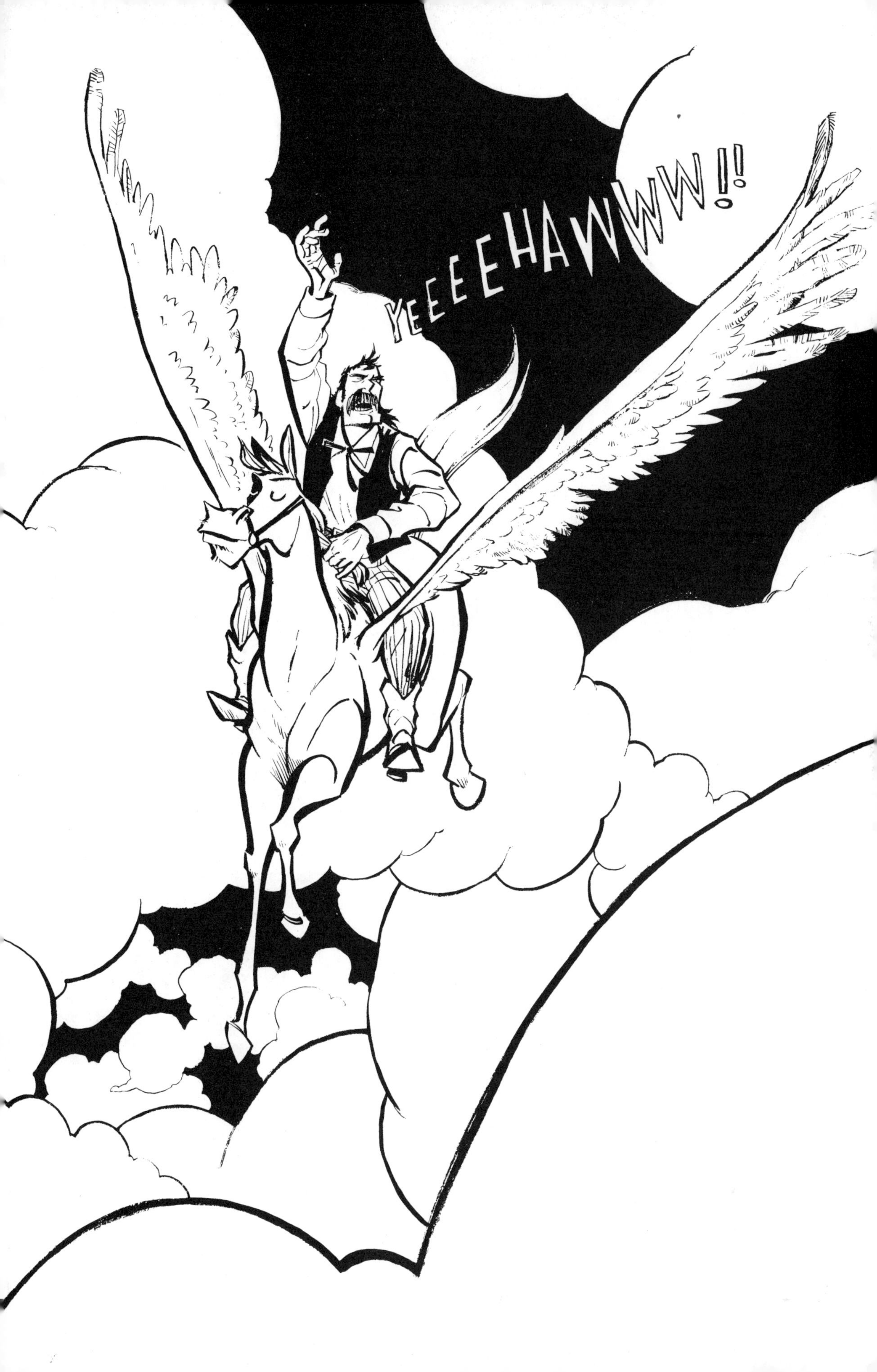
YEEEEHAWWWW!!

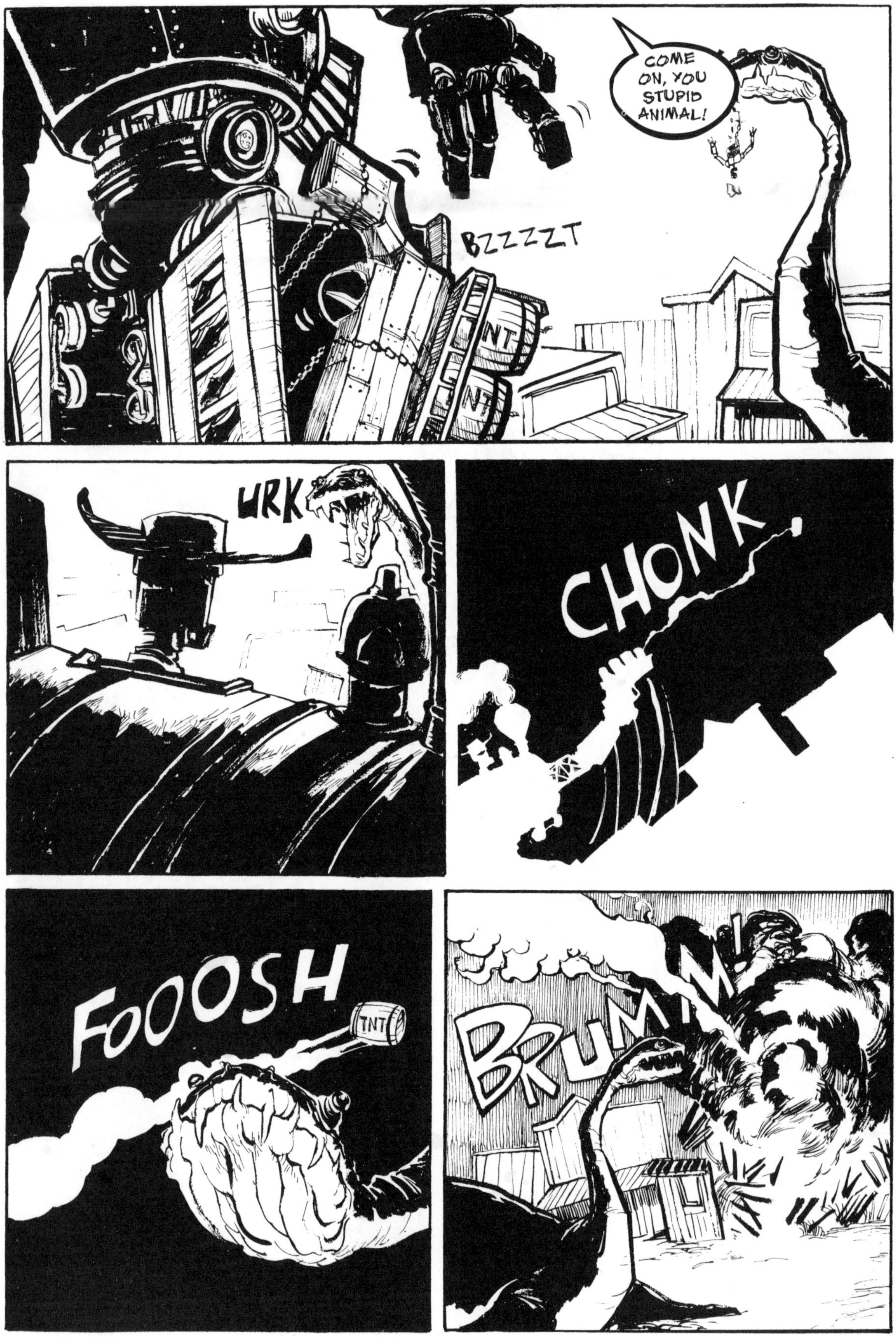
COME ON, YOU STUPID ANIMAL!
BZZZZT
URK
CHONK
FOOOSH
TNT
BRUMM!

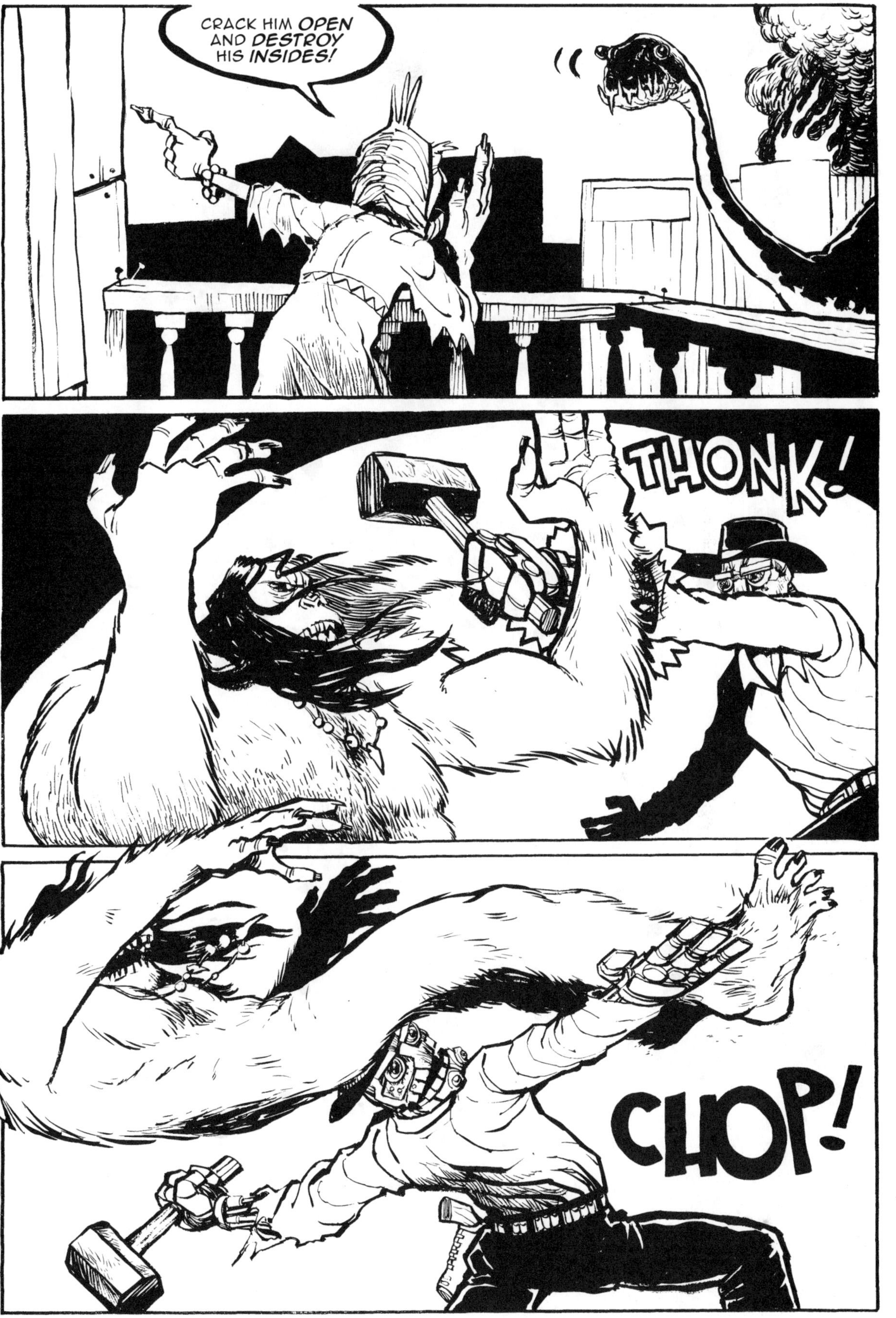
CRACK HIM OPEN AND DESTROY HIS INSIDES!
THONK!
CHOP!

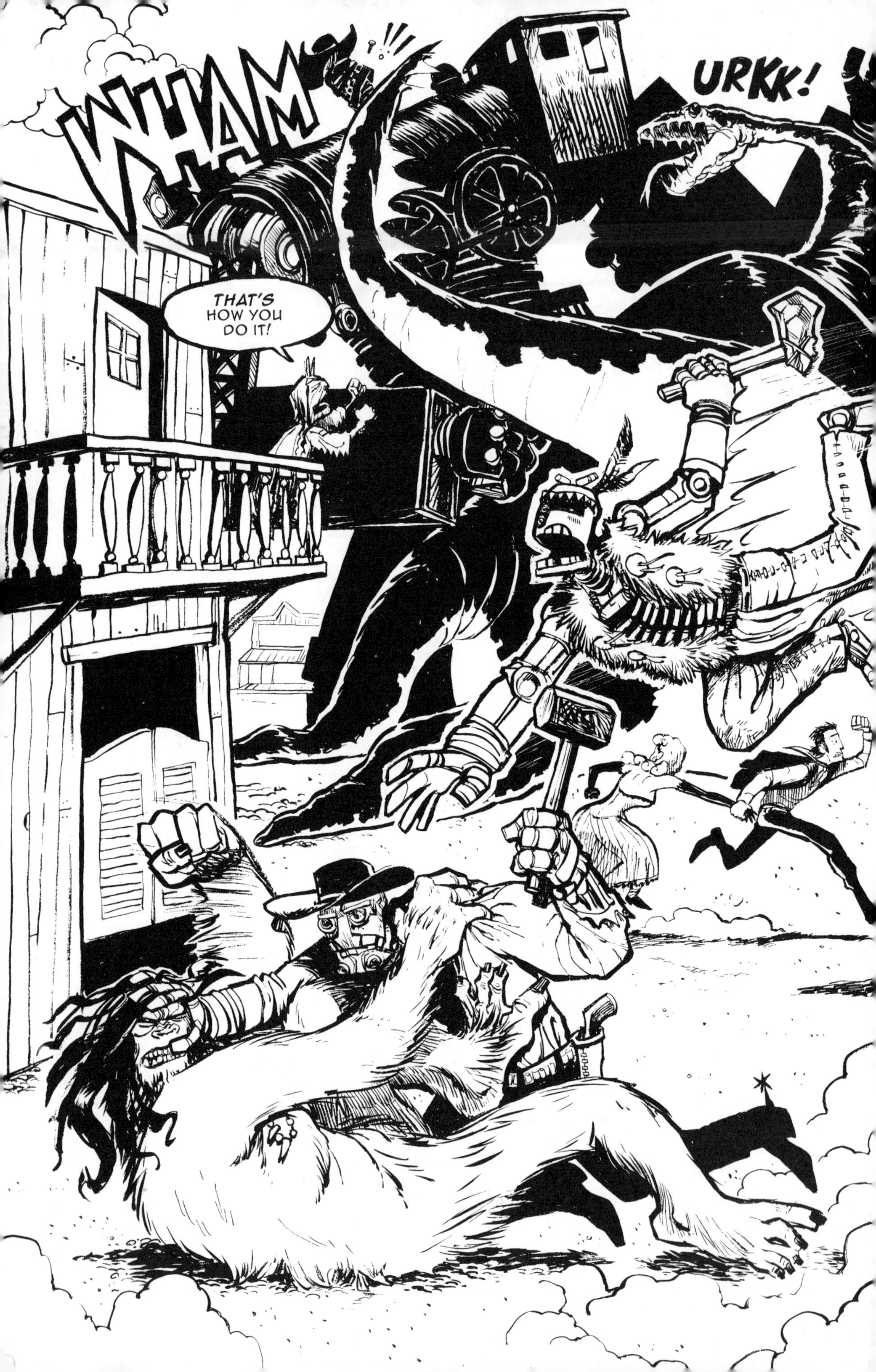
WHAM
URKK!
THAT'S HOW YOU DO IT!

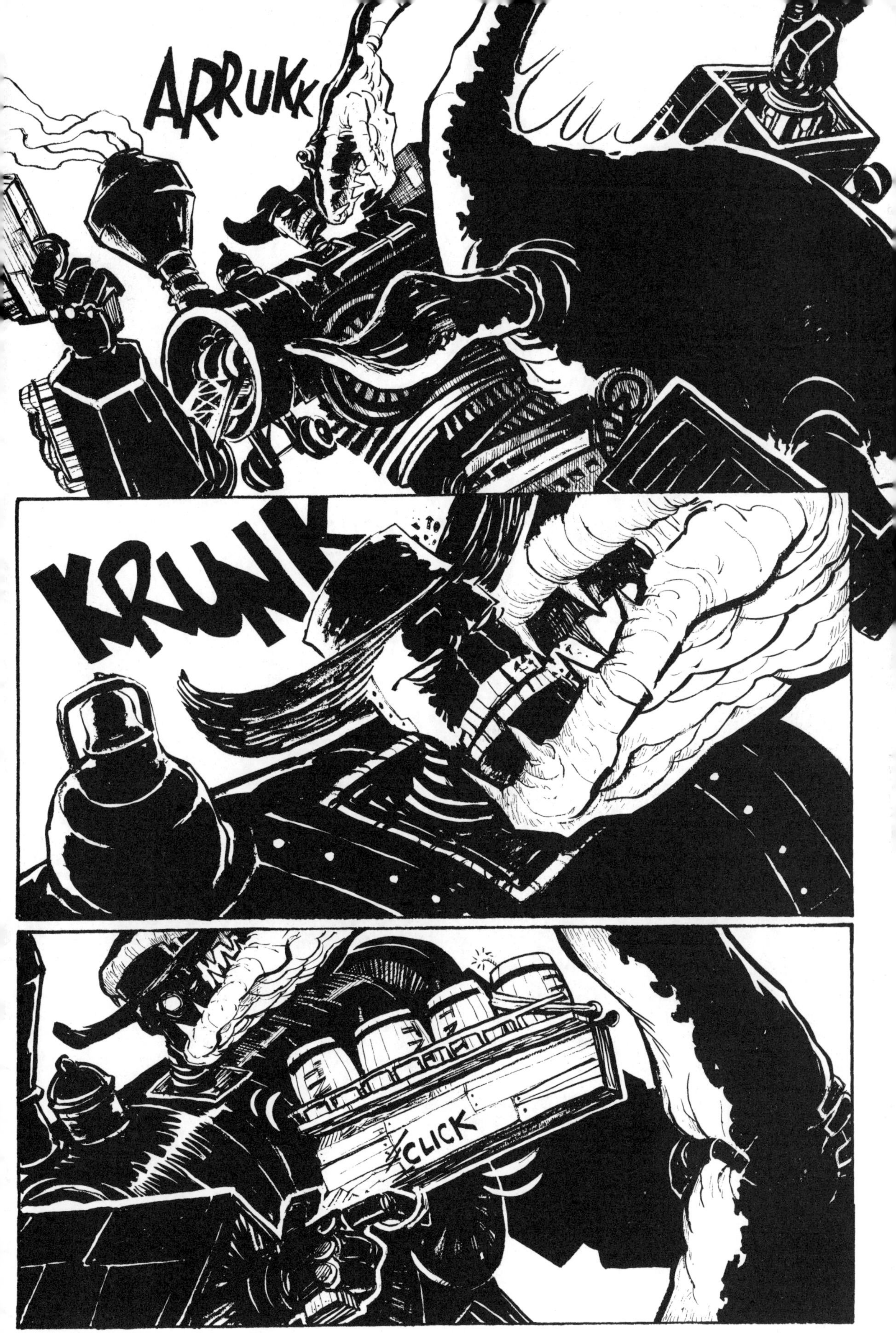
ARRUKK
KRUNK
CLICK

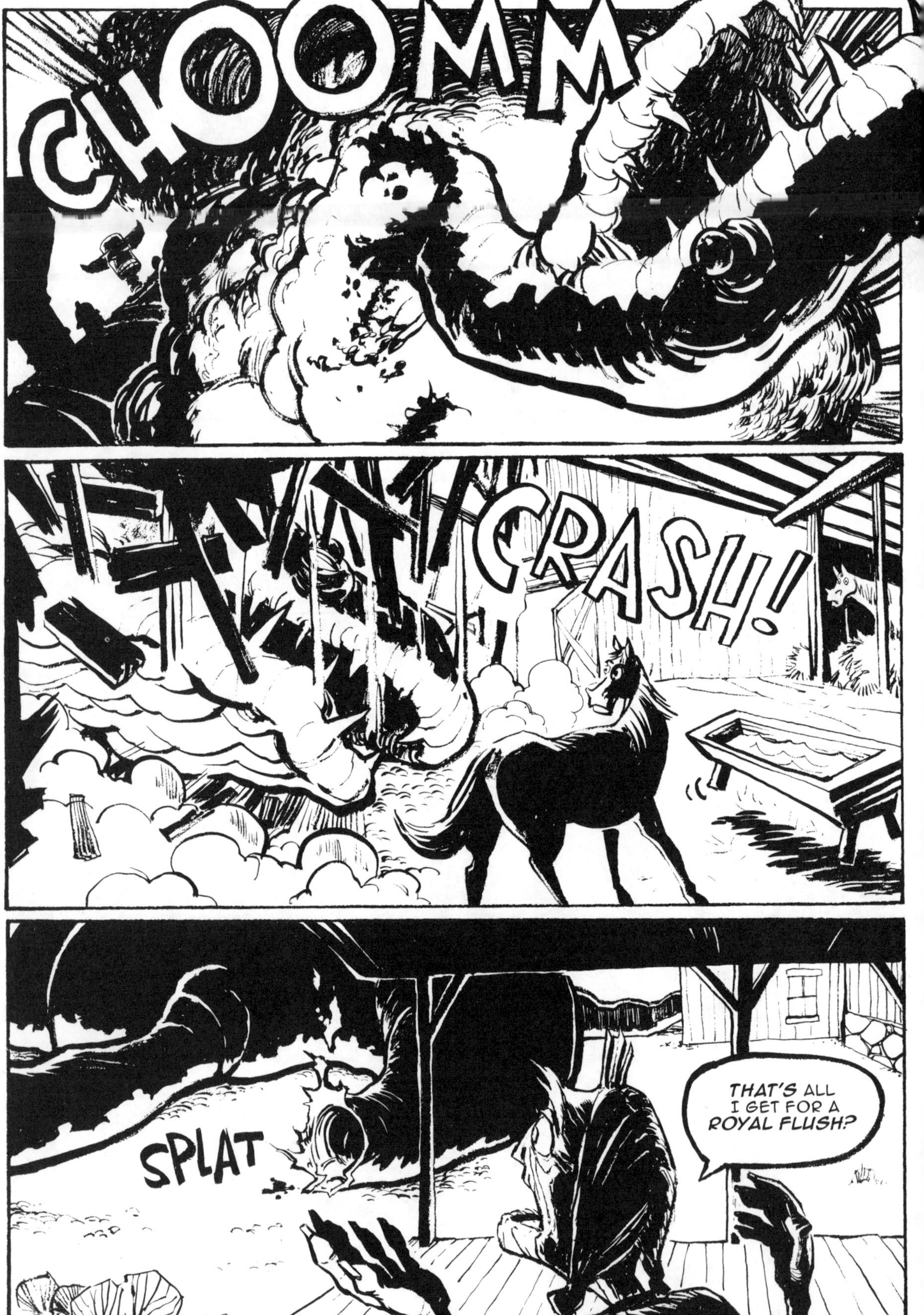
CHOOMM
CRASH!
SPLAT
THAT'S ALL I GET FOR A ROYAL FLUSH?

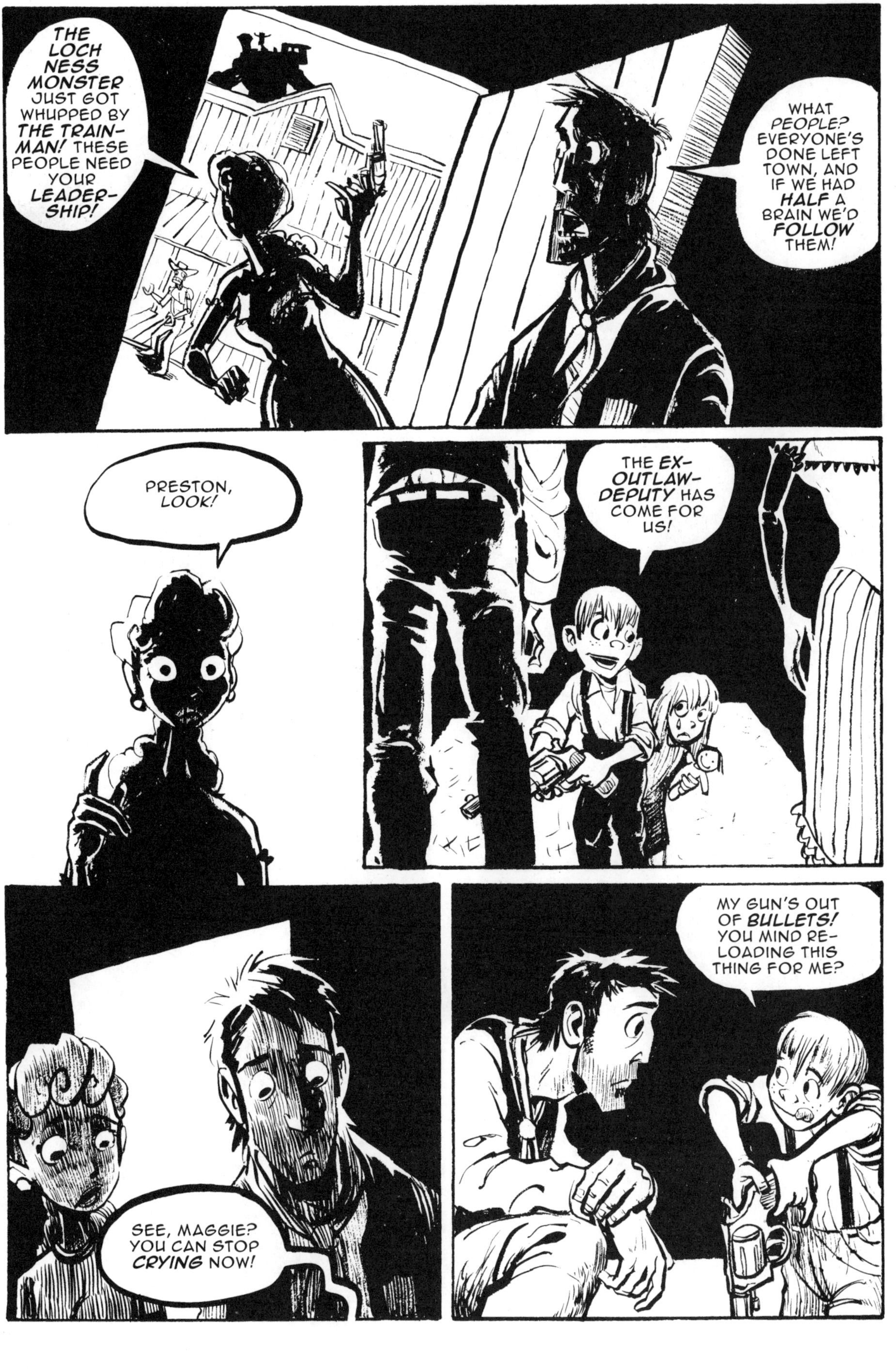
THE LOCH NESS MONSTER JUST GOT WHUPPED BY THE TRAIN-MAN! THESE PEOPLE NEED YOUR LEADER-SHIP!
WHAT PEOPLE? EVERYONE'S DONE LEFT TOWN, AND IF WE HAD HALF A BRAIN WE'D FOLLOW THEM!
PRESTON, LOOK!
THE EX-OUTLAW-DEPUTY HAS COME FOR US!
SEE, MAGGIE? YOU CAN STOP CRYING NOW!
MY GUN'S OUT OF BULLETS! YOU MIND RE-LOADING THIS THING FOR ME?

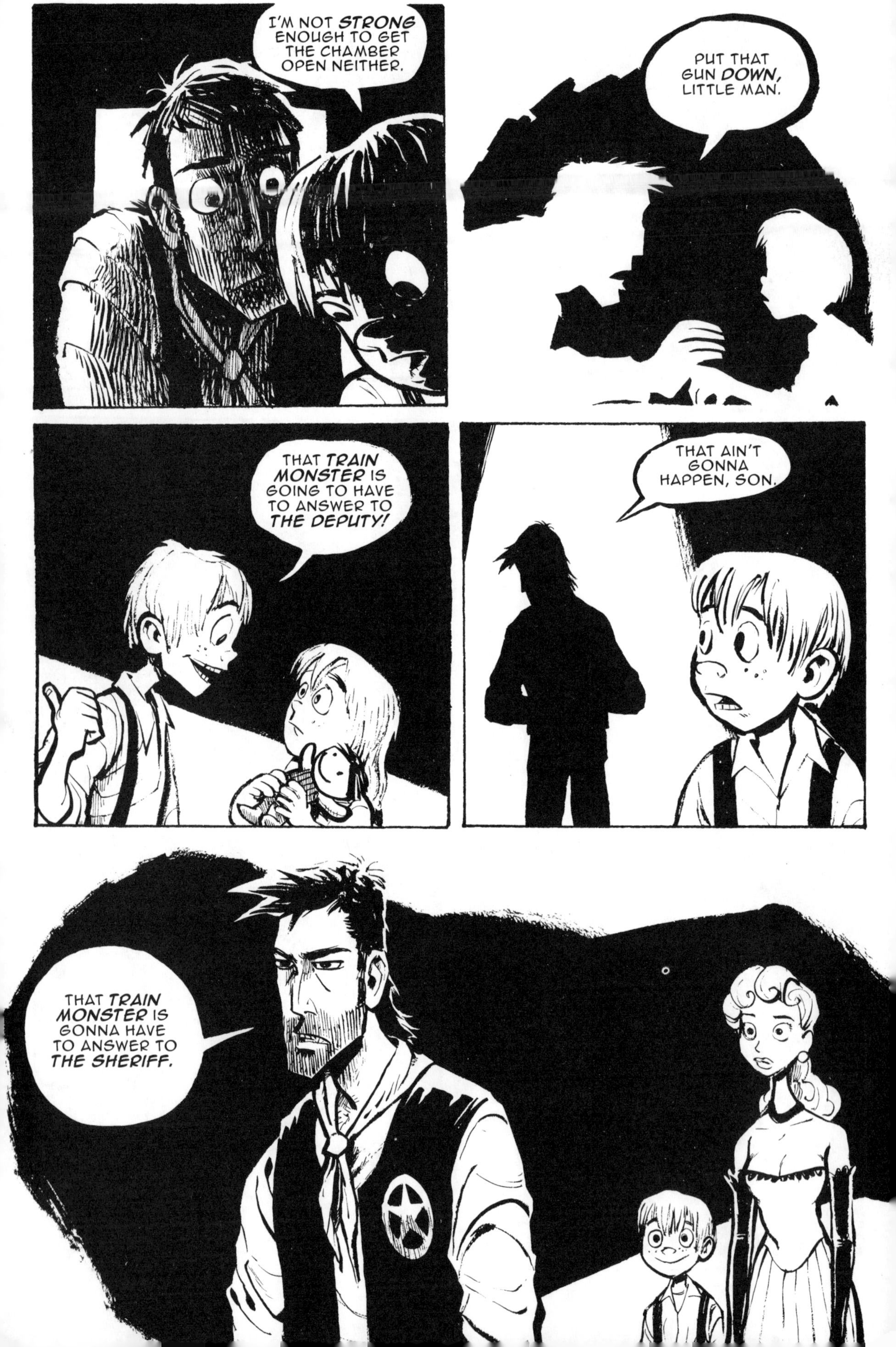
I'M NOT STRONG ENOUGH TO GET THE CHAMBER OPEN NEITHER.
PUT THAT GUN DOWN, LITTLE MAN.
THAT TRAIN MONSTER IS GOING TO HAVE TO ANSWER TO THE DEPUTY!
THAT AIN'T GONNA HAPPEN, SON.
THAT TRAIN MONSTER IS GONNA HAVE TO ANSWER TO THE SHERIFF.

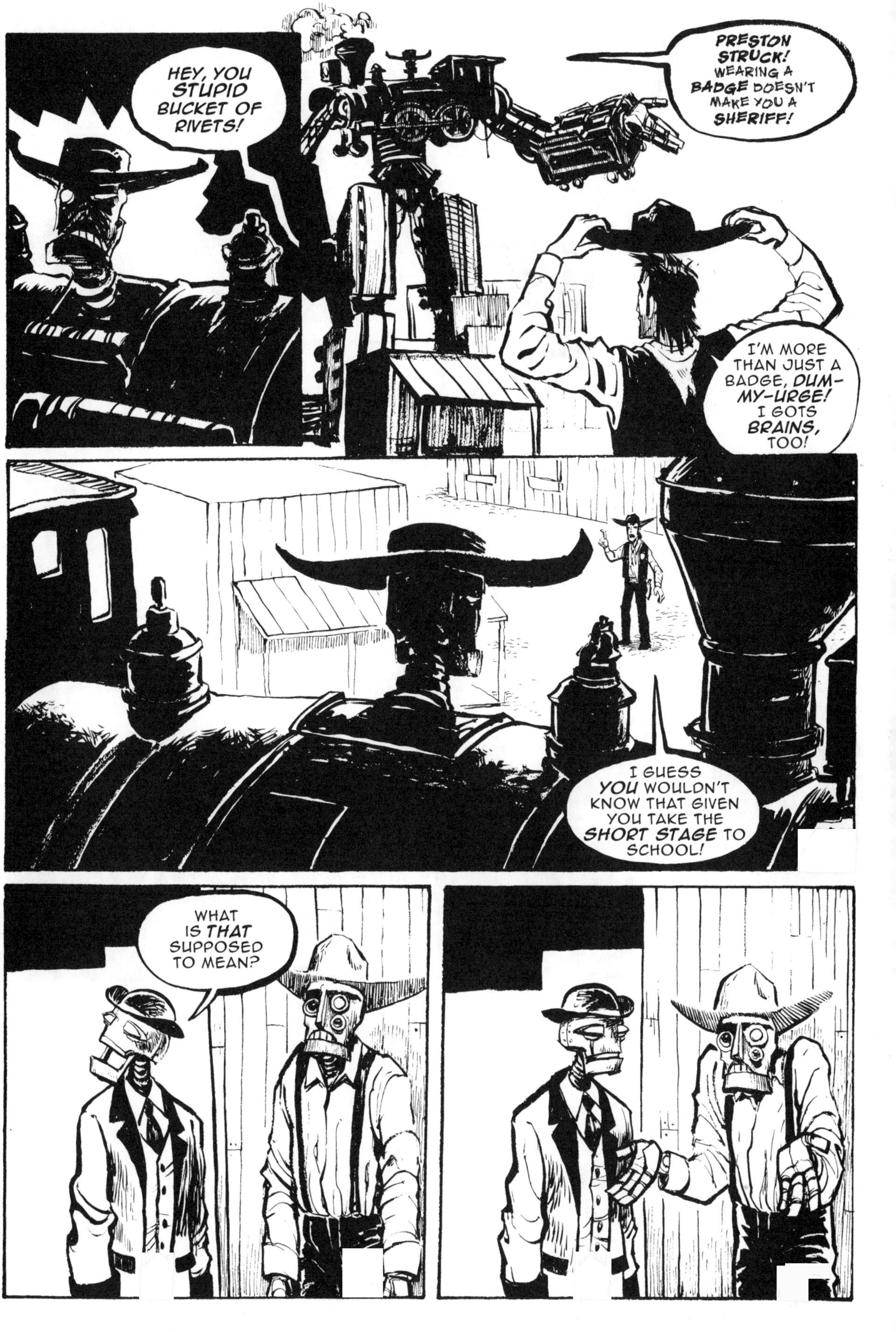
HEY, YOU STUPID BUCKET OF RIVETS!
PRESTON STRUCK! WEARING A BADGE DOESN'T MAKE YOU A SHERIFF!
I'M MORE THAN JUST A BADGE, DUM-MY-URGE! I GOTS BRAINS, TOO!
I GUESS YOU WOULDN'T KNOW THAT GIVEN YOU TAKE THE SHORT STAGE TO SCHOOL!
WHAT IS THAT SUPPOSED TO MEAN?

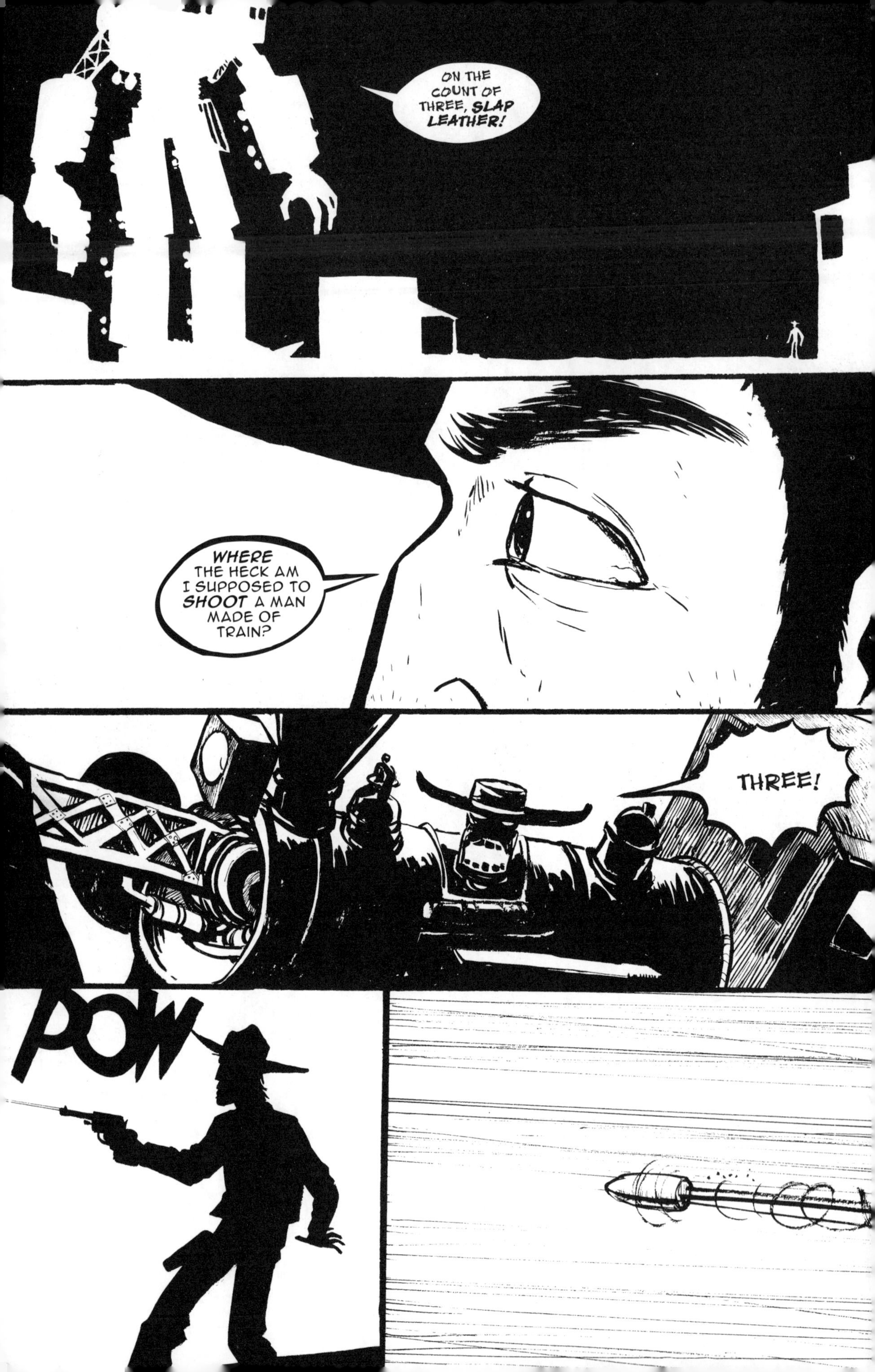
ON THE COUNT OF THREE, SLAP LEATHER!
WHERE THE HECK AM I SUPPOSED TO SHOOT A MAN MADE OF TRAIN?
THREE!
POW

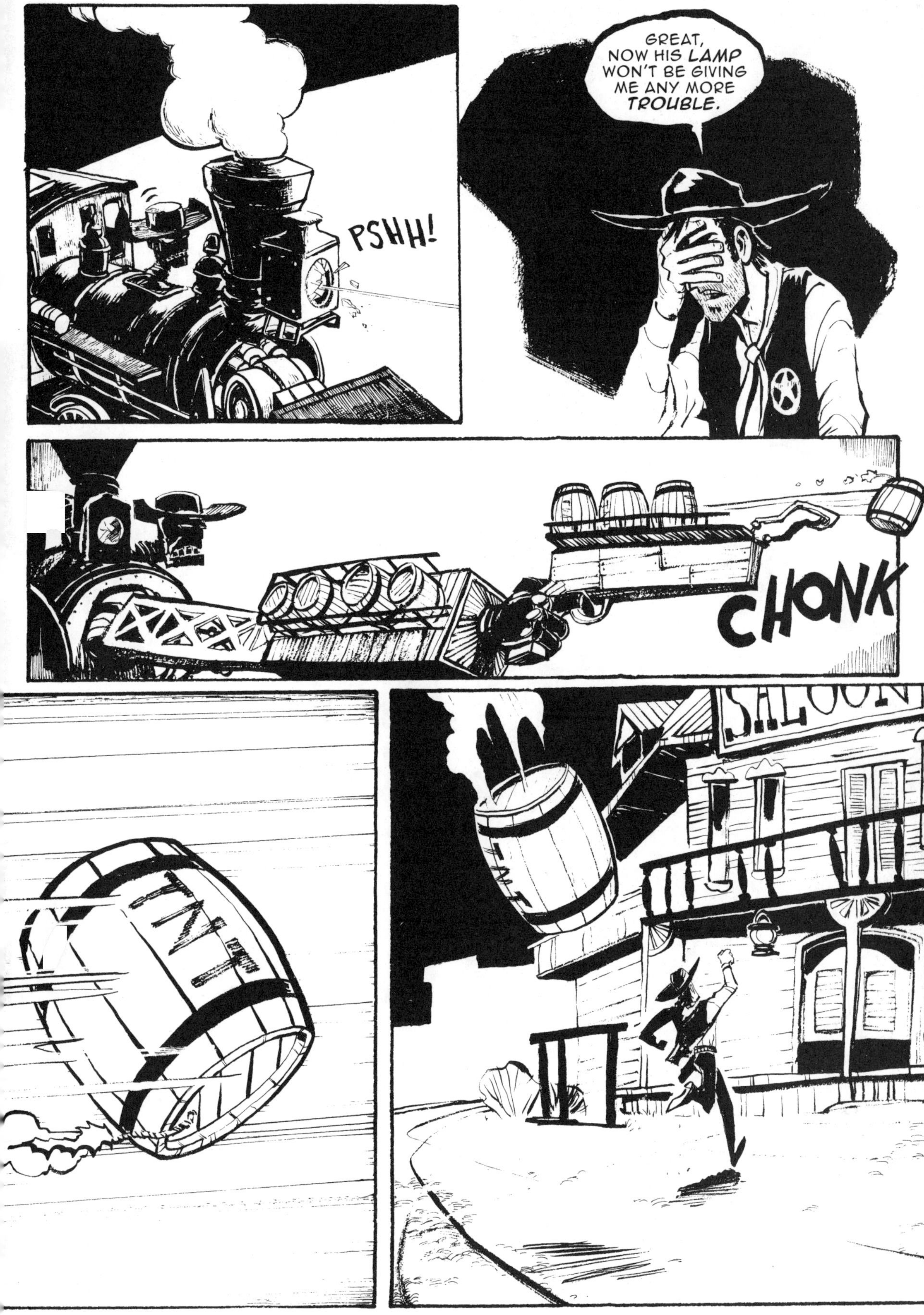

PSHH!
GREAT, NOW HIS LAMP WON'T BE GIVING ME ANY MORE TROUBLE.
CHONK
TNT
SALOON

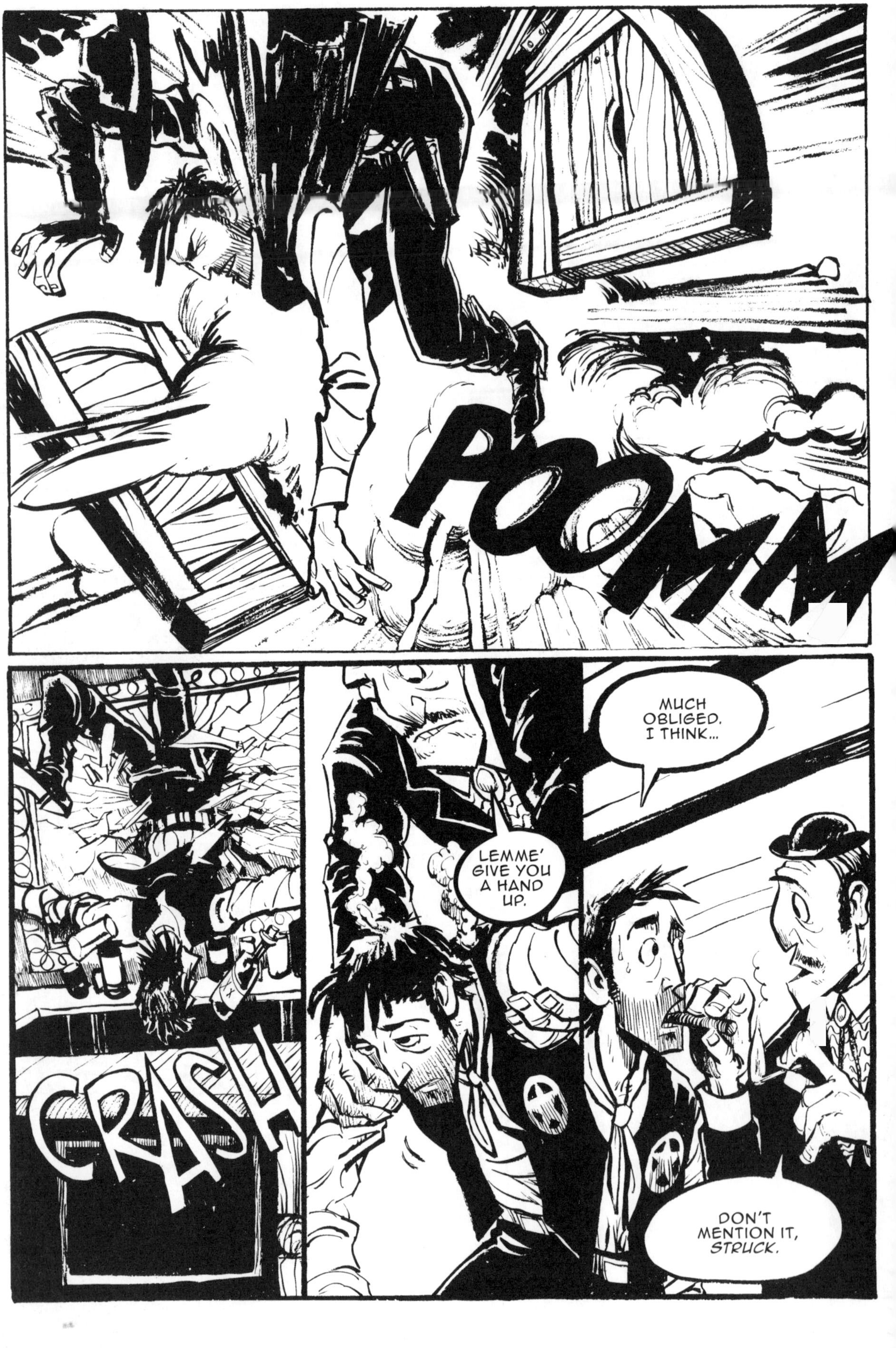
BOOOMM
CRASH
LEMME' GIVE YOU A HAND UP.
MUCH OBLIGED. I THINK...
DON'T MENTION IT, STRUCK.

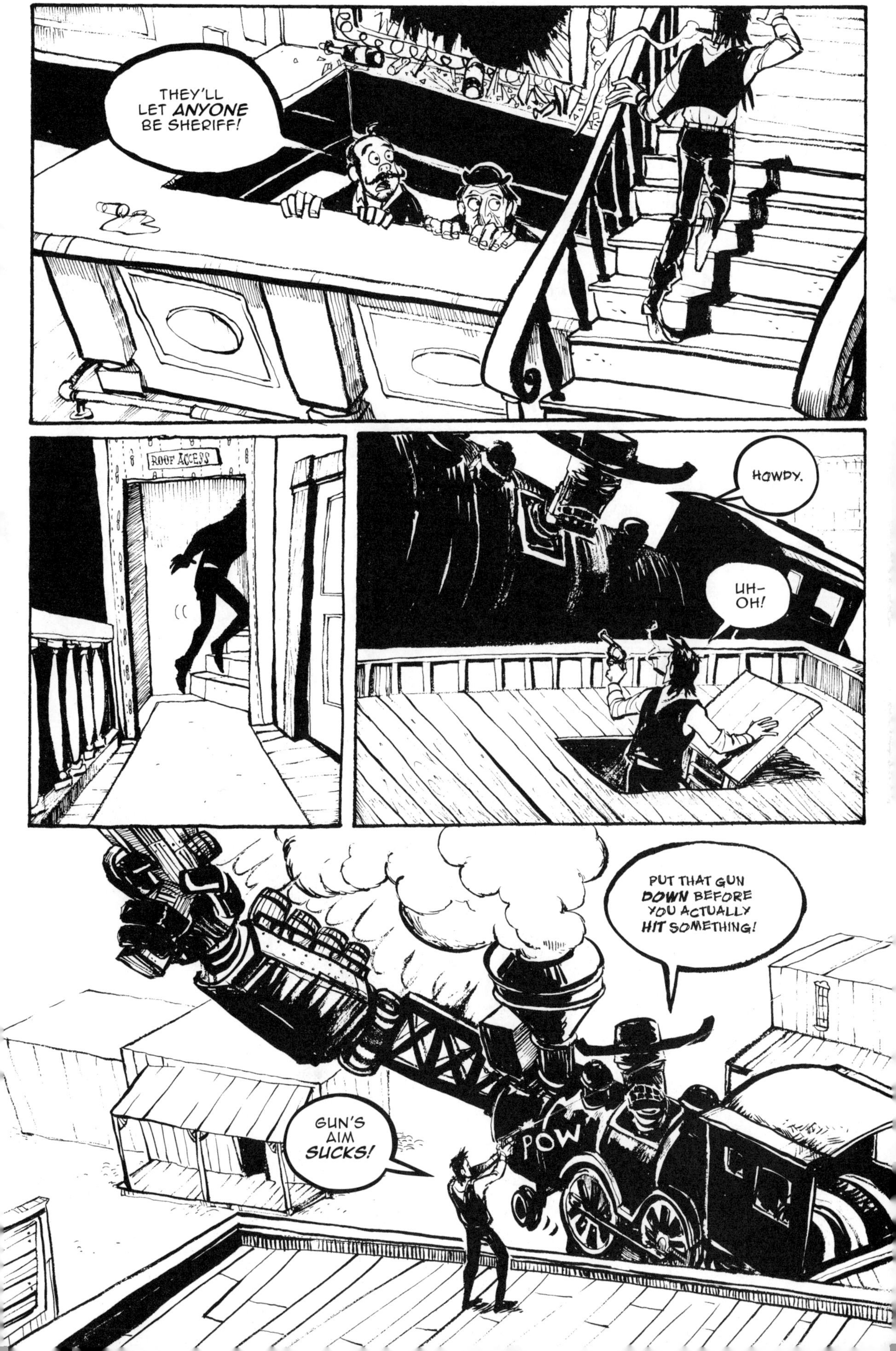
THEY'LL LET ANYONE BE SHERIFF!
ROOF ACCESS
HOWDY.
UH-OH!
PUT THAT GUN DOWN BEFORE YOU ACTUALLY HIT SOMETHING!
GUN'S AIM SUCKS!
POW

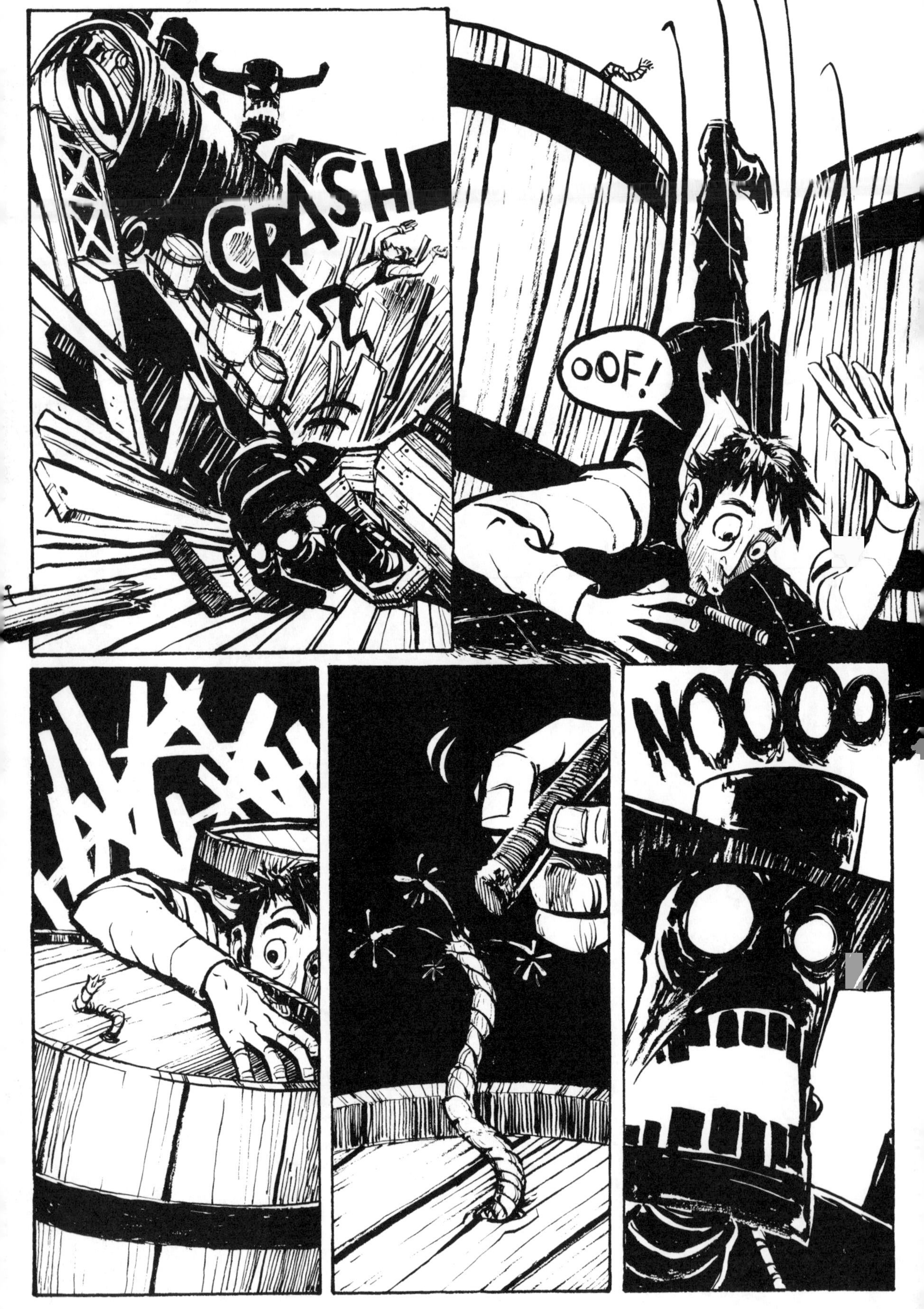
CRASH
OOF!
NOOOO

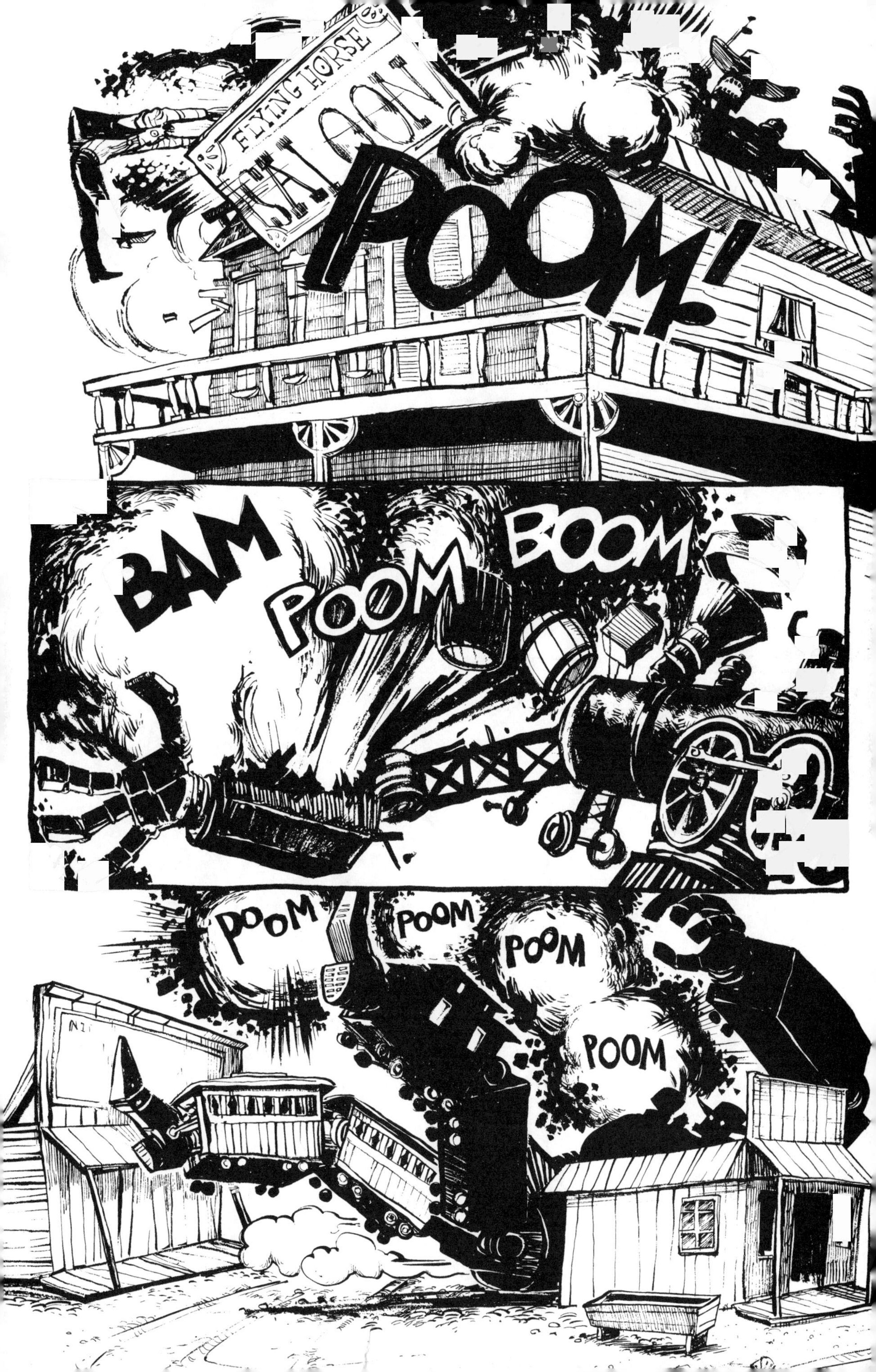
FLYING HORSE
SALOON
POOM!
BAM
POOM
BOOM
POOM
POOM
POOM
POOM

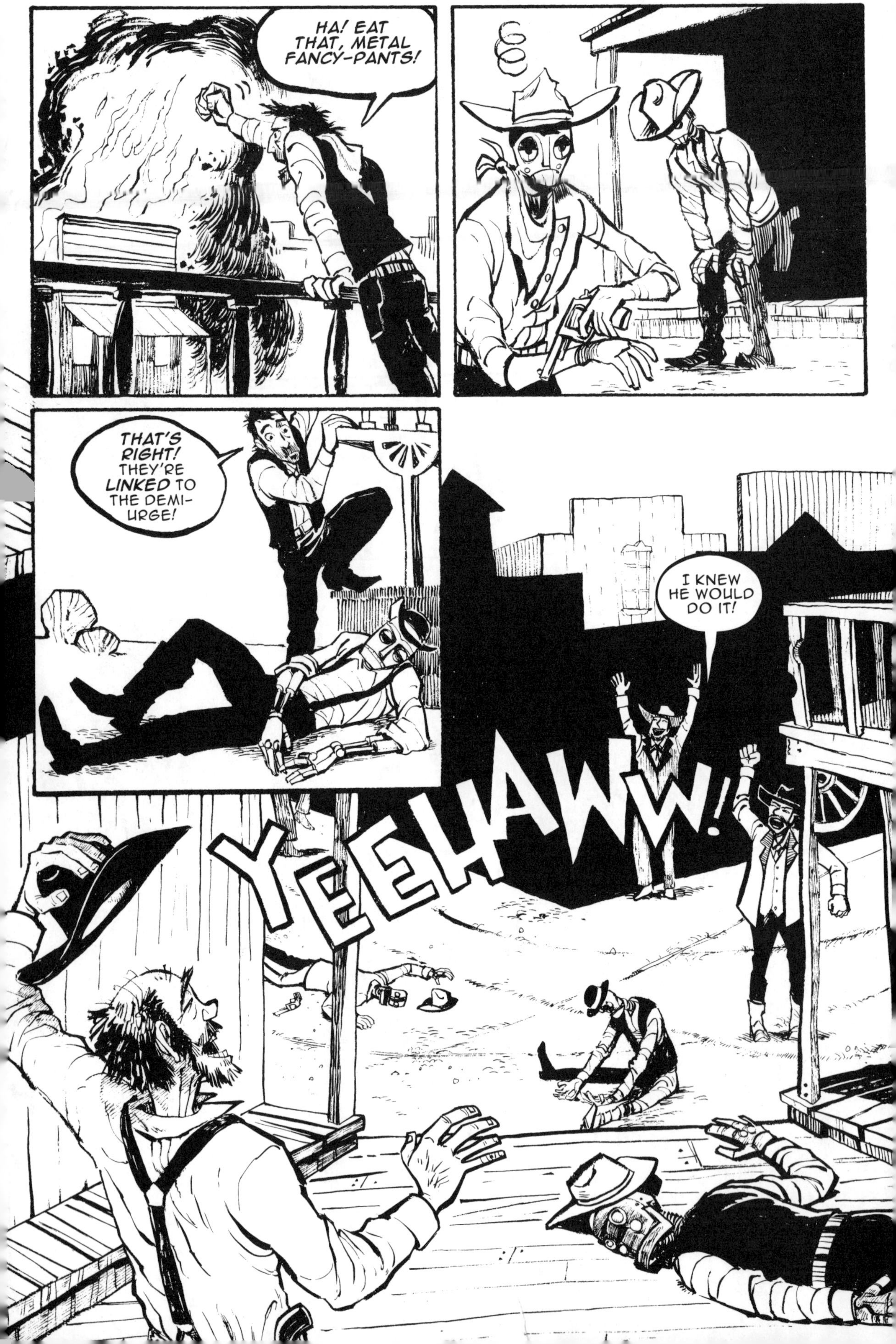
HA! EAT THAT, METAL FANCY-PANTS!
THAT'S RIGHT! THEY'RE LINKED TO THE DEMI-URGE!
I KNEW HE WOULD DO IT!
YEEHAWW!

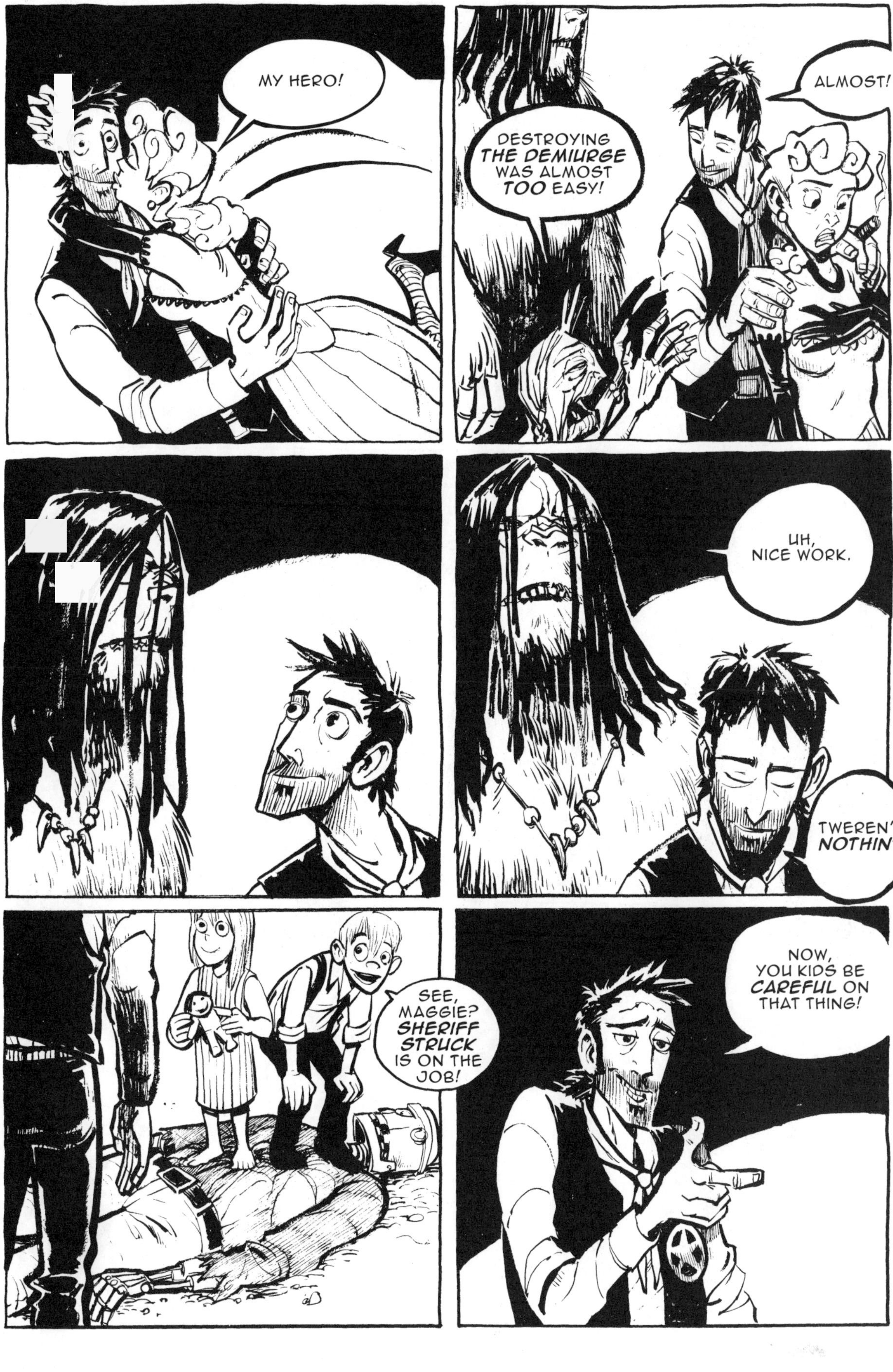
MY HERO!
DESTROYING THE DEMIURGE WAS ALMOST TOO EASY!
ALMOST!
UH, NICE WORK.
TWEREN'T NOTHIN'.
SEE, MAGGIE? SHERIFF STRUCK IS ON THE JOB!
NOW, YOU KIDS BE CAREFUL ON THAT THING!

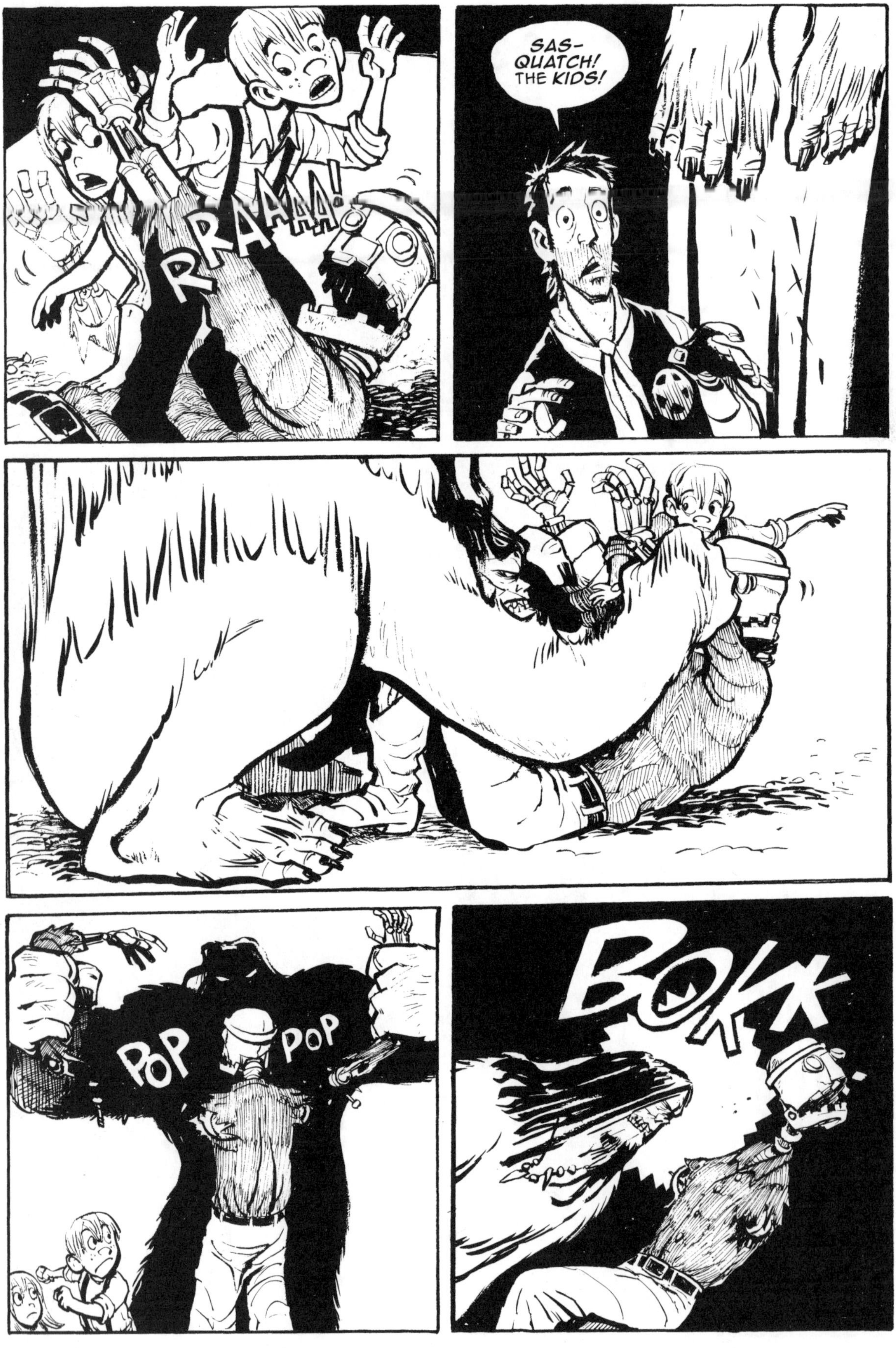
RRAAAA!
SAS-QUATCH! THE KIDS!
POP
POP
BOKK

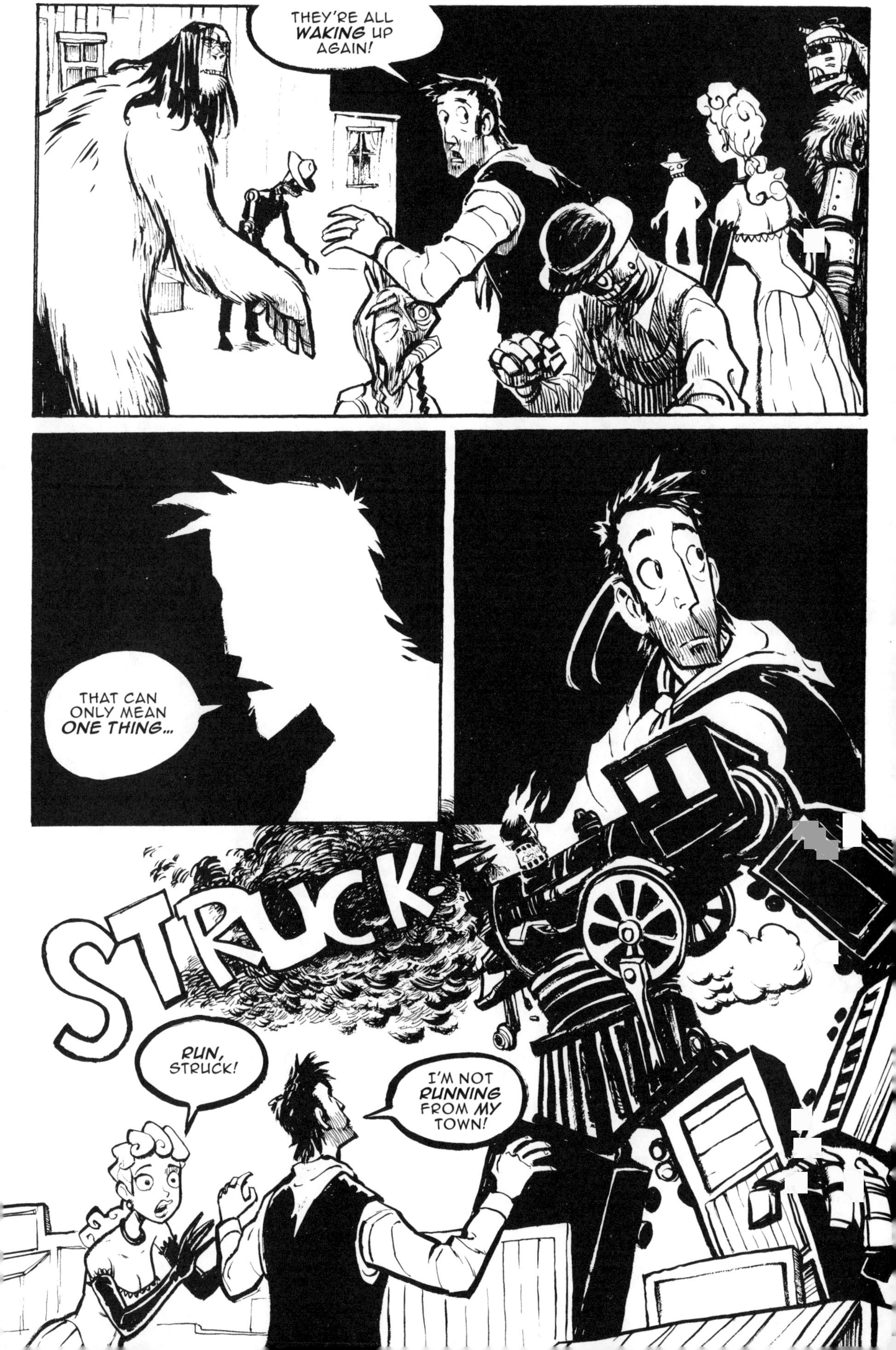
THEY'RE ALL WAKING UP AGAIN!
THAT CAN ONLY MEAN ONE THING...
STRUCK!
RUN, STRUCK!
I'M NOT RUNNING FROM MY TOWN!

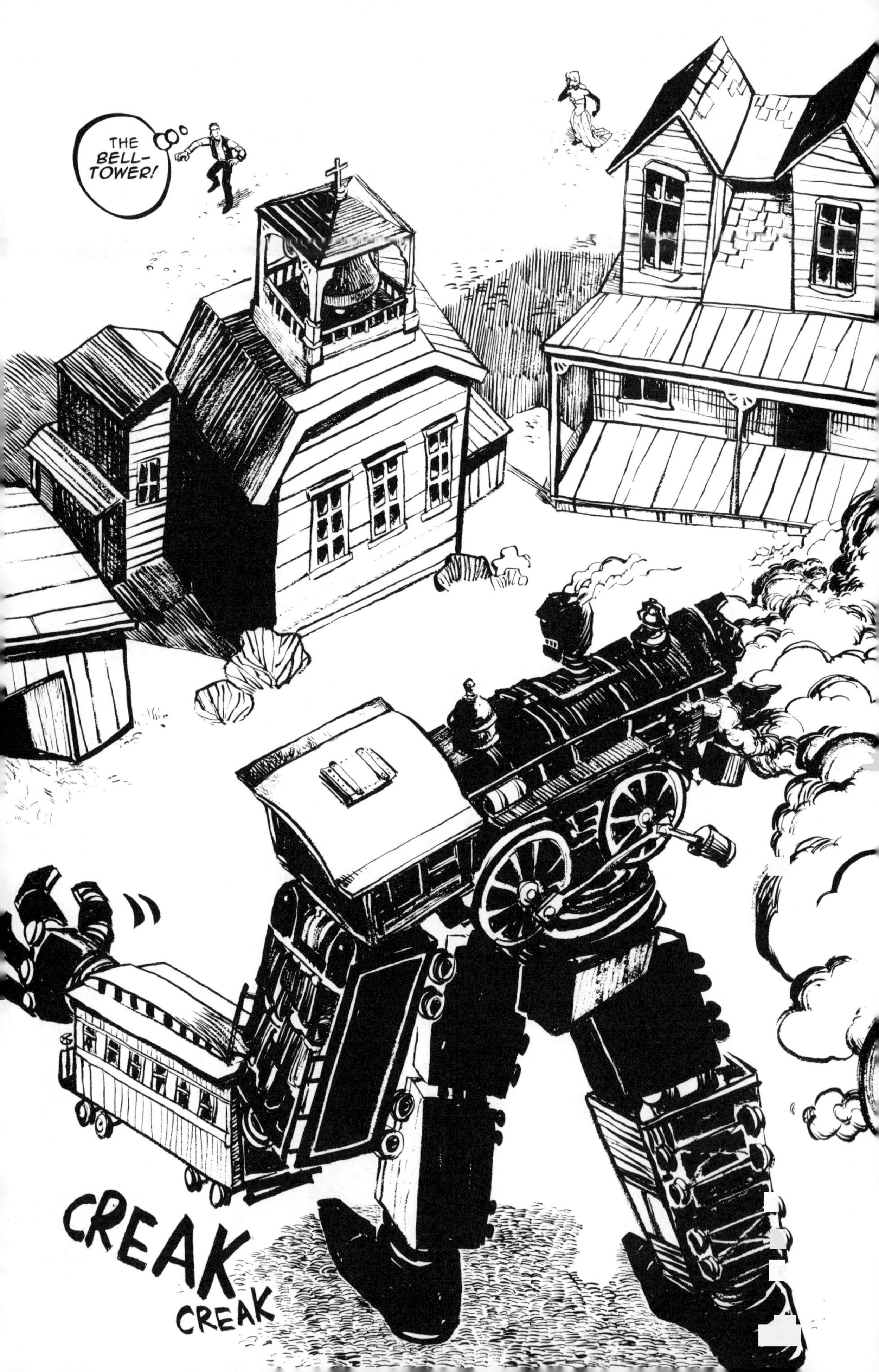
THE BELL-TOWER!
CREAK
CREAK

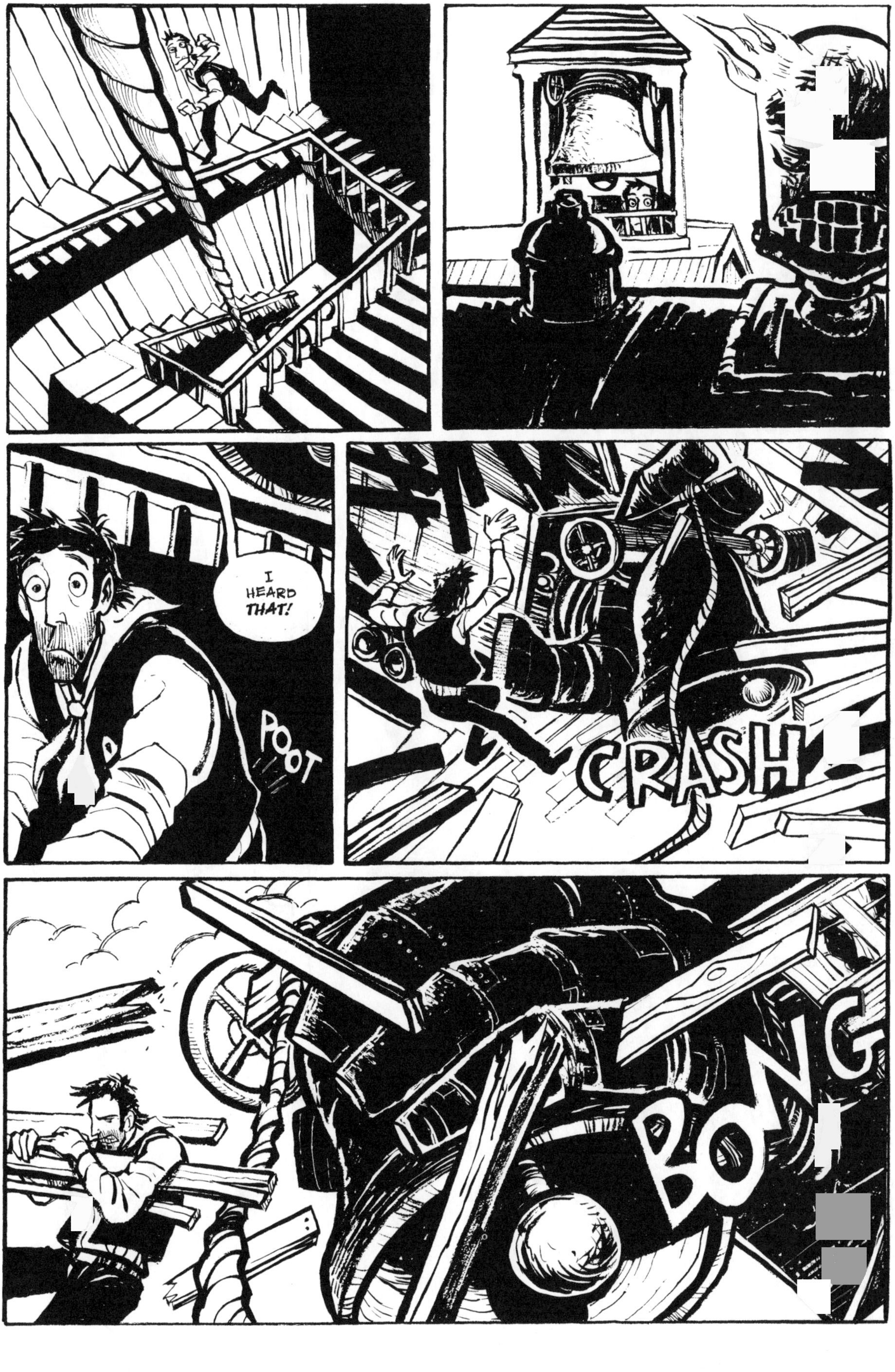
I HEARD THAT!
POOT
CRASH
BONG

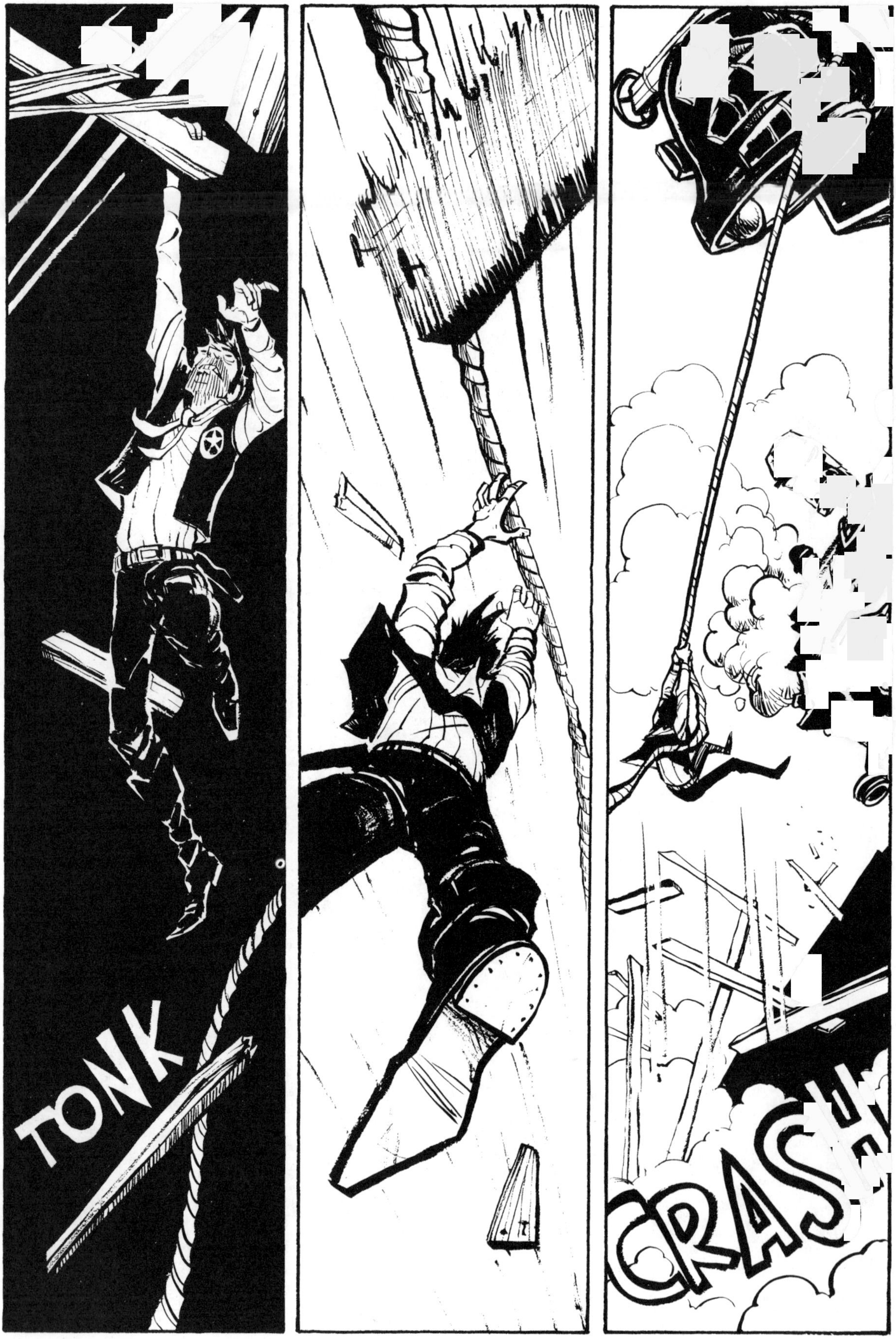
TONK
CRASH

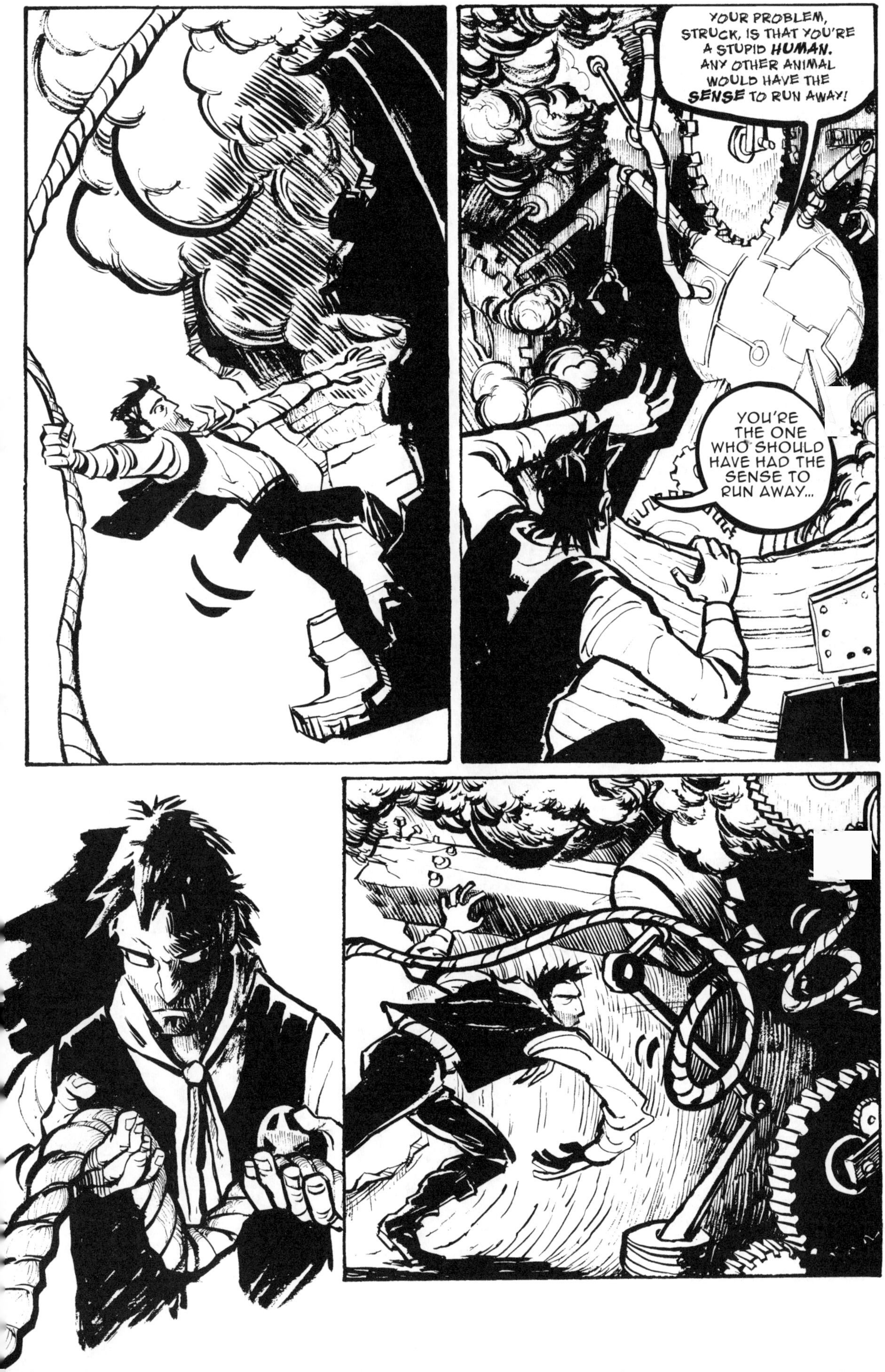
YOUR PROBLEM, STRUCK, IS THAT YOU'RE A STUPID HUMAN. ANY OTHER ANIMAL WOULD HAVE THE SENSE TO RUN AWAY!
YOU'RE THE ONE WHO SHOULD HAVE HAD THE SENSE TO RUN AWAY...

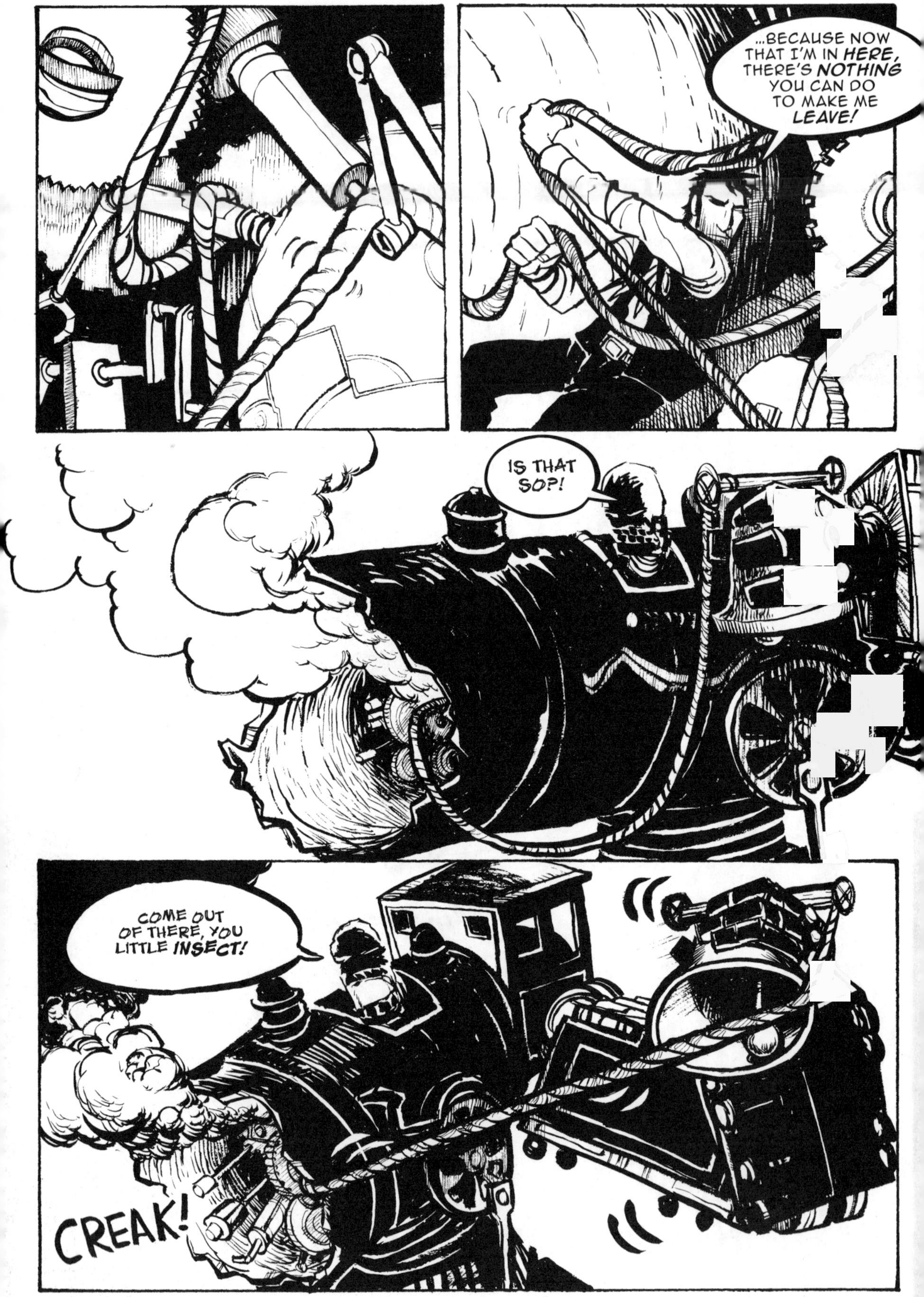
...BECAUSE NOW THAT I'M IN HERE, THERE'S NOTHING YOU CAN DO TO MAKE ME LEAVE!
IS THAT SO?!
COME OUT OF THERE, YOU LITTLE INSECT!
CREAK!

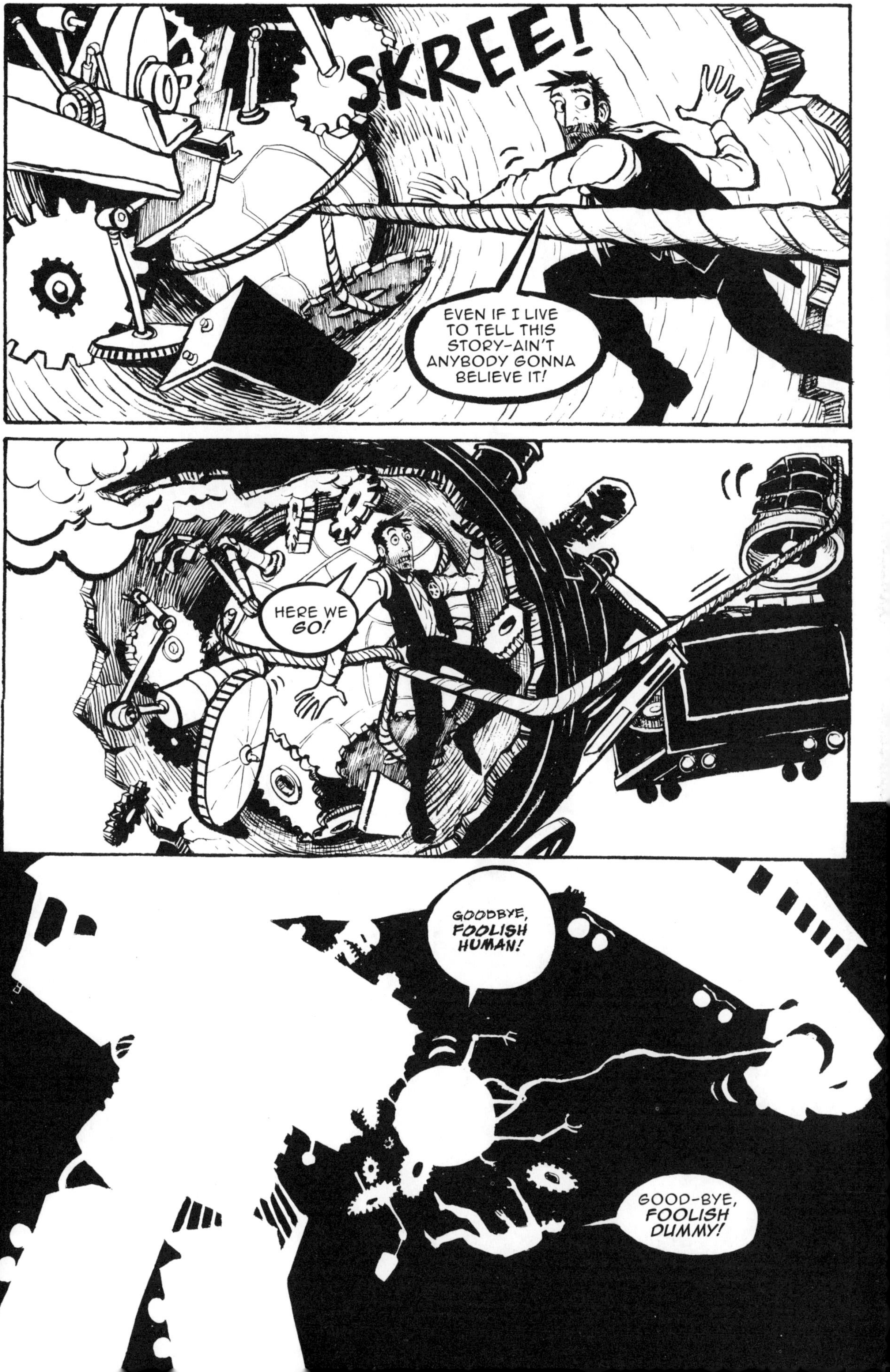
SKREE!
EVEN IF I LIVE TO TELL THIS STORY--AIN'T ANYBODY GONNA BELIEVE IT!
HERE WE GO!
GOODBYE, FOOLISH HUMAN!
GOOD-BYE, FOOLISH DUMMY!

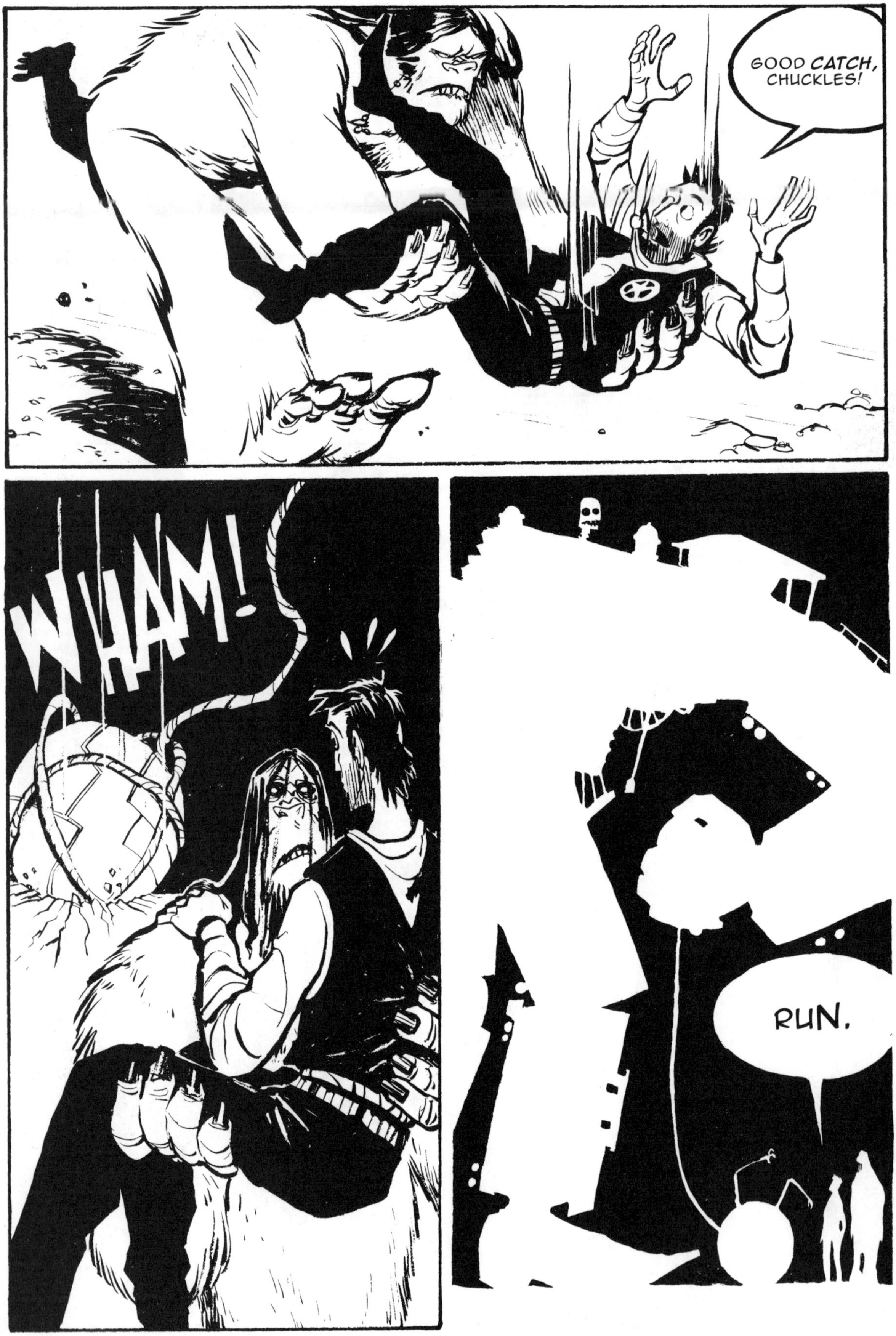
GOOD CATCH, CHUCKLES!
WHAM!
RUN.

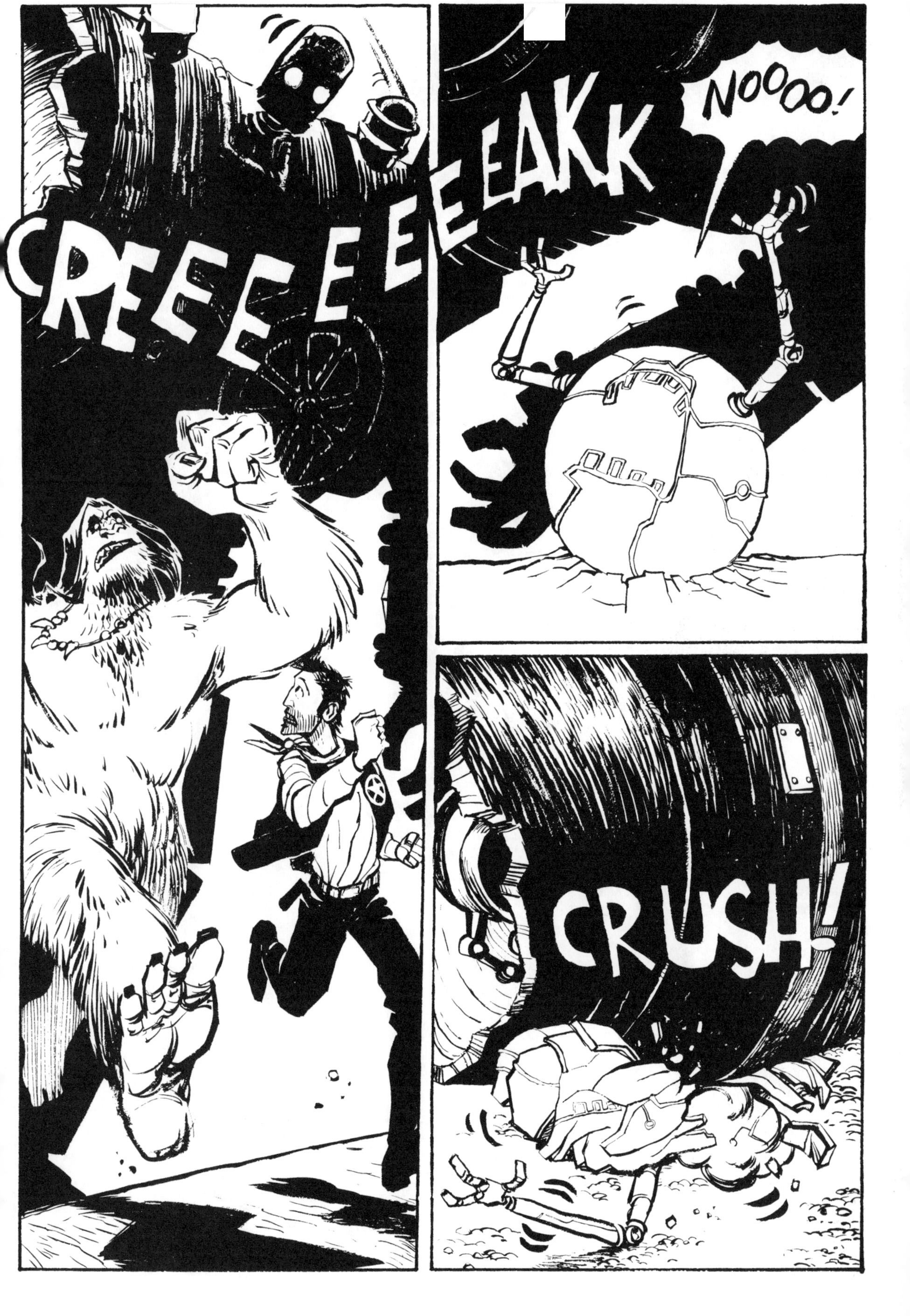
CREEEEEEAKK
NOOOO!
CRUSH!

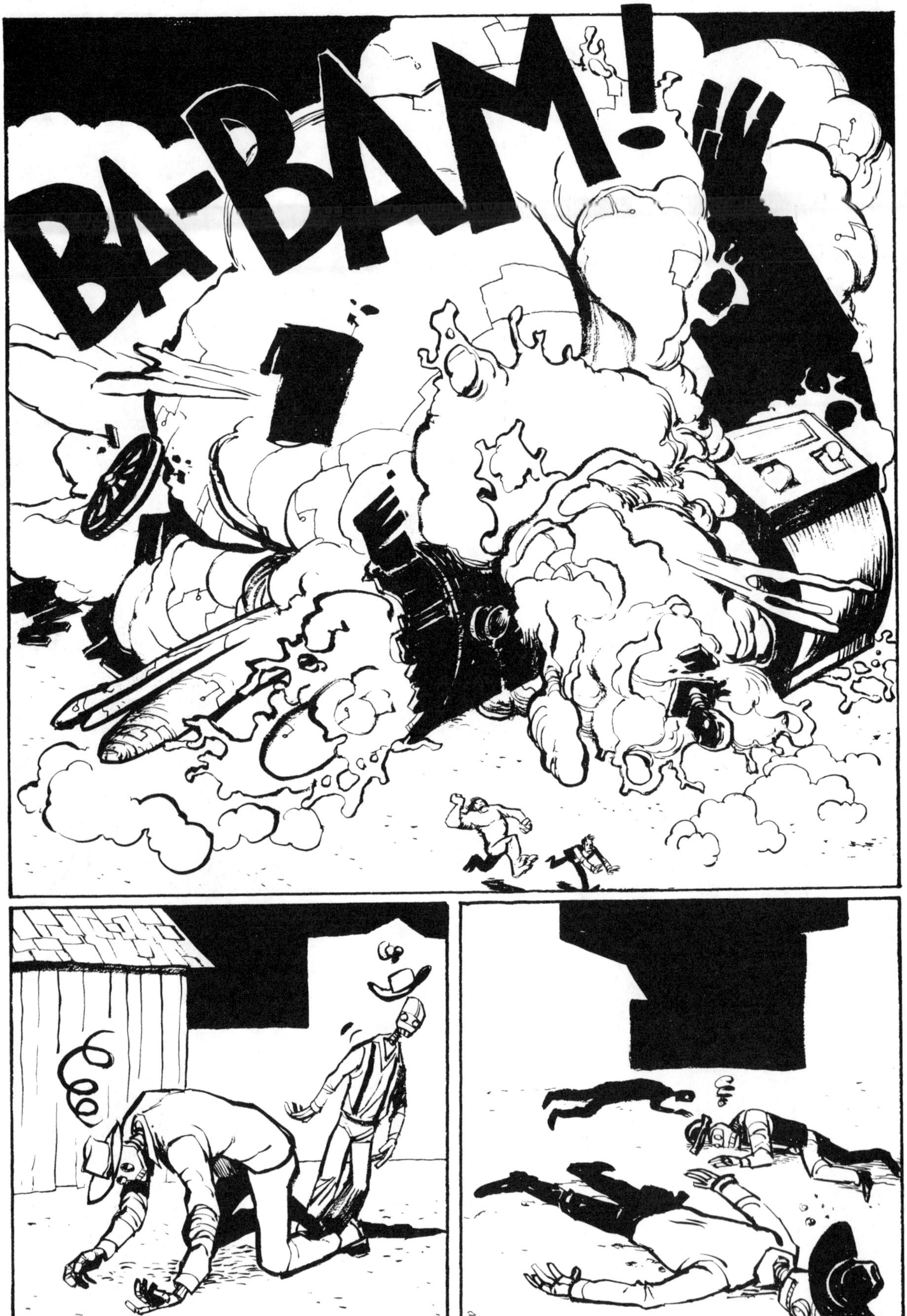
BA-BAM!

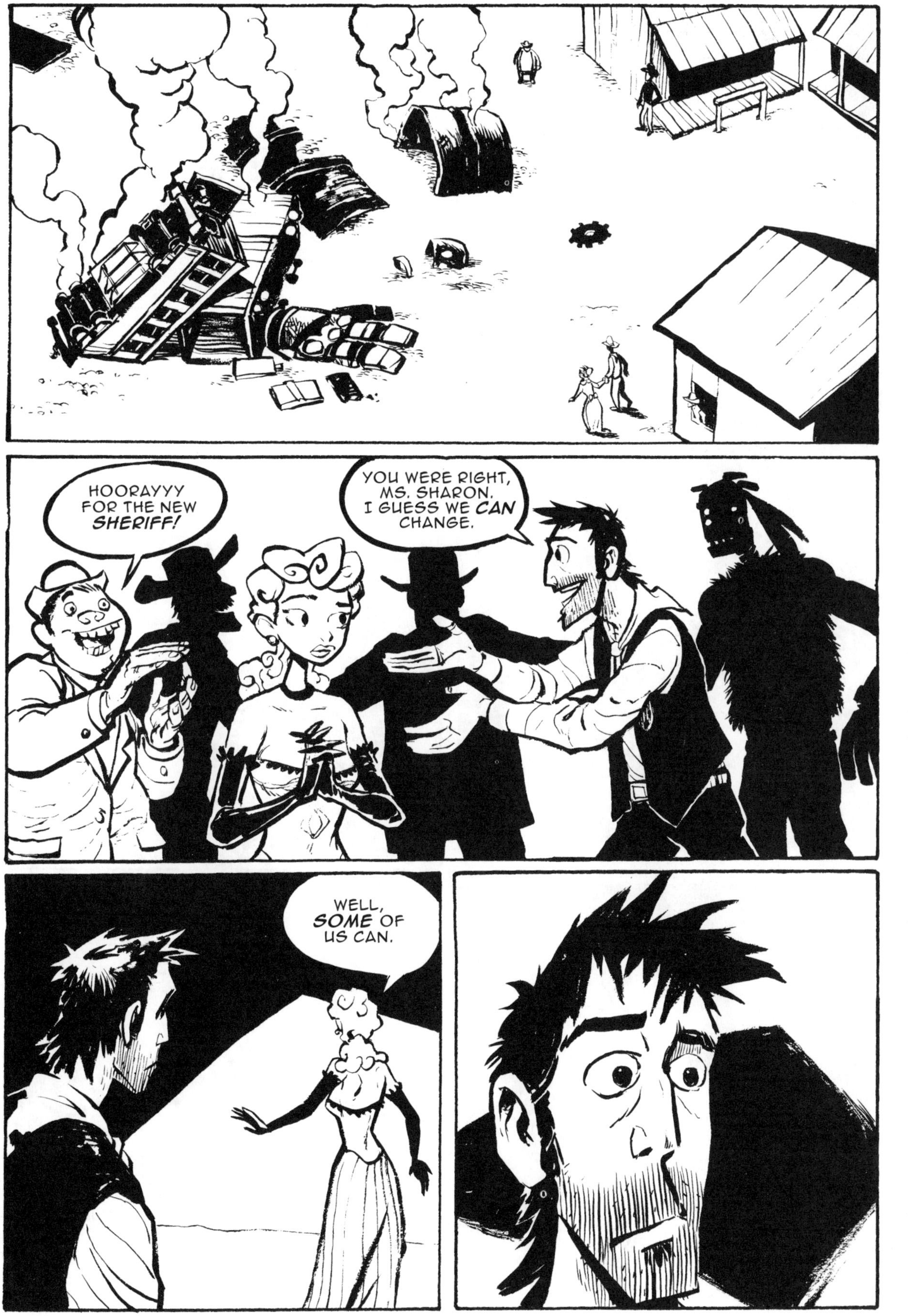

HOORAYYY FOR THE NEW *SHERIFF!*
YOU WERE RIGHT, MS. SHARON. I GUESS WE **CAN** CHANGE.
WELL, **SOME** OF US CAN.

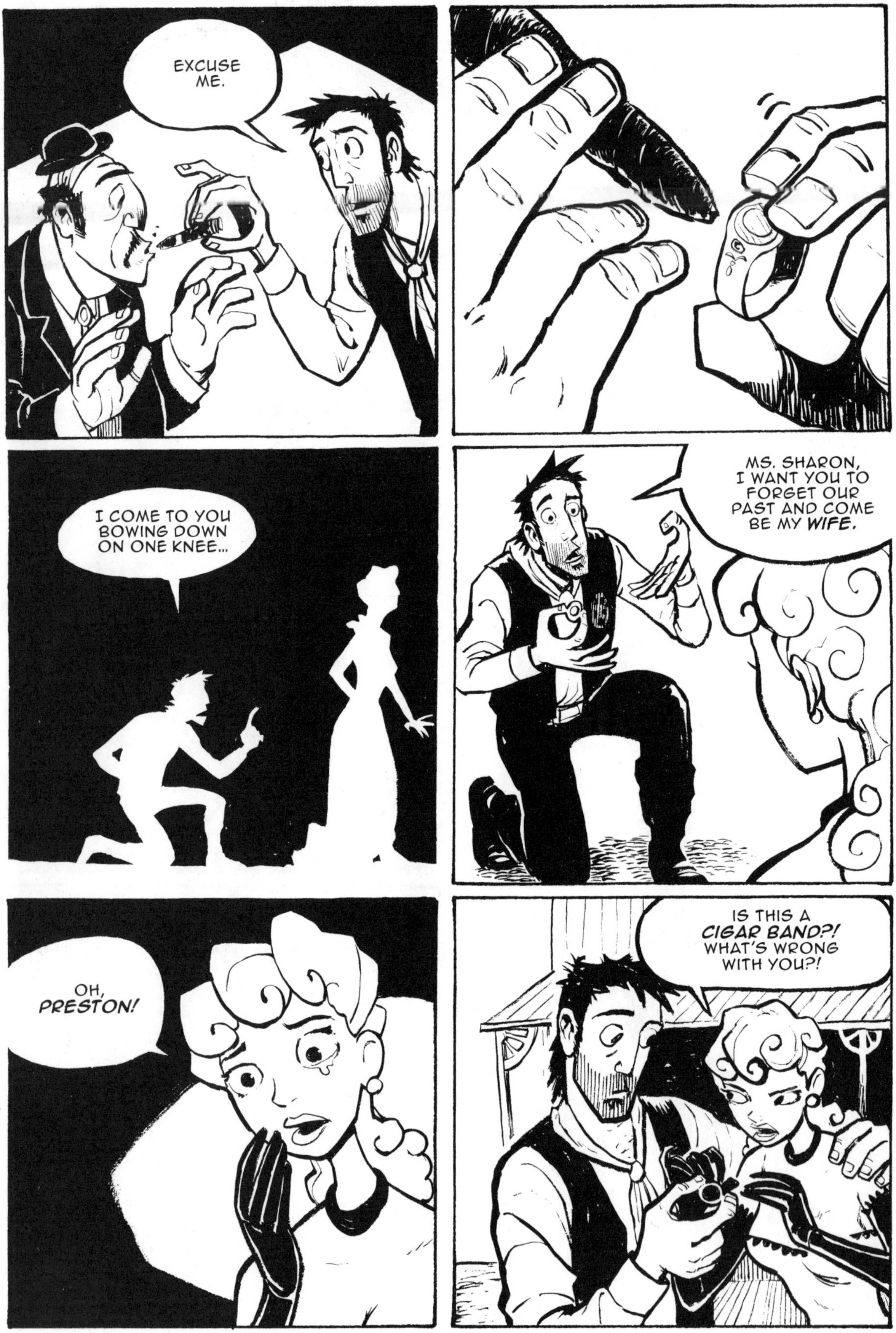
EXCUSE ME.
I COME TO YOU BOWING DOWN ON ONE KNEE...
MS. SHARON, I WANT YOU TO FORGET OUR PAST AND COME BE MY *WIFE.*
OH, *PRESTON!*
IS THIS A *CIGAR BAND?!* WHAT'S WRONG WITH YOU?!

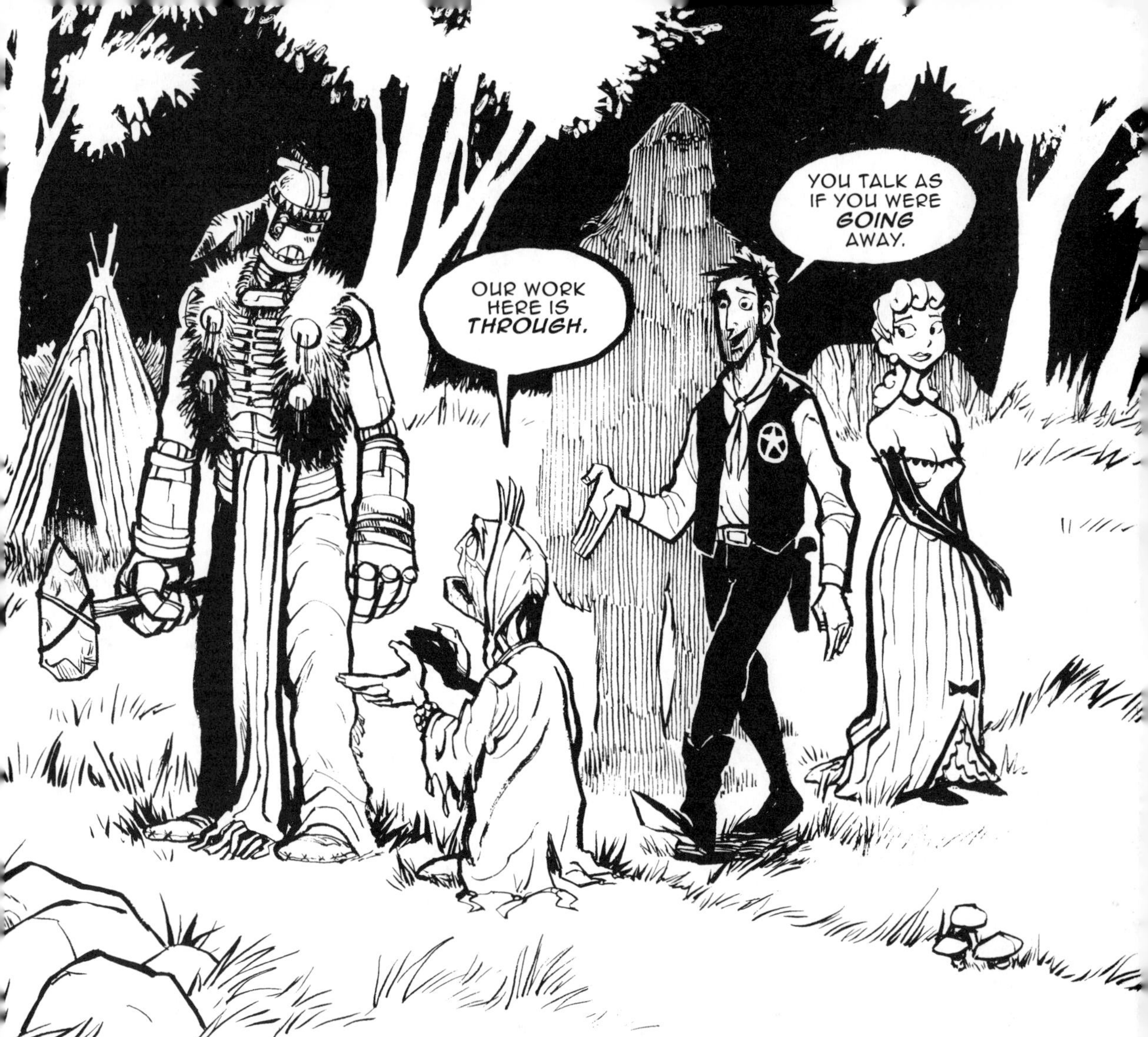
OUR WORK HERE IS THROUGH.
YOU TALK AS IF YOU WERE GOING AWAY.

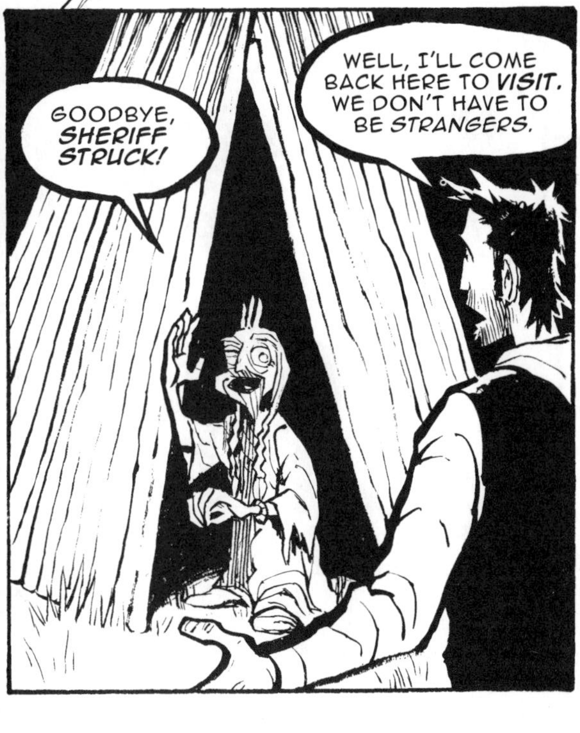
GOODBYE, SHERIFF STRUCK!
WELL, I'LL COME BACK HERE TO VISIT. WE DON'T HAVE TO BE STRANGERS.

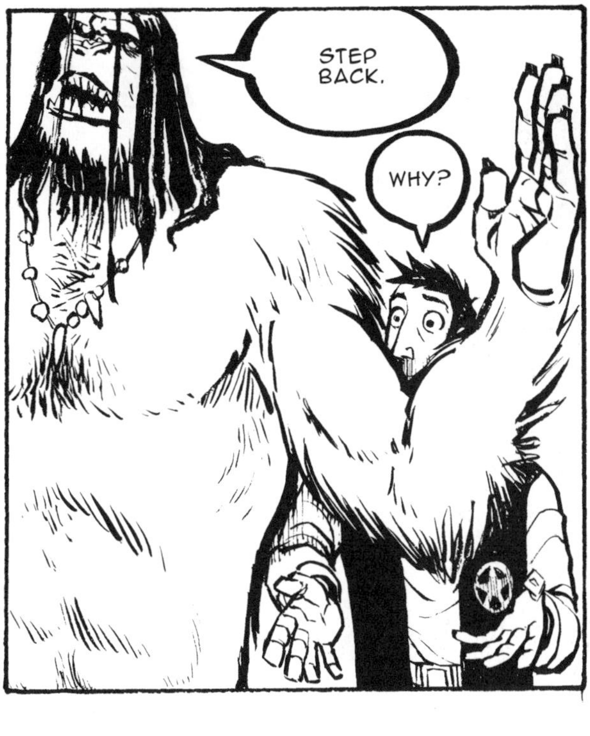
STEP BACK.
WHY?

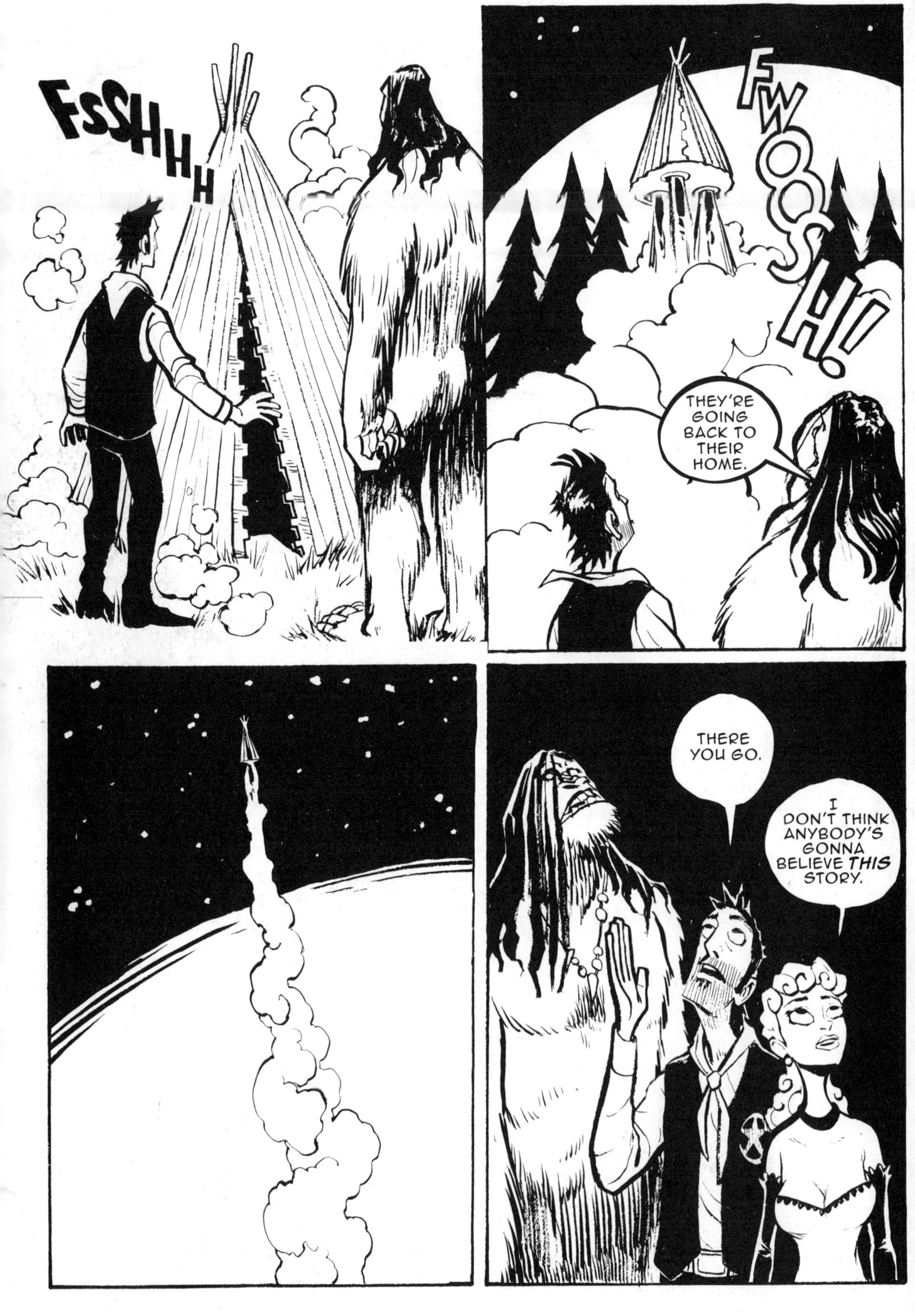
FSSHHHH
FWOOSH!
THEY'RE GOING BACK TO THEIR HOME.
THERE YOU GO.
I DON'T THINK ANYBODY'S GONNA BELIEVE *THIS* STORY.

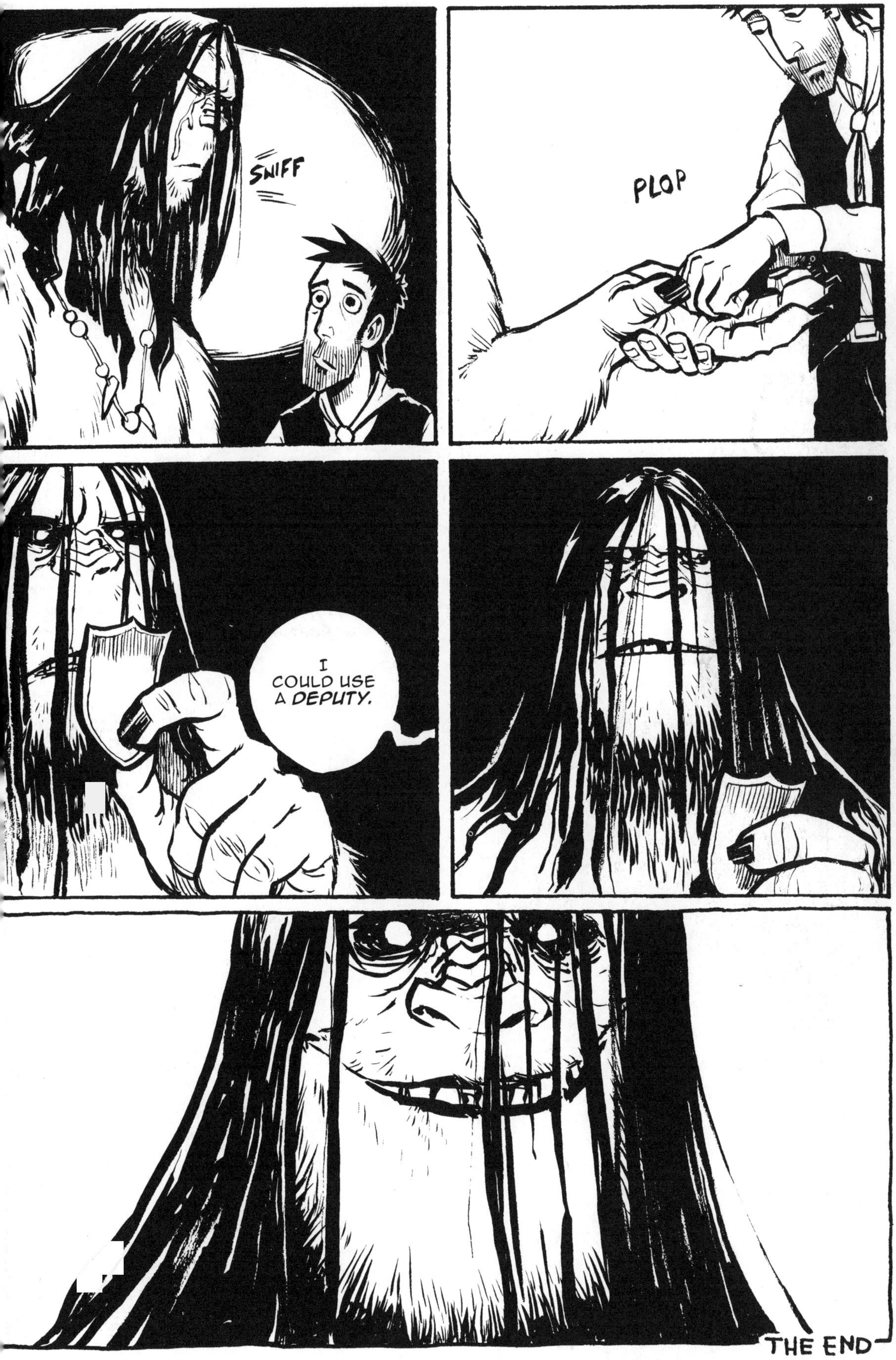
SNIFF
PLOP
I COULD USE A DEPUTY.
THE END

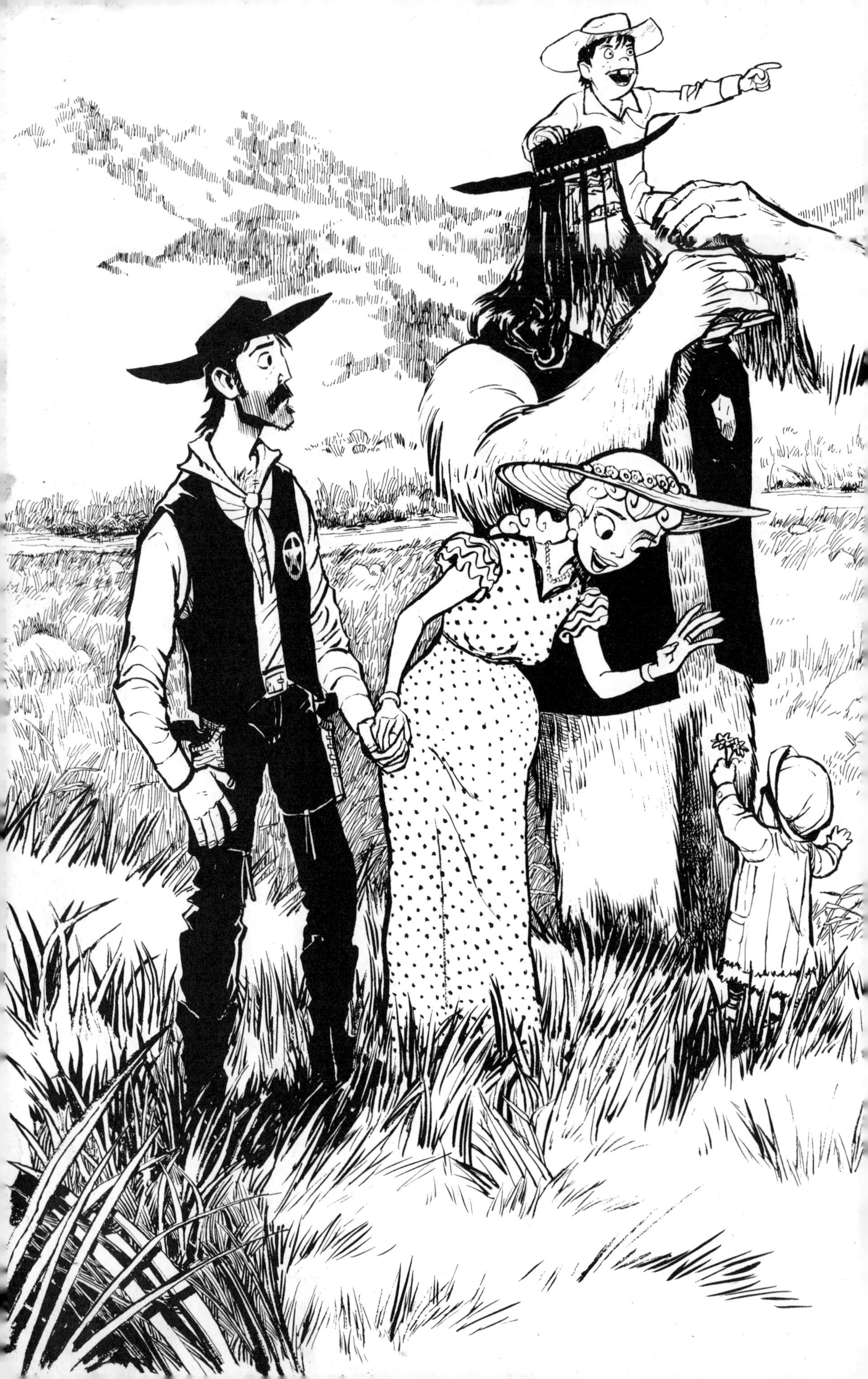